For Sacco and Vanzetti, the nightmare began the night of May 5, 1920. They were riding on a streetcar to Sacco's home when it suddenly stopped. Officer Connolly boarded with his gun drawn. He confronted the two Italians and asked where they came from and where they were going. Then he said, "I want you; you're under arrest as suspicious characters."

The two would never again be free. After their execution seven years later, worldwide riots broke out. American embassies were stoned; cars and American flags were burned.

Although their lives were taken, their spirit has lived on through Vanzetti's words: "That last moment belongs to us; that agony is our triumph."

With Malice Aforethought tells the story of Sacco and Vanzetti, a story that American author and critic Edmund Wilson said "revealed the whole anatomy of American life ... and ... raised almost every fundamental question of our political and social system."

* * * *

With Malice Aforethought has been granted Editor's Choice and Rising Star awards from iUniverse.

With Malice Aforethought

Aforethought

The Execution of Nicola Sacco and Bartolomeo Vanzetti

THEODORE W. GRIPPO

iUniverse, Inc.
Bloomington

With Malice Aforethought
The Execution of Nicola Sacco and Bartolomeo Vanzetti

iUniverse books may be ordered through booksellers or by contacting:

iUniverse
1663 Liberty Drive
Bloomington, IN 47403
www.iuniverse.com
1-800-Authors (1-800-288-4677)

ISBN: 978-1-4502-8067-9 (sc)
ISBN: 978-1-4502-8068-6 (dj)
ISBN: 978-1-4502-8069-3 (e)

Printed in the United States of America

iUniverse rev. date: 06/20/2011

Dedication

To Carmela DeBonis and Donato Grippo, who made that dangerous and fearful crossing and gave their children, Flora and Ted; their grandchildren, Ted, Dan, Tricia, and Teri; and their great grandchildren, Tony, Conor, and Lauren, the blessings of America.

To Marlene, without whose love, patience, tireless devotion, and good counsel, I could not have written this book.

Contents

Author's Note on the Text

When I quote Sacco and Vanzetti, I prefer to use their words, unedited and without use of the [*sic*] designation, even when their words are odd or their statements are ungrammatical. I do this to avoid interrupting the flow of what they said and how they said it.

Preface

Ninety years ago, two Italian immigrant workers, members of a local anarchist group, were arrested for the robbery and murder of a paymaster and his guard in a Boston suburb. Their subsequent trial during the Red Scare challenged Massachusetts and the nation to meet the Constitution's promise of equal justice under the law for all people in America.

I have studied the Sacco-Vanzetti case and written this book to show how that challenge was met. My motive stems from a belief in the Constitution's promise, respect for the law, and my devotion to its practice for over fifty years.

There is also a personal reason for my intense interest in this case. When I was ten years old, I asked my father about Sacco and Vanzetti. I had heard their names, probably on the radio, in connection with the tenth anniversary of their executions. I still remember the look on my father's face as he explained that Nicola Sacco and Bartolomeo Vanzetti had been sentenced to death for robbery and murder, but many believed they were innocent. My father spoke emotionally of the beautiful letters Sacco wrote to his children just before he was executed and of Vanzetti's kind nature and brilliant mind. I believe that my father, an Italian immigrant shoemaker, identified with Sacco, an Italian immigrant shoe trimmer. My father's expression and tone denoted sadness marked with a fear I could not then understand. I later learned he felt threatened by the ill will many Americans displayed toward Italians as a result of that case.

Over the years, I learned bits and pieces about the trial until I felt compelled to learn all that I could about the case. I recently discovered a questionable removal of court papers from the Sacco-Vanzetti case file. These papers consisted of an essentially ignored interim decision by Judge Webster Thayer and related appeal papers regarding his so-called investigation into who switched the barrel of Sacco's gun while it was in an evidence locker. This convinced me of the need for an in-depth analysis of the gun barrel incident. I devote part of the book, especially chapter 16, "The Rosetta Stone," to that endeavor.

Vanzetti's last words to William Thompson, his devoted appellate lawyer, still echo in my mind, "Clear my name." I have used my legal background to explore the guilt or innocence of Sacco and Vanzetti, and I provide my analyses, opinions, and conclusions along the way.

The Sacco-Vanzetti affair has relevance in today's world. It brings into focus the proper role of the public prosecutor and of the judge in criminal proceedings. The case is a reminder that imperfections in human nature, such as blind ambition, can infect a prosecutor and ethnic prejudice can affect the impartiality of a judge. Some recent examples make the point.

Who can forget the injustice visited upon three members of the Duke University lacrosse team in 2006 by a corrupt prosecuting attorney? He fabricated evidence, suborned perjury, and suppressed exculpatory information in order to charge the three students with the rape of a black woman to gain favor with black voters in a close primary election.

An even greater injustice came to light in 2007, when a $102 million civil judgment was entered in the Boston federal court against the United States of America, resulting from the FBI frame-up of Joseph Salvati, Peter Lamone, Henry Tameleo, and Louis Greco for the murder of small-time hoodlum Teddy Deegan. Although the four were exonerated in 2001 for the 1965 murder, they were not vindicated until after Tameleo and Greco died in prison and Salvati and Lamone had each spent over thirty years behind bars.

FBI agents and prosecutors, in their overzealous efforts to fight organized crime, built a case against the four on perjured testimony and false evidence, while concealing information that would have exonerated them. Representative Dan Burton (R-IN), chairman of a congressional committee investigating FBI abuses in 2001, apologized to Salvati and his wife: "I want to express to both of you how deeply sorry we are for everything that was taken away from you and everything you've had to go through the last 30 years."

Since 1990, as a result of improved DNA testing and the efforts of organizations like the Innocence Project, over two hundred prisoners have been found wrongfully convicted of crimes ranging from robbery to rape and murder.

Ambitious prosecutors must be held to the standard demanded by the law. Their role is not to seek convictions at any cost but to seek justice at all costs. And judges must be free of prejudice in order to protect the rights of even those who profess alien ideals.

In today's America, the lessons learned from the case of Sacco and Vanzetti stand as sentinels of our liberty.

Theodore W. Grippo

Acknowledgments

In the course of writing this book, I have received assistance from a number of people whom I want to thank.

Greg Jones, my friend and former law partner of many years, read several early drafts of the manuscript and made many helpful suggestions. His background as a former first assistant United States attorney in Chicago was valuable regarding various aspects of the Plymouth and Dedham trials.

Bill Dal Cerro, my friend and president of the Italic Institute of America, reviewed and gave me valuable comments regarding the manuscript.

Peggy Fox, librarian and researcher, reviewed an early version of the entire manuscript and provided many helpful editorial comments.

I am grateful to my son-in-law, Dave Nichols, who provided invaluable assistance in formatting the manuscript for the publisher. He also originated the design for the cover of this book. My thanks also go to my stepdaughter, Pam Nichols, who reviewed the manuscript and provided valuable editorial comments.

The members of the Barrington Writers' Workshop, Barrington, Illinois, were extremely helpful with their comments regarding the manuscript. Similarly helpful in reviewing early versions of several chapters were members of the writers' group at the Union League Club of Chicago.

Ms. Elizabeth Bouvier, head of archives, Massachusetts Supreme Judicial Court, was extremely helpful in searching for and finding Judge Webster Thayer's decision of March 25, 1924, regarding the switching of gun barrels, and several important appeal documents relating to that decision that appeared to be lost.

I'm grateful to Bruce Watson, author of the recent book *Sacco and Vanzetti: The Men, the Murders, and the Judgment of Mankind,* for sharing with me certain documents relating to Judge Thayer's March 25, 1924, decision.

I want to thank the employees of the following Massachusetts offices, who upon my request searched their files for the fingerprints on the Buick getaway car, and for the Brockton Police Report of May 5, 1920 regarding the arrest of Sacco and Vanzetti, as applicable, even though both searches were unsuccessful: The Norfolk County District Attorney, the Brockton Police Department, the City of Brockton Law Department, the Department of Public Safety, the Massachusetts State Police, the Secretary of the Commonwealth, and the Clerk of the Superior Court of Norfolk County. I'm equally grateful to the Federal Bureau of Investigation for a search of their files for the lost fingerprints, which were not found.

I'm further grateful to the following organizations for permissions I received to use excerpts from published works: The Penguin Group (U.S.A.) for the use of certain letters of Nicola Sacco and Bartolomeo Vanzetti; Bentley Publishers for the use of an excerpt from Upton Sinclair's novel *Boston*; The Kate Sharpley Library for the use of excerpts from *The Story of a Proletarian Life* by Bartolomeo Vanzetti; the *Boston Herald* for the use of an excerpt from F. Lauriston Bullard's editorial "We Submit"; and Random House for the use of an excerpt from Vincent Teresa and Thomas C. Renner's book, *My Life in the Mafia*.

For all other excerpts in the book, I have relied on the doctrine of fair use, with recognition of the source, and I extend my appreciation to the authors and publishers of those excerpts.

I wish to thank the trustees of the Boston Public Library/Rare Books for their permission to use the photographs so identified, including the photograph on the cover of the book. I also thank Commonwealth Editions for its approval to use the scene of the crime map appearing in its Sacco-Vanzetti publication. All other photographs were, to my knowledge pre-1923 publications, or otherwise in the public domain.

All source information, notes, a list of principal characters, and a chronology of major events appear in appendices at the end of the book.

CHAPTER 1

AN OVERVIEW

On April 15, 1920, a brutal crime was committed in South Braintree, a suburb of Boston. Five bandits gunned down and killed a paymaster and his guard while they were delivering a $15,700 payroll. The gang fled with the money. Three weeks later, on the night of May 5, the police arrested Nicola Sacco and his friend Bartolomeo Vanzetti as suspicious persons while they were passengers on a streetcar on the way to Sacco's home. The police quickly identified the two as local immigrant workers associated with a detested anarchist group operating in the Boston area. Thus began the case of Sacco and Vanzetti.

Soon after Vanzetti's arrest, the Commonwealth tried and convicted him for another crime—an attempted armed robbery in nearby Bridgewater some four months earlier. Thereafter, the Commonwealth tried and convicted both Sacco and Vanzetti for the South Braintree murders and six years later executed them for those crimes.

Following Sacco's and Vanzetti's arrest, a reporter sent to cover the story reported back, "[T]here's no story ... just a couple of wops in a jam."[1] After their conviction of the murders on July 14, 1921, the *New York Times* gave the story seven inches on an inside page. However, after their execution on August 23, 1927, the *New York Times* ran a front-page headline and five pages about them, amid outrage and massive protests by millions of workers and supporters throughout America and the rest of the world. They claimed Sacco and Vanzetti were framed and executed for their political beliefs.

The trial became a cause célèbre of American legal history. Edmund Wilson, a noted American writer and critic, observed that the Sacco and

1

Vanzetti case "revealed the whole anatomy of American life with all its classes, professions, and points of view ... and it raised almost every fundamental question of our political and social system."[2]

Historians, scholars, lawyers, and writers continue in a search for evidence to determine their innocence or guilt and whether they got a fair trial. The execution of these two obscure and uneducated Italian immigrants, who were without influence, wealth, or power, inspired many celebrated authors—including Maxwell Anderson, Upton Sinclair, Felix Frankfurter, John Dos Passos, and Edna St. Vincent Millay—to write about this case.

The trial of Sacco and Vanzetti spawned a legion of books. The titles of many convey the intense feelings the case has generated: *The Case That Will Not Die, Tragedy in Dedham, Justice Crucified,* and *The Never-Ending Wrong.* Writers, poets, and artists have authored operas, plays, songs, poems, scores of articles in leading journals, television and film productions, public debates, and thousands of news stories about the Sacco and Vanzetti affair.

Most ironic, on August 23, 1977, Governor Michael Dukakis issued a proclamation on behalf of the Commonwealth of Massachusetts declaring that day "Nicola Sacco and Bartolomeo Vanzetti Memorial Day."[3] The proclamation stated that any stigma and disgrace should be removed from the names of Nicola Sacco and Bartolomeo Vanzetti and from their families and descendants. The proclamation, however, was not without controversy. Apologists in support of the conviction and execution of the two Italians bitterly opposed the proclamation, rejecting its propriety in deference to the honor and memory of the judges, members of the jury, the prosecutors, the governor, and members of his advisory committee who were involved in the case.

The Sacco and Vanzetti affair transcends their deaths and the vicious murders of the two payroll guards. It is an American epic with villains and heroes, "agony" and "triumph."[4] It is a drama that touches on the battle of the American labor movement, the clash of capitalism and socialism, the exploitation of immigrant labor by the remnants of a moribund Puritan elite, and the personal struggle of immigrants seeking acceptance and equality in a country hostile to them.

Frederick Katzmann's successful prosecution of Sacco and Vanzetti and Judge Webster Thayer's death sentences brought a defiant response from Vanzetti: "Sacco's name will live in the hearts of the people and in their gratitude when Katzmann's and yours bones will be dispersed by time, when your name[s] ... are but a deem rememoring of a cursed past in which man was wolf to the man ...".[5]

The Sacco and Vanzetti story embraces not only their murder trial in the Dedham courthouse but also Vanzetti's earlier trial in Plymouth for an attempted armed robbery in Bridgewater and the trial of court interpreter Angelina DeFalco, relating to her shakedown attempt of the two defendants. The public's attention was magnified by six years of unsuccessful motions and appeals and the court's rejection of the confession of Celestino Medeiros, an admitted participant in the South Braintree murders, who tried to exonerate the two Italians with sworn testimony that they were not involved.

A fruitless plea for clemency to the politically ambitious Governor Alvan T. Fuller and a questionable review of the case by his advisory committee exacerbated the affair. Added to the mix were the actions of Frederick Katzmann and Judge Webster Thayer. The establishment saw Katzmann as a fearless prosecutor protecting society from two murdering anarchists. Others saw him as a zealot rather than the people's attorney, whose duty it was to seek justice rather than to convict. Most Americans saw Judge Thayer as the guardian of their venerable institutions. Others viewed him as a prejudiced judge who, in his black robe, was more like a "cobra" poised to strike Sacco and Vanzetti dead than the guarantor of their right to a fair trial.[6]

The times were rife with prejudice against immigrant workers like Sacco and Vanzetti. Following the Great War, a wave of unemployment, labor unrest, and crime swept across the country, centering especially in large urban areas like Boston. The authorities blamed immigrant workers for these conditions. The establishment labeled efforts to achieve reforms for workers the actions of radicals attempting to overthrow the government. The Red Scare that followed the Bolshevik takeover of Russia by revolutionaries known as "the Reds," had fallen upon America, resulting in fear and enmity toward the two Italians.

This story demonstrates how a people caught in a wave of xenophobia reacted in a time of crisis. It reveals that America was not the melting pot once envisioned but a nation of many races and ethnicities—an America that had not yet achieved its ideal of "e pluribus unum."

CHAPTER 2

BOSTON IN THE 1920S

Americans who survived the flu pandemic of 1918 saw glimmerings of good times ahead. The Great War had ended, and the country emerged from the recession that had followed. Americans turned inward, away from the problems of Europe. Prosperity ensued. The "bulls" were on the run, and the stock market soared. The radio, the automobile, and a flood of consumer products reached the masses through easy credit. Prohibition wasn't so bad; it brought speakeasies with flirting flappers and the joy of jazz. Women obtained the right to vote, and they joined the workforce. The country loved Babe Ruth, and Charles Lindbergh was America's hero. Everybody went to the movies, and the talkies made them even better. However, the 1920s were only a glitzy veneer covering hard times for many Americans.

After the Great War, the world changed. Germany, Austro-Hungary, the Ottoman Empire, and Czarist Russia were forever altered or destroyed. A new world order was emerging. The forces of socialism, fascism, anarchism, and democracy were on the march, and they fought to fill the void.

Foreigners, some of whom were immigrant workers from Italy like Sacco and Vanzetti, threatened American democracy on its own soil by promoting opposing ideologies. Boston's withering aristocracy, having come to terms with a hated Irish Catholic peasantry, was confronted with a flood of unschooled Italians and other immigrants they found socially undesirable. New England Yankees, whose roots ran deep into their Puritan past, found these foreigners and their beliefs offensive.[1]

The Puritans and Their Progeny[2]

The hostility of twentieth-century New Englanders toward immigrants had its origin in the Puritan founders of the Massachusetts Bay Colony and the city of Boston three hundred years earlier. Puritans left England primarily to establish a theocracy that excluded nonbelievers. The Puritans were dissatisfied with the failure of Elizabeth I to purify the Anglican Church of all remnants of Catholicism after her father, Henry VIII, broke with Rome.

Puritan theology, with its Calvinistic concept of predestination, held that only Puritans who achieved saving grace could gain heaven; everyone else was destined to hell. The elders of each congregation determined who achieved saving grace. They were the visible saints of their church. The elders controlled each congregation, and the congregations controlled the colony. The colony outlawed other religions and controlled the spiritual and social life of its members. A sinner, depending on the offense, was punished with time in the stocks, forced to wear the scarlet letter, have an ear removed, a tongue bored with a hole, or worse.

During the next 150 years, the laws of the colonies became the laws of most New England states. Government-sanctioned bigotry was the result. Roger Williams, a dissident minister, was banished in 1635 from the Massachusetts Bay Colony because of his objection to its alliance of church and state. Anne Hutchinson was excommunicated and banished in 1637 from the colony because she challenged the right of elders to determine who had saving grace. In 1660, the authorities hanged Mary Dyer, a Quaker follower of Anne Hutchinson, for her beliefs.

As the elders began to lose control of their congregations at the end of the seventeenth century, they sought to divert attention from their own shortcomings. They found a favorite scapegoat of the times, an "accursed group"—the witches. The witch hunts started in Salem in 1692. Before they were over, the elders accused hundreds and hanged nineteen women. In *Justice Crucified*, Roberta Strauss Feuerlicht pointed to what Puritan bigotry begot:

> Calling it God's will, the Puritans planted in the strong soil of New England the seeds of intolerance, injustice, and inequality. The concept of the visible saints would be stretched to embrace wealth and intellect, but the myth that an elect should determine man's fate would endure,

as would the belief that this elect was entitled to choose
who might inhabit their earth. [3]

The exclusion of foreigners remained a tradition in New England for
the better part of three centuries. Nineteenth-century Bostonians, successors
to the Puritans, visited their intolerance first on Irish Catholic immigrants
and then on Italian Catholic newcomers. As Puritan control waned and
democracy took hold, new waves of immigrants streamed into New England
and the rest of America. Although the old barriers began to crumble, hatred
of foreigners (other than those of Anglo-Saxon origin) by New Englanders
did not disappear. Instead, their intolerance found more subtle ways of
expression against these new immigrants: segregated neighborhoods, limited
employment and social opportunities, and quotas for college entrance.

An elite group known as the Brahmins, the visible saints of the times,
achieved the highest social status in Boston.[4] They were the "gentlemen
and gentlewomen of four or five generations" of Anglo-Saxon breeding,
blessed with the divine favor of wealth and education, the progeny of
the Puritans, endowed with saving grace.[5] The Abbotts, Cabots, Lodges,
Lawrences, and Lowells were among the elect. They found little room for
the immigrant newcomers. After the Great War, restricting entry into
America of southern and eastern Europeans, along with arresting and
deporting troublesome immigrants, became the goal of most Bostonians
and other Americans.

Puritan beliefs significantly influenced American culture.[6] This
was evidenced by the continued vitality during the early decades of the
twentieth century of political, social, and religious movements that drew
their strength from Puritan ideals. Chief among these were the Know-
Nothings, the Ku Klux Klan, and the Prohibitionists.

The Know-Nothings, a virulent anti-Catholic, anti-immigrant,
semisecret political party, gathered strength in the years preceding the
Civil War, often under the banner of the American Party. By the 1850s,
the Know-Nothings gained governorships in a number of states and a large
voting bloc in the Congress. Its members divided over the slavery issue,
just as the North and the South did, and the party dissolved following
the Civil War. Former party members, with their prejudices, merged
with Democrats of the South and Republicans of the North, and Know-
Nothing ideals persisted in those groups during the 1920s.

Followers of a revived and growing Ku Klux Klan supported the
nativists' exclusionary attitude in the early decades of the twentieth century.

The Klan, a conceptual ally of the Know-Nothings, emerged as a new force of prejudice and bigotry during this period. Much of the Klan's activities were against blacks, Catholics, and other minorities.

The Prohibitionists, essentially a faith-based group with Puritan values, demonstrated their power by promoting the Eighteenth Amendment, which outlawed the sale of alcoholic beverages. Adoption of the amendment required approval of two-thirds of the Congress and ratification by three-fourths of the states, and the Prohibitionists' success in accomplishing such a difficult task was a reflection of the vitality of Puritan ideals in 1920s America.

It was among the descendants of the Anglo-Saxon founders of New England, steeped in Puritan ideals, that a mixture of southern and eastern European immigrant workers settled in America.

The Immigrant Workers[7]

The immigrants were not completely unwanted. New England elites had mixed feelings; their greed became the seeds of their decline. Decades of cheap immigrant labor that made huge profits for them spawned poverty and disease-ridden ghettos of unskilled workers. The workers were a suffering lot. The mills and factories paid only a dollar or two a day for their labor. Whole families, including unschooled and undernourished children, were put to work. They were barely able to provide scraps of food and inhabited wretched living quarters.

Safety and health standards were nonexistent. The premature death rate in Massachusetts mill and shoe towns had reached epidemic proportions. In 1909, in Lawrence, 17 percent of children died before they were a year old; in the town of Lowell, the annual death rate was 20 percent. Tuberculosis, pneumonia, and woolsorters' disease (anthrax) were rampant; most workers died by the time they were thirty-nine. Driven by these conditions and inflamed by the exploitation of their masters, workers began to organize. Strikes soon spread throughout New England.

Boston and the nation would not forget the 1912 strike at the giant American Woolen Mills in Lawrence, a city of 86,000 mostly immigrant workers, speaking thirty different languages.[8] The workers were crowded into a slum of seven square miles, while the middle and upper classes lived in comfort, and even opulence, in the surrounding areas. The strike took place during one of the coldest and hardest winters in New England's history.

The mill owners contrived a dynamite plot to appear to be the work of the strikers in order to discredit them. Thousands of workers picketed daily. Injuries, and even death, were inflicted on them. Driven by the mill owners' indifference to their suffering, the strikers destroyed looms, machinery, and other property. The government imposed a military siege upon the strikers, during which a soldier bayoneted Dominic Raprada, the young son of Italian immigrant workers, to near death.

The strikers and their families endured severe hunger and bitter cold. Hundreds of parents found it necessary to evacuate their children to caring families in New York and other cities for the duration of the strike because they did not have food and warm clothing for them.

When America and the world learned that Lawrence could not care for its own children, the city became the subject of national and worldwide criticism. City and state leaders were enraged. They ordered the police to stop the further evacuation of children. City officials threatened parents with arrest on grounds of child abuse if they attempted to send their children to the care of others outside the city.

On February 24, when parents and chaperones arrived at the Lawrence train station to send off a wave of forty-six children, the city followed through with its threats. Although many reporters were present, they did not release any photographs to the public showing what happened that morning. However, there were verbal and written accounts. Police grabbed children out of the arms of their mothers, who fought back, reaching for their screaming and crying children, some as young as two or three. To stop the evacuation, police even clubbed some mothers who were pregnant. In seven minutes it was over. The train pulled out of the station without a child on it. The police arrested many of the battered mothers. Strikers vowed revenge. Lawrence was a city seething with rage. It was a cauldron of boiling class hatred.

Despite a congressional investigation, the mill owners were unrelenting. The strike continued until the middle of March. The owners and the workers eventually settled the strike with small benefits for labor but not before inflicting a heavy toll on workers throughout New England. The establishment blamed the radicals for the dispute. Labor activists Joseph Ettor and poet Arturo Giovannitti, leaders of the strike, were arrested and jailed. The police charged them with the murder of Anna Lo Pizzo, a young Italian immigrant worker. She was killed during a gun battle between the police and the strikers. Ettor and Giovannitti were a mile away from where Anna was shot by a stray police bullet. The authorities, nevertheless, charged the two as instigators of the strike. After a dramatic trial, the jury returned not-guilty verdicts, and the court released them.

The Lawrence strike, along with more labor unrest, hardened the New England establishment into a deep hatred of labor leaders, anarchists, socialists, and other radicals. New Englanders believed they were attempting to take over the country. Unions and organized workers continued to clash with owners of businesses. The government sided with the owners, and unions became the scourge of the establishment. As labor became more organized, the owners began moving their mills to the South in order to escape organization of their workers. New England aristocrats saw their fortunes and profits decline. Boston, once the center of American culture, the fountainhead of the Republic, the seat of wisdom, law, and learning, the origin of the abolition movement, was now in decline.[9] Factories were shuttered, and the city's environs were turning into industrial dumps. The elites blamed the radicals and foreign agitators for Boston's fall from grace. Many believed if it were not for those damned dagoes, Boston would still be on top.

The Italians[10]

Italian immigrants had a hard time from the start in America. Businesses shamelessly exploited them for their cheap labor. The workers they displaced hated them, and the more established Americans despised them for their ethnicity, traditions, and religion. As mafia criminals began replacing Irish and Jewish gangs, Italians became the object of disdain by the nativists. Politicians and the media seized on anti-immigrant bias and the criminal activities of a few to blame Italian immigrants for the urban problems of a fast-growing America. They became like the Salem witches, a favorite scapegoat of the times—an "accursed group" of twentieth-century America.

The Italians did not enter the country illegally or uninvited. Virtually all came through Ellis Island. Most were young men, induced to come here by false promises of employers looking for cheap labor. Businesses brought many Italians to America as strikebreakers, earning them a reputation as scabs. Unions denied them membership for that reason and because of their willingness to work for low wages. Even though they shared a common religion, Irish Catholics relegated Italians to segregated religious services in the basements of their churches and barred them from their neighborhoods.

These young Italian workers were often controlled by padroni, Italian agents who arranged their passage to America, obtained jobs and housing for them, and helped them send money back to Italy. Frequently, padroni received and managed their wages, sometimes victimizing their own countrymen for personal gain. Corrupt employers working with corrupt padroni often induced illiterate recruits to enter into unconscionable contracts, making them no better than vassals working for a feudal lord. Many were taken to camps and forced to work under armed guards until advances made under their contracts were repaid through wages withheld by their padroni.

Italian immigrants were often subjected to mob violence because they replaced higher paid workers and because of the low regard the nativists had for Italians. In excess of fifty lynchings and many additional acts of violence were committed throughout the country against Italians and their families during the thirty-year period immediately before the Sacco and Vanzetti trial. During this time, except for blacks, more Italians were lynched in America than persons of any other ethnic group. This deep-seated ill will toward Italians was prevalent among many New Englanders from whom jurors were selected for the murder trial of Sacco and Vanzetti.

The most bloodthirsty violence against Italians occurred in New Orleans in 1892, following the unsolved murder of Chief of Police D. C. Hennessey.[11] This event contributed to a long-lasting negative attitude of many Americans toward Italians. The police rounded up hundreds of Italians as suspects, and nineteen were arrested. Nine of those arrested were tried for the murder; six were exonerated, the jury did not reach a verdict for three, and the rest of the nineteen were never tried. All nineteen were held in jail after the trial on a claim that additional charges would be filed, but it was a setup for the lynchings that followed.

The day after the jury verdicts, the following advertisement appeared in the local papers:

Mass Meeting

All good citizens are invited to attend a mass meeting on Saturday, March 14, at 10 o'clock A.M. at Clay Statue, to take steps to remedy the failure of justice in the Hennessey case.

Come prepared for action.[12]

By ten o'clock Saturday morning, a crowd of eight thousand gathered at the statue of Henry Clay. William S. Parkerson and two assistants, all leading citizens of New Orleans, took charge of the crowd.

Parkerson denounced the jury that freed the Italians and then asked the crowd, "Will every man here follow me, and see the murder of D. C. Hennessey vindicated?"[13]

The crowd responded with a resounding, "Yes, yes, hang the dagoes!"[14]

Parkerson led the crowd to the parish prison. On the way, a prearranged death squad of one hundred men armed with rifles and shotguns joined the crowd.

The throng had grown to a frenzied mob of twenty thousand as they approached the front gate of the prison. Unable to break through the steel doors, they moved to a side entrance, broke that door down, and rammed their way into the prison.

When the warden heard the mob breaking through the side entrance, he locked all prisoners in their cells, except the nineteen Italians. He freed them, but only within the prison, and told them to hide as best they could. He refused to let them have guns to defend themselves.

After the mob broke into the prison, those who were armed pushed the warden and his guards aside and began hunting down the Italians. The leaders organized those who were armed into death squads of twenty-five or thirty. Each went in a different direction hunting for its prey.

Six Italians were in the corridor of the women's section of the prison when they heard an approaching death squad. They ran downstairs into the prison yard. The gates were locked; they were trapped. A death squad caught up with them and fired over a hundred shots into the six Italians. Their bodies were torn to shreds. Another squad in a gallery area trapped and shot three Italians. Two died instantly; the third lived for nine hours before he died.

The roving squads found two others, Emmanuele Polizzi, who had been tried but with no verdict reached, and Antonio Bagnetto, who was tried and found not guilty. Both men were shot but not fatally. While still alive, they were taken out of the prison and turned over to the mob. The mob beat them, threw them about, and then hanged them—Polizzi from a lamppost and Bagnetto from a tree. While the two men were still alive and dangling from the ropes, the armed members of the crowd riddled their bodies with dozens of bullets.

The mob was furious when they were unable to find the other eight prisoners. They had successfully hidden under the floorboards of the women's section of the prison. The mob's attention was diverted when Parkerson emerged from the prison. Cheers and blessings were heard among the crowd at the sight of him. They carried him on their shoulders throughout the city. He was their hero.

No one was ever charged or prosecuted for the lynchings, although the authorities and the media were aware of the leaders of these terrible crimes. Quite the contrary—the press was openly antagonistic, scapegoating Italian immigrants, blaming them for the social and economic ills of the nation. John R. Fellows, former district attorney of New York City, endorsed the mob action in New Orleans.[15] Theodore Roosevelt approved the mass lynchings;[16] he called them "a rather good thing" and boasted that he said so at a party in the presence of "various dago diplomats."[17]

A widely circulated article justified the lynchings.[18] It was authored by then Congressman (and later Senator) Henry Cabot Lodge of Massachusetts and disguised as an immigration policy statement. Another highly publicized article titled "What shall we do with the 'Dago'?" gives a flavor of the times.[19] In 2001, author Michael Barone, in *The New Americans*, provided a deeper insight. He observed that many Americans doubted Italians were white. As Barone pointed out:

> [A] witness in a congressional hearing in the early twentieth century [was] asked if he considered an Italian a white man ... [He] replied, "No, sir, an Italian is a Dago." In the American South, Italians were often segregated like blacks or were classified as another race—"between." As one southern newspaper put it, "the average man will classify the population as whites, dagoes and negroes." [20]

An all-Yankee jury in 1920 New England was well aware of the Italian ethnicity of Sacco and Vanzetti.

The Radicals

The Haymarket affair in 1886 was a defining event for the anarchist movement in America.[21] A lockout at the McCormick Harvester Plant in Chicago resulted in a massive protest by German immigrant workers, many of whom were anarchists. The police fired on the crowd, killing several and wounding many. The next day, a huge demonstration took place at Haymarket Square. Near the end of the event, a bomb was thrown into the crowd killing seven policemen and wounding many participants. Gunfire erupted, killing and wounding more demonstrators. Mass arrests followed. The government charged eight anarchists with murder on the grounds that they were troublemakers and had previously advocated violence. After a trial, the jury found the eight guilty; seven of them were sentenced to death and one to imprisonment. Of the seven sentenced to death, four were hanged, one committed suicide while in prison, and the sentences of two were commuted—one to life and the other to fifteen years.

Seven years later, Governor John Altgeld pardoned the three who remained in prison on the grounds that no evidence had been presented at the trial that any of them had actually thrown the bomb.

The Haymarket affair played a significant role in the Sacco and Vanzetti case. Although it occurred some thirty-five years earlier, the event was fresh in the minds of judges, prosecutors, police, and the public due to continuing anarchist activity. Because Sacco and Vanzetti were anarchists, they were marked men.

Despite the negative impact on Sacco and Vanzetti personally, the Haymarket incident was a boon to the American anarchist movement principally because many found the trial and the sentences against the defendants unjust. This aroused sympathy among young utopian visionaries, resulting in many recruits for the anarchist cause.

Americans viewed anarchism as complete civil disorder produced by murdering and bomb-throwing radicals. Following the assassination of President William McKinley in 1901 by Leon Czolgosz, an avowed anarchist, Congress enacted legislation specifically aimed at restricting the entry of anarchists into this country.

Theodore Roosevelt, upon taking office as president after McKinley's death, charged that anarchism was an intolerable menace: "The anarchist is the enemy of humanity, the enemy of all mankind, and his is a deeper degree of criminality than any other."[22]

Judge Webster Thayer expressed a similar view years later, when he instructed the jury at Vanzetti's Plymouth trial that Vanzetti's "ideals are cognate with the crime."[23]

Yankees and most Americans made few distinctions among the advocates of socialism, whether in the form of Communism or anarchism; they were Reds, they were godless radicals, and they were hated.[24] The 1920 Yankee found the ideology of socialism, with state ownership and control of property and the means of production, anathema. He found the concept of anarchism, with no private property and no governmental authority, even worse. And he feared Communism, with its propensity to revolution and violence.

Immigrant workers who felt exploited by industrial capitalism became the principal advocates of various forms of socialism. For the most part, they turned away from violence and sought redress for their grievances through the organized labor movement.

At the turn of the twentieth century, anarchists were active in all countries of Europe, Asia, and South America. During the early years of the twentieth century, most anarchists in America were of German, Italian, and Russian origin—some with Christian and some with Jewish backgrounds, but by then, most professed atheism.

Sacco's and Vanzetti's involvement in the Italian anarchist movement played a significant role in their arrest and conviction for murder. Italian anarchism spread in America through the activities of Italian intellectuals traveling from state to state preaching their gospel to one Italian enclave after another. Beginning with Carlo Cafiero proselytizing in New York in 1885, Italian anarchist groups spread to East Coast principal port cities, then to the Midwest, especially Cleveland, Detroit, and Chicago, and from there to San Francisco.

The flames of anarchism were spread far and wide by the advent of its most ardent advocate in America.[25] During the first two decades of the twentieth century, the fiery and charismatic Luigi Galleani took center stage.

Galleani was born in 1861 in the town of Vercelli, in the northwestern Piedmont district of Italy. He was drawn to anarchism as a young law student at the University of Turin. After graduation, he shunned the practice of law, devoting his life to fighting capitalism and governmental authority. Galleani was under constant surveillance by the police in every country he settled in because of his support for radical causes. He avoided prosecution in Italy by fleeing to France and then to Switzerland. He returned to Italy in 1900, but was found and convicted of engaging in radical activities and imprisoned. He escaped and, at the age of forty, fled to Egypt, then to London, and finally made his way to Paterson, New Jersey, advocating anarchism and always staying one step ahead of the authorities.

In 1902, Galleani was involved in the Paterson silk workers' strike. During that strike, he was wounded in a clash with the police. He was indicted for inciting a riot at Paterson, but he escaped to Canada. He returned to America under an assumed name and settled in Barre,

Vermont, in a community of stone and marble cutters from Carrara, Italy. In 1903, Galleani founded *Cronaca Sovversiva* (*Subversive Chronicle*) and was its principal editor. It became the leading Italian journal in America supporting anarchism.

In 1906, Galleani's identity was discovered, and he was extradited to New Jersey to stand trial for his role in the Paterson strike. He was set free because the jury could not reach a verdict. Galleani returned to Barre and continued promoting anarchism. In 1912, he moved the publication of *Cronaca Sovversiva* from Barre to Lynn, Massachusetts, where it remained until it was put out of business in 1919 when he was deported to Italy, leaving behind a wife and five children.

Galleani was the author of a bomb-making manual and an advocate of force, if necessary, to bring about his idea of social reform. Because of his association with violence, the public perceived Italian anarchists as bomb-throwing radicals bent on overthrowing the government by force.

Congress adopted the Espionage Act and the Sedition Act after America entered the war in April 1917. This legislation led to a new bureaucracy, joined by a voluntary citizens' army of two hundred thousand. During the war, these citizens helped root out German spies; after the war, this vast force led a crusade against radicals.

The success of a socialist takeover in Russia in 1917 fostered the growth of an assortment of radical movements in America that included Communists, labor syndicalists, Wobblies (International Workers of the World), socialists, and anarchists. These radical groups were principally composed of southern and eastern Europeans, many of whom were supported and financed by the leaders of the Russian Revolution. This concerned Americans, as socialism came to be seen as an international movement funded by the new Soviet Union and backed by the power of that state.

The Red Scare

The Red Scare of 1919–1920 was the result, at least in part, of the rise of aggressive radical activities carried out by exploited immigrant workers.[26] These workers were encouraged by the spread of socialism throughout Europe and to American shores. Americans feared that the radicals would spearhead a Russian-styled workers' revolution and take over the country. The Red Scare had roots in the presidential election of 1912. In that election, Eugene V. Debs, the Socialist candidate, surprised the probusiness establishment and the country by receiving almost a million votes, compared to 6.2 million for President-elect Woodrow Wilson. A series of labor disputes and terrorist bombings followed that election.

The Ludlow incident in 1914 was one of those events.[27] American workers were shocked by what happened during a strike at the Ludlow, Colorado, company mines owned by John D. Rockefeller. Private guards, retained by the company and working with the state militia, machine-gunned a tent colony made up of immigrant striking miners and their families in response to gunfire from the strikers. The militia killed five miners and a boy. The guards and militia set fire to the tents. As a result, eleven more children and two women died. Protests erupted throughout the nation in reaction to what became known as the "Ludlow Massacre." In New York City, anarchists and workers marched in protest on the church regularly attended by Rockefeller. Ironically, a bomb intended for Rockefeller's home in retaliation for the massacre exploded prematurely, killing three anarchists.

In 1914 and 1915, many atrocities occurred in New York City that were believed to be the work of Galleani followers.[28] Bombings took place at St. Alphonsus Church, St. Patrick's Cathedral, the Bronx courthouse, and the Tombs police court. The year 1916 followed with three incidents: the poisoning of two hundred guests at the University Club in Chicago by an anarchist chef, the Mooney-Billings bombing incident in San Francisco, and the December reprisal bombing of the Boston Salutation Street Station, headquarters of the harbor police.

The Mooney-Billings incident was the most serious. Ten innocent people were killed and forty were wounded in that bombing. Tom Mooney and Warren Billings, labor activists, were framed by the authorities for the atrocity. Mooney and Billings were eventually exonerated, but not before Mooney received a death sentence, Billings a life sentence, and each spent over twenty years in prison. Their prosecutor, Edward Cunha, said, "If the thing were done that ought to be done this whole God damn dirty low down bunch would be taken out and strung up without ceremony.[29] They're a bunch of dirty anarchists, every one of them, and they ought to be in jail on general principles."

The clashes between anarchists and state authorities significantly escalated upon America's entry into the World War in April 1917. An era of superpatriotism enveloped the country. Shortly after entering the war, President Wilson put the country and the world on notice, "Woe to the man or group of men that seeks to stand in our way on this day of high resolution."[30] The next day he signed the Espionage Act, which provided penalties for false statements made for the purpose of obstructing the war effort or aiding the enemy. President Wilson's threat, as well as the newly enacted legislation, was directed against anarchists as well as other antiwar sympathizers. Repressive government measures followed an ever-increasing cycle of retaliation in the form of bombings by militant radicals.

The situation got out of hand, as evidenced by the Milwaukee police tragedy in the fall of 1917.[31] An ongoing dispute between anarchists and patriotic members of a local church resulted in the need for police protection for church activities. At a Sunday revival meeting on September 9, a riot broke out between church members and the anarchists, resulting in the police shooting two anarchists to death. In retaliation, on November 24, anarchists planted a bomb at the church, which was discovered and turned over to the police. While the bomb was being examined at police headquarters, it prematurely exploded, killing nine police officers and a woman. In response to the November 24 explosion and killings, the authorities promptly arrested and tried eleven anarchists on assault charges for their earlier encounter with the police on September 9. The jury promptly convicted them, and Judge A. C. Backus excoriated the defendants for being radicals. He sentenced each of them to twenty-five years in prison. Emma Goldman and other anarchists claimed the trial was a frame-up and that the eleven, although charged and tried for the September 9 assault charges, were being punished for the November 24 tragedy. The anarchists vowed revenge.

The year 1918 continued unabated with atrocities, followed by arrests, trials, and convictions of anarchists. The government adopted the Sedition Act in May. It provided a twenty-year sentence for an expressed opinion deemed disloyal to America and any contemptuous reference to its flag, its form of government, or its Constitution. In August, Judge Kenesaw Mountain Landis, in a Chicago trial, sentenced 101 members of the Wobblies to long prison terms for violations of the Act.[32] In the fall, a jury convicted Eugene V. Debs under the Sedition Act, and the court imposed a ten-year sentence for an earlier antiwar speech.

The cycle of violence followed by repression reached a crescendo in 1919.[33] A plot to assassinate President Wilson was uncovered, and the Justice Department announced a roundup of all radicals. The May Day celebration followed a series of bombings intended to force America to recognize Soviet Russia. Galleani was deported and *Cronaca Sovversiva* was finally put out of business. After Galleani's deportation, bombs were set off in seven cities in apparent retaliation. One of the bombs exploded at the doorstep of Attorney General Mitchell Palmer's home, causing extensive damage, and accidentally killed the perpetrator of the act.

In 1919, the radicals committed a most audacious act.[34] They sent bombs through the mail to thirty prominent citizens in America, including Oliver Wendell Holmes, Jr., associate justice of the Supreme Court; four United States senators; two governors; a number of high-ranking federal and state officials; and business leaders John D. Rockefeller and J. P. Morgan. Senator Hardwick's maid opened the bomb package addressed to him, and the blast blew off her hands. The police quickly intercepted the other bombs without harm to anyone.

Attorney General Palmer claimed a conspiracy to overthrow the government by force was in the making. He ordered a dragnet of all Reds, anarchists, and other radicals. The Red Scare shifted into high gear. The first raid took place on November 7, 1919, when an army of government agents raided the headquarters and homes of subversive groups throughout the country.[35] The police arrested many radicals, without warrants, and destroyed the properties of Communists, labor leaders, and anarchists.

One of the most dramatic events involving America's reaction to Russian radicals was the 1919 roundup and deportation to Soviet Russia of 250 Reds aboard the ship *Buford*, nicknamed the "Soviet Ark."[36] The deportees included Emma Goldman, one of the most dangerous radicals in America, and her long-time companion, Alexander Berkman. Berkman had previously attempted the assassination of industrialist Henry Clay Frick, one of the notorious robber barons, during the Homestead Strike of 1892.

While all this turmoil was taking place in 1919, Governor Calvin Coolidge broke the Boston police strike with a tough law-and-order stance. His action brought him national recognition and was instrumental in Warren Harding, candidate for president, selecting Coolidge as his running mate in the 1920 election.

On January 2, 1920, Palmer ordered simultaneous raids in thirty-three cities.[37] Government agents arrested thousands without warrants and held them for deportation. In Massachusetts, there were fourteen raids, and in Boston, over five hundred aliens were marched through the streets in chains and taken to detention facilities where they were isolated, some for months, in barbaric conditions.

The raids struck fear and terror in the hearts of millions of honest, hardworking immigrants. None felt safe from the midnight knock on the door, the nightlong interrogations under the lights, the beatings, the arrests, and the deportations. These were the fears of Sacco and Vanzetti and their friends. It's what they talked about in their homes and at their clubs on Sunday afternoons.

The previous six years of terrorism unleashed by the radicals precipitated the widespread arrests of those believed responsible for the atrocities. The public demanded action and the authorities responded. However, there was clear and convincing evidence that the government's crackdown was indiscriminate and punished many innocent people. This wave of repression, spearheaded by Attorney General Palmer, was one of the most oppressive periods in American history. This is not surprising given Palmer's attitude when speaking of anarchism: "Each and every adherent of this movement is a potential murderer or a potential thief and deserves no consideration."[38]

A committee of twelve leading constitutional lawyers, including Dean Roscoe Pound of Harvard Law School, Felix Frankfurter, and Zechariah Chaffee, condemned Palmer's excessive raids and unlawful arrests. The committee issued a report in May 1920 that summarized their findings. It told the story of an out-of-control government that had no regard for civil and constitutional rights. It reported that under the pretense of curbing radical activities, government agents engaged in indiscriminate arrests and searches without causes or warrants. Innocent men and women were jailed and held without benefit of counsel or friends. Their homes were invaded and their property was seized or destroyed all because they were suspected of radical associations. Government spies infiltrated organizations suspected of subversive activities, and traps were set to snare suspected extremists. The Department of Justice was charged with engaging in the distribution of propaganda to news organizations for the purpose of molding public opinion against suspected radicals and their activities. The committee declared the department's conduct of public persuasion "outside the scope of the Attorney General's duties."[39]

It was clear that the attorney general's actions were undermining public confidence in America's institutions of justice. A group of twenty immigrants arrested during the raids challenged the federal government by filing habeas corpus petitions with Judge George Anderson in the federal district court in Boston. The immigrants claimed unconstitutional arrests, unlawful searches and seizures, and inhumane treatment.

On June 23, 1920, Judge Anderson severely criticized the government's practices and the barbaric treatment of detainees. He decided in favor of the immigrants and declared, "A mob is a mob, whether made up of government officials acting under instructions from the Department of Justice or of criminals and loafers and the vicious classes."[40]

In sum, the year 1920 found the remnants of Puritan intolerance alive among New Englanders, especially against southern and eastern European immigrants. New England Yankees were in a death struggle with radicals who they believed were seeking a new social order in America. This resulted in a fierce, and sometimes cruel, response by those in authority. In this struggle, many in power perverted the institutions of government to protect their own interests and beliefs. They often misused the judiciary to repress undesirables through mass arrests without warrants, illegal searches and seizures, convictions, and deportations without due process.

These were dangerous times for immigrant workers to espouse anarchism and other forms of socialism. These were dangerous times for Sacco and Vanzetti to be charged and tried for murder before a New England judge and jury.

This was the state of the times in Boston in the 1920s.

CHAPTER 3

NICOLA AND BARTOLOMEO

Nicola Sacco and Bartolomeo Vanzetti came from opposite ends of Italy.[1] Sacco was born in 1891 in Torremaggiore, in the south near the spur above the heel of the boot. He was baptized Ferdinando but took the name Nicola after an older brother with that name died. Vanzetti was born in 1888 in Villafalletto, in the Piedmont district of northern Italy. Both villages were nestled in rural settings removed from the fast-paced and rapidly developing industrial cities of northern Italy.

They each had a loving family, and their parents were respected members of their churches and communities. Neither the Saccos nor the Vanzettis were wealthy, but they were comfortable and able to provide for their families and a future for their children.

Sacco and Vanzetti led remarkably similar lives as youngsters. Neither was a lonely child. Sacco, one of seventeen children, and Vanzetti, with two sisters and a brother, each had an active childhood mixing play and learning with family chores. As young boys, they helped with farming, making wine, and in Nicola's case, tending to the family's olive groves. Nicola was essentially homeschooled until his teens. Bartolomeo was an excellent student, but his formal education ended at age thirteen.

Although they were both hard workers, they had different inclinations. Vanzetti was cerebral; Sacco was physical. Beginning at an early age, Vanzetti had a thirst for knowledge that grew more insatiable the older he became. He was a dreamer and an idealist, and as a young man, more religious than Sacco, sometimes "defending his faith with his fists."[2] Sacco was practical. He loved machines and the production of tangible things. Sacco was happy working his strong peasant body in the fields and gardens. Vanzetti was comfortable challenging his mind in a library or classroom.

Sacco and Vanzetti were among the more than five million Italians who came to America between 1880 and the early 1920s during the great tide of Italian immigration. They arrived in America in 1908 but did not meet until 1917.

From 1917 to 1920, Sacco and Vanzetti became close friends as they engaged in activities advancing the cause of anarchism and workers' rights. In 1920, they became enmeshed in a web of circumstances that led to their arrest on May 5. After they were arrested, Vanzetti was quickly tried and convicted in Plymouth for an attempted armed robbery four months earlier in nearby Bridgewater. He vehemently proclaimed his innocence. Following Vanzetti's conviction of the Bridgewater crime, the police charged both of them with murdering a guard and a paymaster during a robbery in South Braintree, Massachusetts, on April 15. A year later, the Commonwealth tried and convicted Sacco and Vanzetti in Dedham for the South Braintree murders.

Many believed the two Italians did not receive a fair trial, that the prosecution fabricated evidence and concealed exculpatory information. Serious doubts as to their guilt persisted. Six years of motions for a new trial, appeals, and clemency hearings followed, to no avail. The Commonwealth executed Sacco and Vanzetti on August 23, 1927, amid worldwide protests.

Because of the ordeal they suffered together, the names of Sacco and Vanzetti are inextricably bound in history. More detail about their lives is necessary to understand their story.

Nicola Sacco

For years, Nicola and his older brother, Sabino, dreamed of coming to America. As soon as Sabino finished his required military service in 1908, he and Nicola, then sixteen, departed for Milford, Massachusetts, a virtual Little Italy. Friends and relatives there helped Sabino and Nicola find jobs and get settled.

Sabino found an immigrant's life in America distasteful and longed to be with his family in Torremaggiore. After a year and a half, Sabino gave up the expedition and returned home. Nicola stayed, working first as a water boy on a road gang, next with a pick and shovel, and then for a year in a foundry at the Draper Company in Hopedale, Massachusetts, trimming slag from pig iron.[3]

Sacco realized the lowly status of an unskilled laborer, and in 1910 he entered a school for immigrants conducted by Michael Kelley to learn the shoemaking trade. In three months, he learned the skills of an edge trimmer and earned forty dollars or more a week, compared to six to eight dollars a week as a laborer. He found steady work at the Milford Shoe Company from 1910 to 1917. Sacco was a skilled worker and one of the best edge trimmers in the business. He regularly sent money to his family in Italy. Sacco was a saver, banking over fifteen hundred dollars by the time of his arrest in 1920.[4]

Although Sacco spent little time in deep reading or writing like Vanzetti, he had a quick and curious mind. He attended evening classes to study English, always well-groomed and courteous. He displayed the enthusiasm of youth and the naïve charm of a man not yet tainted by the disappointments of life. His personality sparkled and he was well liked.

In 1912 Sacco met sixteen-year-old Rosina Zambelli, who had just returned from a convent in Italy to live with her parents. Rosina's gentleness, delicate fine features, and striking auburn hair captivated Sacco. The two became inseparable.

In 1913, a year after their first meeting, Nicola and Rosina eloped. They lost their first child, Alba, shortly after her birth. A year later, their son, Dante, was born. They loved to picnic in the fields with Dante. They gathered wildflowers in the woods and dug for clams at the seashore. Sacco wished he had the words of a poet to describe the beauty of nature. Nicola and Rosina often appeared together as actors in fund-raising plays to help needy immigrants and strikers. The birth of their daughter, Ines, was marred by the fact that it occurred shortly after Sacco was arrested on May 4, 1920. He would never have the joy of living with her as a free man.

Sacco did not come to America as an anarchist. When he arrived, he was just a sixteen-year-old boy eager to see America, the land of his dreams, the land of freedom and opportunity. He succeeded in his trade, made good money, and had a loving family. However, the destitution, suffering, and wretched living conditions he witnessed, especially among immigrant workers in this land of great wealth, turned him toward anarchism.[5] Sacco was drawn more and more into fund-raising and picketing for workers' rights. Eventually, anarchism became his faith and one of the most important matters in his life.

Writings in socialist journals like *Il Proletario* and the poetry of labor activist Arturo Giovannitti moved Sacco. He subscribed to *Cronaca*

Sovversiva, and he admired its radical editor, Luigi Galleani. The bitter strike of mill workers in Lawrence, Massachusetts, in 1912 turned Sacco against industrial capitalism. That strike, led by Italian labor activists Joseph Ettor and Arturo Giovannitti, became Sacco's strike. He picketed before and after a day's work and provided free food from his garden for the strikers. Sacco also participated in the strike at the Draper Company in Hopedale. In 1916 he raised money for striking ironworkers in the Mesabi Range of northeastern Minnesota.

Sacco donated money to Ettor's and Giovannitti's defense of murder charges against them following the Lawrence strike. These charges were an omen of what was forthcoming for Sacco and Vanzetti.[6]

In 1917 Sacco, along with Vanzetti and a group of anarchists from the Boston area, fled to Mexico. This is when Sacco and Vanzetti first met. Their critics claimed they ran to Mexico to avoid the draft or for fear of deportation because of their failure to serve. Neither of these assertions was completely correct. Anarchists were against America's entry into the war, and the Boston anarchist group protested by running to and hiding in Mexico. However, they were also preparing for a return to Italy in order to participate in an anticipated revolution of workers there, which they believed would soon follow the Russian Revolution. They reasoned that they could quickly leave Mexico for Italy when the revolution began, something they would have difficulty doing from America.[7]

Once in Mexico, Sacco immediately missed his family and wanted to return home. Within a few months, it became clear that a workers' revolution in Italy was not about to materialize. As a result, he left Mexico to return to Rosina and Dante. Vanzetti and the other anarchists followed.

Sacco used his mother's maiden name, Mosmacotelli, to hide his identity as a slacker. He found his way back to Michael Kelley, then the owner of the Three K Shoe Company in Stoughton, Massachusetts. Kelley had been his mentor, the man who taught him the shoemaking trade back in 1910. The Three K Shoe Company hired Sacco, and he promptly returned to using his family surname.

Sacco rented a small cottage behind the factory from Kelley, where he, Rosina, and Dante made their home. Kelley trusted Sacco completely and made him the night watchman of the factory. It was in connection with these duties that Sacco obtained and carried a pistol. Kelley told him to get a permit for his gun, but Sacco failed to do so. Sacco earned extra pay for arriving at the factory at 5:00 AM during the winter to bank the furnace and warm the factory for the workers. Kelley allowed Sacco to develop an extensive garden on a large plot of land next to the cottage. He worked in his garden diligently, growing an abundance of vegetables and fruits that he shared freely with the Kelley family and workers in need of food.[8]

When Kelley learned of Sacco's arrest, he remarked that no man who rose at 5:00 in the morning to care for his garden before work, and continued after work sometimes until 10:00 at night, and shared his bounty free of charge to unfortunate workers was the kind of man who would rob and kill. Kelley always believed in Sacco's innocence.[9] He had warned Sacco to stop talking about his radical ideas or he would get into trouble.[10] Sacco told Kelley, "It is in my heart that talks."[11] Kelley remarked, "There was never a better fellow than Nick Sacco nor one with a kinder heart.He couldn't kill a chicken." [12]

Sacco suffered in prison much more than Vanzetti did because of a rule that only prisoners who had been sentenced were eligible for work assignments which were intended to keep them mentally healthy. Sacco, although found guilty in 1921, was not immediately sentenced because of pending motions for a new trial. He was held in the Dedham jail without work or activities to keep him busy. This was very destructive to Sacco, since he had boundless energy and needed work to remain healthy in mind and body. Confinement to a four-foot-by-eight-foot prison cell, with no work or other activities for most of seven years, was cruel punishment for him. Vanzetti, on the other hand, had been sentenced in connection with his Plymouth conviction, and under prison rules he was afforded duties and work responsibilities.

The lows from the despair of facing death and the lack of any success in their case compromised their mental health. Sacco and Vanzetti each suffered mental breakdowns during their seven-year ordeal, and each spent time convalescing in a mental hospital.[13]

By late 1922, Sacco felt persecuted. In February 1923 he wanted to die and began a hunger strike during which he ate nothing for four weeks. He became paranoid and claimed the Commonwealth tried to kill him by torture and then by poisoning his food. He claimed noxious fumes and vapors entered his cell and that electric currents were under his bed. He said he heard Rosina talking to him.

The authorities sent Sacco to the Boston Psychiatric Hospital for ten days of observation. During that time he wounded himself by ramming his head against a wall, proclaiming his innocence and lamenting that there was no justice. The hospital extended his ten-day observation period to thirty days. Sacco threatened suicide. He went through cycles of calmness followed by self-inflicted violence. His doctors concluded that he was suffering from sensory deprivation brought about from the loss of his wife, his children, and his work. This would have been exacerbated if he were innocent, as he claimed. Sacco's isolation and sterile confinement turned him from a gentle and kind individual to a man bent on injuring himself and wanting to die.

On April 10, 1923, Sacco's doctors declared him of unsound mind and in need of hospitalization and treatment. He was committed shortly thereafter to the Bridgewater Hospital for the Criminally Insane. While there, he spent time outdoors working in a garden. He rapidly improved and even became optimistic about the outcome of his case.

By the fall, Sacco had made a full recovery and was discharged from Bridgewater Hospital on September 29, 1923. After he returned to his cell in the county jail at Dedham, he languished until his execution in 1927. During that time, he continued having bouts of depression and despair. Sacco's sanity never became an issue after he was returned to jail from Bridgewater Hospital. His final hunger strike lasted seventeen days and ended shortly before his execution.

Sacco was a simple man, not nearly as complex and as deep a thinker as Vanzetti. Sacco loved his mother, his family, his garden, and good, hard work, but he believed that the upper class would always exploit the working class. He clung to that belief to the end.

Bartolomeo Vanzetti

In his autobiography, *The Story of a Proletarian Life*, written in Italian during his first year in prison, Vanzetti described himself as "nameless, in the crowd of nameless ones."[14]

At the turn of the twentieth century, economic conditions in Italy were bad. Vanzetti's father learned that well-educated lawyers were unable to find work, so he decided that further formal education for his son was a waste. At thirteen, his father introduced Bartolomeo to the rigorous and often exploitative Italian apprentice system:

> [I]n the year 1901 [my father] conducted me to Signor Conino, who ran a pastry shop in the city of Cuneo, and left me there to taste, for the first time, the flavor of hard, relentless labor. I worked for about twenty months there—from seven o'clock each morning until ten at night, every day, except for a three-hour vacation twice a month. [15]

26

From Cuneo, Vanzetti moved to Cavour and worked in a bakery for three years. He did not like his work, but he stayed with it to please his family and because he did not know what else to do. Then he moved on further to Turin, from there to Courgne, and back again to Turin.

It was in Turin, amid the challenges to his faith by his more worldly peers, that he began to question the values instilled in him by his parents. Secular socialism was in the air, and he breathed it in deeply. He believed that, notwithstanding the love his parents had for him, "they teach me many wrong ideas, false principles, and a false divinity."[16]

In Turin, he became sick. His confinement deprived him of "air and sun and joy, like a sad twilight flower."[17] When his family learned of his illness, his father brought him home where his mother nursed him back to health:

> [M]y good, my best-beloved mother ... And so I returned, after six years spent in the fetid atmosphere of bakeries and restaurant kitchens, with rarely a breath of God's air or a glimpse of His glorious world. Six years that might have been beautiful to a boy avid of learning and thirsty for a refreshing draught of the simple country life of his native village. Years of the great miracle which transforms the child into the man ... My mother received me tenderly, weeping from the fullness of her happiness and her sorrow. She put me in bed—I had almost forgotten that hands could caress so tenderly. There I remained for a month, and for two months more I went about with the aid of a heavy walking stick. At last I recovered my health. From then until the day I parted for America I remained in the house of my father. That was one of the happiest periods of my life. I was twenty years old; the magic age of hopes and dreams ... [18]

During his convalescence, Vanzetti read and studied philosophy. He sought new friends among the educated inhabitants of Villafalletto. Soon his formal beliefs in Catholicism faded and secular humanism took its place: "My religion soon needed no temples, altars, and formal prayers."[19]

The development of Vanzetti's newfound concepts regarding religion brought him great satisfaction. However, his happiness soon ended "by the most painful misfortune that can strike a man."[20] His mother fell sick:

"What she, the family and I suffered no pen can describe."[21] Her suffering became so painful that neither friends nor other family members were able to care for her. "I remained alone to comfort her as best I could. Day and night I remained with her, tortured by the sight of her suffering. For two months I did not undress …"[22]

After months of agony, she died in his arms:

> It was I who laid her in her coffin; I who accompanied her to the final resting place; I who threw the first handful of earth over her bier. And it was right that I should do so for I was burying part of myself … The void left has never been filled. [23]

His mother's death became an overwhelming loss to him and the family. Bartolomeo's younger brother and sisters suffered from the loss of their mother's love. His father soon grew old and gray from the tragedy. Without the strength of his mother's love to unify the family, Bartolomeo found strain and discomfort living with his father. He could not help resenting his father for having deployed him to be an apprentice baker at the tender age of thirteen, a circumstance that deprived him of the love of his mother, the joy of growing up with his siblings, and an opportunity to further the education he loved so much.

Bartolomeo was sullen for days. Often he thought of finding his own final resting place in order to be with his mother. It became clear to him that Villafalletto would be a constant reminder of his loss. At the age of twenty, he decided that he must abandon Italy for America and seek a fresh start in life. His was a sorrowful parting. His friends and family tearfully followed him, like a funeral cortege, on the long walk to the railroad station. His farewell was so painful that he was unable to speak. He could only give his followers a parting embrace amid mutual sobs and tears.

After a train ride across France and seven uncomfortable days crossing the Atlantic in steerage class, he arrived in New York. He recalled his first experience in the Promised Land:

> In the immigration station I had my first great surprise. I saw the steerage passengers handled by the officials like so many animals. Not a word of kindness, of encouragement, to lighten the burden of tears that rests heavily upon the newly arrived on American shores. Hope, which lured

these immigrants to the new land, wither under the touch of harsh officials. Little children who should be alert with expectancy, cling instead to their mothers' skirts, weeping with fright. Such is the unfriendly spirit that exists in the immigration barracks. How well I remember standing at the Battery, in lower New York, upon my arrival, alone, with a few poor belongings in the way of clothes, and very little money. Until yesterday I was among folks who understood me. This morning I seemed to have awakened in a land where my language meant little more to the native ... than the pitiful noises of a dumb animal. Where was I to go? What was I to do? Here was the promised land. The elevated rattled by and did not answer. The automobiles and the trolleys sped by, heedless of me ...[24]

Through a friendly countryman he found work in New York as a dishwasher in a rich man's club: "The hours were long; the garret where we slept was suffocatingly hot; and the vermin did not permit me to close an eye. Almost every night I sought escape in the park ..."[25]

Vanzetti soon left the club and found employment at the Mouquin Restaurant, again as a dishwasher. He was often required to work in the dark amid vapors of dust and grime. The garbage gave off foul odors, and the sewage clogged the floor drain, requiring him to trudge through greasy water day after day. He worked over seventy-five hours a week, for which he was paid five or six dollars and leftover scraps to eat. After eight months he left.

He recalled the misery of the poor that year, many of whom slept outdoors and rummaged through garbage for food. He slept in doorways and lined his clothes with newspapers to keep warm. He searched New York in vain for work. While in an employment agency, he met a countryman who had gone without food for days. Out of sympathy, Vanzetti treated him to a meal. His new friend thought it foolish to remain in New York. He argued for the country, where there was more chance of finding work and at least fresh air and sunlight. With the few dollars Vanzetti possessed, they took the next steamboat for Hartford, Connecticut.

From Hartford the two wandered from town to town looking for work, sleeping in parks and barns, and gratefully accepting handouts of bread and water from sympathetic persons. Finally, they found work at the furnaces in a brick factory near Springfield, Massachusetts. The work was so hard that his companion lasted only two weeks. Vanzetti stayed on for ten months. He recalled:

> The work was indeed above my strength, but there were many joys after the day's labor. We had quite a colony of natives from Piedmont, Tuscany, and Venice, and the little colony became almost a family. In the evenings, the sordidness of the day was forgotten. Someone would strike up a tune on the violin, the accordion, or some other instrument. Some of us would dance; I, unfortunately, was never inclined towards this art and sat watching. I have always watched and joyed in other folk's happiness. [26]

Vanzetti's friends urged him to return to his trade as a pastry cook to escape the lot of an unskilled worker, "the lowest animal there was in the social system."[27] This he did, finding work in New York as an assistant pastry chef at Sovarin's Restaurant on Broadway. However, in six months he was discharged with no reason given. He quickly found work at a hotel on Seventh Avenue, but again he was terminated in five months without cause. It was then he learned, "The chefs were, at that time, in league with the employment agencies and got a divvy on every man they placed. The more often they sacked men, the more often they could get new ones and their commission."[28]

Vanzetti was then unable to find work, even as a dishwasher, anywhere in New York. He was forced to work with a pick and shovel with a ragged group of men in Springfield, Massachusetts, building railroad tracks. Eventually, he found his way to Plymouth, where he remained until the time of his arrest.

The journey to Plymouth after Vanzetti landed in New York was a painful odyssey that deeply affected him. He experienced injustice, discrimination, and abuse, suffering the fate of many Italian immigrant workers. They were victims of unscrupulous employment agents, worked beyond their endurance for a pittance, forced to live in vermin-infested hovels, and stripped of their dignity by ethnic slurs and name calling. In Vanzetti's words, "To the bosses I was a dago to be worked to death."[29] He had his reasons for embracing anarchism:

> I underwent all the sufferings, the disillusions, and the privations that come inevitably to one who lands at the age

of twenty, ignorant of life, and something of a dreamer. Here I saw all the brutalities of life, all the injustice, and all the corruption in which humanity struggles, tragically.[30]

Despite his suffering, Vanzetti found solace in studying anarchist thinkers like Kropotkin, Gorki, Merlino, Malatesta, and Reclus.[31] He read Marx's *Capital*, the works of Labriola, the political *Testament* of Pisacane, and Mazzini's *Duties of Man*. He combined reading socialist journals with reading the Bible, *The Life of Jesus,* and *Jesus Christ Has Never Existed*. He studied Greek and Roman history and the revolutions in the United States, France, and Italy. He examined the works of Darwin, Spencer, Laplace, and Flammarion; he read *The Divine Comedy* and *Jerusalem Liberated*. He reread Leopardi, and as he said, "wept with him."[32] The writings of Hugo, Tolstoy, Zola, and Cantu and the poetry of Giusti, Guerrini, Rapisardi, and Carducci were among his favorites.

Vanzetti read and studied after working hard all day and without decent accommodations. Often he read during the night under a flickering gaslight. Many times, he had barely laid his head on the pillow when the whistle sounded calling him back to work.

In his autobiography, Vanzetti shared the essence of his beliefs:

> I championed the weak, the poor, the oppressed, the simple, and the persecuted. I admired heroism, strength, and sacrifice when directed towards the triumph of justice. I understood that in the name of God, of Law, of the Patria, of Liberty, of the purest mental abstractions of the highest human ideals, are perpetrated and will continue to be perpetrated, the most ferocious crimes; until the day when by the acquisition of light it will no longer be possible for the few, in the name of the God, to do wrong to the many …
>
> … I grasped the concept of fraternity, of universal love. I maintained that whosoever benefits or hurts a man, benefits or hurts the whole species. I sought my liberty in the liberty of all; my happiness in the happiness of all. I realized that the equity of deeds, of rights and of duties, is the only moral basis upon which could be erected a just human society. I earned my bread by the honest sweat of my brow. I have not a drop of blood on my hands, nor on my conscience …

> ... I wanted a roof for every family, bread for every mouth, education for every heart, the light for every intellect ... Now? At the age of thirty-three—the age of Christ ... I am scheduled for prison and death. Yet, were I to recommence the "journey of life," I should tread the same road, seeking, however, to lessen the sum of my sins and errors and to multiply that of my good deeds. [33]

Vanzetti's idealistic principles led many to conclude he was a philosophical anarchist, whose nature made him incapable of committing the crimes for which he was charged. On the other hand, Professor Paul Avrich, in his 1991 in-depth study of the anarchist movement in America, *Sacco and Vanzetti: The Anarchist Background*, concluded that Vanzetti was a dedicated revolutionary militant.[34] He argued that Vanzetti was prepared to use force to achieve a new social order. Avrich found evidence for his conclusions in Vanzetti's writings: "We did not come to be vanquished, but to win, to destroy a world of crime and miseries, and to rebuild with its freed atoms a new world."[35]

Vanzetti's supporters have argued that his bellicose attitude at that time was a result of being unjustly imprisoned for five and a half years and facing execution. Except in connection with the Commonwealth's charges against the two, which they denied to their dying day, no one, including the police, the prosecutors, Professor Avrich, or any scholar of the case, has produced any evidence that Sacco or Vanzetti had ever used violence or terrorist tactics. Sacco and Vanzetti lived their lives in accordance with nonviolent beliefs. Vanzetti spoke often of the nonviolent nature of his form of anarchism, that he abhorred violence, deeming it the worst form of coercion and authority.[36] He argued that the goal of anarchism was the elimination of every form of violence, oppression, and exploitation. He said that he would rather be electrocuted for a crime he did not commit than spill innocent blood.[37]

Not only did Vanzetti speak out against violence, he lived and acted as he preached. He was known for his respect for others and for his kindness to children. When young Beltrando Brini, in whose home Vanzetti boarded, showed disrespect to a neighbor by messing up his garden during a ball game, Vanzetti counseled the boy on the virtues of courtesy and respect for the property of others. Vanzetti's examples of respect for others vividly remained with Beltrando throughout his life. He recalled, "He was my ideal. For some boys, it was Ty Cobb, but for me it was Bartolomeo Vanzetti."[38]

Vanzetti's kindness to animals was well-known and remembered by his friends. He taught children by example when he tended an injured and sick kitten back to health.[39] Always willing to help a friend, Vanzetti shared his last dollars to buy dinner for a friend who had not eaten for days.[40] On another occasion, after losing his wallet, he declined to accept a wallet that was found because it had too much money in it.[41] He suggested that it be given to someone in need. When defense attorney Fred Moore told Vanzetti that if he (Moore) sacrificed Sacco, he might get Vanzetti acquitted, Vanzetti replied, "Save Nick, he has the woman and child[ren]."[42] Vanzetti's final and greatest act of charity occurred as the guards strapped him into the electric chair: "I wish to forgive some people for what they are now doing to me."[43]

Vanzetti's mental problems were far less severe than Sacco's. However, after Judge Thayer denied five pending motions for a new trial on October 1, 1924, he fell into a deep depression. In late 1924, Vanzetti displayed signs of paranoia and delusions of persecution. On January 2, 1925, he was committed to the Bridgewater Hospital for the Criminally Insane, where he remained for four months.

During the early period of his hospital confinement he continued to display paranoia, believing everyone had forsaken him and fascists were "out to get him."[44] As treatment took hold, he returned to normal. On May 28, 1925, the hospital discharged Vanzetti, and he returned to prison. He engaged in a brief hunger strike shortly before his execution, primarily to show solidarity with Sacco during his last hunger strike.

There were rumors suggesting that Vanzetti feigned a mental breakdown. It was claimed that he was trying to obtain relief from his dreary existence in Charlestown State Prison, to gain sympathy for his situation, or to simply get bigger and better living conditions.

In 1958, Dr. Ralph Colp, Jr., a psychiatrist, published "Bitter Christmas: A Biological Inquiry into the Life of Bartolomeo Vanzetti." In addition to relying on published materials, he was given access to relevant records at the Bridgewater Hospital for the Criminally Insane and certain unpublished letters at Harvard University. Dr. Colp's publication provides an extensive analysis of Vanzetti's mental breakdown. He found evidence of an early stage of Vanzetti's malady in a letter he wrote in July 1923, the day after the electrocution of a fellow prisoner. It was a letter of despair. Vanzetti wrote, "I was tired, disgusted and furibond."[45] Dr. Colp concluded, "This feeling of 'furibond' then became one of the lineaments of a psychosis."[46] Dr. Colp reviewed Vanzetti's breakdown and gave no hint that he had faked it.

In 1962, Francis Russell, a respected writer and historian who spent a major part of his adult life researching and writing about the Sacco and Vanzetti case, published *Tragedy in Dedham*.[47] He wrote about the facts of Vanzetti's breakdown without any indication that it might have been bogus. To the same effect are the writings of Louis Joughin and Edmund M. Morgan in *The Legacy of Sacco and Vanzetti*, and Eugene Lyons in *The Life and Death of Sacco and Vanzetti*.

* * * *

Much has been said and written about Sacco and Vanzetti these past ninety years. Apologists for their conviction and execution claim they were guilty of two brutal murders; their defenders claim otherwise and argue that the Commonwealth executed them for their political beliefs.

Lacking formal education and witnessing what they believed to be a cruel and indifferent industrial capitalism, particularly toward immigrant workers, Sacco and Vanzetti were drawn to the hope of a workers' utopia. Upton Sinclair thought that Vanzetti was an idealist, a dreamer of justice for the working man.

When Sacco and Vanzetti met in 1917, they did not realize they would soon be caught up in one of the most important trials in American history.

CHAPTER 4

BRIDGEWATER AND THE PLYMOUTH TRIAL

The years immediately following the war resulted in significant unemployment in America. Four million returning soldiers mixing with nine million terminated war workers created uncertainty for anxious men searching for work and economic stability. Many jobless men trained to use a gun were bitter and angry. A string of armed robberies swept across the major cities of America.[1]

Two crimes linked in this story occurred in the Boston suburbs: one, a failed armed robbery in Bridgewater on Christmas Eve, 1919; the other, on April 15, 1920, when two brutal murders occurred during a robbery in nearby South Braintree. Each resulted in a criminal prosecution: the first, in Plymouth, against Vanzetti, for assault with intent to rob and to murder; and the other, in Dedham, against Sacco and Vanzetti, for murder.

The Bridgewater Crime[2]

About seven thirty on the morning of December 24, 1919, four men attempted to rob a truck carrying a thirty thousand dollar payroll destined for the L. Q. White Shoe Company in Bridgewater, Massachusetts. Three men were on the truck: John Graves, age twenty-four, the driver; Ben Bowles, age forty-seven, a policeman; and Alfred Cox, age thirty-two, the paymaster. The streets were slick. A slight fog clouded a cold winter morning.

The payroll truck was headed north on Broad Street closely behind a streetcar. Four bandits in a parked touring car on the right, facing east on

Hale, a cross street, waited to highjack the truck. As the truck approached the corner of Hale, three men jumped out of the bandits' car. The fourth remained in the driver's seat.

One bandit carried a shotgun; the other two were armed with pistols. The man with the shotgun fell to one knee and fired twice at the truck, ordering the driver to stop. Bowles returned two shots, and one of the bandits fired back with his pistol. No one was hit.

Graves immediately pulled the truck to the left of the streetcar, stepped hard on the gas and passed it, blocking the bandits' ability to complete the holdup. When the three bandits realized they could not get at the truck, they aborted the holdup. They scrambled into the waiting getaway car and fled east on Hale Street toward Plymouth. As the truck sped past the streetcar, it skidded on the wet pavement and crashed into a telephone pole about a quarter of a mile north on the west side of Broad Street. No one was hurt.

Promptly after the holdup attempt, Bridgewater Police Chief Michael Stewart opened an investigation. Stewart, a strapping, cigar-chewing Irishman, was the embodiment of a police officer, but his two-man department was not up to carrying on much of an investigation. For that reason, L. Q. White, president of the shoe company, retained the Pinkerton Detective Agency to investigate the crime and apprehend the bandits. Pinkerton operatives interviewed a number of witnesses and issued a series of reports to Mr. White and to Frederick Katzmann, district attorney for Plymouth County, where the crime occurred.

Frank Harding, a salesman in the auto supply business on his way to work that morning, witnessed the event and noted Massachusetts license plate 01173C on the bandits' car. Pinkerton operatives learned that those plates had been stolen a few days before the holdup attempt from George Hassam's garage in Needham, after a man came there looking to borrow license plates.

A Pinkerton informant reported that an Italian in Boston, by the anglicized name of C. A. Barr (for Barasso), claimed he had information about the Bridgewater crime. On January 3, 1920, Chief Stewart, state police Officer Alfred Brouillard, and a Pinkerton detective interviewed Barr. Barr came up with an absurd story, that he had invented a machine that could solve any crime anywhere. He claimed that a Mrs. Vetilia, of 2 Lexington Street, East Boston, looked into the machine and saw the Bridgewater crime being committed, that the bandits had changed their clothes after the attempted holdup, left the getaway car hidden near

Bridgewater, and departed by train. The police were never able to locate Mrs. Vetilia.

Chief Stewart observed that Barr was about forty-five years old, five feet eight, and 150 pounds, with black hair, a dark complexion, and a cropped black moustache streaked with gray. The similarity of Barr's characteristics to the descriptions given of the shotgun bandit and the man who appeared at Hassam's garage should have caused investigators to suspect that Barr was one of the bandits.

Barr may have deliberately told such a preposterous story in order to appear a crank and not be taken seriously. It will never be known if Barr was involved in the Bridgewater crime. What is known is that Chief Stewart had made up his mind very early that the crime was the work of a local gang of anarchists. Barr did not fit that profile, and Chief Stewart never investigated him for the Bridgewater crime.

Except for some minor events, the investigation came to a dead end until April 15, 1920, when the South Braintree murders and robbery burst onto the scene. Since both crimes fell under the jurisdiction of district attorney Katzmann, he instituted an intensive two-track investigation. He placed state police Captain William Proctor, a thirty-year veteran, in charge. The brutality of the South Braintree murders and a possible connection between the two crimes made the investigation a top priority.

During the previous year, Chief Stewart had participated in Attorney General Palmer's infamous Red raids, rounding up radical immigrants for deportation. The chief had arrested Ferruccio Coacci, a local anarchist, during one of the raids. The Immigration Board scheduled Coacci for an appearance on April 15, 1920. On April 16, Chief Stewart learned that Coacci had failed to appear before the board on the day of the South Braintree murders. Stewart also learned that Coacci had, at one time, worked at the L. Q. White Shoe Company and at the Slater & Morrill Shoe Company, targets of the Bridgewater and South Braintree crimes.

That night, Stewart sent one of his officers to check on Coacci. When confronted at his home, Coacci said that he failed to report to the Immigration Board because his wife was sick on April 15 and he had to care for her. He then insisted on leaving for Italy at once, which he did two days later. The investigating officer reported that Coacci's wife did not appear to be sick.

On April 17, two hunters found a Buick touring car later determined to be the getaway car used in the South Braintree murders. They found it less than a mile from the house where Coacci lived with his family. Mike Boda, also a known anarchist, boarded at Coacci's home. This fueled Stewart's suspicion that Coacci, Boda, and their anarchist friends were involved in both crimes. The police found an intact Peters shotgun shell, tire tracks of a smaller car near the Buick, and fingerprints in and about the car.[3] These facts became important evidence a year later at the Dedham trial of Sacco and Vanzetti for murder.

A Pinkerton operative learned that a seven-passenger Buick owned by David Murphy, a shoe salesman, was stolen in Needham on November 22, 1919. In a report regarding the Bridgewater attempted holdup, one of the Pinkertons made a casual comment, "This Buick may have been the car the bandits had."[4] The comment was made despite positive statements by Graves, the driver of the payroll truck, and Frank Harding, who witnessed the crime, both of whom were knowledgeable about the make of automobiles, that the bandits' car was a Hudson.

Chief Stewart seized on the Pinkerton comment to support his theory that the same car, and therefore the same gang, were involved in both crimes. He found two witnesses who said they saw a Buick in Bridgewater around the time of the holdup attempt. Harding eventually changed his previous identification of the car from a Hudson to a Buick when it was time to testify at the Plymouth trial. Graves's untimely death eliminated any testimony to the contrary. Everything fell in place to convince Chief Stewart that the two crimes were the work of the same gang of anarchists, and prosecutor Katzmann bought into Stewart's theory.

The chief returned to the Coacci house on April 20 to find that Coacci had left for Italy, his wife and children had moved out, and only Mike Boda was living there. Boda showed Stewart around the house, including the shack behind it where he usually kept his six-year-old Overland car. Boda indicated that Simon Johnson was repairing the Overland at his garage a few miles away. Stewart noticed a second set of car tracks and that the dirt floor of the shack was newly raked. He jumped to the conclusion that the shack was the hiding place of the stolen Buick and where the loot from the South Braintree crime had been temporarily buried.[5] He believed this was more evidence to support his theory. The chief overlooked the fact that the shack was too small to accommodate two cars at the same time. Moreover, he found no witness who could testify that Boda's Overland was ever parked outside of the shack or that a Buick was ever parked in the shack.

Stewart did not arrest Boda that day, possibly because he knew the Massachusetts legislature intended to introduce a resolution the next day authorizing a fifteen thousand dollar reward for the capture of those responsible for the South Braintree and Bridgewater crimes.[6] Arresting Boda prior to the announcement of the reward would have jeopardized Stewart's ability to claim it. After the legislature announced the reward the next day, he returned to Coacci's place to arrest Boda but found him gone and the house vacated.

The Trap

Chief Stewart was convinced more than ever that he was hot on the trail of the gang responsible for both crimes. He decided to set a trap to arrest Boda and his "godless" anarchist friends.[7] The chief told garageman Simon Johnson and his wife that if anyone called for Boda's Overland, to immediately call the Brockton police. He assumed that anyone calling for the Overland was a member of the gang he was after. Stewart never sought a warrant for the arrest.

The police sprung the trap on May 5, 1920. On that day, Boda and Ricardo Orciani, a fellow anarchist, arrived at Johnson's home by motorcycle, followed by two men on foot, to pick up the Overland. Even though Simon Johnson had repaired the car, he discouraged Boda from taking it because it did not have current license plates. Meanwhile, Johnson's wife called the police from her neighbor's phone. She noticed that the two men who arrived on foot watched and trailed her as she walked to and from her friend's home.

Boda complied with the suggestion to leave the Overland until he obtained license plates. He and Orciani left by motorcycle, and the other two men left on foot. Their departure looked suspicious because it occurred after Mrs. Johnson's phone call to the police. Officer Michael Connolly responded to Ruth Johnson's phone call. He learned that the two men on foot sought directions for a streetcar. At about 10:10 PM, Connolly boarded the streetcar he believed the two men might have taken. He said he saw two men who looked like Italians on that streetcar and arrested them on grounds they were suspicious persons. The two were Sacco and Vanzetti. They were searched, and each was found carrying a loaded pistol, including several shotgun shells on Vanzetti and a number of .32-caliber cartridges on Sacco.[8]

The arresting officer did not know the names of these men or whether they were two of the four men who had visited Johnson's home looking to obtain Boda's Overland. No crime had been committed in the presence of Officer Connolly, and he did not know of any crime they had committed.

That night, Chief Stewart interrogated Vanzetti, and the next morning, prosecutor Katzmann questioned him. None of the questions asked by either Stewart or Katzmann related to the Bridgewater crime or the South Braintree murders. Katzmann directed a number of questions exploring Vanzetti's political beliefs:[9]

> Q: Do you belong to any clubs or societies?
> A: No.
> Q: Are you an Anarchist?
> A: Well, I don't know what you call them. I am a little different.
> Q: Do you like this government?
> A: Well, I like things a little different.
> Q: Do you believe in changing the government by force?
> A: If necessary.
> Q: Do you subscribe for literature or papers of the Anarchist Party?
> A: Sometime I read them.
> Q: How do you get them—through the mail?
> A: A man gave one to me in Boston.

Vanzetti had difficulty understanding English without an interpreter. He had no knowledge of his rights under American law, and he did not have the advice of counsel. Katzmann claimed that Vanzetti gave his consent to the interrogation and that he voluntarily answered his and Stewart's questions after being advised that he was not required to do so.

That night, Vanzetti was required to sleep on a bare board. He asked for blankets, as his cell was cold and unheated. The night officer responded, "Never mind, you catch warm by and by, and tomorrow morning we put you in a line in the hall between the chairs and we shoot you."[10] The officer then slowly loaded his gun, pointed it through the bars at Vanzetti, and spat at him.

Stewart's and Katzmann's questions and the treatment by police led Vanzetti to believe he was arrested because of his association with the anarchist movement and that his detention was part of Attorney General Palmer's program to arrest and deport undesirable radicals. In an effort to protect his friends and fearing for his own safety, Vanzetti lied when asked by the police whether he knew Boda, Coacci, Orciani, and other anarchists, and he lied about whom he and Sacco were with and where they had been that evening.

A well-known police tactic is to ask a suspect questions that he will probably lie about. Katzmann and Stewart could expect that the two would be loath to admit belonging to radical organizations and that they would be reluctant to identify friends who the police might arrest and deport. Lies of this kind by a suspect at the time of arrest could provide the police with apparent evidence of consciousness of guilt.

Katzmann and Stewart made a judgment that the two Italians were part of a gang of anarchists that included Coacci, Boda, and Orciani and that they were responsible for both the Bridgewater and the South Braintree crimes. The authorities issued announcements to that effect to the press. State police Captain Proctor disagreed. He believed that Katzmann had the wrong men and that professional highway robbers had committed the crimes.[11] Proctor's opinion was worth considering. He was the Commonwealth's most experienced investigator, having spent thirty-two years with the state police, probing hundreds of murders and holdups. Katzmann and Stewart chose to ignore Captain Proctor's advice, even though his involvement in the case continued.

The arrest of Sacco and Vanzetti followed a series of events, which upon closer examination by an unbiased investigator should have raised doubts about their guilt. The details of those events follow.

In May 1919, the government deported Luigi Galleani, the principal proponent of anarchism in America. A series of bombings followed in a number of cities. One bomb exploded prematurely on June 2, 1919, at the home of United States Attorney General Mitchell A. Palmer. The explosion scattered body parts of its carrier and a number of printed subversive flyers from the "Anarchist Fighters" throughout the area.[12] After months of investigation, the authorities traced the flyers to a printer in Brooklyn, New York, and two of its employees, Roberto Elia and Andrea Salsedo. The two were arrested: Elia on February 28, 1920, and Salsedo on March 8, 1920, both without a warrant.[13]

After his arrest, Elia pleaded guilty to a minor violation, and the judge issued an order for his deportation. At the request of the Justice Department, based on its claim that Elia possessed information regarding the previous year's bombings, the judge suspended his deportation and remanded him to the Justice Department.

Agents of the Justice Department took Elia to a detention facility at 15 Park Row in Manhattan. While being interrogated, he heard someone being beaten in the next room. Elia recognized the voice of his friend, Andrea Salsedo, amid his cries of pain. Government agents seeking information regarding the bombings of the past year subjected Salsedo to the third degree. Although federal agents denied mistreating Salsedo, immigrant workers provided many testimonials that agents of the Justice Department were brutal to them during this period. Salsedo's wife visited him briefly after his interrogation. She reported her husband's face was badly bruised, he had blackened eyes, and he was in a condition of collapse. Elia's and Salsedo's detention continued.

Narciso Donato, an attorney with an office in the same building, mysteriously appeared as an attorney for Elia and Salsedo. Donato did nothing to protect them or to seek their release. Friends of the two suspected Donato of being a stooge for the government to give the appearance that the anarchists had legal representation during their confinement.

The government altered its files in an effort to cover up the initial confinement of Elia and Salsedo. It indicated that they were under surveillance rather than in custody and that they were being watched instead of held. The government claimed the two were housed at the Park Row facility at their request, for protection, while they voluntarily provided information to the authorities regarding anarchist activities in America.

A week earlier, the anarchist group in Boston had sent Vanzetti, who was then broke and out of work, to New York to determine the fate of Elia and Salsedo. Vanzetti spent several days in New York, but he was not able to learn anything about them. During the trip, New York friends in the movement warned Vanzetti that the government was planning to step up the arrest and deportation of anarchists. They told Vanzetti to warn the Boston group and to urge them to dispose of any radical literature in their possession. He returned to Boston and reported to his comrades the warning he received in New York.

Orciani remembered that Boda owned an Overland, which they could use to collect the literature and take to a safe house. On Sunday, May 2, 1920, the Boston group met and planned that Sacco and Vanzetti should meet with Orciani and Boda the following week to collect and dispose of the literature.

In the meantime, Salsedo's physical and mental condition deteriorated and he became depressed. During the night of May 2, 1920, he fell from his fourteenth-floor bedroom. The next morning, the mangled, dead body of Salsedo was found on the pavement below. The government recorded Salsedo's death as a suicide. The Boston anarchists claimed he was murdered. Eventually, Salsedo's widow sued Attorney General Palmer and his agents for the wrongful death of her husband. She lost the case and returned to Italy with her children. The Justice Department became very secretive after the Salsedo and Elia affair about the procedures its agents used when interrogating radicals, and it became impossible thereafter to obtain information from the government about its role in the Sacco and Vanzetti case.

Fear of deportation as well as physical harm, and even death, spread among the Boston anarchists following the Salsedo tragedy. The urgency to collect and hide the subversive literature became paramount. This led Boda, Orciani, Sacco, and Vanzetti to make the May 5 trip to garageman Johnson's home to pick up Boda's Overland. During the streetcar ride to Johnson's place, Vanzetti drafted a notice in Italian for a typical workers' fund-raising meeting in Brockton on May 9.

Based on the foregoing information, Stewart and Katzmann should have realized the absurdity of claiming that the South Braintree killers, who had access to automobiles, license plates, and over fifteen thousand dollars in cash, would ride streetcars shortly after the crime and plan a public gathering of immigrant workers in order to collect nickels and dimes for the cause of anarchism.

Despite these inconsistencies, Katzmann planned to charge Sacco, Vanzetti, and their fellow anarchists, Boda, Orciani, and Coacci, for the Bridgewater attempted robbery and then prosecute all of them for the South Braintree murders. A trial of that group for the Bridgewater crime first would provide many benefits for the Commonwealth:

- If successful, the gang would stand as convicted felons of the Bridgewater crime, and when prosecuted for the murders at South Braintree, any testimony offered by them in their defense could be impeached.
- It would provide the prosecution with valuable discovery and be a rehearsal for the main event, the Dedham murder trial.
- The prosecution would obtain insight into a local jury's attitude toward Italian immigrant workers, especially if Katzmann connected them to the anarchist movement.

- The related publicity of the Plymouth trial would influence the jury pool available for the Dedham murder trial in favor of the prosecution and against the Italians.
- It would place a heavy financial and emotional burden on Vanzetti and his accomplices, requiring them to defend two trials rather than one.
- The Dedham murder trial would be deferred and provide Katzmann with more time to find evidence against Sacco, Vanzetti, and their accomplices.

Katzmann moved promptly to bring the Bridgewater crime to trial before events overtook the situation and forced him to try the South Braintree murder case first. Katzmann's strategy did not work completely. Boda disappeared; Coacci left for Italy; and Sacco and Orciani had airtight alibis. They both were at work on December 24, 1919, the day of the Bridgewater crime. Katzmann tried but could not break their alibis.

The police arrested Orciani the day after the arrest of Sacco and Vanzetti. However, Katzmann had to release Orciani, as he had no basis to hold him. Vanzetti, however, was vulnerable. Since he was self-employed, he had difficulty establishing independent verification of an alibi. As a result, the court denied him bail. The prosecutor represented to the judge that witnesses saw Sacco in Dedham at the time of the South Braintree crimes. For that reason, the court also denied Sacco bail, and the two were jailed pending action by the grand jury.

Katzmann obtained an indictment against Vanzetti on June 11, 1920, for the Bridgewater crime. Although it was not unheard of for a prosecutor to try someone first for a lesser crime, even if that person was also charged by the same prosecutor with a greater crime, this put a heavy burden on Vanzetti. His lawyers did nothing to prevent or alleviate this burden. It was unusual that Katzmann was able to force Vanzetti to a trial of the Bridgewater crime on June 22, just eleven days after Vanzetti's indictment. Vanzetti and his lawyers had little time to prepare an adequate defense. After the Bridgewater conviction, Vanzetti claimed his lawyer, John P. Vahey, provided him with a poor defense, did little or no investigation, and interviewed few witnesses.

The Commonwealth never sought an indictment of the other three anarchists who Katzmann announced were responsible for the Bridgewater and South Braintree crimes. This signaled a weakness in the government's evidence in both cases. In pretrial publicity, Katzmann and his team of prosecutors painted a picture of a gang of five anarchists as responsible for these crimes. The publicity lent credibility to the prosecution's charges against Vanzetti in the Bridgewater attempted robbery and against Sacco and Vanzetti in the South Braintree murders. However, in neither trial did Katzmann present evidence that Coacci, Boda, and Orciani were members of the gang that committed those crimes.

The Plymouth Trial

Judge Webster Thayer presided at the Plymouth trial, and Frederick Katzmann and his assistant, William Kane, were the prosecutors. J. P. Vahey and J. M. Graham, two locally connected criminal lawyers, represented Vanzetti. Katzmann continued his parallel investigation of the South Braintree murders during the Plymouth trial.

Jury selection was uneventful; none of the jurors selected were challenged, even though Arthur Nickerson was a foreman at the Plymouth Cordage Company. Because Vanzetti actively participated in a bitter strike at that plant in 1916, he was blackballed and denied employment after the strike was settled. Defense counsel should have challenged Nickerson's participation as a juror, since it was likely that he would be prejudiced against Vanzetti.

No effort was made by Vanzetti's counsel to suppress the gun and shell evidence obtained by the police at the time of his arrest, notwithstanding that the arrest and search were conducted without a warrant.

Assistant prosecutor William Kane, in his opening statement to the jury, outlined the Commonwealth's case against Vanzetti.[14] He said it was based on the following four points:

- Identification testimony linked Vanzetti to the crime.
- A spent Winchester shotgun shell found on December 24, 1919, at the crime scene and one intact Peters shotgun shell found on April 17, 1920, near the abandoned Buick were of the same make as one intact Winchester and three intact Peters shotgun shells found on Vanzetti the night he was arrested.
- Vanzetti owned a cap that was similar to a cap worn by the shotgun bandit.
- Vanzetti showed consciousness of guilt when he lied to police at the time of his arrest.

Identification of Vanzetti

The eyewitnesses to the shooting were Ben Bowles, the guard; Alfred Cox, the paymaster; Frank Harding, a salesman on his way to work; and Maynard Shaw, a fourteen-year-old newsboy near the scene. John Graves, the driver of the payroll truck, had died in the meantime from causes unrelated to the attempted holdup and truck crash.

The testimony of Bowles, Cox, and Harding at the Plymouth trial in June 1920 was very different from the statements they made to Pinkerton detectives immediately after the crime in late December 1919 and from their testimony at the preliminary hearing on May 18, 1920.[15] Katzmann concealed the Pinkerton reports from defense counsel until shortly before Vanzetti's execution on August 23, 1927. As a result, Vanzetti's lawyers were not able to impeach the testimony of those witnesses at the Plymouth trial because of their previous inconsistent statements to the Pinkertons.

The four prosecution witnesses who identified Vanzetti as the shotgun bandit gave reasonably consistent descriptions, with minor exceptions, of the bandit's general characteristics—height, weight, age, and dress. However, the conflict between their earlier descriptions of the moustache of the man the prosecution claimed was Vanzetti, and their testimony at the trial, reflected evidence of coaching by the prosecution.

At the trial, Bowles described the shotgun bandit as having a "dark moustache ... the moustache was trimmed on the side," and that Vanzetti was positively that man.[16] However, when Bowles gave a statement to Pinkerton agent J. J. H. on the day of the crime, he described the shotgun bandit as having a "black, closely cropped moustache."[17] And, when Bowles testified under oath at the preliminary hearing, he described the shotgun bandit as having a "short, croppy moustache ... Dark."[18] Vanzetti kept a huge, flowing, walrus-type moustache that could not be mistaken for a "closely cropped" or "short, croppy" moustache.

Although Vanzetti's lawyer did not have the benefit at the trial of J. J. H.'s Pinkerton report regarding Bowles's first description of the shotgun bandit, he was able to cross-examine Bowles at the trial based on his conflicting sworn testimony at the preliminary hearing. When asked by Vahey at the trial to describe the shotgun bandit's moustache, Bowles responded:[19]

A: The moustache looked trimmed on the side.
Q: It was not a close-cropped moustache?

A: I believed I made the remark cropped. It was not cropped, I mean trimmed on the side here (indicating) or short here.

Q: You know there is a difference between a cropped moustache and a trimmed one?

A: Yes, but at the time I did not stop to think I meant trimmed instead of cropped.

Cox, the paymaster, went through a similar transformation in his testimony. Cox testified at the trial that the shotgun bandit had a "short and well-trimmed moustache."[20] Asked if he had seen the man with the shotgun since the day of the crime, Cox answered, "I feel that I have,"[21] indicating, "the man in the dock here," pointing to Vanzetti in the prisoner's cage in the courtroom.

When interviewed by Pinkerton agent J. J. H. on the day of the crime, Cox said that he saw the shotgun bandit within ten to fifteen feet and that he had a "closely cropped moustache, which might have been slightly gray."[22] At the preliminary hearing, he testified that the shotgun bandit had a "short, croppy moustache. Well trimmed."[23] At that hearing, Cox had difficulty identifying Vanzetti as the shotgun bandit,[24] stating that "the man might look different today"[25] and "I think there is a doubt." When asked by Vahey at the preliminary hearing if he was sure he could "swear positively" that Vanzetti was the man he saw on December 24 carrying a shotgun, Cox answered, "No. I am not."[26]

When cross-examined at the trial on these inconsistencies, Cox was evasive, often denying he was doubtful of being able to identify Vanzetti as the shotgun bandit. Cox tried to deny his previous description of the shotgun bandit's moustache as "croppy," but rather as "short and well trimmed." Finally, he admitted, "I might have used the word croppy. I have left that word out because I don't know at this moment just what it means—because I don't know that I know just what a croppy moustache is."[27]

The testimony of the prosecution's key witnesses continued. Speaking of the shotgun bandit, Harding told Pinkerton agent J. J. H. that on December 24, 1919, the day of the crime, "I did not get much of a look at his face, but I think he was a Pole."[28] On January 3, 1920, he told Pinkerton agent A. B. M. that he did not see their faces on the day of the holdup.[29] Yet, at the preliminary hearing on May 18, 1920, he testified that the man with a shotgun had a "moustache, dark—call it medium."[30] It seemed to be croppy." Then, at the trial in June 1920, Harding was positive about identifying Vanzetti as the shotgun bandit. On cross-examination, he was evasive regarding his previous testimony at the preliminary hearing that the shotgun bandit had a "croppy moustache."[31]

The prosecution's final eyewitness to the shooting was Maynard Shaw. At the trial, he said he had a "fleeting glance" at the shotgun bandit and could tell he was a foreigner by the way he ran. He described the man as having a "dark ... well-kept moustache."[32] On the basis of Shaw's "fleeting glance," he identified Vanzetti as the shotgun bandit.

The defense produced a number of witnesses who testified that the style of Vanzetti's moustache at the time of the trial was the same at the time of the crime. This testimony was presented to avoid any claim that Vanzetti changed the look of his moustache after the crime.[33] These witnesses also testified that Vanzetti always maintained a flowing, walrus-like moustache.

Georgiana Brook testified for the prosecution that while walking with her five-year-old son that morning, she saw Vanzetti at the wheel of the bandit car shortly before the shooting. Her testimony contradicted Bowles's statement that the driver was a light-complected person. It also conflicted with testimony of other witnesses that the driver remained at the wheel while the shotgun bandit (who the other witnesses claimed was Vanzetti) came out of the car with the two other bandits. Moreover, it was undisputed that Vanzetti did not know how to drive a car. Mrs. Brook also testified that after she and her son passed the bandit car, they walked to the train station and from there witnessed the shooting and attempted robbery. It was later determined—though not in the court record—that because of obstructions from two buildings, it was impossible for anyone to observe the crime scene from the railroad station.[34]

Vanzetti's Shotgun Shells

The Commonwealth's second charge had a dual purpose:[35] 1) to connect a spent Winchester shotgun shell found by Dr. Murphy on December 24, 1919, at the Bridgewater crime scene to an intact Winchester shotgun shell Officer Connolly claimed he found on Vanzetti at the time of his arrest on May 5, 1920, and 2) to connect an intact Peters shotgun shell found near the abandoned Buick on April 17, 1920, to three intact Peters shotgun shells found on Vanzetti when Officer Connolly arrested him. The prosecution claimed the abandoned Buick was the getaway car used in the Bridgewater crime. By establishing these connections, the prosecution intended to provide the jury with a basis to infer that Vanzetti was present at the crime scene and at the location of the abandoned getaway car. The evidence relating to the spent Winchester shell found by Dr. John Murphy follows.

Dr. Murphy testified that he awoke the morning of December 24, 1919, at about quarter to eight, to what sounded like "two blow-outs."[36] He observed the scene of the crime from his bedroom window as the getaway car sped away. Dr. Murphy immediately ran outside to help anyone who might have been hurt. He said, "I saw a ... shell, a common Winchester shell ... that had been discharged, and picked it up."[37] Prosecutor Kane then showed Dr. Murphy a spent Winchester shell that the doctor identified as the shell he found.[38] That shell was offered into evidence despite objection from defense counsel. The judge never formally admitted it into evidence, and it was not given an exhibit number.

On cross-examination, Dr. Murphy further testified regarding the spent shell:[39]

> Q: [by Vahey] Do you do any hunting, Doctor?
> A: I do.
> Q: It is the ordinary bird shell, is it not?
> A: It is an ordinary paper shell.
> Q: It is an ordinary bird shell, is it not?
> A: No, I don't know what shot it is.
> Q: Such a shell you use in hunting for birds, isn't it?
> A: Use it for anything.
> Q: Small birds?
> A: Sure.

Oddly, neither assistant prosecutor Kane nor defense attorney Vahey asked Dr. Murphy if he found anything else at the crime scene. Several reports issued by a Pinkerton detective provide an answer.

In his report dated May 10, 1920, Pinkerton agent H. H. stated, "the shell was found by Dr. Murphy near the scene of the attempted holdup along with the wad and a number of shot ... as he [Dr. Murphy] now recalls it was a #12 gauge Winchester repeating shell and the shot apparently was #10."[40] In other reports, H. H. indicated that Dr. Murphy turned over an envelope to Kane containing number 10 shot and that he gave the spent Winchester shell to Captain Proctor.[41] Kane never produced, mentioned, or accounted for the number 10 shot at or after the trial.

Dr. Murphy's testimony was vague and ambiguous. It bordered on false testimony when he answered, "No, I don't know what shot it is."[42] The doctor was an experienced hunter. When he answered, "Sure," to Vahey's question whether he used such a shell to hunt small birds, Dr. Murphy betrayed his attempt at ignorance regarding the kind of shot contained in the spent Winchester shell. He knew that shell had contained birdshot because he found number 10 shot with the shell and because that is the only kind of shot used to hunt small birds. Buckshot would obliterate a small bird, and a hunter would never use it for that purpose.

Number 10 shot—birdshot—is very small and cannot ordinarily do significant harm to a human.[43] Buckshot, on the other hand, can be deadly. The Commonwealth had reason to conceal the birdshot because it faced a dilemma.

The Commonwealth's charge against Vanzetti of assault with intent to murder would be defeated if the Winchester shell found by Dr. Murphy had contained nonlethal birdshot. Katzmann knew that the intact Winchester shell found on Vanzetti contained buckshot. If that were known, the two shells could not be connected, and Katzmann's attempt to place Vanzetti at the crime scene through the Winchester shell evidence would fail. In addition, disclosure of the birdshot might reveal the existence of the Pinkerton reports to the defense. Katzmann wanted those reports concealed from Vanzetti's counsel because they contained information contrary to the anticipated testimony of his identification witnesses. The dilemma could be resolved if the birdshot was concealed and never mentioned at the trial.

To further the prosecution's case,[44] Kane presented testimony from Captain Proctor that the spent Winchester shell found by Dr. Murphy was "identical" to the Winchester shell found on Vanzetti, "only that one is loaded and the other empty."[45]

The Plymouth trial took a surprising turn regarding the second purpose of the prosecution's shell evidence. In his opening statement to the jury, assistant prosecutor Kane promised that the Commonwealth:

> shall produce evidence from the State Officer that when this car was found in the woods off Manley Street, he found a shell near it on the ground and that it was ... a Peters shell ... and that the defendant had three Peters shells on his person when arrested ...[46]

The prosecution never produced evidence of finding a Peters shell on the ground near the car. The reason may be that when arrested, Vanzetti claimed he had only three shotgun shells, not four, as Officer Connolly testified.[47] The prosecution may not have wanted to open up that dispute. In addition, a dispute over the Peters shell might reveal the existence of the birdshot.

A colloquy between Judge Thayer and both counsel relating to the shotgun shells interrupted Connolly's testimony during the Plymouth trial. The issue discussed was whether the four shotgun shells the police claimed they found on Vanzetti should be admitted into evidence.[48]

Vanzetti's lawyer argued that four and a half months had elapsed between the Bridgewater crime and the arrest of Vanzetti and that shotgun shells found at those separate and distinct events were too remote in time and space to prove that Vanzetti was the shotgun bandit. Vahey also noted that many hunters were active in the Bridgewater area, and any one of them could have dropped the spent Winchester shell Dr. Murphy found in the road.[49] Moreover, Dr. Murphy found only one spent shell even though the shotgun bandit fired at least twice.

The judge eventually allowed the four shells into evidence, holding that it was for the jury to decide the weight of that evidence. This was a highly prejudicial and erroneous ruling by Judge Thayer, certainly as to the three Peters shells, because the prosecution failed to produce any evidence that the authorities found an intact Peters shell near the abandoned Buick getaway car.

The implications and inferences applicable to the shell evidence were not exhausted. The shells played a role during the deliberations of the jury in both the Plymouth and Dedham trials.

Vanzetti's Cap

The next element of the prosecution's case against Vanzetti was the claim that the shotgun bandit wore a cap during the holdup that was similar to a cap owned by Vanzetti.[50]

Graves, Cox, and Bowles each told Pinkerton agent J. J. H. on the day of the crime that the shotgun bandit was bareheaded.[51] Later, at the preliminary hearing, Cox testified that the shotgun bandit's hat had fallen off on the ground near him;[52] at the trial, Cox testified that the shotgun bandit had no hat on his head.[53] Bowles also testified at the trial that the shotgun bandit was bareheaded.[54] Harding told a Pinkerton agent on the day of the crime that the shotgun bandit wore a black derby hat.[55] At the trial, Harding testified that the shotgun bandit did not wear a hat.[56]

Maynard Shaw also testified at the trial that the shotgun bandit was bareheaded.[57] Georgiana Brooks testified at the trial that she saw Vanzetti at the wheel of the bandit car wearing a dark, soft hat just before the shooting began.[58] However, her description of the hat worn by the man that she identified as Vanzetti did not conform to any hat or cap that Vanzetti owned.

Katzmann tried to connect Vanzetti to the Bridgewater crime through the cap testimony of Chief Michael Stewart and college student Richard Casey, a friend of Stewart's family.[59]

Stewart testified that he went to Vanzetti's room and took possession of some clothing, including a brown cap.[60] At the trial, that cap was identified by Richard Casey as similar to a brown cap that he had seen on a passenger in a large Buick in Bridgewater on the morning of the crime. Casey testified that he picked the Vanzetti cap out of a group of six caps that Chief Stewart displayed in his office. He described the driver of the Buick as smaller than the passenger and that he had dark hair, a short, well-trimmed moustache, and a prominent nose.[61] He indicated that the driver wore a soft, black velour hat. Katzmann used Stewart's and Casey's testimony to claim that Boda was the driver of the Buick and Vanzetti was Boda's passenger.

Boda's neighbor, Napoleon Ensher, followed Casey's testimony. He testified that during the spring of that year, Boda drove a Buick around the Bridgewater area. This was the prosecutor's attempt to link Boda to the bandits' car.[62] Following that link, Katzmann tried to connect Boda and Vanzetti through garageman Johnson's testimony that identified Vanzetti as one of the four men who showed up at his home on the night of May 5, with Boda, to pick up the Overland. Piling inference upon inference creates no more substance than "soup made from the shadow of a dead pigeon."[63]

Consciousness of Guilt

The final element of the prosecution's case was evidence of Vanzetti's consciousness of guilt. This was based on Vanzetti's lies to Chief Stewart and prosecutor Katzmann at the time of his arrest and by Vanzetti's alleged suspicious conduct when he, Boda, and others arrived at garageman Johnson's home to pick up the Overland.[64] While rather insignificant in

Vanzetti's Plymouth trial, consciousness of guilt was critical evidence in the Dedham trial.

Vanzetti did not take the stand at the Plymouth trial to defend his innocence. This, too, would have raised a consciousness of guilt issue in the minds of the jury. Jurors often find criminal defendants guilty who do not take the stand in their own defense. Vanzetti blamed his lawyers for this error until his dying day, a charge that his lawyers denied, claiming that the decision was entirely Vanzetti's after being fully advised.

To the contrary, Vahey told Vanzetti that if he took the stand, there was a risk his anarchist beliefs would become known to the jury, and then surely, he would be found guilty not only of the Bridgewater crime but of the South Braintree murders as well. Vanzetti's suspicion that he had been sold out by Vahey to help Katzmann was reinforced when Vahey and Katzmann became law partners after the Dedham trial.[65]

Vahey's advice was disingenuous at best. Vanzetti's ignorant and unschooled mind in American law accepted Vahey's warning in good faith. However, just two months earlier, before the same Judge Thayer, Sergie Zagroff, an avowed anarchist, was charged and tried by Katzmann's office for advocating the overthrow of the government. Zagroff took the stand in his own defense, admitted that he was a Bolshevik, that he advocated a revolution in this country, and that the government should be overthrown.

When the jury announced its not-guilty verdict, Judge Thayer became furious. Showing his bias, he demanded, "Mr. Foreman, did you take into consideration the testimony … that he did not like this form of government and that the only true government was the kind run by working men? How did you arrive at the verdict that you announce?"[66]

The foreman replied, "The jurors … understood the definition of 'advocating anarchy' [based on Judge Thayer's instructions] … to be the act of a person who actually used violence in bringing about this aim and not the advocacy of those aims …"[67]

Some will argue that the Zagroff and Vanzetti cases are not comparable, that Zagroff was a First Amendment–free speech case, and that Vanzetti's case was about an attempted holdup. The verdict in the Zagroff case suggests that Vanzetti should have testified and that his explanations, although dependent on admissions of radicalism, might well have been acceptable to a local jury under freedom of speech principles.

Vanzetti's Alibi

A dozen witnesses testified that Vanzetti was in Plymouth on the morning of December 24, delivering eels and fish. This should have been a complete defense, but it did not prevail. The reason given by one member of the jury was that the alibi witnesses did not stand up to Katzmann's vigorous cross-examination. The jurors apparently concluded that the memories of all twelve witnesses were not reliable because Katzmann was able to cast doubt on their ability to accurately recall events on days other than December 24.[68]

This explanation was not credible, considering that Christmas Eve was a most important "Day of Remembrance" among members of the Italian community.[69] It was a fast day during which Italians eat only eels or fish during their noon and evening meals. An important day that an Italian, and indeed, any Christian, would remember.

Vanzetti's alibi witnesses testified in Italian, and that alone may have diminished their credibility. An interpreter translated the questions and answers, making it difficult for the jury to follow. A more likely reason for the rejection of their testimony is that all of the witnesses were Italian, and the jury did not trust them to be truthful, especially when one of their own was involved. Because of long-standing anti-Italian bias among New Englanders, it was a common belief that, "The dagoes stand together."[70]

Mrs. Adeladi Bonjionanni testified that Vanzetti's helper, Beltrando Brini, delivered eels to her home between 9:00 and 10:00 on the morning of December 24. She said Vanzetti was in her front yard and made change for her purchase.[71]

It was easy for Katzmann to discredit Mrs. Bonjionanni's testimony before a local Yankee jury. He imposed impossible memory tests to show her inability to recall what she was doing on other days and on which days of the week the twenty-fourth fell during other months. As if those tests had any relevance to what she testified had occurred on Christmas Eve. Katzmann got away with these tricks because defense counsel failed to object and Judge Thayer failed to stop Katzmann's chicanery. The following are examples of twenty-seven similar questions testing Mrs. Bonjionanni's memory:[72]

> Q: (By Katzmann through an interpreter) What were you doing between nine and ten on the 24th day of last February?
>
> Q: What were you doing on the 24th day of April last between nine and ten in the morning?

Q: What were you doing on the 24th day of last month between nine and ten in the morning—of May?

Q: Were you boiling polen[t]a on the 17th day of March?

Q: Was that a fast day?

Not surprisingly, the witness was unable to answer these questions. Since Vanzetti's lawyers did not object, the jury would assume these questions were appropriate even though they were repetitive, badgering, and irrelevant.

The following alibi witnesses gave consistent and certain testimony that Vanzetti was in Plymouth the morning of December 24, 1919, delivering eels and fish when the Bridgewater crime was taking place at 7:30 AM.

Mary Fortini testified that Vanzetti boarded at her home and that she woke him at about 6:15 on the morning of December 24 to tell him that Carlo Balboni was at the house asking for the eels he ordered.[73] Vanzetti dressed and took care of Balboni's order, had breakfast, and prepared to make other deliveries. She saw Vanzetti several times in and about the house that morning, between 8:00 and noon, working with his helper, Beltrando Brini. She confirmed that the night before, Vanzetti was at the kitchen sink preparing fish and eels for delivery the next day.

Carlo Balboni, a fireman at Plymouth Cordage Company, confirmed that after finishing work at 6:00 the morning of December 24, he went to the Fortini home to pick up a package of eels that he had ordered from Vanzetti and that Vanzetti delivered the eels to him at that time.[74]

John DiCarli, a shoemaker, testified that Vanzetti delivered a package of eels to him at his shop between 7:00 and 7:40 on the morning of December 24.[75]

Enrico Bastoni, a baker, confirmed that Vanzetti was at his store the morning of December 24, shortly before 8:00.[76] Bastoni testified that Vanzetti asked to borrow a horse and wagon in order to make his deliveries.

Rosa Balboni, wife of Joseph Balboni, saw Vanzetti in Bastoni's bakery after 7:00 AM on December 24.[77] She testified that Vanzetti delivered eels to her home at about 3:00 or 4:00 in the afternoon.

Beltrando Brini, Vanzetti's thirteen-year-old helper, confirmed that beginning at about 8:00 AM on December 24, he worked for at least four hours with Vanzetti, delivering eels and fish.[78]

Vincent Longhi left for work shortly after 7:00 on the morning of December 24, at which time he saw Vanzetti deliver eels to his mother.[79]

Four women testified that Vanzetti delivered eels or fish to their homes on December 24, at the times indicated: Terese Malaquci, after 7:00 AM;[80] Margaretta Fiochi, around 9:00 or 10:00 AM;[81] Emma Borsari, between 10:30 and 10:45 AM;[82] Esteno Christophori, just after 11:00 AM.[83]

Katzmann tried to discredit all of these witnesses by posing many trick questions like the following to Mary Fortini during her cross-examination.[84] She could not answer any of them:

> Q: On the day before Christmas what were you doing at half past seven in the morning?
> Q: What time did Vanzetti get up on the day after Christmas?
> Q: What time did Vanzetti get up the first day of this year?
> Q: What time did Vanzetti get up on Washington's birthday of this year?
> Q: What time did he get up Easter Sunday morning this year?
> Q: What time did he go to bed the Saturday night before Easter morning of this year?

Beltrando Brini provided detailed testimony during his direct examination that he and Vanzetti delivered fish and eels the morning of December 24, 1919. He spoke in English, making it easier for the jury to follow. Beltrando told his story in response to a series of questions put forth by Vanzetti's lawyer. Katzmann cross-examined Beltrando for hours. He made Beltrando's testimony appear a made-up story composed by his parents and rehearsed many times.[85] First, Katzmann encouraged the boy to admit he had a good memory. He then made Beltrando recite the events of December 24, which he easily did in narrative detail. The trap was set:

> Q: [by Katzmann] That is just the same story, isn't it?
> A: Sure.
> Q: How many times did you tell that story?
> A: I told it to Mr. Vahey [Vanzetti's lawyer].
> Q: How many times did you tell it to Mr. Vahey?
> A: Twice.

Q: Told it here twice, that is four times. How many other times?

A: I told it at home ...

Q: Maybe ten times?

A: No ...

Q: Did you tell it when Bastoni and Esther were there?

A: Mr. Bastoni was there ...

Q: When you left out something at first would not he [his father] tell you there was something you had left out?

A: Sure, at first ...

Q: And your papa would say "be sure and put that in"?

A: Yes sir, sure.

Q: And your mother would say it?

A: Sure ...

Q: You learned it just like a piece at school?

A: Sure.

In all, Katzmann peppered the thirteen-year-old with 293 questions during his cross-examination.[86] He even imposed a memory test on the boy:[87] "Q: Which day of the week was the 26th of last November? I am not asking about December, but November. A: I don't remember."

Judge Thayer gave Katzmann's cross-examination of Beltrando Brini an unwarranted boost when, in response to an objection, the judge declared in the presence of the jury, "It seems to me that this may have bearing on the question that it [Beltrando's testimony] is a story that has been practically given to him, taught to him. I will allow it."[88]

Those in support of the fairness of Vanzetti's Plymouth trial have argued that it was free from prejudicial evidence relating to his political beliefs or his association with the anarchist movement. Katzmann's cross-examination of three of Vanzetti's alibi witnesses belies that conclusion.

Katzmann asked John DiCarli, a shoemaker, these questions on cross-examination:[89]

Q: Have you ever heard Vanzetti make any speech?

A: No.

Q: Are you sure of that, Mr. DiCarli?

A: Yes.

> Q: I asked you last night when the court adjourned if you had ever heard Vanzetti making any speeches. What is your answer?
>
> A: No.
>
> Q: Do you belong to any organization that he belongs to?
>
> A: No ...
>
> Q: Have you not discussed Government theories over there between you?
>
> A: No.
>
> Q: Have you not discussed between you and Vanzetti the question of supply and demand?
>
> A: No.
>
> Q: Have you discussed the question of the poor man and the rich man between you?
>
> A: No, sir.
>
> Q: Do you mean that answer, Mr. witness?
>
> A: Yes.

Katzmann's cross-examination of Beltrando Brini implied that Vanzetti had engaged in political activities:[90]

> Q: Did you hear them [Vanzetti and others] talk about our Government?
>
> A: No.
>
> Q: Did your papa and Vanzetti and the baker belong to any society or organization?
>
> A: No.
>
> Q: Did you ever hear Mr. Vanzetti making any speeches to the Italians?
>
> A: No.

Finally, Katzmann cross-examined Matthew Sassi, Vanzetti's friend and neighbor:[91]

> Q: Do you belong to any organization that Vanzetti belongs to?
>
> A: No, I don't know anything about him.
>
> Q: Do you know anything of his political beliefs?
>
> A: No, sir.

Q: Have you ever heard him make any speeches to fellow
   workers at the Cordage?

A: No.

After the defense witnesses testified and Katzmann had completed his cross-examination of them, the case was ready for the jury.

Jury Deliberations

One of the mysteries of the Plymouth trial is the absence of an official transcript. All that has been available is an incomplete copy of the transcript found among the papers of Fred Moore, Sacco's counsel. The available transcript lacks portions dealing with the selection of the jury, the arguments of counsel, and certain rulings and jury instructions by Judge Thayer. It is not known how Katzmann presented his arguments to the jury regarding controversial aspects of the testimony that related to identification of Vanzetti, the shell evidence, or the cap evidence.[92]

A considerable portion of Judge Thayer's instructions to the jury is missing, raising the suspicion that those instructions contained prejudicial comments. Observers of the Plymouth trial have reported that Judge Thayer instructed the jury, "Vanzetti's ideals are cognate with the crime."[93] This instruction gave the jury a way to find Vanzetti guilty based on his beliefs.

After the Plymouth jury retired for its deliberations, they requested further instructions regarding the Commonwealth's charge of assault with intent to murder. Judge Thayer instructed the jury that Vanzetti could be found with "intent" to murder if the weapon he carried and used was capable of causing great bodily harm or death to his victim. After returning to the jury room for further deliberations, the jurors decided to determine what was contained in the shotgun shells found on Vanzetti at the time of his arrest four months after the Bridgewater crime. They opened those shells, one of which was the Winchester, and saw that it contained buckshot. The jurors knew birdshot was not deadly, but buckshot was. This convinced them that the shooter intended great bodily harm or death. Some of the jurors took buckshot as a souvenir.[94]

The jury returned guilty verdicts against Vanzetti on July 1, 1920, for assault with intent to murder and for assault with intent to rob. Shortly after the trial ended, Judge Thayer and Katzmann learned from juror Sullivan of the jury's out-of-court tampering with the shell evidence.

Judge Thayer did nothing to protect Vanzetti's rights, and in collusion with Katzmann, concealed the jury's misconduct.[95] Katzmann told Sullivan not to say anything more about the matter. The judge and Katzmann knew that the verdict of assault with intent to murder could not stand because the jury's decision was influenced by tampering with evidence outside of the presence of the judge and the parties. Judge Thayer, with Katzmann's participation and consent, voided the verdict of assault with intent to murder but let stand the verdict of assault with intent to rob.

In an apparent attempt to compensate for eliminating the attempted murder charge, Judge Thayer sentenced Vanzetti to twelve to fifteen years, an overly severe punishment for attempted robbery by a first-time offender, where no one was harmed and nothing was stolen. Vanzetti's sentence was the longest that Judge Thayer had imposed for comparable, and even more serious, crimes since coming to the bench. For example, in May of the same year, Judge Thayer sentenced a man to three years for assault with intent to murder.[96] In another case, a man charged with assault with intent to murder pled guilty to assault with a dangerous weapon, and the judge sentenced him to six months. In December 1919, the judge sentenced a man to six to eight years on a guilty plea to armed robbery.

Judge Thayer correctly concluded that the jury's misconduct should void its verdict of assault with intent to murder. However, there is a strong argument that he should have voided the jury's verdict of assault with intent to rob as well. The shotgun bandit's single act of shooting at the guards and ordering the driver of the payroll truck to stop, resulted in the simultaneous commission of two crimes—assault with intent to rob and assault with intent to murder. These two crimes were inextricably bound in fact and in logic. The jury was persuaded that Vanzetti was guilty of the greater crime of assault with intent to murder because they found buckshot when they tampered with the shells in evidence. Can it be said without reasonable doubt that the jury's discovery of buckshot showing intent to murder did not influence their guilty verdict of assault with intent to rob?

At the very least, Vanzetti should have had the opportunity to raise the issue on appeal. Vanzetti was deprived of this argument because the prosecution and the judge concealed the jury's misconduct, and Vanzetti's lawyers failed to appeal his conviction. This convenient and suspicious failure benefited the prosecution and was never explained by Vanzetti's counsel. There were grounds for an appeal that included the conflicting testimony relating to the identification of Vanzetti as the shotgun bandit, the jury's improper tampering with the shell evidence, Dr. Murphy's ambiguous testimony regarding birdshot, Vanzetti's airtight alibi supported by a dozen witnesses, and the missing portions of the transcript. Vanzetti's lawyers knew that an appeal would have ameliorated the deleterious affect of his felony conviction in the upcoming Dedham trial. Why didn't Vanzetti's lawyers appeal the conviction?

A group of loyalists formed the Sacco-Vanzetti Defense Committee shortly after the two were arrested. Its purpose was to establish a defense fund, retain legal counsel, and provide public relations support for the two Italians. The defense committee viewed Vanzetti's conviction a disaster. They saw it as an omen—a foreshadowing of the Dedham trial. The committee dismissed Vahey and Graham as Vanzetti's attorneys because they were incompetent, ineffective, and unwilling to take on prosecutor Katzmann and Judge Thayer.

In a search for new counsel, Aldino Felicani, treasurer of the defense committee, turned to his friends in New York for a recommendation.[97] Anarchist leader and labor activist Carlo Tresca, and his friend, liberal firebrand Elizabeth Gurley Flynn, the "East Side Joan of Arc," recommended Fred Moore. He was the pugnacious and indefatigable California lawyer who was part of the team that successfully defended Italian labor activists Joseph Ettor and Arturo Giovannitti of murder charges stemming from the bitter strike of mill workers in Lawrence in 1912.

Felicani followed the advice of Tresca and Flynn, and the defense committee retained Moore as counsel for both Sacco and Vanzetti. Moore moved quickly to assure his control of the case. He appointed William Callahan, a local attorney, to assist him in the representation of Sacco and attorneys Tom and Jeremiah McAnarney, two local politically connected brothers, to represent Vanzetti. Moore made sure, through these arrangements, that he would be in charge of the entire defense of the two Italians.

The Dedham trial would have immediately followed, except for the intervention of parasites gnawing on the underside of the Massachusetts judicial system planning a shakedown of Sacco and Vanzetti.

CHAPTER 5

THE SHAKEDOWN

For a brief time, the Sacco and Vanzetti case lost its news appeal. Then, in early 1921, Angelina DeFalco, an interpreter at the Dedham court, put the story back in the headlines.[1] Fred Moore, Sacco's and Vanzetti's new lawyer, urged the police to arrest Mrs. DeFalco. Moore acted in response to the following events.

On January 2, 1921, Benjiamino Cicchetti, a relative of Mrs. DeFalco and a known "fixer" for Italians in trouble, introduced Mrs. DeFalco to his friend, Aldino Felicani, treasurer of the defense committee. Mrs. DeFalco claimed that she was in a position to help Sacco and Vanzetti because she had a special relationship with prosecutor Fred Katzmann, his lawyer brother Percy, and attorney Francis J. Squires, clerk of the Dedham court. She indicated that if the defense committee would pay a sum of money to two lawyers recommended by her to represent Sacco and Vanzetti, she could guarantee Sacco's freedom, and even Vanzetti's, but that would be more difficult because of Vanzetti's conviction of the Bridgewater crime.

Members of the defense committee met with Mrs. DeFalco during the following days. The committee sought to determine how to free the two Italians and negotiate the fee, although no money passed hands. A defense committee secretary secretly recorded the meetings at the other end of a listening device in the basement.

Mrs. DeFalco told the defense committee they would have to pay fifty thousand dollars to free Sacco and Vanzetti. After negotiations, that amount was reduced to forty thousand dollars, and then thirty-five thousand dollars, payable in installments. Mrs. DeFalco indicated that

Percy Katzmann and Squires would have to represent Sacco and Vanzetti in place of Fred Moore. The money had to be paid to them as a retainer and must not be paid to Fred Katzmann. She said Fred Katzmann would recuse himself and turn the prosecution over to an assistant. There would be a trial of sorts with a rigged jury that would include a foreman who was part of their "county ring." She told them it was easy to fix a jury. Interestingly, whenever Percy Katzmann represented a criminal defendant in Norfolk or Plymouth counties, his brother Fred would conveniently recuse himself. Percy Katzmann became very successful in his defense practice under this arrangement.

To seal the deal, Mrs. DeFalco organized a dinner at her home for the evening of January 7. She invited the Katzmann brothers, Squires, Felicani, and another member of the defense committee to the dinner. When Fred Moore learned of these events, he feared a trap and was opposed to Felicani or any member of the defense committee attending the meeting at DeFalco's home. After much debate, Felicani agreed not to attend the event. He gave Mrs. DeFalco an excuse at the last minute that he would not attend the dinner because he had to meet an out-of-town benefactor who pledged financial support for DeFalco's deal. Since the benefactor had not yet arrived, Felicani indicated he was not in a position to talk financial terms.

Felicani wanted to know who attended the DeFalco dinner. Felicani, accompanied by Riccardo Orciani, who was now acting as Fred Moore's chauffeur, and Robert Reid, Moore's detective, surreptitiously drove past the DeFalco home that evening. They saw a line of parked cars and took down the license numbers. In the morning, Reid checked out the numbers and found that three of the cars parked at DeFalco's home belonged to Fred Katzmann, Percy Katzmann, and Francis Squires.

Following these events, Fred Moore filed a complaint with the police that resulted in the arrest of Mrs. DeFalco. The charge against her was the solicitation of law business by a nonlawyer. Judge Michael Murray quickly held a short trial without a jury. The Katzmann brothers, as well as Squires, took the stand. The Norfolk County prosecutor and his office were on trial, and the Boston papers carried the story on their front pages.

Fred Katzmann testified that he never knew or even heard of Mrs. DeFalco until these charges were brought against her and that he had no part in her activities. No one asked Katzmann to explain why his car was parked in front of the DeFalco home the night of January 7, well before charges were brought against Mrs. DeFalco.

At the trial, Percy Katzmann and Francis Squires acknowledged that they knew Mrs. DeFalco. They claimed that she had tried to interest them earlier in representing Sacco and Vanzetti, but they had declined. However, they were willing to talk to her out of consideration for her past activities as a court interpreter. Hearing this testimony, Judge Murray found that Mrs. DeFalco had used bad judgment, but he found her not guilty of criminal conduct and dismissed the charges.

The arrest and trial of Mrs. DeFalco proved to be a disaster for the Sacco and Vanzetti defense. It put the Norfolk County prosecutor's office on trial and backed Fred Katzmann into a corner to prove he was not part of a shakedown operation.

This was a particularly sensitive time for a county prosecutor in Massachusetts to be charged with a shakedown. During 1920 and 1921, widespread corruption of justice within the Commonwealth had surfaced. The Massachusetts attorney general brought charges against Nathan A. Tufts, the elected district attorney of Middlesex County (Cambridge), and Joseph C. Pelletier, the elected district attorney for Suffolk County (Boston). They were found guilty of collaborating with crooked lawyers to extort payoffs from vulnerable persons targeted by these prosecutors for some real and some fabricated crimes. Both prosecutors were convicted, removed from office, and disbarred from the legal profession.

This kind of corruption was well known and had spread among members of the Massachusetts bar and other so-called county rings of chasers and bag men, some of whom included court interpreters active in Norfolk County, where Sacco and Vanzetti were to be tried for murder. One such interpreter was Joseph Ross, who also acted as Judge Webster Thayer's chauffeur. There had been quiet rumors about Judge Thayer touching on the integrity of his courtroom and his relationship with Ross. Some years later, Ross was convicted of courtroom corruption.

If there was ever a chance to save Sacco and Vanzetti from the death penalty, it was lost. District Attorney Fred Katzmann was fighting to save his reputation. Sacco and Vanzetti had to be found guilty; otherwise, the district attorney would be viewed as having thrown the case. Katzmann now had a personal stake in the outcome of the Dedham trial. Because of such a conflict of interest, Fred Katzmann should have been barred as a prosecutor in a case involving Sacco and Vanzetti.

With the benefit of historical perspective, it is difficult to conclude that the DeFalco trial was anything other than a fix to absolve what looked like a Norfolk County ring. The quickness of the trial before a judge without a jury on charges of the improper solicitation of law business, along with the judge's ruling exonerating all parties, was all too convenient to be genuine. The big losers were Sacco and Vanzetti, who were innocent of any wrongdoing in the shakedown attempt but forced to suffer the consequences of the wrongful actions of others.

After obtaining the conviction of Vanzetti in the Plymouth trial, Katzmann had Sacco and Vanzetti perfectly positioned for the main event, the trial of the two for murder. No one realized that the Dedham trial—which would take place before the same Judge Thayer, a judge with a bias, and which would be prosecuted by the same Frederick Katzmann, a prosecutor with a vengeance—would become the trial of the century.

CHAPTER 6

South Braintree and the Dedham Trial

The Dedham murder trial did not begin until almost a year after the Plymouth jury convicted Vanzetti. This gave Katzmann time to continue his search for evidence and to reorganize his team. Katzmann replaced Captain Proctor of the state police with Chief Stewart of Bridgewater's two-man police department as his chief investigator. Proctor had become troublesome because of his insistence that Sacco and Vanzetti were the wrong men. He argued that professional highwaymen committed the South Braintree robbery and murders.[1] Katzmann permitted Proctor to continue with the investigation but in a subordinated role.

The DeFalco affair, with its related trial and adverse publicity for the Norfolk County prosecutor's office during the early months of 1921, was an unanticipated distraction for Katzmann. It put pressure on him to complete his investigation and prepare for the Dedham trial set to begin on May 31, 1921.

The start of the trial the day after Memorial Day, in the shadow of the armistice that ended World War I, was not the best time for these two defendants to face judge and jury. The people of Boston were in a dual mood—a state of mind that mixed superpatriotism honoring their heroes with continuing fears brought on by the Red Scare. Labor unrest, the bombings, the murders, the anarchist agitation, and the Palmer raids were all fresh in the minds of the people. While Bostonians decorated graves of the fallen, could Sacco and Vanzetti, two draft-dodging Italian immigrant workers espousing atheistic anarchism, get a fair trial before a New England jury? A few lines from the then popular poet, Jim Seymour, provide a clue:

> What's all this fuss they're making about them guys? ...
> ... they got what was comin to 'em ...
> They're only a couple o' God damn dagoes! ...
> We don't care whether they done it or not.
> To hell with 'em!
> They're dagoes.[2]

The South Braintree Crime[3]

The core facts of the South Braintree murders and robbery are straightforward and undisputed. The crime occurred at about 3:00 PM on Thursday, April 15, 1920. Bandits gunned down Frederick Parmenter, paymaster at the Slater & Morrill Shoe Company, and Allessandro Berardelli, his guard, and the gang stole a $15,700 payroll.

American Express delivered the payroll by train earlier that morning. It was packaged at the company's main office for payment to its employees at its factory located a short distance west on Pearl Street. Later that afternoon, Parmenter and the guard each carried a payroll box on foot to the factory when two bandits shot and killed them. A third bandit helped the other two pick up the payroll boxes, which they threw into an approaching Buick touring sedan occupied by two confederates. The three bandits then piled into the getaway car. One of them shot at horrified witnesses as the five sped east on Pearl Street toward South Braintree Square and beyond. The gangsters dumped large tacks, weighted to stand upright, out of the Buick to puncture the tires of any cars that might follow.

Two days later, hunters Charles Fuller and Max Wind found the getaway car abandoned in the Manley Woods, twenty miles from South Braintree and about a mile from the Coacci home.[4] The police and the hunters carefully examined the Buick. They did not find a bullet hole on the car. Yet, after the police impounded the Buick, they reported finding a bullet hole in the right rear door.

The bullet hole became the subject of scrutiny during the Dedham trial. The following exchange occurred when defense counsel questioned Charles Fuller:[5]

Q: [by McAnarney] Have you told us all the marks you saw on that car?

A: I think I have.

Q: ... Were there any bullet marks on that car?

A: I do not recollect any.

Q: You examined it pretty carefully?

A: Fairly carefully.

Q: So the car you looked at, there was no bullet hole through the door, was there?

A: Not that I saw.

Counsel also cross-examined Max Wind, the other hunter.[6] He testified that during his examination of the Buick, which he conducted with Fuller and the police, they did not find a bullet hole in the side of the automobile.

William Hill, a police officer, accompanied by City Marshall Ryan, had also examined the Buick in the presence of Fuller and Wind.[7] Hill testified that he did not see a bullet hole in the Buick until after he examined the car in the garage, at which time he found a bullet hole in the right rear door.

The bullet hole could not have been made during the South Braintree crime, since no one returned fire against the bandits or shot at the getaway car during that event. Was this an indication that the police tampered with the Buick to make it appear that the car used in the South Braintree murders was also used in the Bridgewater shootout, where shots were exchanged between the guards and the bandits?

"Snowflaking," the practice of police planting false evidence against a suspect to fortify an arrest, is a well-known, unscrupulous tactic.[8] The bullet hole in the getaway car was one of several snowflaking claims made against the police in the Sacco and Vanzetti case.

Witnesses presented the first version of the South Braintree crime at an inquest held on April 17, 1920.[9] Pinkerton detectives hired by the company were also gathering information. Unfortunately for Sacco and Vanzetti, the inquest minutes and the Pinkerton reports (like the Pinkerton reports regarding the Bridgewater crime) were not known or made available to them or their counsel until 1927, shortly before the two were executed.[10]

The inquest testimony and the Pinkerton reports provided reliable information, as the facts were fresh in the minds of the witnesses and free from the manipulation of anyone bent on proving Sacco and Vanzetti guilty. During the course of the Dedham trial, prosecutor Katzmann had the benefit of that information and was able to fashion his theories, spin his arguments, and prepare his witnesses in a way most favorable for the conviction of the two suspects. Counsel for Sacco and Vanzetti did not have that information, and therefore they were unable to cross-examine witnesses whose testimony at the trial conflicted with their earlier testimony at the inquest or with their statements to the Pinkerton detectives.

While the core facts of the South Braintree crimes were undisputed, the details varied considerably in important ways, depending on which witness testified and when. Some witnesses testified at the inquest immediately after the event, some before the grand jury on September 10, 1920, others at the trial a year later, and still others at clemency hearings six years later before Governor Fuller and his advisory committee.

Shelly Neal, the American Express local agent, testified at the inquest that on the morning of the crime he saw two unfamiliar cars, a Hudson and a Buick, parked next to each other. He said that the drivers spoke while their cars faced in opposite directions outside of the company's main office.[11] A year later, at the Dedham trial, Neal omitted mentioning a second car.[12] Focus on two cars would not occur until 1926, when Celestino Medeiros, a self-confessed participant in the South Braintree murders, testified as to the use of two cars during the South Braintree crime.[13]

An important witness at the inquest was Thomas Fraher, superintendent at the Slater & Morrill factory. He provided some details as to what happened the day of the crime. When asked by the judge if there was anything more he could add that would help find the killers, Fraher testified that he had a talk the morning of the inquest with Fred Loring, an employee at the factory, concerning some remarks made by a group of cabdrivers Loring overheard in a Boston restaurant, but he had nothing else worth noting.[14]

Fraher did not mention that Fred Loring had delivered a cap to him an hour after Loring claimed he found it next to Berardelli's body immediately after the shooting. However, Loring testified to that effect at the Dedham trial as part of Katzmann's attempt to prove the cap belonged to Sacco.[15] Fraher's failure to mention the cap at the inquest would, with other evidence that came to light during the clemency hearings six years later, establish that Loring's cap testimony at the trial was false.[16] Possibly another example of snowflaking.

At the inquest, Lewis Wade,[17] a shoemaker at Slater & Morrill, identified the driver of the getaway car as a young man with light hair, a pale fellow who looked sickly, stating, "he looked as though he was in consumption."[18] Numerous witnesses confirmed this unusual description of the driver.[19] Steve "the Pole" Benkosky, a member of the notorious Morelli gang of thieves from Providence, Rhode Island, precisely fit this description.

Dr. John Frazer, a medical examiner, testified at the inquest that he attended the autopsies and that Berardelli was shot four times.[20] He stated that all the bullets were .32 caliber and steel jacketed, indicating that an automatic pistol had been used rather than a revolver. This ruled out Vanzetti's gun, a .38-caliber revolver.[21]

A second medical examiner, Dr. Frederick Jones, also attended the autopsies.[22] He testified at the inquest that the six bullets extracted from the two victims were identical and that he believed they were fired from the same pistol. Dr. Jones was quick to point out that the pistol may not have been a Colt.[23] If he was correct, none of the six bullets were fired from Sacco's gun, since it was a Colt. But how could Dr. Jones have concluded that none of the bullets were fired from a Colt by simply looking at the bullets? It was well known that a Colt automatic pistol produced left-twist markings on bullets fired through its barrel.[24] Bullets have twist markings because the inside of a gun's barrel has grooves that spiral to the right or to the left.[25] Between the grooves, upgraded portions of the barrel are called lands. These lands and grooves put spin on a bullet that causes it to fly straight rather than tumble end over end. The lands and grooves create contra lands and grooves on a spent bullet. Because of the right or left spiraling of the lands and grooves, a rightward or leftward slant to the contra lands and grooves is embedded in a bullet. The slant of the contra lands and grooves is obvious to the naked eye. All six bullets should have had right-twist markings in order for Dr. Jones to comment that the gun may not have been a Colt. Observers of the case have doggedly followed this clue for ninety years.

The autopsies of the two victims were conducted by Dr. George Burgess Magrath, medical examiner for Suffolk County.[26] Each of the four bullets removed by Dr. Magrath from Berardelli's body, was marked on its base with a roman numeral. The third bullet had killed Berardelli; it was marked with a roman numeral III and later identified as Bullet III.

Dr. Magrath's testimony provided to the grand jury on September 10, 1920, was consistent with Dr. Jones's opinion that all four bullets fired into Berardelli were shot from the same pistol.[27]

According to Dr. Magrath:

> These four bullets … [were] all alike, they were jacketed and weighed 4 and 1/10 grammes; the dimensions and weight are consistent with what is known as a .32 caliber made to be used in an automatic pistol … I have an opinion that they all may have been fired by the same gun, but I have no proof. The bullets were all of the same size and weight. A final determination I did not make, but I have a belief that they were fired from the same weapon and they very well could have been, judging from the size and weight … They looked exactly alike.

Since Berardelli might have been shot by two guns with the same twist, Dr. Magrath could not be certain that all four Berardelli bullets were shot from the same weapon. However, because he stated twice that he believed the four Berardelli bullets were shot from the same gun, and that "[T]hey looked exactly alike," the fatal bullet must have shown the same twist as the other Berardelli bullets which were identified at the trial as having right-twist markings.

Given these circumstances, Sacco's gun should have been ruled out as the source of the fatal bullet. However, that was not how the case was prosecuted.

Police searched the clothing of the murdered men and did not find firearms or cartridges.[28] None of the witnesses at the inquest testified that either Parmenter or Berardelli showed any signs that they were carrying weapons, that the bandits picked up any weapons from the victims, or that any of the bandits wore gloves.

Overlooked Clues

Neither the prosecution nor defense counsel followed up on two important clues:[29] 1) fingerprints found on the Buick, and 2) a few days before the crime, a police officer saw a member of the Morelli gang driving a Buick touring car that fit the description of the South Braintree getaway car.

The first clue surfaced in news stories in various editions of the *Brockton Times* and other press reports indicating that the state police had obtained very good photographs of fingerprints on the abandoned Buick.[30] The May 7, 1920, edition of the *Brockton Times* reported on a conference involving the district attorney's office and high police officials, and that Inspector George C. Chase had completed the comparison of fingerprints found on the Buick with those of Sacco and Vanzetti.[31]

No report was publicly issued on the results of the fingerprint comparisons. The existence of Sacco's or Vanzetti's fingerprints on the Buick would have been conclusive evidence of their participation in the murders. Obviously, the fingerprints of Sacco and Vanzetti were not among those found; if they were, the police would have either publicly revealed those results or that evidence would have been presented during the trial. Conversely, the absence of their prints would have been exculpatory evidence, since the killers were not seen wearing gloves. One prosecution witness was specific in describing the bare hand of a bandit in the getaway car, who she claimed was Sacco.[32]

The failure to announce the results of the fingerprint analysis should have raised a negative inference against the Commonwealth, since it indicated that the prosecution had something to hide. Katzmann was successful in suppressing the release of this information. Defense counsel never complained on the record about its concealment. This was significant, because it not only reflected prosecutorial misconduct in the suppression of exculpatory evidence but also incompetence on the part of defense counsel for failing to aggressively pursue an apparent obstruction of justice.

The author of this book made diligent efforts to locate the missing fingerprints.[33] Beginning in early February 2006, he filed information requests under the Massachusetts Public Record Law for the missing fingerprints and any related information or materials with the following agencies: the Brockton Police Department, the Norfolk County District Attorney, the Massachusetts Department of Public Safety, the Massachusetts State Police, the state archives, and the Secretary of the Commonwealth. All requests failed to produce any information or materials regarding the missing fingerprints.

On the chance that local authorities sent the fingerprints to the FBI for a search against its more extensive database, the author filed a request under the Freedom of Information Act for the fingerprints and any related information with that agency in early February 2006. After he pursued that request for a year, including an administrative appeal, no information regarding the missing fingerprints was produced.

How is it possible that such critical evidence, including any information, transmittal letters, or receipts, can be missing and not accounted for? More likely than not, authorities took deliberate actions to destroy this exculpatory evidence.

The second clue was contained in the notebook of Inspector E. C. Jacobs of the New Bedford police.[34] A few days before the South Braintree murders, Inspector Jacobs saw Michael Morelli, a known thief, driving a Buick touring car in New Bedford with two other men in it. The inspector suspected that Morelli had stolen the car, and he made an entry in his notebook: "R.I. 154 E Buick touring car, Mike Morelli."[35]

Mike, along with his four brothers, made up the core of the Morelli gang of Providence, Rhode Island. When news of the South Braintree murders and robbery reached Inspector Jacobs, he immediately suspected the Morellis because of their reputation and because Mike Morelli was driving a Buick similar to the getaway vehicle shortly before the crime.[36]

On the day of the murders, Jacobs said he saw a black touring car in New Bedford, between 5:00 and 5:30 PM, bearing the same Rhode Island license plate he saw on the Buick.[37] He suspected Mike Morelli was driving the Buick he saw a few days earlier, and he noted the license number in his notebook. Jacobs, however, did not get a full view of the car. He said, "I caught a rear view of the car as it passed me going by the post office and noted the number 154 E in my notebook."[38] Although Jacobs assumed it was the same Buick, he did not indicate that the rear window was broken out, which should have been obvious if the car he saw was the Buick getaway car. Then, on April 24, Jacobs saw a black Cole 8 touring car with the same Rhode Island plate on it parked in front of Joe Fiore's restaurant, a Morelli gang hangout in New Bedford.[39] He made an entry in his notebook: "April 24, 1920, 154 E, Black Cole 8, touring."[40] He wondered what happened to the Buick touring car that carried that same license plate just a week or so earlier.

Jacobs investigated the matter. He found Frank Morelli, Mike's brother, in Fiore's restaurant and asked him how it was that plate R.I. 154 E, registered in the Morelli name, was on a Buick and later on a Cole 8. Frank Morelli told Jacobs that he was in the car business, and the license plate was a dealer plate that he transferred from car to car in his business.[41] Jacobs had no way at the time to challenge Frank, but he continued to suspect the Morelli gang of the South Braintree robbery and murders.

If the car Jacobs saw in New Bedford on April 15 between 5:00 and 5:30 PM was the Buick getaway car, it means the bandits bypassed the Manley Woods on their way to New Bedford after committing the South Braintree murders. It also means that the bandits switched plates on the Buick to license plate 154 E some time during their escape and that the driver of the getaway car doubled back from New Bedford between 5:30

Thursday evening, the day of the crime, and early Saturday morning, when the abandoned Buick was found in the Manley Woods. Such a scenario would have had the bandits driving around New Bedford in the Buick getaway car on the day of the crime, displaying license plate 154 E traceable to the Morellis. This would have been foolish and illogical. Moreover, it was contrary to the sequence of towns and areas of the bandits' escape route, which is described hereafter in assistant prosecutor Williams's opening statement.

There were those who argued that when Sacco and Vanzetti were arrested, amid press announcements that the South Braintree killers had been caught, Jacobs dropped his investigation of the Morellis, and for that reason, the information in his notebook never reached those in charge of the South Braintree investigation before the Dedham trial.[42]

The supposed unilateral decision by the New Bedford police to withhold this important evidence from the Norfolk County prosecutor is not credible. The murders were highly publicized, and the arrest of Sacco and Vanzetti would have stimulated Inspector Jacobs to share his information with Katzmann. The urge to do so would have been irresistible. For all Jacobs knew, Sacco and Vanzetti were working with the Morelli gang. And wouldn't Jacobs have wanted to share in the glory of catching the South Braintree gang of killers and share in an almost certain reward?

It is reasonable to assume that Inspector Jacobs contacted Katzmann's office to share the Morelli information and that someone in his office told Jacobs they had the killers and to drop the matter. Chief Stewart would have been concerned that disclosure of Jacobs's information would make it more difficult to convict the two Italians. He was busy building a case against an anarchist group from West Bridgewater that included Sacco, Vanzetti, Boda, Orciani, and Coacci, not the Morelli gang from Providence, Rhode Island.[43] This is precisely the theory that assistant prosecutor Harold Williams presented to the jury in his opening statement.[44] Katzmann and Stewart would have had to reconsider their theory of the South Braintree crime if they pursued the Morelli gang theory. Besides, a conviction of Sacco and Vanzetti would be a way to get rid of two troublemakers and send an unmistakable message to other radicals that the law was closing in on them.

This was the mood of New Englanders at the time of the Dedham trial. They saw the Reds—the socialists, the Bolsheviks, the anarchists, the labor agitators, the bomb throwers, the radical immigrant workers—as a threat to American values, the greatest threat to the Republic since the

Civil War. Even if Sacco and Vanzetti were innocent of the South Braintree murders, because they were part of the Red menace, the public sentiment was to "treat 'em rough!...Stand the goddam Bolsheviks against a wall and shoot them full of holes!" [45]

The entries in Jacobs's notebook remained unknown until 1926, when Herbert Ehrmann, a young lawyer on the Sacco and Vanzetti appellate team, discovered the notebook after a thorough investigation.[46] He also obtained information that at the time of the South Braintree murders, members of the Morelli gang were under indictment for stealing shoes from Slater & Morrill and Rice & Hutchins shoe companies, both located in South Braintree, and that members of the gang were out on bond.[47] This meant that not only were the Morellis available to commit the crime, but they needed money to pay legal fees and bond premiums. It also showed that the Morellis were familiar with the scene of the crime and payroll procedures of the Slater & Morrill Shoe Company.

These facts pointed to the Morelli gang as responsible for the murders and became the basis, in 1926, of a motion by Sacco's and Vanzetti's lawyer for a new trial.[48] By that time however, the prosecutors, Judge Thayer, and the Massachusetts Supreme Judicial Court were not about to acknowledge they were wrong and that the two Italians were innocent.

After the arrest of Sacco and Vanzetti, the prosecution made all-out efforts to find evidence to prove them guilty of the murders. Katzmann ignored clues and suspects to the contrary. Although the headlines of major newspapers blared that the police arrested Sacco and Vanzetti for the South Braintree murders, Katzmann knew he could not convict them merely because they lied about their evening at Johnson's garage and because they were armed on the night of their arrest.

The Search for Evidence[49]

Eyewitness testimony identifying the murderers would be a big part of the prosecution's case; such evidence, however, is notoriously unreliable in a fast-action crime of this kind. That would have been particularly true since none of the witnesses knew Sacco or Vanzetti before the crime occurred. The prosecution's eyewitness accounts of these events were jumbled, conflicting, and contradictory, even more so than the prosecution's eyewitness accounts of Vanzetti at the Plymouth trial. The vagaries of eyewitness identification are well known;[50] the annals of criminal law are rife with instances of mistaken identification. Eminent legal scholars, in their published treatises, have reported that some of the most tragic miscarriages of justice have been due to eyewitnesses providing false identification testimony.[51]

The unreliability of the Commonwealth's eyewitness testimony was compounded by the way the two Italians were subjected to identification procedures after their arrest. None of the prosecution's witnesses identified the suspects out of a lineup of men with similar physical characteristics and dress, with only one known exception.[52] This occurred when Vanzetti, viewed among a group, was the only man with a moustache, and the witness had a picture of Vanzetti in his pocket. Instead, witnesses to the murders observed Sacco and Vanzetti standing alone.[53] They were required to assume positions mimicking a shooter or otherwise imitating the actions of the killers. It is not surprising that such viewings resulted in witnesses identifying Sacco as the shooter and Vanzetti as his accomplice.

The prosecutors prodded uncertain witnesses to reconsider their doubts amid suggestions consistent with a positive identification.[54] They only called witnesses at the trial who gave satisfactory responses to Katzmann or his staff.[55] And they summarily dismissed uncertain witnesses and witnesses who were positive that Sacco and Vanzetti were not the killers, without disclosure of their identities to the defense.[56]

In order to establish guilt of capital murder beyond a reasonable doubt to twelve jurors and the public at large, Katzmann needed physical evidence connecting Sacco and Vanzetti to the crime. Eyewitness testimony could then be vindicated, and the concept of consciousness of guilt could be convincingly applied to their lies and the fact that they carried guns the night they were arrested.

Katzmann's initial attempts to obtain evidence against Sacco and Vanzetti kept coming up empty.[57] In addition to the failure of the fingerprint evidence to connect them to the murders, the police never found or traced any of the stolen payroll to the defendants or their families, friends, or associates.[58] Sacco's and Vanzetti's lifestyles after the robbery and murders never changed in the slightest. They continued to ride streetcars, work at their jobs, and seek contributions in dribs and drabs for their cause.[59] The Commonwealth never proved the identities of the other gang members.

Katzmann even recruited the Department of Justice to determine if anarchists in New York were in receipt of large sums of money,[60] and he caused Coacci's luggage to be searched by the Italian police when it arrived in Italy after Coacci was deported, both with negative results.[61] The government placed spies among members of the defense committee to find clues or admissions of guilt. None was obtained.[62]

Katzmann considered placing a spy in the home of Rosina Sacco.[63] John Ruzzamenti, the proposed spy, deposed under oath that Katzmann told him "he [Katzmann] was right hard up against it;[64] that he had no evidence against the said Nicola Sacco or against the said Bartolomeo Vanzetti ... that he had been unable to get anything out of them or out of any other person."

Katzmann suggested that Ruzzamenti find work in Sacco's hometown and seek to board at Sacco's home. Katzmann, according to Ruzzamenti's affidavit, made the following proposition to him:

> [That] Rose Sacco was undergoing great physical, mental and spiritual suffering by reason of the incarceration of her husband, [and that] it should be easy for the affiant to establish friendly relations with her, and ... secure confidential communications from her as to any criminal activities of her husband ...[65]

Ruzzamenti agreed to undertake the plan, but it was never carried out.[66] Katzmann admitted interviewing Ruzzamenti but claimed he did so only to place him as a spy in the cell next to Sacco. Katzmann denied that he ever considered placing a spy in Sacco's home.

Katzmann eventually placed Anthony Carbone, an undercover agent, in the cell next to Sacco to seek possible admissions of guilt from him, again to no avail.[67] Nevertheless, the search for evidence continued because Katzmann and Stewart had made up their minds that Sacco and Vanzetti were guilty even though they still had no convincing evidence to prove it.

The Dedham Trial

The trial of Sacco and Vanzetti for the South Braintree murders began at the Dedham courthouse on May 31, 1921. The classic courthouse, with its Roman dome and Grecian columns, stood at the center of Dedham, a sentinel of American values. Arching elms, giant oaks, and well-kept lawns bordered the town's streets. Elegant mansions were dotted among old colonials and white steepled churches. Dedham was the perfect picture of a New England village.

Throughout the trial, the police housed the defendants in the county jail located in Dedham. Each day, Sacco and Vanzetti, handcuffed to each other, walked from the jail to the courthouse through Dedham streets surrounded by a small army of armed guards.[68] During the early days of the trial, curious spectors lined the streets, along with the press. Women and children peered at the so-called killers of South Braintree from behind drawn curtains in the the safety of their homes. The walks occurred four times each day: from the jail to the courthouse in the morning, to and from the jail at noon, and back to jail following adjournment. After a time, spectators and the press thinned out until the closing days of the trial, when they reemerged in large numbers.

The courthouse was heavily guarded by police, and body searches were conducted of all those entering the building.[69] As if their daily walks to court surrounded by armed guards were not enough to send a message that these men were dangerous killers, throughout the trial Sacco and Vanzetti were required to defend themselves from within a steel cage[70]—a throwback to Massachusetts' Puritan roots. Massachusetts was the only state in America to continue such a prejudicial practice. The entire process turned the presumption of innocence on its head.

The strong personalities of Judge Webster Thayer, prosecutor Frederick Katzmann, and chief defense counsel Fred Moore dominated the trial.

Judge Thayer was only five feet two inches tall, but his Napoleon complex more than made up for his diminutive stature. Although he was prep-school and Dartmouth educated, his family was not among the Boston elite. He spent his life seeking acceptance from the Mayflower descendants who dominated Boston society. His family's middle-class status and his father's occupation—a meat wholesaler, who some derisively called a butcher—kept him from achieving the high regard and acceptance he sought from the Brahmins. As a result, Judge Thayer was a bitter man in his sixties when the trial began.[71] His thin lips, set in a wrinkled face with a high forehead and deep-set eyes, gave him an austere appearance.

Judge Thayer had a mediocre legal background. He never attended law school; instead, he read the law and tutored under a lawyer in preparation for the bar examination. He developed a rather pedestrian law practice and eventually found his way into local politics. In 1917, the governor, a former classmate at Dartmouth, appointed Webster Thayer to the bench.[72] Given to flowery language, he issued verbose, pompous rulings and decisions. Like his New England peers, he had a deep hatred, or perhaps fear, of Communism in all its variations. He projected those feelings on southern and eastern European immigrants espousing alien philosophies. He held himself out as a man of duty and loyalty to his country.

Frederick Katzmann tried to represent himself as Mayflower connected, but he was not.[73] A German father and a Scottish mother raised him in Roxbury, a lower-middle-class area. Although the family was poor, he was able to work his way through Harvard College, tending furnaces. Following graduation, he held mundane jobs while attending night law school at Boston University. He developed a modest law practice and became active in local politics. Eventually, the voters elected him district attorney for Norfolk and Plymouth counties. During the war years, he used his mother's maiden name to identify himself as Frederick Gunn Katzmann, to lessen the negative impact of his German surname. Katzmann was of at least average intelligence, with a modest command of the language, but he had a certain cunning and street savvy that made him brilliant in the art of cross-examination.

Although he was ambitious, the higher levels of Boston society never accepted Katzmann. He had his eye on the office of attorney general of Massachusetts, and perhaps even more. The portly Katzmann projected strength through his Teutonic features with a look of confidence and self-satisfaction.

Fred Moore had started his legal career as a corporate railroad lawyer out West, but he soon turned to defending radicals, labor activists, and members of the Wobblies caught up in the struggles of the growing labor movement. He was controversial, with a bohemian lifestyle, marrying and divorcing a series of his secretaries. More important, his demeanor and courtroom style during the Dedham trial (barefoot in court one day, no jacket or tie another day, and sleeping on the courthouse lawn during lunch hour) infuriated Judge Thayer.[74] He came to hate Moore. According to observers, the judge angrily complained that no long-haired radical from California was going to tell him how to run his court.[75] Thomas McAnarney, one of Vanzetti's lawyers, recalled, "Mr. Moore would ... make some remark and it would be perfectly clear that it got under Judge Thayer's skin."[76] Sacco and Vanzetti bore the brunt of Judge Thayer's wrath against Moore.

Moore's reputation among his followers was that of a brilliant lawyer. That reputation, upon scrutiny, was not justified. However, even if he was not a great lawyer, he was accomplished at promoting a cause. His genius for public relations developed the Sacco and Vanzetti case into the national, and then international, cause célèbre that it became. Through Moore's association with the American labor movement and his connections with socialists and Communists worldwide, he was able to gain support and financial backing for Sacco and Vanzetti from those groups. Through his efforts, the defense committee raised well over three hundred thousand dollars, a large sum in 1920.[77]

Fred Moore's motive for representing Sacco and Vanzetti was often questioned. There were those who believed he was an idealist and found it noble to defend the working man against the oppression of capitalists. There were others, including Sacco and his wife, who saw a more sinister side to him. They thought he was in it for the money and personal fame. Some thought he was primarily interested in advancing the cause of socialism, that he sought to prolong the Sacco and Vanzetti court battles in order to provide socialists with a propaganda tool. Whatever conclusions one might make about Moore's intentions and conduct in the case, he had a significant role in making it a part of history.

Fred Moore engaged Tom and Jeremiah McAnarney to represent Vanzetti. They were two brothers who, with their brother John, formed a trio of successful second-generation Irish, politically connected attorneys in the Boston area. Contrary to expectations, the McAnarneys were active members of the Republican Party.[78] It was obvious that the McAnarney brothers sought acceptance from the highest levels of Boston society. Governor Calvin Coolidge appointed the oldest brother, John, a judge. He was the leader of the family. It was his belief in the innocence of the two Italians that cleared the way for Tom and Jeremiah to represent Vanzetti. Tom was passive in the case, with Jeremiah, the trial lawyer, taking the major role in Vanzetti's defense. Jeremiah's eagerness and energy often found him stumbling with grammar as he fought to express himself in dynamic terms.

Preliminary Matters

At the beginning of the Dedham trial, a number of preliminary issues needed to be addressed by lawyers for the defense:

- whether a change of venue should be pursued because of Judge Thayer's bias against the two Italians;
- whether a new jury should be selected because of the prejudicial way the jury pool was created;
- whether Katzmann's personal interest in the case, resulting from the DeFalco affair, should disqualify him as a prosecutor;

- whether ambiguities in the indictments should require a dismissal of the charges; and
- whether arrest and search and seizure procedures should be questioned.

The defense did not vigorously confront these issues, and the course of the Dedham trial was not altered. Judge Thayer continued as the presiding judge; a motion to disqualify the jury was overruled; Katzmann and his staff prosecuted the case; and ambiguities in the indictments were deemed waived because defense counsel had ignored them.

One of Moore's early mistakes was his failure to move the court to suppress evidence of the guns and ammunition found on the defendants the night they were arrested. Moore had grounds to argue that the searches following the arrest of Sacco and Vanzetti were illegal and that the evidence found should be suppressed.

Massachusetts courts in 1921 still clung to the reactionary rule that "courts do not pause ... to investigate whether physical evidence ... was obtained lawfully or unlawfully ... courts do not impose an indirect penalty upon competent evidence because of illegality in obtaining it."[79] This concept, however, was in the process of change at the federal level. Moore should have argued that Massachusetts ought to follow the exclusionary rule adopted in 1914 by the United States Supreme Court in *Weeks v. United States*.[80]

In the *Weeks* case, evidence obtained in violation of the Fourth Amendment of the United States Constitution (unreasonable search and seizure) must be excluded from, and may not be used in, a federal criminal case. Although the limitations of the Fourth Amendment were not then held applicable to state conduct as they are today, Article XIV of the Constitution of the Commonwealth of Massachusetts provided an equal alternative: "Every subject has the right to be secure from all unreasonable searches, and seizures, of his person, his houses, his papers, and all his possessions." Accordingly, an unreasonable search and seizure claim under the state constitution was available to exclude the guns and bullets found on the two Italians when they were arrested.

State constitutional litigation developed the exclusionary rule as early as 1901 in Vermont and in 1903 in Iowa.[81] In 1921, Moore had the support of state supreme court decisions and the United States Supreme Court in the *Weeks* case to argue for the adoption of an exclusionary rule under the Massachusetts Constitution.

From the early days of the Republic, arrests and searches without a warrant or probable cause were held unreasonable and illegal. In order for an arrest without a warrant to be legal, a crime had to be committed in the presence of the arresting officer, or the officer had to have probable cause that the person to be arrested had committed a felony.[82] The requirement of probable cause has deep roots in American history. The general warrant, which left blank the name of the person to be arrested, perpetuated the oppressive practice of allowing the police to arrest and search on suspicion. Police control took the place of judicial control, since no showing of probable cause before a magistrate was required.[83]

In the 1959 case of *Henry v. United States*, the United States Supreme Court held:

> [A]s the early American decisions both before and immediately after its adoption [the Fourth Amendment] show, common rumor or report, of suspicion or even strong reason to suspect was not adequate to support warrant for arrest ... Arrest on mere suspicion collides violently with the basic human right of liberty. Evidence required to establish guilt [beyond a reasonable doubt] is not necessary ... On the other hand, good faith on the part of the arresting officer is not enough. Probable cause exists if the facts and circumstances known to the officer warrant a prudent man in believing that the offense has been committed ... And while a search without a warrant, is within limits, permissible if incidental to a lawful arrest, if an arrest without a warrant is to support an incidental search, it must be made with probable cause.[84]

Although the *Henry* case was decided well after the Sacco-Vanzetti case, the arrest of the two Italians should be measured against the teaching of that case because it expresses well the legal rules applicable to arrest, search, and seizure. A review of the arrest of the two Italians is appropriate.

Officer Michael Connolly, with drawn gun, stopped and boarded a streetcar near Brockton. He was looking for two men who had tried to pick up Boda's Overland housed at Johnson's garage for repairs. Connolly was acting on Chief Stewart's suspicion that anyone calling for Boda's car was a member of the gang of anarchists who committed the Bridgewater and South Braintree crimes.

Connolly approached Sacco and Vanzetti and asked where they had been and where they were going.[85] After Vanzetti's nonthreatening response, Connolly arrested them as "suspicious characters."[86] The two were then searched and found carrying weapons and cartridges.

Connolly had not obtained a warrant for their arrest or search. He did not know their names or if they were the men who had visited Johnson's garage. No crime had been committed in the presence of Officer Connolly, and he knew of no facts that the two had committed a felony. There was no probable cause for Officer Connolly to have arrested the two men.

There were after the fact anecdotal comments that someone told Officer Connolly some Italians were trying to steal a car, which they claimed would have justified Connolly's arrest of Sacco and Vanzetti, but there is no evidence of that claim in the record of the trial. These hearsay comments appear to be nothing more than an afterthought by apologists for Connolly's conduct to justify the arrests and the searches he made without a warrant. Officer Connolly never claimed that was the basis of the arrests. His testimony is clear. He testified under oath that he arrested Sacco and Vanzetti "as suspicious characters," for that reason and that reason alone.

Why didn't Fred Moore claim the arrests and searches were illegal, and why didn't he seek to exclude the evidence so obtained? Moore was responsible for the failure to raise the issue, as he was the chief counsel for the defense team at that time. The issue would have been ideal for review by the Massachusetts Supreme Judicial Court and by the United States Supreme Court as well, if Moore had raised a violation of the Fourth (unlawful search and seizure) and Fourteenth amendments (loss of life, liberty, or property is prohibited without due process of law) of the United States Constitution. There has been much speculation as to why Moore failed to raise these constitutional issues. Incompetence, lack of attention to details, and distractions because of fund raising and public relations work could have all contributed to his negligence.

A disturbing element of the Dedham trial related to the jury pool. After the first pool of five hundred proposed jurors resulted in the selection of only seven jurors, an additional pool of prospective jurors was, by law, required to be selected randomly from the highways and byways. However, it was learned that this second group of five jurors was selected from special places—in one case, a Masonic lodge. Clearly, prospective jurors so selected might be prejudiced against the two immigrants and their radical ideas. Judge Thayer summarily overruled Moore's objection to this process.

Another unsettling event relating to the jury involved its foreman, Harry Ripley. He was a retired police officer and a former client of an assistant prosecutor on the case. Just before the trial began, when Ripley was told by his friend William Daly that he (Daly) believed the two Italians were innocent,[87] Ripley replied, "Damn them, they should hang them anyway."[88] This attitude was consistent with the fact that Ripley stood at attention and saluted the American flag in the courtroom each day before he entered the jury box and was a clue as to how he would react to two radical slackers who fled to Mexico to avoid service during the war. Ripley reflected the mood of New Englanders on the eve of the trial—a populace revved up to a state of hysteria as a result of terrorist bombings, clashes with immigrant workers, and the Red Scare.

Even before the Dedham trial began, Judge Thayer, in one of his uncontrolled outbursts, told a group of assembled reporters with reference to Sacco and Vanzetti, "You wait 'til I give my charge to the jury. I'll show 'em!"[89] The members of the press agreed to say nothing about the incident, and none of the newspapers or the reporters in attendance mentioned the incident at that time—an indication of how Judge Thayer marginalized the press in this case.

* * * *

The trial began with Assistant District Attorney Harold Williams making an opening statement to the jury. He outlined the Commonwealth's case and the evidence he would present to prove it. Williams advanced the theory that a gang of five anarchists from the Bridgewater area committed the South Braintree robbery and murders and that the Buick found two days later in the Manley Woods was the getaway car.[90]

Williams identified Shelly Neal as the American Express agent who delivered the payroll to the company for packaging the morning of April 15, 1920. Williams said that Neal noticed a suspicious car (only one car) outside of the main office that morning, and that a slight man with an emaciated, yellowish face stood near that car.[91] He told the jury that while the shooting was going on, a big black car, which had been down at the Slater & Morrill factory, drove up Pearl Street and picked up the bandits with the payroll and that it was the same car Neal had seen in front of the American Express office earlier in the day.

Williams charged that Sacco, Vanzetti, Boda, Coacci, and Orciani were members of the gang and that the shed next to Coacci's home was used to hide the Buick. In his description of the escape route, Williams said the bandits bypassed Randolph and the Manley Woods, and then drove to the Matfield Crossing. He gave a weak reason why the bandits drove over the railroad crossing and immediately doubled back and recrossed it. He suggested they crossed at Matfield to "take Vanzetti over to Plymouth,"[92] or for the purpose of "disposing of something in the Matfield River," or "some other reason ..." He then posited that the bandits drove back to the Manley Woods, which was about a mile from Coacci's home, and abandoned the Buick.

Critical to the prosecution's case was avoiding any testimony from Mabel Hewins. Mrs. Hewins lived at the corner of Oak and Orchard streets in Randolph. The prosecution learned she would have testified that, on the afternoon of the crime, a car with five men fitting the descriptions of the bandits stopped at her home and asked directions to Providence, Rhode Island.[93] She also believed that Sacco was the driver of the car.[94] Many witnesses to the crime later indicated that Joe Morelli looked like Sacco. The prosecution did not call her because a disclosure that the bandits were on their way to Providence would have conflicted with its claim that the gang abandoned the Buick within a mile of Coacci's home after they made the recrossing at Matfield. In addition, it was well known that Sacco did not know how to drive a car. At the time of the trial, the prosecution concealed from the defense Mabel Hewins's knowledge of the events of April 15. It was not until 1926 that William Thompson, appellate counsel for the defense, learned of her story when he was working on Sacco and Vanzetti's clemency petition to Governor Fuller.

Contrary to the prosecution's theory of the case, and contrary to Inspector Jacobs's claim that he saw the getaway car in New Bedford the evening of the crime, what makes sense is that the bandits drove the Buick getaway car to the Manley Woods immediately after the crime, stripped off the stolen license plate, and abandoned the car. In an effort to throw off the police, the bandits switched to a previously parked car or a waiting car with a driver, the second car, the Hudson, that Shelly Neal saw the morning of the crime. In either case, the bandits continued their escape in the Hudson to Providence.

That two cars were involved explains the second set of smaller car tracks found near the abandoned Buick. It also explains that the mistaken crossing by the bandits at Matfield and their immediate turnaround was because they lost their way to Providence, which is consistent with Mabel Hewins's story. The two-car theory is also compatible with Neal's inquest testimony that he observed two suspicious cars on the morning of the crime.

Providence was the home base of the Morelli gang. Sacco, Vanzetti, Boda, Coacci, and Orciani had no known connections with Providence or any reason to travel there. Finally, it is consistent with the testimony six years later of Celestino Medeiros, the self-confessed participant in the crime, that the gang used two cars and that they switched cars in the woods after the holdup in their escape to Providence.

CHAPTER 7

DEDHAM: THE CASE AGAINST VANZETTI

Before Williams made his opening statement in the Dedham trial, he took the jury on a tour of what he considered important sites. This included Coacci's home and the shed next to it, where Williams claimed the bandits hid the getaway Buick pending its use in the South Braintree crime. This gave credibility to the prosecution's claim that Coacci and his boarder, Boda, together with Sacco and Vanzetti, were members of the gang responsible for the robbery and murders at South Braintree. However, the prosecution never produced any evidence during the trial to support the involvement of Coacci and Boda in the crime.

Williams attempted to prove the Commonwealth's case against Vanzetti, based on the following claims:

- Six witnesses identified Vanzetti at or near South Braintree on the day of, or the day before, the crime.
- The gun found on Vanzetti the night the police arrested him belonged to the slain guard, Berardelli.
- Four intact shotgun shells found on Vanzetti the night of his arrest connected him to the crime.
- The lies Vanzetti told police on the night of his arrest showed consciousness of guilt.

Identification of Vanzetti

A total of one hundred and sixty-eight witnesses testified at the trial, forty-three of whom were identification witnesses. Only five witnesses testified they saw Vanzetti in the vicinity of the crime on April 15. One additional witness testified he saw Vanzetti in the South Braintree area on either April 14 or 15.

Michael Levangie, gate tender at the Pearl Street railroad crossing, was an important identification witness for the prosecution. He stated that Vanzetti was the driver of the getaway Buick,[1] even though it was undisputed that Vanzetti did not know how to drive a car.[2] Every other witness who identified the driver described him with light hair, a light complexion, and sickly looking like someone with consumption[3]—a description that did not fit Vanzetti. In his summation to the jury, Katzmann admitted that Vanzetti was not the driver of the bandit car. In an attempt to salvage Levangie's testimony, Katzmann suggested that he saw Vanzetti in the backseat just behind the driver and confused him with being the driver.[4]

Levangie said that, when the getaway car approached the shanty he was in, someone in the car pointed a revolver at his head. However, he could not identify that person or tell how many men were in the car.[5] He said that the driver was dark complected, with cheekbones sticking out, black hair, and a heavy brown moustache, and Vanzetti was that man. He testified he had seen Vanzetti before the trial at the Brockton police station in one of those non-lineup viewings.[6] Only Levangie placed Vanzetti near the scene of the crime.

On cross-examination, Vanzetti's counsel, Jeremiah McAnarney, tested Levangie's veracity by asking him if he recalled talking to him (McAnarney) before the trial. Levangie denied speaking to him[7] or that he told McAnarney the only man he saw in the car was a "light complected man, Swedish or Norwegian type of person."[8]

Three defense witnesses rebutted Levangie's testimony. Edward Carter, a Slater & Morrill employee, said Levangie told him right after the shooting that the driver was a "light complected man."[9] Just after the shooting, Alexander Victorson, a freight and ticket clerk, heard Levangie say that "it would be hard to identify these men."[10] John Sullivan, Levangie's co-worker, testified that he had seen Levangie talking with McAnarney about two weeks prior to the trial and that he (Sullivan) had talked to Levangie the next day and Levangie acknowledged that fact.[11]

Two other witnesses claimed that Vanzetti was in the South Braintree vicinity the day of the crime. John Faulkner, from Cohasset, testified he boarded a train for Boston on the Plymouth Line at 9:20 AM on April 15, the day of the crime. He said he was sitting in a combination smoking and baggage car, and a man sitting next to him had remarked that a man behind him wanted to know if the upcoming stop was East Braintree. Faulkner testified the man asking about the next stop looked like a foreigner, had a black moustache, and got off at East Braintree at about 10:00 AM carrying a leather bag. He identified Vanzetti as that man.[12]

On cross-examination, Faulkner could not describe any other passenger on the train that morning.[13] Edward Brooks, a ticket agent, testified on rebuttal that the smoking car Faulkner was in was not a combination smoking and baggage car, that he (Brooks) had seen a dark man with a bag getting off at East Braintree on several occasions after April 15, and that Vanzetti was *not* that man.[14]

The defense established that no passenger paid a cash fare on the trains that morning traveling from Plymouth or neighboring stations to East Braintree, South Braintree, or Braintree.[15] The ticket agents at Plymouth and nearby stations deposed that they had not seen Vanzetti at their station that day.

Harry Dolbeare, a South Braintree resident, testified he saw Vanzetti in a car the morning of April 15 between 10:00 and noon, near South Braintree Square, with several other foreigners.[16] Dolbeare could not describe anyone else in the car, except to say they were a tough-looking bunch.

Austin Reed, the gate tender at the Matfield railroad crossing, some twenty miles from South Braintree, said that on April 15 at about 4:15 PM, a car full of men approached the crossing just as he was letting down the gates because of an approaching train.[17] The driver of the car did not want to stop. Reed testified that one of the men in the car shouted at him, "What to hell I was holding him up for."[18] Reed described that man as sitting in the front seat next to the driver, that he was a dark-complected man with high cheekbones, a stubbed moustache, and black hair. Reed said he saw that man in the Brockton police station about three weeks later in one of those non-lineup viewings and the man was Vanzetti. He could not describe the other four men in the car. On cross-examination, Reed admitted the man he claimed was Vanzetti was the man who yelled at him and that he spoke in unmistakable and clear English.[19] Vanzetti spoke broken English with a heavy Italian accent.[20]

Austin Cole, a trolley conductor, testified to having seen both Sacco and Vanzetti on his run from Bridgewater to Brockton the night of April

14 or 15.[21] The prosecution used this testimony to support its claim that Vanzetti lied the night of his arrest when he told the police he had never been in Brockton and that Sacco and Vanzetti were in the area either the day of, or the day before, the crime was committed.

Katzmann had to have been aware that Vanzetti could not be convicted of capital murder based on the slim identification testimony of those witnesses. He was still searching for physical evidence connecting Vanzetti to the crime, especially since no one saw Vanzetti at the crime scene during the actual shooting.

The prosecution developed two theories to implicate Vanzetti: 1) the .38-caliber revolver found on Vanzetti on the night of his arrest belonged to the slain guard Berardelli, and Sacco picked it up after he shot Berardelli and gave it to Vanzetti, and 2) four shotgun shells the police found on Vanzetti the night of his arrest connected him to the South Braintree crimes.

Berardelli Gun Theory

Assistant prosecutor Williams did not raise the Berardelli gun theory in his opening statement to the jury. This leads to suspicion that the prosecution planned to hold this claim until the last minute in order to leave the defense little opportunity to disprove it.

The prosecution advanced the Berardelli gun theory through the testimony of several witnesses. Sarah Berardelli, the guard's wife, said that Parmenter, the murdered paymaster, gave her husband a nickel-plated revolver six months before the shooting, when the company hired her husband to protect the payroll, and that her husband's revolver looked like the revolver found on Vanzetti.[22] Three weeks before the crime, she and her husband had taken his gun to the Iver-Johnson Company in Boston for the repair of a broken spring. They gave the receipt for the gun to Parmenter.[23]

There is unrebutted evidence that Berardelli was not carrying a gun at the time the crime was committed. Aldeah Florence, a friend and neighbor, testified that Mrs. Berardelli told her after the murders that "he [Berardelli] had a revolver and that he never carried it, and that it was broken, and she was going to have it taken into Boston to have it fixed.[24] Well, three or four days after she [Mrs. Berardelli] came back from the funeral she said 'Oh, dear,' she says, 'If he had taken my advice and taken the revolver out of the shop he would not be, maybe he would not be in the same condition he is today."[25]

Katzmann challenged Mrs. Florence on cross-examination, but could not shake her testimony. The final exchange between the two makes that clear:[26]

> Q: [by Katzmann] I am asking you if after her husband's death she said that the revolver was still in the shop where it had been taken for repair?
> A: Yes, sir.

James Bostock, a machine worker at Slater & Morrill, testified that he believed he saw Berardelli with a gun on the Saturday before April 15.[27] However, on cross-examination, Bostock did not testify that gun was the gun in evidence as Exhibit 27, claimed by the prosecutor to have been found on Vanzetti when he was arrested.[28]

Witness Lincoln Wadsworth, in charge of repairs to firearms at Iver-Johnson Sporting Goods, testified company records showed that on March 20, 1920, Berardelli brought in a .38 Harrington & Richardson revolver, like the one found on Vanzetti, for repair.[29] However, George F. Fitzmeyer, gunsmith at the company, said its records showed the company repaired the hammer of a .32 Harrington & Richardson revolver between March 19 and March 22, not that it repaired the spring of a .38 Harrington & Richardson revolver.[30]

The company's records showed that the gun brought in by Berardelli had not been delivered or picked up by anyone.[31] James Jones, manager at Iver-Johnson, testified that if a repaired gun was not picked up or delivered by the following January, it would have been sold. Since the company had no record of such a sale, Jones reasoned that the company delivered the gun or someone picked it up.[32]

The confusing testimony put into question the reliability of the prosecution's theory that the gun found on Vanzetti was really Berardelli's gun. Nevertheless, Katzmann continued to pursue his theory so that the jury could infer Vanzetti's connection to the shooting.

Six years later, Lincoln Wadsworth told the governor's advisory committee that there were "thousands of times more chances" that the revolver found on Vanzetti was not the gun that Berardelli brought in for repair than that it was Berardelli's gun.[33] He stated that assistant prosecutor

Williams had discouraged him from giving such an opinion at the time of the trial.

Wadsworth was right.[34] Evidence discovered fifty years after the execution of Sacco and Vanzetti confirms that the prosecution knew from the beginning of the trial that the revolver found on Vanzetti did not belong to Berardelli. William Young and David Kaiser, in *Postmortem: New Evidence in the Case of Sacco and Vanzetti*, published in 1985, revealed a February 18, 1921, memorandum by Chief Stewart, the lead investigator for Katzmann, released by the Massachusetts State Police in 1977. The memo identified a revolver Parmenter bought at the time Berardelli went to work for Slater & Morrill:

> Thursday, February 16th, found on the revolver book of C. A. Noyes Hardware Company in Brockton an entry showing that on October 10, 1919 F. A. Parmenter purchased a Harrington and Richardson, .32 caliber, nickel finish, center fire revolver, No. 394717.[35]

The memo disclosed that Parmenter purchased the revolver six months before the South Braintree murders. Mrs. Berardelli testified that this was the time Slater & Morrill hired her husband as a payroll guard and Parmenter gave him a gun. Young and Kaiser concluded the gun referred to in the memo was most certainly the gun Parmenter gave to Berardelli and not the gun found on Vanzetti, which was a .38 caliber, serial number G-82581.[36]

Katzmann and his team of prosecutors withheld from defense counsel documentary exculpatory evidence in its files that would have rebutted the Commonwealth's claim that the gun found on Vanzetti belonged to Berardelli. The withholding of this evidence by the prosecution was more, much more, than a failure to disclose. It was an act of fraud by the prosecution on the court, on the jury, on the people, and on Vanzetti. The fact that the Commonwealth concealed this information for fifty years speaks volumes about its willful participation in this fraud.

Vanzetti's Shotgun Shells

The third prong of the Commonwealth's case against Vanzetti was based on shotgun shells. Officer Connolly testified that on the night he arrested Vanzetti, he found four intact shotgun shells on him: three Peters and one Winchester.[37] Vanzetti's lawyer objected to this testimony as irrelevant. The prosecution argued that the earlier testimony of a witness indicating that he saw the barrel of a shotgun protruding from the rear window of the getaway car made relevant the shotgun shells found on Vanzetti.

After the defendant's objection and the prosecutor's response, the judge admitted only two of the four shotgun shells into evidence. They were admitted without the Commonwealth establishing a chain of custody, without identification marks on the shells made by the person who found them, and without identifying the caliber of the shot.[38] The two shells not admitted into evidence were the shells that the jurors improperly opened during their deliberations at the Plymouth trial.

Vanzetti testified in his direct examination that when the police arrested him, he was in possession of three, not four, shotgun shells.[39] Through aggressive cross-examination of Vanzetti, Katzmann developed a basis to argue that Vanzetti did not deny he was in possession of four shotgun shells that night.[40] Katzmann was determined to keep Officer Connolly's testimony at the Dedham trial consistent with his testimony a year earlier at the Plymouth trial, when he said he found four shells when he arrested Vanzetti, one of which was a Winchester. Finding a Winchester shell on Vanzetti was important for the prosecution's claim in the Plymouth trial because that would connect Vanzetti to the Bridgewater crime scene where Dr. Murphy found a spent Winchester shell.[41] Katzmann could not afford to have shell evidence at the Dedham trial contradict Connolly's previous testimony at the Plymouth trial.

Vanzetti's possession of shotgun shells had an additional purpose at the Dedham trial. Katzmann argued that those shells connected Vanzetti to the South Braintree murders because of Hans Behrsin's earlier testimony that he saw the back of the getaway car "with a gun or shotgun, whatever it was"[42] protruding out of the back window. The strength of the shell evidence at the Dedham trial rested on whomever the jury believed told the truth about the number and kind of shells found on Vanzetti when the police arrested him.

Overall, the case against Vanzetti was weak. The Commonwealth's claim that the gun found on Vanzetti belonged to Berardelli was not convincing. Chief Stewart's February 18, 1921, memo released in 1977, shows this claim was false. The Vanzetti shell evidence was dubious. Defense counsel discredited Levangie's identification of Vanzetti as the driver of the getaway car. The vague testimony of the other three identification witnesses

(John Faulkner, Harry Dolbeare, and Austin Reed) was of little value in the face of strong cross-examination and rebuttal testimony.

Consciousness of guilt, based on Vanzetti's lies the night of his arrest, the fourth claim of the Commonwealth's case against him, would have had little force or effect if Vanzetti's alibi witnesses placed him in Plymouth at the time of the South Braintree crimes. Katzmann had to destroy Vanzetti's alibi if he hoped to convict him.

Vanzetti's Alibi

Vanzetti testified that on April 15, he spent the morning and early afternoon in Plymouth, selling fish along Cherry and Castle streets, Standish Avenue, and Suosso Lane.[43] He said that about noontime, Joseph Rosen, a peddler, approached him and offered to sell cloth to him for a suit. Rosen posed a good price because of a small imperfection in the cloth. Vanzetti was not familiar with good quality cloth, so he sought help from his friend Alphonsine Brini, who worked in the woolen mills and could give him good advice.

Vanzetti and Rosen met with Alphonsine Brini and her daughter LeFavre at their home around noon on April 15. After receiving favorable advice from Alphonsine, Vanzetti bought the cloth from Rosen. Thereafter, Vanzetti continued to hawk fish along the streets of Plymouth.[44]

Vanzetti finished selling fish at about 1:00 PM. That's when he joined Melvin Corl, a fisherman, who was painting his boat along the shore of Plymouth Bay. Vanzetti spent about an hour and a half visiting with Corl.[45] Mr. Holmes, a local lumberyard employee, joined them for a short time.[46] Vanzetti also talked to Frank Jesse, a boatbuilder, while Corl painted his boat.[47]

The defense called the following witnesses to corroborate Vanzetti's alibi: Melvin Corl, Angel Guidobone, Alphonsine Brini, LeFavre Brini, Nurses Gertrude Matthews and Ella Urquhart, and Joseph Rosen.

Melvin Corl had a clear recollection that he finished painting his boat in time for his wife's birthday, which was Saturday, April 17.[48] He testified that he met and talked with Vanzetti two days before, on Thursday, April 15, while he painted his boat. Corl also said he delivered a boat owned by Joseph Morey to Duxbury on Saturday, April 17.[49]

Angel Guidobone testified that he bought fish from Vanzetti in Plymouth about noon on April 15.[50] On cross-examination, he fixed the day of his purchase as four days before he had surgery at the Plymouth hospital.

Alphonsine Brini fixed the date of her meeting with Vanzetti on April 15 because it was a week after she had come home from the hospital on April 8.[51]

LeFavre Brini fixed the date of April 15 as the date Vanzetti met her and her mother with Rosen because it was the day that Gertrude Matthews, the nurse from Plymouth Cordage Company, had visited her mother.[52]

Nurse Gertrude Matthews testified that she visited Alphonsine Brini several times between April 15 and April 25, but could not recall the exact date of the first visit.[53]

Nurse Ella Urquhart, keeper of the records of Plymouth Cordage Company's nurses department, was barred by Judge Thayer from testifying to the date of Nurse Matthews's visit.[54] If allowed, she would have testified that the records of her department showed that Nurse Matthews had visited Mrs. Brini on April 15, corroborating the testimony of Mrs. Brini and her daughter, and thereby corroborating Vanzetti's alibi. Of all the alibi witnesses, only Nurse Urquhart's testimony was barred by Judge Thayer.

An extensive colloquy between Judge Thayer, Katzmann, and William Callahan (a Vanzetti lawyer) occurred regarding the propriety of Nurse Urquhart's proposed testimony. Judge Thayer ruled that even though Nurse Urquhart was the official keeper of the records and the entries were the original entries in her own hand, he would not let her testify as to what that record showed because she did not have personal knowledge of the event. The judge held that while such records might be admissible in a civil case, they would not be admissible in this criminal case.[55] Vanzetti's lawyer made no effort to recall Nurse Matthews and have her refresh her memory by reviewing the official records as to the dates she visited Mrs. Brini.

Joseph Rosen testified he was able to fix April 15 as the date he met Vanzetti in Plymouth because his wife paid his poll tax on that day and because he spent that night at a rooming house in Whitman.[56] He remembered that everyone at the rooming house talked about the robbery and murders that had taken place at South Braintree that afternoon.

In an attempt to discredit the Brinis' testimony, Katzmann brought out that Vanzetti was a close friend of the Brini family, implying that their testimony was tainted. Counsel for the defense objected. This led the lawyers for the parties to confer with Judge Thayer. As a result, the following stipulation between the lawyers was read to the jury:

It is agreed by counsel for the Commonwealth and counsel for the defendant as follows: that this witness, Alphonsine Brini has, in another case, testified on behalf of the defendant Vanzetti as to his whereabouts different from the place set forth in that case.[57]

The "other case" was the Plymouth trial. Alphonsine testified in that case on Vanzetti's close ties to the Brini family; however, she never testified as to his "whereabouts different from the place set forth in that case."[57]

It is inexplicable why Vanzetti's lawyers agreed to the stipulation. It had the prejudicial effect of bringing Vanzetti's Plymouth trial into the Dedham trial. The stipulation diminished the credibility of Alphonsine Brini and nullified her corroboration of Vanzetti's alibi. Because of this stipulation, Katzmann was able to discredit Mrs. Brini's testimony in his closing argument to the jury with these words:

I want to discuss the manner in which an alibi may be put together … take Mrs. Brini—Mrs. Brini, a convenient witness for this defendant Vanzetti. You remember … he was the most intimate friend and was like one of the family and there most every evening and once or twice in the daytime—Mrs. Brini, it is agreed in another case when another date was alleged, testified to the whereabouts of this same Vanzetti on that other date there involved, a stock, convenient and ready witness as well as friend of the defendant Vanzetti.[58]

In the absence of the stipulation, Katzmann would never have been able to make that argument. It was a damaging charge against an important Vanzetti alibi witness, and it went unanswered by defense counsel. Not only did the lawyers for these defendants make such a foolish mistake, but they also seldom objected to the improper cross-examination of witnesses testifying on behalf of their clients when they should have. The lack of preparation of the defendants' witnesses, a responsibility of defense counsel, became obvious as the case proceeded. This was disastrous for the two Italians, as Katzmann was a most effective interrogator, particularly when he went unchallenged and the witnesses were unprepared.

Katzmann consistently badgered Vanzetti's alibi witnesses. At times, his attacks were vicious. LeFavre Brini, the fifteen-year-old daughter of Mrs. Brini, was brought to tears during the following exchange:[59]

> Q: [by Katzmann] Two months before that date [April 15] daytimes were you working at the Gorton-Pew Fisheries?
>
> A: Yes.
>
> Q: So you were not at home daytimes at all except when your mother was ill, were you?
>
> A: Yes.
>
> Q: That is true, isn't it? And how long before that had you been working for the Gorton-Pew Fisheries? How long before your mother became ill?
>
> A: I worked there all summer.
>
> Q: All what summer?
>
> A: All that summer.
>
> Q: Well, I say before March 18?
>
> A: March 18?
>
> Q: Yes.
>
> A: How do you fix March 18?
>
> Q: Don't you fix March 18? Doesn't that date mean anything to you, March 18, 1920? (Doesn't that date mean to you, Miss Brini?)
>
> A: [Witness hesitates] Why should it?
>
> Q: Is that your answer to me? Do you love your mother, Miss Brini?
>
> A: Yes.
>
> Q: Don't you know that was the day that she says she went to the hospital?
>
> A: Yes.
>
> Q: And that date doesn't mean anything to you?
>
> A: Why, yes.
>
> Q: Well, why didn't you remember it when I asked you?
>
> A: [Witness hesitates.]
>
> Q: Excuse me for raising my voice to you, I didn't mean to frighten you. Why didn't you remember it, Miss Brini, when I told you the day?
>
> A: I did not know what you meant by that.

Q: You know what March means, don't you?

A: Yes.

Q: You know what 18th means, don't you?

A: Yes.

Q: You know March 18 is a date, don't you?

A: Yes.

Q: When I asked you about March 18, you did not remember, did you, that that was the day your mother was taken out to the hospital—was taken out of the house to the Jordan Hospital did you?

MR. CALLAHAN [Vanzetti's counsel]. Wait a minute. I pray your Honor's judgement.

Q: That your mother went to the Jordan Hospital?

A: [Witness hesitates.]

Q: You did not remember that, did you, Miss Brini?

A: [Witness hesitates.]

Q: Is that too hard to answer?

A: No.

Q: Will you please answer it?

A: [Witness hesitates.]

THE COURT: I wish you would please answer it if you can.

THE WITNESS: I did not remember when you first asked me.

Q: You did not. And that is why you said to me, 'Why should I remember March 18?'

A: Yes.

Q: Don't you think you should have remembered March 18th more than April 15th?

A: [Witness hesitates.]

THE COURT: Won't you please answer the question so we can go along?

MR. KATZMANN: I won't press it your Honor.

This is an example of badgering the witness with argumentative, irrelevant, and confusing questions. All the witness got from the lawyer who should have been defending her was a milquetoast prayer to the judge, and all the judge did was plead for the witness to "please answer" Katzmann's questions.

Vanzetti's alibi should have carried the day. However, like the alibi witnesses at the Plymouth trial, the jury did not believe his witnesses. Was it because the jury found that the witnesses did not correctly recall April 15 as the date of their encounter with Vanzetti, or was it because most of the alibi witnesses were Italians and could not be trusted? Regardless, the case against Vanzetti left doubts as to his guilt. It had to be apparent to Katzmann that the conviction of Sacco was vital to the Commonwealth's effort to send the two Italians to the death chamber. Katzmann devoted the bulk of his resources to convict Sacco. Clearly, a conviction of Sacco would carry Vanzetti to the chair as well.

CHAPTER 8

DEDHAM: THE CASE AGAINST SACCO

The weakness of the prosecution's charges against Vanzetti imposed a heavy burden on District Attorney Frederick Katzmann to use all his ingenuity and skills to build a conclusive case against Sacco. To achieve this, he relied on five claims:

- A number of witnesses identified Sacco as being near the crime scene on April 15, 1920, and one witness identified him as the gunman who shot Berardelli.
- A worker found a cap next to Berardelli's body, immediately after the shootings, that belonged to Sacco.
- The gun found on Sacco the night of his arrest fired Bullet III that killed Berardelli.
- The six intact Winchester cartridges found on Sacco when he was arrested connected him to Shell W, the spent Winchester shell found at the crime scene.
- Sacco showed consciousness of guilt the night of his arrest.

Identification of Sacco

The prosecution introduced seven witnesses placing Sacco at or near the crime scene.[1] Seven additional witnesses were introduced for the same purpose; however, their testimony backfired against the prosecution.[2]

Of the first group of seven prosecution witnesses, the most important—in fact, the prosecution's star identification witness—was Lola Andrews, who, with her friend Julia Campbell, had gone to South Braintree on the morning of the murders looking for work at the shoe factories. Mrs. Andrews said that as she and Mrs. Campbell entered the Slater & Morrill factory, she noticed two men at a nearby automobile. One was light skinned, sickly looking, and wearing a long coat and a cap; the other was dark complected and was working on the car.[3]

When the women finished their business at the factory and left, the man with a dark complexion was working under the front of the car and the sickly looking man stood at the rear of the car. Mrs. Andrews testified that she asked the dark-complected man directions to Rice & Hutchins and that he got up from under the car and directed her to that factory.[4]

Mrs. Andrews's testimony was important because if the man she spoke to was Sacco, she was the *only* witness who got a close face-to-face look at him while he was supposedly in South Braintree on the day of the crime.[5] Her testimony also connected Sacco to what was later determined to be the bandits' car.

Mrs. Andrews's testimony was subject to such significant contradictions that she should have been a disaster for the prosecution. Instead, Katzmann was allowed to promote her credibility to the jury in his closing argument by his personal endorsement. He told the jury:

> And then there is Lola Andrews. I have been in this office, gentlemen, for now more than 11 years. I cannot recall in that too long service for the Commonwealth that ever before I have laid eye or given ear to so convincing a witness as Lola Andrews.[6]

The prosecutor's statement was legally incompetent. He provided testimony not subject to cross-examination and not under oath. It should not have been allowed.

The following events should have undermined the credibility of Mrs. Andrews as a witness for the prosecution. Fred Moore, Sacco's attorney, with a stenographer and two assistants, interviewed Mrs. Andrews on January 14, before the trial, as a possible witness for the defense. At that time, Mrs. Andrews told Moore that she could not identify the two men she had seen near the car in front of the Slater & Morrill factory on the day of the crime. Shown pictures of Sacco and Vanzetti, she stated they were not the men. The stenographic record of her answers at that meeting verified those statements.[7] But then in court, she denied that she ever said any such thing, claiming instead that she had identified the man in the pictures shown to her by Moore as the man who got up from under the car.

Moore rebutted Mrs. Andrews's testimony with a surprise witness—Julia Campbell, the friend who had accompanied Mrs. Andrews on April 15. Mrs. Campbell unequivocally testified that neither of them spoke—ever—to the man working under or on the car, either before entering or after leaving the Slater & Morrill factory.[8] Katzmann could not shake her testimony on cross-examination. She was positive and adamant that neither she nor Mrs. Andrews spoke to either man: "We simply walked out by them and walked into Rice & Hutchins."[9]

A mugger attacked Mrs. Andrews in February 1921. After the attack, Officer George Fay interviewed her and asked if the mugger might have been one of the men that she had seen in South Braintree the day of the murders. Mrs. Andrews told Officer Fay that she had not seen the faces of the men at South Braintree.[10] Officer Fay testified to that effect in rebuttal to her identification of Sacco as the man she saw when she left the Slater & Morrill factory on April 15.

The night before Mrs. Andrews appeared in court, she met with Jeremiah McAnarney, a Vanzetti attorney, and told him she could not testify that Sacco and Vanzetti were the men she and Mrs. Campbell had seen by the car when they visited Slater & Morrill looking for work on April 15. [11]

Judge Thayer engaged in an extraordinary exchange with rebuttal witness Harry Kurlansky. He testified that on the evening Mrs. Andrews returned from observing Sacco in jail at the request of the prosecutor, she entered his tailor shop. He told her she looked tired, and she responded, "Yes, they bothering the life out of me. The Government took me down and want me to recognize those men—I don't know a thing about them. I had never seen them and I can't recognize them."[12]

After Katzmann cross-examined Kurlansky, Judge Thayer interjected:[13]

> Mr. Witness, I would like to ask one question. Did you attempt to find out who this person was who represented the Government who was trying to get her to take and state that which was false? ... Did

you try to find out who it was who represented the Government?

[Kurlansky]: No.

[Judge Thayer]: Why not? I am trying to find out why you didn't do it.

Kurlansky clearly damaged the credibility of Mrs. Andrews's testimony. Judge Thayer's bias surfaced when he aided the prosecution by discrediting Kurlansky in the presence of the jury. The judge's questions suggested Kurlansky was remiss for his failure to investigate the government's attempt to have Mrs. Andrews present perjured testimony.

Alfred LaBrecque rebutted Mrs. Andrews's testimony.[14] LaBrecque was a newspaper reporter and, at one time, a neighbor of Mrs. Andrews. He testified that he interviewed her after she was assaulted. In response to LaBrecque's question whether the man who assaulted her resembled the man she was supposed to have seen at South Braintree, she responded that she did not see the faces of the men in South Braintree. He also testified before the Governor's Advisory Committee on July 18, 1927, that Mrs. Andrews's reputation for truthfulness was not good. He gave several examples, including that she had committed insurance fraud by claiming compensation for injuries she had not sustained.

After the jury returned its guilty verdicts against Sacco and Vanzetti, their lawyers filed a number of supplementary motions seeking a new trial for the defendants. One motion contained an affidavit of Mrs. Andrews repudiating her trial testimony in which she identified Sacco as the man working on the car.[15] Judge Thayer denied the motion principally because Mrs. Andrews had later retracted her repudiation.[16]

There was more to discredit Mrs. Andrews's credibility. Katzmann concealed evidence he had in his possession that flatly contradicted Mrs. Andrews.[17] It was revealed that Minnie Kennedy and Louise (Hayes) Kelly, employees at Slater & Morrill, observed a car about ten feet from them in front of the factory, shortly before the shooting. They noticed the driver of the car whom they both described as having a light complexion and slight build. They also noticed another man working on the car and indicated that neither Sacco nor Vanzetti was that other man. Mrs. Kennedy and Mrs. Kelly deposed that they had provided statements to that effect to Katzmann shortly after April 15.[18] At that time, they picked out a picture of Steve "the Pole" Benkosky, a known member of the Morelli gang of Providence, Rhode Island, as the driver of that car.

On appeal to the supreme judicial court, William Thompson, then appellate counsel for Sacco and Vanzetti, in a challenge to the testimony of Mrs. Andrews, argued that District Attorney Katzmann had concealed the Kennedy-Kelly evidence.[19] This was a serious charge of prosecutorial misconduct. The supreme judicial court overruled Thompson's argument, holding that a district attorney is not bound to call witnesses "in whom he has no confidence, whose testimony contradicts what he is trying to prove"— [20] a non sequitur response by the supreme judicial court.

The second important prosecution witness was Lewis Pelser, a shoe worker at Rice & Hutchins. He was the only witness who claimed Sacco shot Berardelli. He testified that he saw the shooting from the factory's first-floor window: "I seen this fellow shoot this fellow.[21] It was the last shot. He put four bullets into him …" Pelser described the shooter as having a dark complexion. When asked if he saw the man in the courtroom who shot Berardelli, Pelser answered (referring to Sacco), "Well, I wouldn't say it was him, but he is a dead image of him …"[22]

On cross-examination, Pelser admitted that Mr. Robert Reid, an investigator for the defense, interviewed him about two months before the trial and that he did not tell Reid everything he knew about the shooting. Pelser admitted telling Reid that he did not see any of the shooting, stating, "Why no, I just seen him [Berardelli] laying there, that is all."[23] Pelser's explanation for his false statement was that he did not know Reid and did not want to have to go to court and testify.[24]

Pelser told Reid that when the shooting started, he ducked under a bench and saw nothing;[25] then in court, he first denied that he ducked under a bench but later stated that he had. He also admitted that after the arrest of Sacco and Vanzetti, he told the police he was unable to identify any of the killers.[26]

Pelser claimed he talked to no one, including the prosecuting attorneys, about his testimony before his appearance on the stand.[27] Pelser's testimony revealed that although Rice & Hutchins terminated his employment after the crime, the company had recently rehired him.[28] In addition, Pelser testified that he talked with his boss a few days before he came to court. Defense counsel did not pursue the reason for Pelser's termination or if there were any conditions to his reemployment.

The defense produced three rebuttal witnesses to Pelser's testimony,[29] all fellow workers who testified that Pelser was not at the window at the time of the shooting because they had all ducked under the benches when the shooting started. Dominic Constantino, one of the three, said he heard Pelser say after the shooting that he had not seen anything.[30]

After the trial, Fred Moore obtained a deposition under oath from Pelser repudiating his testimony at the trial that Sacco was the "dead image" of the man he saw shoot Berardelli.[31] In his repudiation, Pelser reaffirmed his statements to Mr. Reid before the trial, that he ducked under the bench and saw nothing[32]. Pelser indicated that Assistant District Attorney Williams had urged him to make the identification of Sacco.[33]

In a complete turnabout a few days later, Pelser retracted his repudiation.[34] Pelser claimed Moore plied him with liquor and tricked him into making his denial. Shortly thereafter, Pelser absolved Mr. Williams, in writing, from any wrongdoing in connection with his identification of Sacco.[35]

The third important prosecution witness was Carlos Goodridge, a salesman. At the time of the South Braintree murders, he was in a poolroom near the railroad crossing in the center of town. As Goodridge was leaving the poolroom, the getaway car came within twenty feet of him, and a man in the car pointed a gun at him. Goodridge identified Sacco as that man.[36] He said he first saw Sacco the previous September or October, after the shooting, at Sacco's arraignment.[37] Goodrich was at the courthouse at that time on personal business.

On cross-examination, Sacco's lawyer attempted to impeach Goodridge's testimony by showing that his personal business at the courthouse had to do with pleading guilty to grand larceny charges filed by Katzmann and that he was now on probation.[38] Judge Thayer would permit none of it, ruling that because the court had not entered a judgment of conviction against Goodridge, such evidence was not competent.[39] This ruling barred Sacco's lawyer from inquiring whether Katzmann offered probation to Goodridge in exchange for his identification of Sacco.

The defense produced four rebuttal witnesses who contradicted Goodridge's testimony. Harry Arrogni, a barber, testified that Goodridge told him right after the shooting, "I saw a man in the car but if I have got to say who the man was, I can't say."[40] Peter Magazu, owner of the poolroom, stated that Goodridge told him, "This job wasn't pulled by any foreign people."[41] Andrew Manganio, Goodridge's employer, said that Goodridge told him he could not identify the killers because he had been so scared.[42] And Nicola Damato, another barber, testified that Goodridge told him he had not seen anyone in the getaway car.[43]

After the trial, Goodridge's criminal background became the subject of a supplementary motion for a new trial.[44] During the motion, the defense argued that given Goodridge's life of crime and the current charges of grand larceny, no prosecutor would have recommended probation for him unless something more was involved. Defense counsel charged that Goodridge obtained probation in exchange for his identification of Sacco.

Following are the facts of Goodridge's life of crime and deception.[45] In 1893, he was sentenced for larceny of gold watches; in 1908, he was sentenced for larceny of money; in 1909, he was divorced for adultery; in 1911, he was indicted for larceny in New York but fled to avoid prosecution; and in 1913, he was implicated in an arson charge with intent to defraud an insurance company. He lived in Vermont under various names with a woman to whom he was not married; he committed perjury to obtain a license to marry; in 1919, he was divorced from his second wife for cruel and inhumane treatment. "Goodridge" was an assumed name; Erastus Corning Whitney was his real name. His former wife, Grace Mary Rackliff, recalled, "[H]e hated all persons that were of Italian nativity ... on many and diverse occasions [he] said that Italians coming over on the ships to America ought to be sunk in the harbors."[46]

Four additional prosecution witnesses, William Tracy, William Heron, Mary Splaine, and Frances Devlin, testified that Sacco was in South Braintree on the day of the murders. Tracy, a local real estate agent, on cross-examination, repeatedly equivocated about identifying Sacco, stating "I did not say positively," "Well, he looks like the man," and "but I wouldn't positively say so."[47]

William Heron, a railroad detective, said he was "pretty sure" that he saw Sacco smoking at the railroad station with another man on the day of the crime.[48] Sacco was not a smoker. Heron was hostile when cross-examined by defense counsel.

Mary Splaine and Frances Devlin were bookkeepers for Slater & Morrill. They each testified that after the shooting, they observed Sacco in the getaway car from the window of their office some sixty feet away.[49] Mary Splaine described the man she claimed was Sacco as follows:

> He was ... slightly taller than I am ... possibly ... 140 to 145 pounds. He was muscular ... I noticed particularly the left hand was a good sized hand, a hand that denoted strength ... The left hand, that was placed on the back of the front seat ... He had a gray ... shirt and [a] clean-cut face ... The forehead was high. The hair was brushed back and it was between ... two inches and two and one-half

inches in length and had dark eyebrows, but the complexion was a white, peculiar white that looked greenish. [50]

Dr. Morton Prince, world famous psychiatry professor at Harvard, criticized Miss Splaine's attempt to provide the details of whom and what she saw.[51] He noted that Miss Splaine had seen Sacco from a distance of about sixty feet, for only one and a half to three seconds, in a car moving between fifteen to eighteen miles an hour.[52] Yet at the end of a year, she remembered sixteen different details, even to the size of his hand, the length of his hair, and the shade of his eyebrows. He claimed that "such perception and memory under such conditions can easily be proved to be psychologically impossible."[53] He questioned the "animus and honesty of the state that introduces such testimony to convict, knowing that the jury is too ignorant to disbelieve ..."[54] It is also worth noting that Sacco did not have a large left hand; he wore a size 7-3/4 glove.

Dr. Prince explained how Miss Splaine became acquainted with the personal characteristics of Sacco:

> Sacco had been shown to her on several occasions.She had had an opportunity to study him carefully ... he sat before her in court. At the preliminary hearing in the police court she was not asked to pick Sacco from among a group of other men. Sacco was shown to her alone. Everyone knows that under such circumstances the image of a person later develops ... in an observer's mind and becomes a false memory ... produced by suggestion. [55]

The prosecution presented a second group of seven witnesses, all of whom had seen the bandits, but none of whom identified Sacco as one of them, and four of whom also indicated that Vanzetti was not one of the bandits.

Hans Behrsin, chauffeur for Mr. Slater, described the two bandits standing by the fence near the Rice & Hutchins factory:[56] "[B]oth of them seemed to be pretty well light complexioned fellows," and "[Y]es, one had an army shirt on." Behrsin did not identify Sacco and Vanzetti as the bandits.

James Bostock saw the shooting and the bandits from within fifty feet, and he could only say that the bandits looked like Italian fruit peddlers. When asked if he could identify the bandits after he observed Sacco and

Vanzetti, Bostock answered, "No sir, I could not tell whether or not they was, no sir."[57]

Lewis Wade, a shoe worker at Slater & Morrill, saw one of the bandits shoot Berardelli, and he saw the getaway car and its driver. Wade said the man at the wheel was a pale-faced man and he looked sick. When asked if he could tell the jury if the man he saw doing the shooting was in the courtroom, he answered, referring to Sacco, "I would not say for sure."[58] Even after he was pressured by the judge, he answered, "Well, I ain't sure. I have a little doubt.—I have a doubt, I don't think he is the man."

In 1926, Wade picked a picture of Joe Morelli as strikingly like the man he had seen shooting Berardelli.[59] He said that he resembled Sacco.

James McGlone was working on an excavation across the street from the shooting and had seen the bandits.[60] He testified on cross-examination that he did not see in the courtroom the men he had seen on April 15.

Edgar Langlois, foreman at Rice & Hutchins, was asked to identify the defendants at the Brockton police station after their arrest and stated that Vanzetti was not like either of the men and that he was unable to identify Sacco.[61]

Mark Carrigon, a shoe worker at Slater & Morrill who had seen the getaway car and its passenger after the shooting, testified on cross-examination that he was unable to identify either Sacco or Vanzetti when taken to see them after their arrest.[62]

Louis DeBeradinis, a cobbler, saw the getaway car from his shop just after the shooting.[63] He saw one man leaning out of the car, pointing a gun at him. DeBeradinis described the gunman: "Well, the man I saw he had a long face.[64] That is what I said in the Brockton police station, it was a long face, and awful white, and light hair combed in the back. It was a thin fellow I saw."

The prosecutor then asked DeBeradinis:[65]

Q: Now, have you seen that man since, that you saw that day?

A: No sir.

Q: Have you seen anybody that looked like him?

A: No sir.

Q: Now, just a minute. Were you taken down to Brockton police court?

A: Yes sir.

Q: Did you see anybody there?

A: Yes sir.

Q: How did that man that you saw there compare with the man that you saw that day on Pearl Street?

A: There is a lot of difference.

Q: What?

A: There is a lot of difference between the one I saw on Pearl Street [the gunman in the car] and the one I seen at Brockton [Sacco].

Following these questions, the transcript records a bizarre exchange between the prosecutor and his own witness, with the prosecutor attempting to force DeBeradinis to identify Sacco as the gunman in the getaway car.[66] Eventually, Sacco's lawyer entered the fray and moved the court to stop further questioning by the prosecutor because he was attacking the credibility of his own witness.

The defense presented twenty-five rebuttal witnesses in response to the Commonwealth's identification witnesses. Their testimony, subject to some ambiguities when cross-examined, is briefly summarized as follows: twenty-three testified that neither Sacco nor Vanzetti was one of the killers,[67] and two were uncertain whether Sacco or Vanzetti was one of the killers.[68] Albert Frantello and Barbara Liscomb were the two most important witnesses of that group.

Albert Frantello, a former Slater & Morrill worker, saw two men leaning against the fence outside of Rice & Hutchins shortly before 3:00 PM on the day of the crime.[69] He testified that he was close enough to touch them, that neither Sacco nor Vanzetti was one of the men he saw, and that the two men were "speaking in the American language."

Katzmann put Frantello through a fierce cross-examination.[70] He attempted to show that Frantello had previously identified the men at the fence as Italians, indeed, as low-class "wops."

Katzmann tried to discredit Frantello's testimony that the men were speaking in English.[71] The witness would not bend, instead asserting, "Well, I will tell you the truth. He was speaking the American language, that is the truth."

Katzmann showed that Frantello, although born and raised in America, was of Italian heritage, implying bias in favor of the two Italian defendants. Katzmann asked the witness about the two men at the fence, "[W]ere [they] what may be called in the vernacular 'wops' or were they Americans?"[72] Katzmann reminded the jury repeatedly that the defendants were low-class Italians—wops. Katzmann used the offensive word "wop" no less than twenty-two times on six pages of the printed transcript in his questions to Frantello, thereby connecting that offensive reference to Frantello's Italian heritage as many times.[73]

Barbara Liscomb, a Rice & Hutchins worker, observed one of the killers as she looked out of a window at the factory right after the shooting. He was "a short dark man ... holding a revolver in his hands."[74] She testified that he looked right up at her and that she had a clear view of his face. She said, "I would always remember his face."[75] Asked if either man in the dock was that man, she answered, "No sir."[76] She was asked again, "Are you sure about that?" She answered, "I am positively sure."

It had to be clear to Katzmann that the defense discredited the Commonwealth's identification witnesses during their cross-examination and that those witnesses were vulnerable to the testimony of rebuttal witnesses. Katzmann had to present physical evidence connecting Sacco to the murder of at least one of the victims if he hoped to win this case.

The Sacco Cap Evidence

Harold Williams told the jury in his opening statement that a cap was found next to Berardelli's body just after he was shot and that Sacco owned and wore a cap like the one found.[77]

The first witness to present testimony to that effect was Fred Loring, a shoe worker at Slater & Morrill. He testified that he arrived on the scene moments after the shooting and that he found a cap about eighteen inches from Berardelli's body, which he picked up and carried to the shop. He looked it over, and about an hour later he gave it to Thomas Fraher, the superintendent at the factory.[78]

At the trial, Loring identified a cap as the one he found at the scene of the crime. He testified that the cap was in the same condition at the time of the trial as it was at the time he found it.[79] The prosecution offered the cap into evidence during Loring's testimony, but it was not admitted because of objections from defense counsel.[80] It is significant that the prosecution did not call Fraher as a witness to verify that Loring gave him the cap about an hour after the shootings. Following Loring's testimony, the wives of the slain paymaster and his guard each testified that the cap did not belong to their husbands.[81]

George Kelley, Michael Kelley's son and superintendent of the Three-K shoe factory that employed Sacco, testified at the trial.[82] He stated there were times when Sacco wore a cap to work and times when he wore a hat. Kelley could tell little more about Sacco's cap other than it was dark and dirty and Sacco hung it on a nail.[83] When asked at the trial to examine the lining of the cap offered in evidence, Kelley said he noticed it was torn.[84] Based on Kelley's testimony, Williams offered the cap into evidence, but Sacco's lawyer again objected.[85] Then Judge Thayer left the neutrality that he should have maintained and again interjected himself for the prosecution:[86]

> [Judge Thayer]: I would like to ask [Kelley] one question: Whether,—I wish you [prosecutor Williams] would ask him, rather,—according to your best judgment, is it your opinion that the cap which Mr. Williams now holds in his hand is like the one that was worn by the defendant, Sacco?
>
> Mr. Moore: I object to that question, your honor.
>
> [Judge Thayer to Mr. Williams]: did you put it? I would rather it came from Mr. Williams. Will you put that question?
>
> Q: [by Williams] Mr. Kelley, according to your best judgment, is the cap I show you alike in appearance to the cap worn by Sacco?
>
> A: [Kelley] In color only.
>
> [Judge Thayer]: That is not responsive to the question. I wish you would answer it if you can.
>
> [Kelley]: I can't answer it when I don't know right down in my heart that that is the cap.
>
> [Judge Thayer]: I don't want you to. I want you should answer according to what is in your heart.
>
> [Kelley]: General appearance, that is all I can say. I never saw the cap so close in my life as I do now.
>
> [Judge Thayer]: In its general appearance, is it the same?
>
> [Kelley]: Yes sir.
>
> Mr. Moore: I object to that last question and answer.
>
> [Judge Thayer]: You may put the question so it comes from counsel rather than the Court.
>
> Q: [by Williams] In its general appearance, is it the same?
>
> A: [Kelley] Yes.
>
> Mr. Williams: I now offer the cap, if your honor please.

[Judge Thayer]: Admitted. [into evidence as Exhibit 29]

This is another example of how Judge Thayer assisted the prosecution. Here the judge used his position of authority to encourage the witness to provide testimony to support admission of the cap into evidence.

When Sacco's lawyer asked him on direct examination whether the cap introduced into evidence as Exhibit 29 was his, he denied that it was.[87] Sacco said he never saw the cap before and he never owned a cap with a fur lining. He was asked to try it on, which he did, but said, "[C]ould not go in. My size is 7-1/8."[88] The jury was not told that the cap in evidence as Exhibit 29 was size 6-7/8, based on the Pinkerton report of H. H., issued on April 19, 1920.[89] Katzmann concealed all the Pinkerton reports from the defense until shortly before the execution of Sacco and Vanzetti on August 23, 1927.[90]

On cross-examination, Katzmann showed Sacco a second cap that Sacco identified as his, even though he said it looked "too dirty."[91] Sacco was told to try the second cap on, which he had no difficulty doing. Then, Sacco was again asked to try on the first cap marked Exhibit 29 in evidence and found it difficult, saying, "[C]an't go in … Oh, but it is too tight."[92]

Katzmann then asked that the cap Sacco admitted was his (the second cap) be marked as Exhibit 27 for identification, and he proceeded to question Sacco about it [93] (exhibits marked for identification take a different sequence of numbers than those admitted into evidence). Katzmann called Sacco's attention to a hole in its lining and asked him if he had ever seen it before.[94] Sacco denied ever seeing a hole in the lining of his cap, but he admitted that he had worn it to work and hung that cap on two stakes.[95]

Sacco's wife also testified about the two caps. She said that the second cap looked like her husband's cap, but the first cap did not, and that she never saw a hole in the lining of his cap.[96]

Katzmann called Lieutenant Daniel Guerin to the stand.[97] He testified that the day after Sacco's arrest, he entered Sacco's home and obtained one of his caps. He identified that cap as the one marked Exhibit 27 for identification and that it was in the same condition at the trial as it was on May 6, when he had taken it from Sacco's home. Katzmann then offered the second cap into evidence. Moore objected because the police obtained the cap through an unlawful search and seizure. Without ruling on Moore's objection, Judge Thayer admitted the second cap into evidence as Exhibit 43.[98]

When Katzmann made his closing argument to the jury, he implied that Sacco denied ownership of the cap taken from his home. Katzmann was not truthful. Sacco admitted that cap was his but said that it looked "too dirty."

To summarize: Exhibit 29 in evidence was the cap Loring claimed he found on Pearl Street after the shooting; Exhibit 27 marked for identification, later marked Exhibit 43 when admitted into evidence, was a cap the police took from Sacco's home on May 6, 1920, without a warrant.

As a result of information that surfaced six years later before the advisory committee, it was determined that Loring's cap evidence was false. The Sacco defense attorneys discovered that Loring did not find the controversial cap next to Berardelli's dead body after the shooting.

On July 18, 1927, President A. Lawrence Lowell, of Harvard, chairman of the advisory committee, questioned former Chief of Police Jeremiah Gallivan about the controversial cap marked Exhibit 29 in evidence:[99]

> A: [By Gallivan] Now, I suppose you want to know something about that cap?
> Q: [By Lowell] Yes.
> A: It was Saturday morning [April 17, 1921] when Tom Fraher, Superintendent of Slater & Morrill's factory, called me on the telephone down there.
> [By Lowell.] When, Saturday morning?
> Q: What day was this murder?
> A: Thursday afternoon.
> Q: How do you spell his name?
> A: ... F-r-a-h-e-r ... I think that's the way to spell it. I know him very well; he called me down and says, 'Jerry, here's a cap that was picked up there'—Now, I understand him to say 'last night, last evening but I don't know whether it amounts to anything or not, but I thought you better keep it here.'
> Q: 'Picked up last evening.' That would be Friday evening?
> A: Yes, sir. So I took the cap and looked at it, and if you were to put the cap before me now I wouldn't know it; I haven't seen that cap for seven years.

News accounts in the Saturday, April 17, editions of local newspapers confirmed Gallivan's testimony before the advisory committee that someone had found a cap on Pearl Street, *on Friday, April 16.*[100] This, in turn, confirmed a story by several Slater & and Morrill employees that Loring had told them he did not find the controversial cap and that someone else found it on *April 16.*[101]

Gallivan further testified at the advisory committee hearing that he had made a hole in the lining of the cap that Loring claimed he found (Exhibit 29 in evidence) to see if he could find any identifying marks that might lead to its owner. After that, he put the cap under the back seat of his car and kept it there for two weeks before he turned it over to state police Officer John Scott.[102] Gallivan told Scott at that time that he made the hole in the lining.[103]

It appears that someone fabricated the hole in the second cap, the one found in Sacco's home, in an attempt to support the Commonwealth's claim that the cap that Loring alleged he found belonged to Sacco. The inference for the jury was that the hole in the controversial cap (the first cap) resulted from the nail that put a hole in the cap that Sacco admitted was his. The following summarizes the Exhibit 29 cap evidence:

- Loring did not find that cap on April 15, the day of the shootings.
- Someone other than Loring found that cap on April 16, after hundreds of people had milled around the scene of the crime.
- When Fraher gave that cap to Gallivan, there was no hole in the lining, and Gallivan made the hole in an attempt to find identifying marks.
- Gallivan told Officer Scott that he made the hole in the lining of that cap when he turned it over to Scott.
- Loring testified falsely at the trial that that cap was in the same condition it was when he claimed to have found it because the hole in its lining was made later by Gallivan.
- That cap was a size 6-7/8. Sacco's cap size was 7-1/8.

How much about the Exhibit 29 cap in evidence did the prosecution know? Did the prosecution participate in what appears to be a fraud on the court, on the people, and on Sacco? Why didn't Sacco's trial lawyers discover the news accounts that reported the controversial cap was found on Friday, April 16? Herbert Ehrmann, Sacco and Vanzetti's appellate lawyer, uncovered that important fact six years after the trial when he reviewed news accounts of the crime in preparation for the governor's advisory committee's hearings.[104]

Neither the advisory committee members, following their hearings, nor the governor, following his clemency hearings, took any of these facts into account in deciding the fate of Sacco and Vanzetti. They minimized the importance of the controversial cap notwithstanding that:

- Katzmann's closing argument to the jury depended heavily on the cap evidence for the conviction of Sacco.[105]
- Judge Thayer used the cap evidence in three separate decisions to justify his denials of motions for a new trial.[106]
- The supreme judicial court concluded that if the jury found favorably on the cap evidence, that would support a finding that Sacco was present at the time of the shooting.[107]

The inconsistencies surrounding the cap evidence raised doubts whether the murder verdicts were justified. The ballistics evidence raised more doubts.

Sacco's Gun and Bullet III

Early in the Dedham trial, prosecutor Katzmann told Fred Moore that he would not claim that any particular gun fired any particular bullet.[108] Katzmann had to make that concession because Captain William Proctor, the Commonwealth's most experienced ballistics expert, repeatedly told Katzmann he could find no evidence that Sacco's pistol shot Bullet III.[109] It was an accepted fact that ballistics technology at the time of the Dedham trial could not indicate if a particular gun shot a particular bullet. Despite Proctor's negative conclusion, he testified at the Dedham trial to the contrary.[110] On November 8, 1923, during Thompson's presentation of the fifth supplementary motion for a new trial, he learned the truth behind Proctor's reversal. A major controversy erupted at that time. Following are details of how events unfolded.

Sacco initiated an offer during the trial to submit his Colt .32, then in evidence as Exhibit 27, to ballistics tests.[111] Fred Moore argued that because Sacco knew he did not use his gun to kill anyone, he agreed to submit the gun for tests. Sacco was sure the results would prove his innocence. Because Sacco's gun was already in evidence, his consent was necessary to perform tests on it.[112] Sacco's initiation of the tests was a powerful showing of his consciousness of innocence, although Moore never made that point during the trial.

Sacco's offer created a predicament for Katzmann. If he refused to proceed with the tests, it would show that the Commonwealth doubted Sacco's guilt, and that might be used to exonerate him. On the other hand, if Katzmann participated and the results were negative, the case could be lost. Because Captain Proctor could find no evidence that Bullet III was shot from Sacco's gun, Katzmann sought a second expert, one more amenable to the prosecution's point of view. This led to the hiring of Captain Charles VanAmburgh, a retired army captain, who had spent some years in military procurement of guns and ammunition.[113] At the time he was hired, he was in private industry doing similar work. VanAmburgh's credentials were dubious; he was not a ballistics engineer, he had a high school education at most, and he had no experience with ballistics matters in a criminal case.[114] Captain Proctor had to show VanAmburgh how to make various ballistic measurements when he joined the prosecution's team.[115]

The tests were held in the city of Lowell on June 18, 1921, in the midst of the Dedham trial.[116] Captain Proctor and Captain VanAmburgh conducted the tests for the Commonwealth, and James Burns, a ballistics engineer at the United States Cartridge Company, acted for the defense. A second expert, Henry Fitzgerald, in charge of testing at the Colt Firearms Company, was also retained by the defense. While Fitzgerald did not attend the tests, he testified at the trial based on his review and analysis of the results of the Lowell tests.[117]

After the tests, Captain Proctor told Katzmann he was still unable to find any evidence that Sacco's pistol fired the fatal bullet.[118] Captain VanAmburgh expressed a weak opinion that Sacco's gun fired Bullet III.[119] Neither VanAmburgh nor Proctor expressed an opinion at that time regarding Shell W, the spent Winchester shell found at the crime scene. The defense experts concluded that Bullet III and Shell W were not fired through Sacco's gun.[120]

Katzmann had a problem. Since both his experts participated in the Lowell tests, they had to testify, even though Proctor and VanAmburgh did not agree on the results. Katzmann's solution was to present Captain Proctor and Captain VanAmburgh as the last two prosecution witnesses in the Commonwealth's case and to prearrange Proctor's testimony to seem consistent with VanAmburgh's testimony.

Proctor took the stand first. He testified as to his background in order to qualify as an expert. He described in detail his study of Bullet III. Then, Proctor testified:[121]

> Q: [by Williams] Have you an opinion as to whether
>   bullet 3[III] was fired from the Colt Automatic
>   [Sacco's] which is in evidence?
> A: I have.
> Q: And what is your opinion?
> A: My opinion is that it is consistent with being fired by
>   that pistol.

Notice Proctor's opinion: "consistent with being fired by that [Sacco's] pistol," not consistent with being fired by a Colt .32 pistol.

VanAmburgh was the prosecution's last witness.[122] After he provided his background, qualified as an expert, and described his study of Bullet III, he testified:

> Q: [by Williams] Have you formed an opinion, Captain,
>   as to whether or not No. 3[III] bullet was fired from
>   that particular Colt [Sacco's] automatic?
> A: I have an opinion.
> Q: And what is your opinion?
> A: I am inclined to believe that it was fired, No. 3[III] bullet
>   was fired, from this Colt [Sacco's] automatic pistol.

VanAmburgh's last words to the jury were, "No. 3 [III] bullet was fired from this Colt [Sacco's] automatic pistol." Defense counsel did not cross-examine VanAmburgh on his use of the words, "inclined to believe," and VanAmburgh did not explain his words of limitation to the jury. An opinion is essentially a belief, as distinguished from a fact. To use the phrase "inclined to believe" in an opinion results in a double qualifier and diminishes the strength of the opinion.

In addition, defense counsel did not cross-examine Proctor on the meaning of his words "consistent with." John Dever, a member of the jury, conceded that the ballistics evidence presented by the prosecutor played a crucial role in the jury deciding that the defendants were guilty of murder.[123] One juror reported it was "the deciding factor" and "there was no getting around that evidence."

After Sacco and Vanzetti were convicted, William Thompson and his co-counsel Herbert Ehrmann learned the truth behind Proctor's ambiguous phrase "consistent with" while they prepared the fifth supplementary motion for a new trial. Thompson obtained an affidavit from Captain Proctor dated October 20, 1923, in which he admitted these facts:

> During the preparation for the trial, my attention was repeatedly called by the District Attorney and his assistants to the question: whether I could find any evidence which would justify the opinion that the particular bullet taken from the body of Berardelli, which came from a Colt automatic pistol, came from the particular Colt automatic pistol taken from Sacco. I used every means available to me for forming an opinion on this subject. I conducted, with Captain VanAmburgh, certain tests at Lowell, about which I testified, consisting in firing certain cartridges through Sacco's pistol. At no time was I able to find any evidence whatever which tended to convince me that the particular mortal bullet found in Berardelli's body, which came from a Colt automatic pistol, which I think was numbered [III] and had some other exhibit number, came from Sacco's pistol and I so informed the district attorney and his assistant before the trial ...
>
> ... At the trial, the District Attorney did not ask me whether I had found any evidence that the so-called mortal bullet which I have referred to as number [III] passed through Sacco's pistol, nor was I asked that question on cross-examination. The District Attorney desired to ask me that question, but I had repeatedly told him that if he did I should be obliged to answer in the negative. That is still my opinion for the reason that bullet number [III], in my judgment, passed through some Colt automatic pistol, but I do not intend by that answer to imply that I had found any evidence that the so-called mortal bullet had passed through this particular Colt automatic pistol and the District

Attorney well knew that I did not so intend and framed his question accordingly. Had I been asked the direct question: whether I had found any affirmative evidence whatever that this so-called mortal bullet had passed through this particular Sacco's pistol, I should have answered then, as I do now without hesitation, in the negative. [124]

Katzmann and Williams each responded to Proctor's affidavit with separate affidavits that denied they had "repeatedly" asked Proctor to find evidence that Bullet III came from Sacco's gun.[125] Katzmann avoided saying anything more of substance, and Williams added that Proctor suggested the form of the disputed questions and answers.[126]

Captain Proctor's opinion became even more controversial following testimony by Albert Hamilton (Sacco's ballistics expert) before the governor's advisory committee four years later. Hamilton informed them that in an automobile ride Captain Proctor had told him that "in his real opinion the fatal bullet [Bullet III] had not been fired through Sacco's pistol."[127] The committee members did not want to hear that. Proctor died shortly thereafter, and the committee's report, released shortly before the execution of the two Italians, simply stated regarding that issue, "We do not believe Hamilton's testimony."[128]

Captain Proctor's "real opinion" regarding Bullet III should be evaluated against an earlier statement he made to Hamilton: "I have been too old in the game, I have been too long in the game, and I'm getting to be too old to want to see a couple of fellows go to the chair for something I don't think they did."[129] Proctor had expressed his view a number of times to Katzmann and others that Katzmann had the wrong men.

The deception worked. Proctor's and VanAmburgh's opinions led the jury and the public to conclude that the fatal bullet came from Sacco's gun. Judge Thayer used these opinions to the detriment of the defendants when he instructed the jury that the prosecution experts testified to the "effect" that Sacco's Colt fired the bullet that killed Berardelli.[130]

When Proctor's contrived and misleading ballistics testimony, aided and abetted by the prosecution and misused by the judge, became public, it outraged Harvard Professor Felix Frankfurter.[131] In response, he wrote a critical article in 1927 shortly before the execution of Sacco and Vanzetti. The article appeared in the *Atlantic Monthly*, followed by his book on the case condemning the misconduct of prosecutor Katzmann and Judge Thayer.

Professor Edmund Morgan, in the 1948 publication of *The Legacy of Sacco and Vanzetti*, decried the action of the prosecutor as "monstrous misconduct which no discretionary power of a trial judge should be allowed to conceal or condone."[132]

Shell W

The next piece of evidence presented by the Commonwealth was a spent Winchester shell (Shell W) found at the crime scene. The prosecution connected it to the Winchester bullet that killed Berardelli and to Sacco because of the Winchester bullets he carried the night of his arrest. James Bostock, a Slater & Morrill worker, claimed he found Shell W at the scene of the crime with other spent shells. Bostock testified on June 9, 1921:[133]

Q: [by Williams] Did you pick up any shells there?
A: Yes, I picked up some shells.
Q: Where abouts did you pick them up?
A: I picked them up just close to where the shooting was, about two or three feet from the shooting.
Q: What did you do with them?
A: I think Mr. Fraher had them.
Q: Mr. Fraher?
A: I left them in Slater & Morrill's office.
Q: How many did you pick up?
A: Three or four.
Q: You turned them over to Mr. Fraher?
A: No. I left them in the office of Slater & Morrill, in one of the desks.
Q: Is that all you found there?
A: That is all. I saw some others picked up. I saw some others had some others, but that is all I picked up.

This was strange testimony. It is clear that Bostock was not comfortable answering these questions. He said he picked up "some shells," then when pressed, he changed it to "three or four" shells. He must have known how many shells he picked up. Thomas Fraher, superintendent of the Slater & Morrill factory, contradicted Bostock's testimony six weeks later:[134]

Q: [by Williams] Do you know a man named Bostock?

A: James Bostock, yes.

Q: Shortly after the shooting, did Bostock deliver anything to you?

A: Four empty shells ...

Q: Shells of what general character?

A: Well, four brass shells; I should say they were .32 calibre ...

Q: You took those shells.

A: I took those shells.

Q: What did you do with them?

A: I kept them until Captain Proctor of the state police arrived, and turned them over to him.

Captain Proctor confirmed that he received four spent shells from Fraher on the day of the murders and kept them for about a year until he turned them over to the sheriff at the beginning of the Dedham trial.[135]

Amateur historian Lincoln A. Robbins uncovered evidence in 1977 consisting of a trial notebook belonging to assistant prosecutor Harold Williams. The notebook contained a handwritten entry made a few months before the Dedham trial: "Shay picked up 3 shells where Ber fell and gave them to Sherlock."[136] (Shay and Sherlock were police officers.) A subsequent typewritten document found with the notebook included the entry "shells found on street: Shay to Fraher to Proctor."[137] Apparently, upon further review, Williams or some associate corrected the chain of custody of the shells to Shay to Fraher to Proctor, rather than Shay to Sherlock to Fraher to Proctor. However, neither document indicated Bostock was in the chain of custody. This was another example of the prosecution concealing crucial documentary evidence to the prejudice of the defendants.

Bostock testified he placed three or four shells in a desk and said, "I think Mr. Fraher had them."[138] Bostock did not say how or when Fraher got the shells. Fraher testified that Bostock delivered "four empty shells" to him.[139] Fraher's testimony does not square with the documentary evidence that Lincoln Robbins found, which makes no mention of Bostock finding any shells, but rather indicates that Officer John Shay picked up three shells (not four) where Berardelli fell.

Bostock's and Fraher's testimonies are in conflict. The fourth shell, probably Shell W, looks very much like a plant that the prosecutor used to match the Winchester brand of Bullet III, thereby connecting Sacco to the crime because he carried six intact Winchester cartridges when arrested.

This questionable evidence was used to support the prosecution's claim that Bullet III was shot from Sacco's gun.

Consciousness of Guilt

Consciousness of guilt is circumstantial evidence based on the conduct of a defendant from which the jury may infer that the defendant was conscious of the crime in question and that his conduct was a manifestation of his guilt of that crime.[140] This kind of evidence is probative only if no other reasonable explanation exists for the defendant's actions.[141] Prosecutor Katzmann used consciousness of guilt to convict Sacco and Vanzetti because of the weakness of the Commonwealth's identification and other evidence.

Throughout the trial, Judge Thayer acknowledged that the verdicts in this case did not rest on the testimony of eyewitnesses but on evidence of the defendants' consciousness of guilt.[142] He cited as evidence showing their consciousness of guilt the attempt by Sacco and Vanzetti to draw their guns at the time they were arrested, the conduct of the two at Johnson's garage earlier that evening, and the various lies they told the police after they were arrested.[143]

An analysis of the Commonwealth's claim that Sacco and Vanzetti tried to use their guns at the time of their arrest begins with the fact that both defendants were armed with loaded weapons at that time. Sacco was found with a loaded Colt .32 automatic and an assortment of twenty-two cartridges,[144] and Vanzetti had a loaded Harrington & Richardson .38 revolver and four (Vanzetti claimed only three) intact shotgun shells.[145] Neither of them had a permit to carry their weapons. Carrying guns would not, without more concrete evidence, have been enough to convict them of the murders of Parmenter and Berardelli. The times were bad, and it was common for many men, especially immigrants, to carry weapons.[146]

Since the end of the war, crimes of violence were prevalent in the industrial towns of New England.[147] Vanzetti regularly traveled to Boston to buy fish for his business and often carried cash of one hundred dollars or more. He said he carried a gun for protection.[148] In Sacco's case, since he worked as the night watchman at the Three K shoe factory, he armed himself when he inspected the plant late in the evening and on weekends.[149] His boss, Michael Kelley, knew he owned a gun and often reminded him to get a permit.[150]

Sacco and Vanzetti each had an explanation for the ammunition they carried. The Saccos were preparing for a trip to Italy in a few days. Mrs. Sacco, while cleaning the house, found loose cartridges and shotgun shells. She gave the cartridges to her husband for disposal.[151] Sacco testified that he intended to shoot them off in the woods before leaving on their trip. Sacco carried the cartridges and his gun in his clothing and said he didn't think anything of it when he left with Vanzetti for Johnson's garage to pick up Boda's Overland.[152] Mrs. Sacco gave the shotgun shells to Vanzetti. He said he intended to sell them to friends for a few quarters, which he planned to contribute to the cause.[153]

While these explanations seemed innocent, Sacco and Vanzetti were vulnerable to speculation that they had armed themselves and sought Boda's Overland the night of May 5 in order to commit crimes like the South Braintree robbery. This left them open to Officer Michael Connolly's claim that they attempted to draw their weapons when they were arrested.[154]

In order to establish consciousness of guilt, the prosecution offered Officer Connolly's testimony at the Dedham trial. Connolly testified as to the events on the night of May 5, 1920, when in response to Mrs. Johnson's phone call, he boarded a streetcar and arrested Sacco and Vanzetti:

> I went down through the car and when I got opposite to the seat I stopped and I asked them where they came from. They said "Bridgewater." I said "What was you doing in Bridgewater?" They said "We went down to see a friend of mine." I said "Who is your friend?" He said "A man by the—they call him Poppy." "Well" I said "I want you, you are under arrest." Vanzetti was sitting on the inside seat and he went, put his hand in his hip pocket and I says, "Keep your hands out on your lap, or you'll be sorry." [155]

Vanzetti interrupted Connolly's testimony—he jumped up in open court and shouted, "You are a liar!"[156]

Connolly continued, "They wanted to know what they were arrested for. I says 'suspicious characters' ...Officer Vaughn got on... and when he got on I told him [Vanzetti] to stand up, and I told Officer Vaughn to fish Vanzetti; and I just gave Sacco a slight going over ..."[157]

Connolly testified that Vaughn found a revolver on Vanzetti and continued:

> I put Sacco and Vanzetti in the back seat of our light machine, and Officer Snow got in the back seat with them. I took the front seat with the driver ... I turned around and faced Sacco and Vanzetti ... I told them when we started that the first false move I would put a bullet in them. On the way to the station Sacco reached his hand to put under his overcoat and I told him to keep his hands outside of his clothes and on his lap ... I says to him, "Have you got a gun there?" He says, "No." He says "I ain't got no gun." ... We went along a little further and he done the same thing. I gets up on my knees on the front seat and I reaches over and I puts my hand under his coat but I did not see any gun. "Now," I says "Mister, if you put your hand in there again you are going to get into trouble." He says "I don't want no trouble." We reached the station, brought them up to the office, searched them. [158]

Connolly said that after they reached the station, Officer Merle Spear searched Sacco and found twenty-two cartridges in his hip pocket and a fully loaded Colt automatic "down between his pants and his shirt, underneath his vest and coat."[159]

The details Connolly provided of these events lent credibility to his testimony. Yet Connolly's testimony of the same events at Vanzetti's Plymouth trial a year earlier did not mention that Vanzetti attempted to draw his weapon when Connolly arrested him.

More to the point, Connolly's testimony before the grand jury on September 10, 1920, three months after the Plymouth trial, was far different from his Dedham testimony.[160]

> Q: [by Katzmann] As a result of what you had been told, what did you do?
> A: I placed two men—two Italians, Vanzetti and Sacco, under arrest.
> Q: Did you search them?
> A: I did.

Q: What did you find?

A: Further up the line another officer got on the car to help me, and we found two guns ...

Q: Did you ask them where they had been?

A: I asked them where they had come from.

Q: What did they say?

A: From Bridgewater. I said, "Well, you are under arrest as suspicious persons, and we are going to hold you for the Bridgewater police."

Q: Did you have any talk with them?

A: No, I did not have any talk with them until we got up to the central station ...

Q: Did you then?

A: Yes.

Q: What was it?

A: I asked where they lived, and Sacco said he lived in Stoughton and Vanzetti said he lived in Plymouth.

Q: Go on.

A: That is all I had to do with it ...

Although lawyers for the defendants sought to obtain the September 10, 1920, grand jury minutes, Katzmann claimed he was not required by law to provide them. It's clear why Katzmann refused to release the minutes: Connolly could not have testified at Dedham that Sacco and Vanzetti tried to draw their guns when they were arrested if those grand jury minutes were released showing Connolly's testimony to the contrary regarding that event.

After the trial, Officer Curron, who had witnessed the arrest of Sacco and Vanzetti by Officer Connolly, told a defense investigator that a number of Brockton police officers would no longer speak to Connolly because of his testimony that the two Italians tried to draw their weapons when they were arrested.[161] The fabrication of Connolly's Dedham testimony and the concealment of his grand jury testimony are more examples of prosecutorial misconduct.

Connolly's false testimony gave Katzmann the opening to make the following comments in his closing argument to the jury:

What was Vanzetti going to do with the gun if he had drawn it? What was the defendant Sacco going to do with the automatic if he had drawn it? Can you conceive of but one purpose gentlemen? They were going to draw their respective weapons to kill those police officers and make their escape. Consciousness of guilt! [162]

Judge Thayer built on Connolly's testimony and Katzmann's argument in his charge to the jury:

> The Commonwealth claims that the defendant Vanzetti put his hand in his hip pocket for the purpose of using a revolver upon the arresting officer ... If the defendant Vanzetti intended to do violence to the arresting officers ... from this evidence you may find consciousness of guilt on the part of the defendant Vanzetti ...[163]

Even without knowing the existence of Connolly's grand jury testimony, Osmond Fraenkel, in his 1933 seminal treatise, *The Sacco-Vanzetti Case*, found that Connolly's Dedham testimony made no sense.[164] Fraenkel thought it absurd and not credible to believe that after Vanzetti had been disarmed, Sacco would attempt to draw his gun while in the presence of three armed policemen. What would Fraenkel have said had he known of Connolly's grand jury testimony? What would an impartial jury have concluded if they knew of Connolly's grand jury testimony?

There is even more reason to reject Connolly's Dedham testimony. It is not credible that the two officers who searched Sacco and Vanzetti at the time of their arrest on the streetcar would not have discovered Sacco's gun and his possession of twenty-two bullets, particularly after the officers found a gun and shells upon searching Vanzetti.[165] Connolly's grand jury testimony explicitly indicated, in contradiction to his Dedham testimony, that he and another officer searched the two Italians "and we found two guns." Vanzetti was right. Connolly lied at the Dedham trial, and Katzmann knew it.

The final prop Katzmann used to build a claim of consciousness of guilt was the lies Sacco and Vanzetti told authorities the night of their arrest. They both lied about the same things:[166] what they were doing in West Bridgewater the night of their arrest; whether they knew Boda or Orciani; whether they saw a motorcycle near the Johnson home that night; and where, when, and from whom they purchased the guns and ammunition found on them. At the trial, they explained their lies as an attempt to protect themselves and their friends from deportation, jail, or worse, the fate of Andrea Salsedo, whose dead body was found below the fourteenth floor of the government's detention center.[167]

The effect of all these falsehoods on the jury was devastating to the credibility of Sacco's and Vanzetti's testimony. Katzmann wove the trivial and irrelevant falsehoods among relevant ones, giving the jury the impression that the defendants were capable of lying about everything.

As Herbert Ehrmann indicated in *The Case That Will Not Die*, Sacco and Vanzetti had good reasons to lie that had nothing to do with the murders and robbery at South Braintree:

> They were indeed conscious of guilt—the guilt of being hunted and hated radicals and draft dodgers ... their affiliation with anarchists was a fact, their agitation against the existing order was a fact, the Mitchell Palmer raids were a fact, the arrest of fellow anarchists and their deportation were facts, the long detention of Elia and Salsedo was a fact ... the crushed body of Salsedo ... was a fact.[168]

And for those lies that appear to have no logical basis, not knowing how such information would be used, they would have lied about everything out of fear—the kind of fear that envelops outcast immigrants in the grip of the police. These were the lies of immigrants, hated for their political beliefs and ethnicity, who barely understood the language, who knew little or nothing of due process or the legal system, and who were without power, influence, or wealth.

The most critical point is that consciousness of guilt is not applicable if there is any rational or reasonable basis for the lies other than the defendant's guilt of the crime. And there were other rational or reasonable explanations for their lies. Of equal importance is the fact that at the time of their arrest, neither the police nor prosecutor Katzmann advised them that they were suspects of the South Braintree robbery and murders, and no evidence was presented that the two were aware of those crimes. From the questions of the police and the prosecutor, the two thought they were arrested for their radical beliefs and activities and as part of Attorney General Palmer's raid on radicals. The attempt to prove Sacco and Vanzetti guilty of the South Braintree crimes on the basis of their consciousness of guilt on these facts was a distortion, like looking through the wrong end of a telescope.

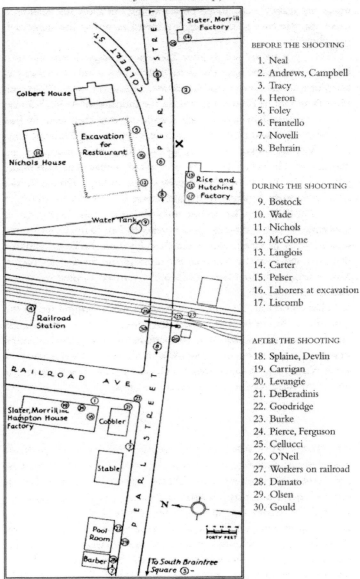

THE NEIGHBORHOOD OF THE CRIME
(from the trial transcript)

BEFORE THE SHOOTING

1. Neal
2. Andrews, Campbell
3. Tracy
4. Heron
5. Foley
6. Frantello
7. Novelli
8. Behrain

DURING THE SHOOTING

9. Bostock
10. Wade
11. Nichols
12. McGlone
13. Langlois
14. Carter
15. Pelser
16. Laborers at excavation
17. Liscomb

AFTER THE SHOOTING

18. Splaine, Devlin
19. Carrigan
20. Levangie
21. DeBeradinis
22. Goodridge
23. Burke
24. Pierce, Ferguson
25. Cellucci
26. O'Neil
27. Workers on railroad
28. Damato
29. Olsen
30. Gould

Courtesy Commonwealth Editions, Beverly, Massachusetts.

128

Nicola Sacco, circa 1920.

Rosina Sacco, circa 1920.

Bartolomeo Vanzetti, circa 1920.

Nicola, Dante, and Rosina Sacco, circa 1920.

Judge Webster Thayer, circa 1920.
Courtesy of the trustees of the Boston Public Library/Rare Books.

District Attorney Frederick Katzmann, circa 1920.
Courtesy of the trustees of the Boston Public Library/Rare Books.

SACCO FLAYS CAPITALISTS IN FIERY SPEECH IN COURT

Holds Courtroom Spellbound by Address---Went to Mexico to Escape War Service, He States--- Proud of Having Been a Slacker

This cartoon, published in the *Boston Post,* depicts various aspects of the Dedham trial, including Sacco's attempt to try on a cap found at the scene of the crime. The prosecution claimed the cap belonged to Sacco. Sacco claimed it was too small for him.

Sacco and Vanzetti funeral.
Courtesy of the trustees of the Boston Public Library/Rare Books.

Over one hundred thousand people viewed the bodies, and an additional
two hundred fifty thousand to a million people lined the streets as the
cortege moved through Boston for the trip to the crematory. The mourners
followed amidst a falling rain that likened the streets to a valley of tears.
They called it "the march of sorrows." It was a funeral of regal dimensions.

Mug shots of Nicola Sacco (top) taken at time of his arrest in 1920 and of Joseph Morelli (bottom) when he was arrested, circa 1920.

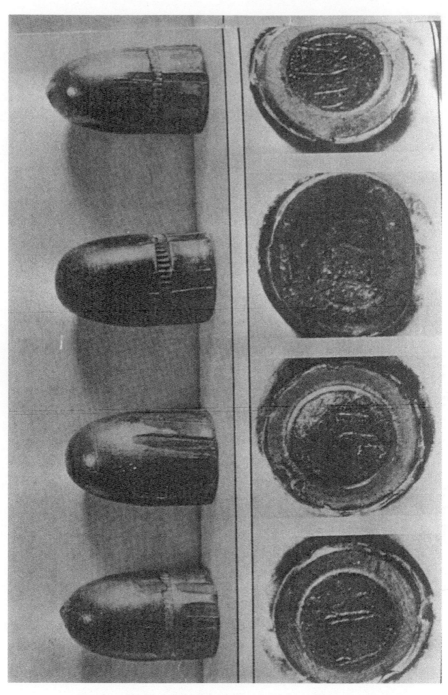

The four "Berardelli" bullets. The third from the left was
the fatal bullet, later identified as Bullet III.

CHAPTER 9

DEDHAM: KATZMANN'S VICTORY

As the end of the trial approached, Katzmann had to be aware of the defects in his case;[1] the negative implications resulting from his inability to account for the loot and his failure to formally charge and prove who the other members of the gang were.[2] And he could not ignore the following:

- Inconclusive testimony regarding the identification of Sacco and Vanzetti as the killers;
- unconvincing evidence that the gun found on Vanzetti had been taken from the slain guard, Berardelli;
- suspicion that the fourth shotgun shell Connolly claimed he found on Vanzetti was a plant;
- doubt that the cap Loring supposedly found right after the shooting, next to Berardelli's body, belonged to Sacco;
- growing doubt that Bullet III was shot from Sacco's gun.

If Sacco could establish he was in Boston at the time of the South Braintree murders, the prosecution's case would be lost. Katzmann knew he had to destroy Sacco's alibi that he was visiting the office of the Italian consulate on April 15, 1920, seeking a family passport.

Sacco's Alibi

Sacco learned of his mother's death in March and felt that he should return home to comfort his father.[3] Sacco found a replacement worker and caught up on all his work.[4] He arranged with Michael Kelley, his employer, to take the day off on April 15 for a trip to Boston to obtain a family passport. Sacco indicated he would try to make it back to work in the afternoon.[5]

On April 15, Sacco had a brief encounter at the Stoughton station with Dominick Ricci, his friend and a local carpenter, while he waited for the 8:56 AM train to Boston.[6] When he arrived in Boston, he walked to the North End and bought an Italian language newspaper, *La Notizia*. Shortly thereafter, he met a friend, Angelo Monello, and they talked for a short while.[7] Sacco said he did some window shopping, and at noon he decided to have lunch at Boni's restaurant and visit the Italian consulate for his passport in the afternoon.

As Sacco approached Boni's restaurant, he said he met his friend, Professor Felice Guadagni, and they decided to have lunch together.[8] Entering the restaurant, they encountered Albert Bosco, a friend of Professor Guadagni.[9] The three chatted and, during their conversation, Sacco told Bosco that he was planning a trip to Italy and was heading to the Italian consulate to obtain a passport. Bosco left the restaurant at about 1:00 PM, and Sacco and the professor continued with lunch.[10] Then, John Williams, an advertising agent for foreign language newspapers in America and a friend of Professor Guadagni, joined them at their table for awhile.[11]

After lunch, Sacco said he went to the consulate's office, arriving there at 2:00 PM.[12] He met with Guiseppe Andrower, a passport clerk. He brought a large picture of himself with his wife and son for a family passport. The picture was too large, and he said he left the consulate intending to come back another day with a correctly sized picture.[13]

On his way back to the train station, Sacco stopped at Giordiani's coffee shop for a brief cup of coffee.[14] At 2:45 PM, he met Professor Guadagni, who was with Antonio Dentamore. Guadagni introduced him to Dentamore, and he learned that Dentamore was a foreign exchange clerk at the Haymarket National Bank, a former editor of *La Notizia*, and a Catholic priest.

Sacco, Dentamore, and Professor Guadagni spent time talking about Sacco's pending trip to Italy and that his visit to the Italian consulate, seeking a family passport, was unsuccessful.[15] After that encounter, Sacco said he headed home.

The last person Sacco met on his way to the train station was Carlo Affe, a fruit and vegetable peddler.[16] Sacco had an outstanding account of $15.67 for produce he previously purchased from Affe. He paid the outstanding balance on his account and then caught the 4:12 PM train back to Stoughton.[17] He arrived at home at 6:00 PM.

Katzmann did not challenge Sacco directly on his claim that he went to the Italian consulate in Boston; rather, he challenged whether he went there on April 15. In order to make his challenge credible, Katzmann required each witness who testified in support of Sacco's alibi to explain how the witness fixed April 15 as the date of his meeting with Sacco. Then Katzmann vigorously cross-examined each witness as to how the witness fixed that date. Katzmann imposed unreasonable memory tests on each of the witnesses, making their testimony appear incredible, confused, or false.

The cross-examination of Dentamore is a good example.[18] Dentamore explained on direct examination that he fixed the date of meeting Sacco with Professor Guadagni at April 15 because that was the day of a banquet awarding James T. Williams, Jr., editor of the *Boston Transcript*, the title of commandante by the Italian government for his efforts during the war. Dentamore said that he had an argument about the banquet with Professor Guadagni at Giordiani's coffee shop shortly before 3:00 PM and that Sacco was there at that time.

Then Katzmann took Dentamore over the hurdles.[19] He strode back and forth across the courtroom, firing over eighty questions of the following kind at Dentamore, who could not provide satisfactory answers:

> Q: Was there anybody with you at ten minutes of three the day after you received the invitation to the banquet?
> ...
> Q: Or the day after? ...
> Q: Or the day after that? ...
> Q: Where were you—with whom were you talking if anybody, at ten minutes to three twenty-two days ago from today? ...
> Q: Twenty-one days ago? ...

These questions would be impossible for anyone to answer. Besides, the questions were irrelevant as to how Dentamore was able to fix his April 15 encounter with Sacco. None of Katzmann's dates involved a memorable event like the banquet honoring James T. Williams, Jr., on April 15.

The trial became a game, and the members of the jury enjoyed the sport, often laughing during Katzmann's performance and giving each other a friendly elbow in recognition of a good job by Katzmann.

Defense counsel read Guiseppe Andrower's affidavit to the jury. He was the passport clerk in the office of the Italian consulate. Andrower claimed that he was able to fix Sacco's visit at April 15 since he noticed a calendar on the desk of a secretary the day Sacco came to the office. In his closing argument to the jury, Katzmann denigrated the affidavit:

> Gentlemen, if I were to be hanged because I could not tell the day I have looked at a diary or a calendar since this trial first opened, I would be hanged 40 times a day. If you can tell me what day ... you looked at a calendar pad on the 15th day of May you possess mental attainments that are not human ... [20]

What is ironic about Katzmann's statement is his acknowledgment of the absurdity of the type of memory tests he applied so vigorously to Sacco's alibi witnesses.

Affe, the fruit and vegetable peddler, kept irregular records, and Katzmann highlighted that fact through his examination.[21] Nevertheless, Affe's records did show that Sacco paid off an outstanding account on April 15, and Affe fixed his meeting with Sacco in Boston on that date by reviewing his records.

John Williams, the advertising agent, gave impartial testimony supporting Sacco's alibi during his cross-examination.[22] His records showed that he took an order on April 15 in Boston from the Washington Knitting Mills for an ad to run the following weekend. He testified that he fixed April 15 as the day he met Sacco and Professor Guadagni at Boni's because that was the day he was in Boston selling an ad to his client. In addition, Williams testified that he was regularly treated in Boston for asthma by Dr. Howard Gibbs and that he was treated by the doctor on April 15, 1920. Dr. Gibbs provided corroboration from his records that showed Williams had visited him in Boston on April 15 for an asthma treatment.[23]

If nothing else, the testimony of John Williams, verified by his business records and corroborated by the records of Dr. Gibbs, should have raised a reasonable doubt whether Sacco was in South Braintree on April 15, as the prosecution claimed. Neither John Williams nor Dr. Gibbs had any prior connection with Sacco or any of Sacco's associates. They were not

Italians, an apparent impediment to truthfulness to an all-Yankee jury. There is no evidence or any reason to believe that John Williams and Dr. Gibbs committed perjury for a lowly immigrant shoe worker.

Albert Bosco also supported Sacco's alibi.[24] He fixed his meeting with Sacco as April 15, the day of the banquet honoring editor James T. Williams, Jr. Katzmann challenged, but could not shake, Bosco's testimony on cross-examination.

Professor Felice Guadagni also corroborated Sacco's alibi.[25] He testified he was able to fix the date he met Sacco for lunch at Boni's as April 15 because that was the date of the banquet honoring James T. Williams, Jr.

Angelo Monello walked briefly with Sacco in Boston the morning of April 15.[26] He fixed the date by remembering that the following Sunday was April 18, when he went to New York to see Mimi Aguglia, a world-famous artist, in the play *Madame X*. Katzmann challenged Monello to identify ten other dates and people with whom he had discussed the play *Madame X*.[27] He was unable to do so.

Dominick Ricci, the carpenter who met Sacco the morning of April 15 at the Stoughton train station, established that date with reference to work he was doing on a customer's home.[28] On cross-examination, Ricci was asked whether he was working as a carpenter on a series of dates, including April 18, to which he answered yes. Then Katzmann asked if he worked on thirty-eight subsequent dates, specifically identifying each date without disclosing which day of the week each date fell on. Ricci answered yes to each date. At the conclusion of this test, Katzmann announced to the court and the jury that each of those dates fell on a Sunday. Sacco's counsel did not object to Katzmann's improper rebuttal testimony. Katzmann made Ricci look dishonest, like someone who would answer yes to any question that favored Sacco.

Katzmann was mistaken or he lied.[29] August 2, 9, 16, and December 6 of 1920 were dates Katzmann claimed fell on a Sunday, but those dates all fell on a Monday.

* * * *

Katzmann's ultimate tactic was to denigrate the patriotism and character of Sacco and Vanzetti in order to win his case. He had a powerful weapon in his arsenal to achieve this goal—the ability to mount an effective cross-examination of the defendants. He planned to use his skills to force compromising testimony from Sacco and Vanzetti to gain guilty verdicts if they dared to testify in their own defense.

Katzmann's opportunity became a reality when the two Italians testified.[30] They each indicated they needed Boda's Overland to dispose of radical literature. Vanzetti stated he carried a gun for protection because the times were bad.[31] Sacco claimed he needed a gun because of his night watchman duties. They both testified that when arrested, they lied to the police to protect their friends and themselves from deportation, and even worse, from the fate of Andrea Salsedo.[32] Sacco and Vanzetti had to testify in order to explain that their lies and actions were based on those reasons and not to conceal robbery and murder. Katzmann, through his cross-examination, would attempt to show that those explanations were false and illogical, thereby establishing consciousness of guilt.

Katzmann's treatment of Sacco and Vanzetti cannot be fully appreciated without reading the entire 170 pages of the transcript devoted to those interrogations.[33] A summary of some of the more controversial portions of Katzmann's cross of the two Italians follows.

Cross-Examination of Vanzetti

Katzmann recognized that Vanzetti was more facile with the English language than Sacco. Although he vigorously engaged Vanzetti, he saved a savage examination for Sacco, who was more vulnerable and easily manipulated due to his poor facility with English and his limited education.

Katzmann questioned Vanzetti principally on three topics: 1) that he was a draft dodger; 2) that he possessed four (not three) intact shotgun shells when arrested; and 3) that the real purpose to obtain Boda's Overland on the night of May 5, 1920, was to commit further crimes, not to dispose of radical literature.

Katzmann began by challenging Vanzetti's character and patriotism:[34]

> Q: [by Katzmann] So you left Plymouth, Mr. Vanzetti, in May 1917, to dodge the draft, did you?
> A: Yes, sir …
> Q: Physically sound as you were, and after you had been in this country since 1908?
> A: Yes, sir.
> Q: When this country was at war, you ran away so you would not have to fight as a soldier?

A: Yes.
Q: Is that true?
A: It is true.

To reignite the jury's disdain for a slacker, Katzmann returned to the draft-dodging theme on the second day of Vanzetti's grilling with these kinds of questions:[35]

> Q: [by Katzmann] Did I ask you at Brockton anything about where you were at the time of the registration under the selective service draft?
> Q: Had you any reason to believe that night that I knew that you had run away to avoid the draft?
> Q: Was there a single question asked by any police officer about your evasion of the draft, when you were arrested? ...
> Q: Well, has the fact you told me an untruth about how long you knew Nick Sacco anything to do with your evasion of the draft? ...
> Q: What has it to do with your evasion of the draft? ...

Katzmann shifted his questioning. He wanted Vanzetti to acknowledge that on the night of his arrest, he was carrying four (not three) intact shotgun shells. Over and over, Katzmann so structured his questions, notwithstanding Vanzetti's direct testimony and previous responses that he had only three shells.[36]

Vanzetti capitulated:[37]

> Q: [by Katzmann] Will you say, Mr. Vanzetti, you did not get four shells at the Sacco house?
> A: I say I don't at all insist. I don't remember exactly.
> Q: You won't say it isn't four, will you?
> A: No ...

Vanzetti seemed to lose interest; the issue had no relevance to the murders in South Braintree. Why was Katzmann so adamant about pursuing this matter? Katzmann had a purpose. Now there was a record in Vanzetti's own words, if not supporting, certainly not opposing, Officer Connolly's controversial testimony in the Plymouth trial that he found four shells—

three Peters and one Winchester—on Vanzetti the night he was arrested.[38] Vanzetti's surrender would stand in opposition to any future claim by him or others that he had only three shells and that the fourth shell was a plant.

Katzmann challenged Vanzetti's purpose for attempting to obtain the Overland the night he and Sacco were arrested. Vanzetti testified on direct that he and Sacco traveled by streetcar to Johnson's garage to meet Boda and Orciani. He said that the purpose of the meeting was to pick up Boda's Overland, which had been at Johnson's garage for repairs, and that they intended to use the Overland to collect radical literature from their friends and hide it in a safe place.[39] He also indicated that on the way to Johnson's place, he had written an invitation for a public meeting of Italian immigrant workers to be held the following Sunday.[40]

Katzmann questioned Vanzetti whether it was his intention to pick up the radical literature that evening:[41]

> Q: [by Katzmann] Did you state … that Boda's purpose was to take the automobile to take the literature?
> A: Yes.
> Q: Doesn't that mean he was to take the literature that night?
> A: No, that don't mean that necessarily, at all.
> Q: Then what was your purpose … to get an automobile that was not to be used for that purpose that night?
> A: We want to take the automobile, and then my intention is to take the automobile with Boda, because I do not know how to drive the automobile, to go to Bridgewater and if we will be able to find the party [Pappi], because I do not remember the address of [Pappi]. I do not know exactly where he lived. We will tell to Pappi about telling the Italian people of Bridgewater to come in Brockton next Sunday at the speech, and after I found Pappi, and speak to Pappi, go toward Plymouth and speak with my friends if I can find some friends who want to take the responsibility of receiving such books [the socialist literature] in their house, in his house.

Katzmann had his opening to move in with the implication that Vanzetti, Sacco, Boda, and Orciani had a different purpose for the Overland:[42]

Q: Couldn't you, Mr. Vanzetti, have done everything that you say you intended to do by starting in Orciani's motorcycle with the side-car that was at the Sacco house before you ever started to go to West Bridgewater?

A: I don't understand what you say.

Katzmann repeated the essence of the question a number of times in different ways without receiving a clear answer from Vanzetti, leaving the impression with the jury there was another purpose for the use of the Overland that night. The fact that both Sacco and Vanzetti were armed played into the implication that the two anarchists, along with their two friends, were out to commit another armed robbery. And Katzmann made that suggestion to the jury in his closing argument that dripped with sarcasm:

> But they had arsenals upon them.Vanzetti had a loaded .38 calibre revolver, this man who ran to Mexico because he did not want to shoot a fellow human being ...
>
> And ... Nicola Sacco, another lover of peace ... had with him ... 32 death dealing automatic cartridges, 9 of them in the gun ready for action ...
>
> ... Maybe, gentlemen, you think that is the way men would be armed who were going on an innocent trip... going to make a social trip down to see Pappi, the friend of Vanzetti, and he did not know where he lived ... [43]

Cross-Examination of Sacco

Katzmann's cross-examination of Sacco was marked by intense animosity. It was "bitter and cruel ... surely one of the most extraordinary cross-examinations in a capital case that ever took place in a modern courtroom."[44] Katzmann opened by attacking Sacco's patriotism and character, just as he had done with Vanzetti. On direct examination Sacco had declared, "I was crazy to come to this country, because I liked a free country."[45] Katzmann, a master at the art of twisting testimony, portrayed Sacco a liar and an ingrate. He skillfully turned Sacco's statement that he liked a free country into a declaration that he loved the United States of America.[46] Then Katzmann tried to show Sacco's love for America was not genuine, that he was dishonest, a coward, a thankless slacker. These inflammatory charges were made to a jury of self-proclaimed patriotic Yankees in the shadow of the war's end, remarks that were sure to arouse enmity against an ungrateful immigrant.

Katzmann pounded Sacco with these kinds of questions:[47]

> Q: [by Katzmann] Did you say yesterday you love a free country?
>
> A: Yes, sir.
>
> Q: Did you love this country in the month of May 1917?
>
> A: I did not say—I don't want to say I did not love this country …
>
> Q: Do you understand that question?
>
> A: Yes.
>
> Q: Then will you please answer it.
>
> A: I can't answer in one word.
>
> Q: You can't say whether you loved the United States of America one week before the day you enlisted for the first draft?
>
> A: I can't say in one word, Mr. Katzmann.
>
> Q: You can't tell this jury whether you loved this country or not? …
>
> A: I could explain that, yes, if I loved—
>
> Q: What?
>
> A: I could explain that, yes, if I loved, if you give me a chance.
>
> Q: I ask you first to answer that question. Did you love this United States of America in May 1917?
>
> A: I can't answer in one word …

Katzmann set a trap. If Sacco answered no, he would offend twelve "patriotic" jurors; if he answered yes, he would be branded a liar for fleeing to Mexico to avoid the draft.

Sacco stepped into the snare:[48]

> Q: There are two words you can use, Mr. Sacco, yes or no. Which one is it?
>
> A: Yes.

Then the onslaught began:[49]

> Q: And in order to show your love for this United States
> of America when she was about to call upon you to
> become a soldier you ran away to Mexico? ...
> Q: You still loved America did you? ...
> Q: Is that your idea of showing your love for
> America? ...
> Q: And would it be your idea of showing your love for
> your wife that when she needed you, you ran away
> from her? ...
> Q: Don't you think going away from your country is a
> vulgar thing to do when she needs you? ...
> Q: Do you think it is a cowardly thing to do what you
> did? ...
> Q: Do you think it is a brave thing to do what you
> did? ...
> Q: Do you think it would be a brave thing to go away
> from your own wife? ...

Even though Katzmann eventually changed the subject, he found ways
to return to the same theme:[50]

> Q: Is your love for the United States of America
> commensurate with the amount of money you can
> get in this country per week? ...
> Q: Better country to make money, isn't it? ...
> Q: Mr. Sacco, that is the extent of your love of this
> country, isn't it, measured in dollars and cents? ...

It mattered not how Sacco answered. The repeated form of these
questions told the jurors all they needed to hear to turn against him.

Sacco was not tried for draft dodging. What could his failure to sign
up for the draft in 1917 or whether he loved this country have to do with
robbery and murder in South Braintree in 1920? Dedham began as a trial
for murder, but with the full support of Judge Thayer, Dedham became a
trial of Sacco's patriotism, character, and beliefs.[51]

Sacco's cross-examination lasted two days and covered ninety-seven
pages of the transcript.[52] At times his answers were barely audible. Unable

to explain himself well because of his difficulty with the language and his apparent misunderstanding of many questions, he ended by testifying through an interpreter.[53]

Judge Thayer inappropriately took over prosecution of the case for a time. Over the repeated objections of Sacco's lawyer, Judge Thayer asked eight different times during Sacco's cross-examination, while in the presence of the jury, whether Sacco's lawyer was going to claim that the collection of the socialist literature by the defendant was in the interest of the United States.[54]

Judge Thayer demanded to know:

> Is that not your claim, that the defendant, as a reason that he has given for going to the Johnson house, that they wanted the automobile to prevent people from being deported and to get this literature all out of the way? Does he not claim that this was done in the interest of the United States, to prevent violation of the law by the distribution of this literature? I understood that was the [reason]. [55]

Neither Sacco nor Vanzetti ever made such a claim.

William Thompson, appellate counsel for Sacco and Vanzetti, challenged Judge Thayer's actions in his brief to the Massachusetts Supreme Judicial Court:

> It seems incredible that the Court could have believed from any testimony that had been given by Vanzetti or Sacco that their purpose in collecting and suppressing the Socialist literature had anything to do with the interest of the United States. *If anything had been made plain, it was that they were actuated by personal fear of sharing the fate of Salsedo, not merely deportation, but death by violence while awaiting deportation.* Yet the Court *eight times*, in the face of as many explicit disclaimers from McAnarney [defense trial counsel], suggested that that was the defendants' claim. Had that claim been made it would, of course, have been the grossest hypocrisy, and might well have sealed the fate of both defendants with the jury. The repeated suggestion of the Court in the presence of the jury that that *was the claim amounted to a* violation by the

Court of the defendants' elementary constitutional right
to a fair and impartial trial. (Emphasis added by William
Thompson in his brief to the supreme judicial court.) [56]

It was obvious that Sacco wanted an opportunity to tell the jurors of
his plight as an immigrant worker in America. Restricting Sacco to yes or
no answers as to whether or not he loved this country caused him great
anxiety. Katzmann correctly anticipated that Sacco's pent-up compulsion
to tell his story would explode out of control if given the opportunity.
Sacco took the bait when Katzmann invited him to speak.[57]

Sacco broke into a long, rambling rant against the injustices of America
toward the working man before a stunned and silent courtroom. In broken
English, punctuated with an Italian accent, Sacco complained that the
quality of food in America for the average worker was not good:[58] "In
Italy is more opportunity to laborer to eat vegetable, more fresh …" Sacco
complained that "Debs he is in prison, still away in prison because he
is a Socialist …" He charged that capitalists exploited the workers, that
Rockefeller and Morgan gave millions to Harvard for the education of the
wealthy but nothing for the working man, and that these men of wealth
fostered wars for their personal profits: "Rockefellers, Morgans, and some
of the peoples, high class, they send to war. Why? … What right we have
to kill each other? … why should I kill them men? …" Sacco espoused
pacifism, and he ended, "That is why my idea I love Socialists …"

The cross-examination became a debate between Katzmann and Sacco
on the virtues of Harvard's contributions to the education of underprivileged
children.[59] Sacco was no match for Katzmann. He provided fodder for an
endless array of questions, irrelevant to murder in South Braintree but
fuel for a bonfire of animus against himself. Sacco's tirade was a disaster
for the defense.

In this sequence, Katzmann stuck Sacco one more time. He inquired
if Sacco was familiar with a Mr. Giovanni Fruzetti of Bridgewater.[60]
Sacco answered that he was and knew Fruzetti had been deported because
he supported anarchism. Katzmann established that Sacco's views on
anarchism were the same as Fruzetti's. Herbert Ehrmann, co-appellate
counsel for the defendants, later explained why Katzmann pursued this
line of questioning: "Mr. Katzmann was not acting as the district attorney
of Norfolk County prosecuting a murder case, but as an agent for the
Department of Justice attempting to secure admissions for a federal case."[61]
If the Dedham jury found Sacco not guilty, the federal authorities would

have grounds to deport him for the same reason that Fruzetti had been deported.

Vanzetti was spared from this treatment because he was already in prison as a result of the Plymouth conviction. The federal government and the Commonwealth wanted these two anarchists out of circulation, and they were doing all they could to make that happen.

Sacco and Vanzetti testified that at the time of their arrest they feared their socialist literature would be discovered and expose them and their associates to deportation, harm, or even death.[62] Katzmann had to discredit those explanations. He knew if the defendants could establish any believable reason for their lies other than to hide murder and robbery, consciousness of guilt would not be a credible charge by the Commonwealth.[63] Katzmann devised a strategy to preserve the Commonwealth's claim. He would cross-examine Sacco to test the authenticity of his radicalism in order to determine if his claimed fear of deportation or harm was genuine.[64]

Judge Thayer supported and further rationalized Katzmann's strategy with these comments:

> [T]here seemed to be no limit to which they [Sacco and Vanzetti] had a right to go in explanation of their professed belief in radicalism as a reason for telling falsehoods ... Counsel [Katzmann and his assistants] were allowed to cross-examine the defendants, particularly Sacco ... in order to test the truthfulness of his testimony ... the defendants having introduced the subject of radicalism to show their fear of deportation or some other punishment ... then the Commonwealth had a right to cross-examine for the purpose of showing that his or their beliefs, acts, conduct and the character of the literature they possessed were not of such a character or nature that would subject either of them to deportation or to any other punishment and if the Commonwealth did not succeed in showing this fact, it still had the right to show that there was no logical or reasonable connection between the falsehoods told and radicalism. [65]

Judge Thayer knew Sacco's and Vanzetti's radicalism was genuine. Regarding Vanzetti, the judge had charged the Plymouth jury a year earlier, "His ideals are cognate with the crime."[66] During the Dedham trial, the judge, in out-of-court statements, had referred to the defendants as bastards and Bolsheviks.[67] Moreover, Katzmann's files were full of information about the anarchist beliefs and activities of the two defendants, much of which had been provided by federal authorities.[68] Dedham became a trial of Sacco's and Vanzetti's radicalism instead of a trial to determine whether Sacco and Vanzetti were guilty of murder. The excuse that the authenticity of Sacco's and Vanzetti's radicalism had to be tested through Katzmann's cross-examination was a ploy to justify bringing the hated political beliefs of the two Italians before the jury.

In his book, *The Case of Sacco and Vanzetti: A Critical Analysis for Lawyers and Laymen,* published shortly before their execution, Felix Frankfurter, then professor of law at Harvard, criticized Katzmann and Judge Thayer's conduct.[69] He charged Katzmann with deliberately painting Sacco and Vanzetti as unpatriotic anarchists, and he criticized Judge Thayer for allowing Katzmann to make such prejudicial charges to the jury.[70] Frankfurter denounced the judge's opinion as "a farrago of misquotations, misrepresentations, suppressions and mutilations."[71]

The Trial Ends

Wednesday, July 13, 1921, was the thirty-sixth day of the Dedham trial. The day was set aside for closing arguments. The lawyers agreed, and the court approved, four hours of argument for each side. The defendants divided their time equally; Fred Moore closed for Sacco, and Jeremiah McAnarney for Vanzetti. However, defense counsel did not divide the coverage of their closing arguments and needlessly duplicated the matters they covered.

Counsel for Sacco and Vanzetti faced a daunting task as they prepared their respective closing arguments to the jury. That body alone would decide which witnesses told the truth, whether Sacco and Vanzetti were at the crime scene, if Bullet III was the genuine fatal bullet and whether it was shot from Sacco's gun, and if the two atheist, draft-dodging, Italian immigrant anarchists were guilty of murder. Under Massachusetts law, it was the jury's responsibility to determine the facts of the case, and neither Judge Thayer nor the supreme judicial court could change the factual findings of the jury, with rare exceptions not applicable in this case.

Moore and McAnarney had to organize, evaluate, and explain a mass of complicated and conflicting evidence to a jury of laymen in ways most favorable to their clients. Equally important, defense counsel had to logically argue how the law should be applied to ambiguous events. Sacco and Vanzetti's lawyers had to use all their intelligence, powers of persuasion, knowledge of history, literature, and science to seek justice for their clients.

In this case, the defense made their closing arguments first. Katzmann's closing followed. There was no reply by the defense. This worked as a disadvantage for Moore and McAnarney because they didn't know how the government would argue its case. Moore showed his frustration when, during his closing argument, he said, "Mr. Katzmann is going to say that a man—I don't know ... I do not know what he is going to say. I wish I did.[72] I wish I had some capacity to read his mind and dispute what he is going to say. I can't." Moore and McAnarney should have argued that since the Commonwealth had the burden to prove guilt beyond a reasonable doubt, it should have been required to argue first.

Moore did not meet the challenge of the closing. His argument for Sacco's life was ineffective, incomplete, and not well prepared. He rambled. He spent over three-quarters of his time analyzing the testimony of identification witnesses.[73] He claimed identification was the "primary issue and the only issue." He argued, "Gentlemen, there isn't a single witness called by the government who had an unqualified opportunity of observation who gives an identification. Not one."[74]

Moore paid undue deference to Katzmann when he said that "the attitude of the district attorney's office has been of unfailing courtesy and unfailing fairness."[75] He said that Sacco's lies were a result of his fear of Selective Service violations, his possession of radical literature, and of being deported.[76] He devoted a brief paragraph to Sacco's alibi, arguing that all Sacco's alibi witnesses would be committing perjury if their testimony was false.[77]

Moore's response to the ballistics evidence was similarly vapid. The best he could muster was, "If the time has come when a microscope must be used to determine whether a human life is going to continue to function ... ordinary men ... should well hesitate to take a human life."[78] Moore said not a word in his closing argument about the cap evidence against Sacco, the episode at Johnson's garage, or Connolly's claim that Sacco reached for his gun when arrested.

Moore left these final thoughts with the jury: "The man that committed that crime must go to the chair[79] ... If that boy [Sacco] committed this crime, there is no penalty too severe to visit upon him ... You are the judges of the facts ... the facts as you believe them to be found on the witness stand." Hardly a rousing defense for Sacco.

McAnarney's closing was no better. He delivered platitudes and generalities sprinkled with rhetorical questions but no answers. He praised the judge as learned and paid excessive deference to Katzmann.[80]

On substance, McAnarney spent too much time analyzing the same identification witnesses Moore had previously covered. He did not mention Vanzetti's alibi, thus giving it away. He made little effort against the prosecution's claim that Vanzetti's gun was really Berardelli's—the only physical evidence connecting Vanzetti to the crime. That should have been McAnarney's main target. His argument frequently wandered unconnected from one point to another. He often made arguments for Sacco's position as if he forgot that Vanzetti was his client.

McAnarney, as he often did, stumbled over his grammar during his final comments to the jury:

> I will take all the blame—I will take all the lies that they say we lied about, we have lied all through every time they asked us where we were or our whereabouts, we lied just as well as that little wife did, and for that very reason. I am not asking sympathy for her in any way, remarkable little woman that she is. If her husband is a murderer, that is unfortunate for her, but that cannot stop justice being done ... [81]

How did such ramblings advance the cause of Vanzetti or Sacco?

Finally, McAnarney's closing came to an end: "I want every man, too of this panel to treat these two defendants as if they were your own individual brother[82] ... He came to this world by the same power that created you, and may he go from this world by the same power that takes you."

Katzmann was well prepared. He covered all the key issues. He was thorough—from the witnesses who identified the defendants at the scene, to technical ballistics evidence, to Sacco's and Vanzetti's alibis, to their consciousness of guilt.

The following day, July 14, Judge Webster Thayer delivered his instructions to the jury, and he finished by early afternoon. His charge, carefully prepared as it was, could not disguise his deeper sentiments that surfaced at that crucial moment. America was still in the spell of war fever, the Red Scare, and superpatriotism.

Judge Thayer exalted the jury for their service, reminding them of the nobility of loyalty to America:

[Y]ou, like the true soldier, responded to that call in the spirit of supreme American loyalty. There is no better word in the English language than "loyalty." For he who is loyal to God, to country, to his state and to his fellowmen, represents the highest and noblest type of true American citizenship, than which there is none grander in the entire world. [83]

Beyond those introductory remarks that set the stage for the jury's deliberations, the judge outlined the duties of the jurors, providing them with the meaning of fundamental legal terms needed for their work. Although Judge Thayer's general instructions carried an air of reasonableness, many of his specific instructions were in error. In particular, the judge instructed the jury on the law of conspiracy, even though the indictments did not charge a conspiracy and the prosecution never offered evidence to support such a crime. He instructed the jurors that "each conspirator is legally bound by the result of the shooting by one or more conspirators to the same effect and in the same manner as though each conspirator fired a shot himself which, in fact caused death."[84] Couching the murders as the result of a conspiracy made each defendant equally guilty of murder without requiring the Commonwealth to prove which defendant was the primary actor who committed the killings.

Judge Thayer committed further errors:

- He misrepresented Proctor's and VanAmburgh's ballistics testimony by stating that their expert opinions were to the "effect" that fatal Bullet III was shot from Sacco's gun.[85]
- He misstated Bostock's testimony, stating that the Saturday night before the murders, Bostock saw Berardelli with a revolver that was similar to the revolver that Berardelli always carried.[86] This gave support to the Commonwealth's argument that Berardelli carried his gun during the holdup and that Sacco took it after shooting him and gave it to Vanzetti.
- He failed to remind the jury that a cap, supposedly found at the scene immediately after the shooting, did not fit Sacco's head when he tried it on at the trial.[87]

- He made no analysis of the extensive alibi testimony provided by numerous witnesses for both Sacco and Vanzetti. The judge barely mentioned the alibi evidence.[88]
- He mischaracterized and overemphasized Sacco's and Vanzetti's conduct as signs of their consciousness of guilt, devoting more attention to that charge than to all the other charges combined.[89]

The following factors left little doubt as to the outcome of the case: the cumulative effect of Katzmann's prosecutorial misconduct, Judge Thayer's prejudicial actions throughout the trial, including his erroneous jury instructions, and defense counsel's incompetence.

After receiving the judge's charge, the jurors retired for their deliberation at about 3:30 PM, and by 5:00 PM they had concluded that the two Italians were guilty of murder in the first degree.[90] The jurors decided to hold off making an announcement of their verdicts until after dinner, to avoid criticism of not taking enough time for their deliberations.[91] At 7:55 PM they announced that they had reached a verdict.[92] Nicola Sacco found guilty of murder in the first degree; Bartolomeo Vanzetti found guilty of murder in the first degree.

Sacco responded loudly in open court, *"Sono innocente! Sono innocente!"*[93] Rosina ran to him and threw her arms over the edge of the cage that enclosed him and Vanzetti, holding Sacco as best she could. She cried, "What am I going to do?[94] I've got two children. Oh, Nick. They kill my man." She sobbed uncontrollably as the bailiffs led her away. Vanzetti stood by, grim and pale, and said nothing. Then, Sacco shouted again to the jury as they left the courtroom, this time in English, "They kill an innocent men.[95] They kill two innocent men."

After guards removed Sacco and Vanzetti, the courtroom emptied, except for Jeremiah McAnarney and assistant prosecutor Harold Williams. McAnarney moved across the darkened room toward Williams with an outstretched hand to offer congratulations for the Commonwealth's victory, a common courtesy between opposing lawyers after a trial. Williams responded with tears in his eyes, "For God's sake, don't rub it in, this is the saddest thing that ever happened to me in my life."[96]

So ended the Dedham trial.

CHAPTER 10

MOTIONS AND APPEALS

After the guilty verdicts, the authorities sent Vanzetti back to Charlestown State Prison, where he continued to serve his sentence for the Plymouth conviction. He returned to a prison life of work assignments, with some free time for study and letter writing. Prison rules forced Sacco to languish in the Dedham jail with nothing to do for most of his time because he was not yet sentenced for the Dedham conviction.[1]

Except for infrequent court appearances, Sacco and Vanzetti remained separated for the next six years until shortly before their execution. Though physically apart, the outside world linked them together to such an extent that Rosina Sacco was frequently referred to as Mrs. Sacco-Vanzetti and Luiga Vanzetti as the sister of Sacco-Vanzetti.

The case shifted to a new phase, focusing on life or death, not on legal concepts of guilty or not guilty. The strategy going forward fell on Fred Moore. He immediately filed a motion for a new trial, arguing that the verdicts were against the weight of the evidence. The motion was filed on July 18, 1921, argued on November 5, 1921, and denied on December 24, 1921.[2]

The symbolism of Judge Thayer's Christmas Eve denial was not lost. Even in the case of avowed atheistic anarchists like Sacco and Vanzetti, Christmas Eve held a special place in their hearts—a place of respect and reverence for family—reaching back to their youth. Sacco and Vanzetti believed Judge Thayer chose that special day to show his disdain for them. He took an additional step to show the two Italians what was in store for them. He wrote a sixteen-page decision denying the motion. This was not necessary. A motion of this type is typical and required in most, if not all, jurisdictions. Following a conviction, a defendant must file a perfunctory motion to set aside the verdict. The trial judge must be given an opportunity to correct any errors at the trial level before an appeal can be perfected. The motion may be denied in a short, final order. Judge Thayer, however, fortified the guilty verdicts with a detailed opinion, thereby providing the supreme judicial court with support for the verdicts and showing that he properly exercised his discretion regarding his rulings. This sent a message to Sacco's and Vanzetti's lawyers that there would be little hope to reverse the guilty verdicts.

Under Massachusetts law, the scope of appellate review even in a capital murder case was very narrow; only matters of law, not the facts, were reviewable.[3] When adhered to literally, a jury's guilty verdict would be very difficult to modify unless the trial judge was found to have abused his discretion. This changed in 1939 because of the Sacco-Vanzetti case. Pursuant to legislation adopted at that time, the Commonwealth's appellate procedures were expanded in ways that would have enabled Sacco and Vanzetti to obtain a new trial in the light of new evidence.

Fred Moore developed a strategy to significantly prolong the time within which Sacco and Vanzetti would have to file an appeal to the high court. Judge Thayer's delay of almost six months before issuing his denial of the defendants' perfunctory motion resulted in some unintended consequences. It gave Moore the opportunity to file the Ripley-Daly supplementary motion, and before the judge acted on the Ripley-Daly motion, Moore filed additional supplementary motions.[4] This caused jurisdiction of the case to remain with Judge Thayer at the trial level for over three years, which, with the filing of two additional motions and three appeals, delayed the sentencing of Sacco and Vanzetti until April 9, 1927.

The supplementary motions and appeals required responses from the Commonwealth, frequently calling for hearings, briefs, and oral arguments. This activity created ongoing publicity; it drew attention and scrutiny to the case throughout the country and abroad. Consequently, posttrial evidence, new arguments, and analyses developed questioning the guilt of Sacco and Vanzetti.

Each of the following supplementary motions made a claim of prosecutorial abuse or judicial error:

The Ripley-Daly Motion:[5] Shortly after the verdicts were handed down at the Dedham trial, Jeremiah McAnarney learned from Harry

Ripley, the foreman of the jury, that he had brought three .38-caliber cartridges he owned into the jury room. McAnarney found that at least two other jurors had seen these cartridges and one other juror had heard talk about them during their deliberations. Markings on these cartridges confirmed that one or more members of the jury had pushed them through Vanzetti's gun. Ripley died ten days after the jury concluded its deliberations. McAnarney provided his affidavit regarding Ripley's actions and a number of other affidavits to support the motion. The main argument for a new trial was that the jury engaged in one or more experiments with evidence that was not subject to cross-examination by defense counsel.

The Daly part of the motion established that William Daly had known Ripley for thirty-eight years. He deposed that he met Ripley a few days before the Dedham trial and asked him if he was going to be a juror in the case involving the "two ginneys"; Ripley said that he was. Daly told Ripley he did not believe they were guilty because it was not reasonable to believe that a man would rob a factory in broad daylight, where he had worked and was known, whereupon Ripley replied, "Damn them, they ought to hang them anyway."[6]

Judge Thayer denied the motion on the following grounds:

> [T]he mere production of the Ripley cartridges and the talk or discussion about them did not create such disturbing or prejudicial influence that might in any way affect the verdict or operate in any way whatsoever to the prejudice of the defendants, or either of them.[7]

Judge Thayer did not mention the Daly affidavit in his decision. Defense counsel appealed the denial of this motion.

The Gould-Pelser Motion:[8] Shortly after Parmenter and Berardelli were shot, one of the bandits in the getaway car fired a shot at Roy Gould, a bystander. The bullet went through Gould's overcoat. He gave his name and address to the police and told them what had happened, but Gould was never called by the prosecution. Moreover, the prosecution did not provide the defense with the name of this witness. When Fred Moore learned of Gould's story, he took Gould to view Sacco in jail and obtained an affidavit from him describing the shooter as someone different from Sacco. Gould also indicated that the shooter did not resemble Vanzetti.

Judge Thayer denied this motion as it related to Gould on the ground that this new evidence was merely cumulative and would not have affected the verdicts.[9]

The second part of this motion related to the witness, Lewis Pelser, who had testified at the Dedham trial that Sacco was the "dead image" of the bandit who shot Berardelli.[10] Shortly after the trial, Moore obtained an affidavit from Pelser retracting that testimony. Pelser told Moore that assistant prosecutor Williams had coerced him to make the identification of Sacco. In a complete turnabout a few days later, Pelser repudiated his retraction and absolved Williams of attempting to force his testimony against Sacco.[11]

Judge Thayer denied this motion, and an appeal was taken by the defendants only as to the Gould affidavit.

The Goodridge Motion:[12] Carlos Goodridge was a prosecution witness who identified Sacco as one of the bandits. Through affidavits and other records, Moore moved to impeach Goodridge's testimony because he had a criminal record of felonies, misrepresentations, and perjuries. Moore learned that Goodridge was the subject of a pending felony charge before the superior court in Dedham, which Katzmann's office was prosecuting. Moore argued that Katzmann granted Goodridge probation in exchange for favorable testimony for the prosecution in the Sacco-Vanzetti trial. The prosecution responded that Moore had used threats of intimidation and arrest against Goodridge in order to obtain information from him about his past. For this, Judge Thayer condemned Moore.[13] At the same time, the judge exonerated the Commonwealth's conduct in the matter.[14] The motion was denied, and no appeal was taken.

The Andrews Motion:[15] Lola Andrews was the witness who identified Sacco as the man working on the getaway car on the day of the crime. Moore obtained a series of affidavits indicating that the prosecution had forced the testimony of Mrs. Andrews through intimidation. Moore also obtained an affidavit from Mrs. Andrews repudiating her testimony that identified Sacco as the man working on the getaway car. However, shortly thereafter, she revoked her repudiation.[16] Judge Thayer criticized the conduct of both the defense and the prosecution in the treatment of Mrs. Andrews; however, he found the charges against prosecutor Williams without merit.[17] Judge Thayer denied the motion on the basis that Mrs. Andrews's affidavit was worthless. No appeal was taken.

The Hamilton-Proctor Motion:[18] The court treated the Hamilton-Proctor motion as two separate matters. The first involved Albert Hamilton and

Augustus Gill, additional ballistics experts for the defense. During the Dedham trial, the prosecution presented the testimony of two experts: Captain Proctor of the state police and Captain VanAmburgh (U.S. Army Ret.). Burns and Fitzgerald were the original experts on behalf of Sacco. These experts provided sharply divided opinions for and against the defendants regarding the guns, cartridges, shells, and bullets. The controversy continued in this supplementary motion with new ballistics experts Hamilton and Gill presenting their analysis for the defense, and VanAmburgh, with new expert Merton Robinson, for the prosecution. The affidavits, arguments, and decision on this motion cover more than one hundred pages of the trial record.[19]

Judge Thayer denied the Hamilton part of the motion,[20] principally because he said he did not believe the prosecution's expert witnesses would knowingly commit perjury, and he was unconvinced by Hamilton and Gill's new analysis.

Defense counsel based the Proctor part of the motion on Captain Proctor's affidavit of self-impeachment. He confessed his opinion given at the trial, that Bullet III was "consistent with" having been fired through Sacco's gun, was only intended to mean that it was shot through some Colt .32 automatic. He deposed that prior to the trial he had repeatedly told prosecutors Williams and Katzmann that he found no evidence that Sacco's gun shot the fatal bullet and that the prosecutors had prearranged his testimony.[21] (See chapter 8 for a review of Proctor's misleading ballistics opinion and his affidavit of self-impeachment.)

Judge Thayer's decision denying the Proctor part of the motion stated that it was "a most unusual one" because it charged the prosecutors with "unprofessional conduct" by allegedly presenting testimony they knew was false and prejudicial to the defendants.[22] The judge rationalized Proctor's testimony by presenting a series of his own questions followed by his own answers favorable to the prosecution and in support of Proctor's misleading "consistent with" ballistics opinion. For the most part, Judge Thayer ignored or made little of Proctor's affidavit of self-impeachment.[23] The judge found, "The questions propounded by Mr. Williams [to Captain Proctor] were clearly put, fairly expressed and easily understood." The judge concluded that Proctor's opinion was to prove a proposition "that was clearly within the province of the jury."[24]

Felix Frankfurter, in 1927, saw the Proctor incident as one "which shake[s] one's confidence in the whole course of the proceedings ..."[25] Twenty years later, Professor Edmund Morgan, a leading expert in the law of evidence, labeled Proctor's misleading testimony as "monstrous misconduct."

Judge Thayer denied all five supplementary motions on October 1, 1924. This sobering event resulted in a reevaluation by the defense committee and by Sacco and Vanzetti of continuing with Fred Moore as counsel for the defense.[26]

Many questioned Moore's ability as a lawyer, with considerable justification, even though his skill in successfully promoting the Sacco and Vanzetti case nationally and internationally as a cause célèbre was unquestioned. During Moore's four years in charge of the case, liberals, intellectuals, and labor leaders throughout the world gave their support, both vocally and financially, to Sacco and Vanzetti. Moore convincingly argued to these groups that the Commonwealth prosecuted the two Italians for their political beliefs.

An unfortunate aspect of the internationalization of the case was the open support for Sacco and Vanzetti by the Communist Party. The Communists rode on the coattails of the two Italian workers and used them for propaganda to show the evils of the capitalistic system. This worked against Sacco and Vanzetti gaining broad public support, as most Americans hated Communism.[27]

The irony was that Sacco and Vanzetti were opposed to all governing authority. They wanted humanity to be free of authoritarian ruling bodies. They believed that the Communists and other radicals were exploiting their struggle to advance the cause of their own authoritarian organizations. The two Italians were unhappily aware that their execution as martyrs of the working class would make their deaths valuable to the cause of Communism.[28]

The relationship between Moore and Sacco had never been good. Sacco and his wife, Rosina, did not like him from the start, and as time went on their relationship got worse. Since the defense committee brought Moore into the case and because the committee was paying his legal fees and expenses, the Saccos were constrained to put up with Moore.[29]

Moore acted as general counsel of the Sacco and Vanzetti case; it was his vehicle to fame and fortune. Sacco's letters showed that he saw Moore as more of an opportunist for his own aggrandizement than a believer in his innocence. And Sacco's beliefs were justified. Moore spent money with abandon, often on useless and irrelevant investigations.[30] His strategy prolonged the case, but it did not provide Sacco and Vanzetti with a strong defense.

The defense committee had asked William Thompson to represent Sacco and Vanzetti on the eve of the Dedham trial, but he declined because he had no time to prepare.[31] As a result of the guilty verdicts and Judge Thayer's denial of all motions for a new trial, as well as Moore's otherwise controversial representation, Sacco and Vanzetti decided to change defense counsel. Thompson agreed to enter his special appearance on March 16, 1923, to help argue some of Moore's supplementary motions. Thompson was a respected member of the Boston Bar Association, a Brahmin, and a Harvard-educated lawyer with honors; he stood for maintaining the highest standards of conduct in criminal cases. Although he respected the law, he sought justice even more.

During the summer of 1924, Sacco officially discharged Moore by letter, criticizing his selfish motives. Sacco signed his letter, "your implacable enemy, now and forever."[32] During the following months, Moore used his association with the case to raise funds for his personal use. When the defense committee learned of this, it forced Moore to officially withdraw from the case on November 8, 1924.[33] On November 25, 1924, Thompson entered his appearance as general counsel for the defense of both Sacco and Vanzetti.[34] Moore left Boston bitter and financially broke.

The McAnarney brothers withdrew their appearance from the case as Vanzetti's lawyers on December 9, 1924.[35] For the next three and a half years, Thompson and his associate, Herbert Ehrmann, gave Sacco and Vanzetti the benefit of their brilliant minds and faithful hearts.[36] They were all Sacco and Vanzetti could have expected or hoped for as lawyers for their defense. Thompson and Ehrmann believed in their innocence.

After Thompson took charge, his first order of business was the preparation of an appeal to the supreme judicial court.[37] The appeal included the verdicts of conviction as well as the denial of the Ripley-Daly, Gould-Pelser, and Hamilton-Proctor motions for a new trial. Thompson filed initial appeal papers on September 13, 1924; however, final papers were not filed until November 10, 1925. On January 11, 12, and 13, 1926, the parties presented oral arguments before the high court.

On May 12, 1926, the Massachusetts Supreme Judicial Court, through its five judges speaking unanimously, issued its decision: "Exceptions overruled. Verdicts to stand."[38] It was like a giant wave sweeping away all grounds for appeal.[39] The ninety-page opinion was artfully written, neatly denying exceptions to dozens of issues against the convictions of Sacco and Vanzetti. The decision took no account of the cumulative effect of Judge Thayer's adverse rulings and prejudicial conduct identified in Thompson's appeal papers. The high court separately considered each issue Thompson raised and found it within the discretion of the trial judge.[40]

There were two additional appeals to the Massachusetts Supreme Judicial Court. One was based on the Medeiros confession, the other on Judge Thayer's bias. Both appeals are discussed in subsequent chapters.

CHAPTER 11

TRUE CONFESSIONS?

If Sacco and Vanzetti were innocent, who were the guilty parties? A high-profile criminal case will often stimulate confessions to the crime. The motives vary. A deranged individual, though innocent, may confess to a crime to obtain attention and fame. On the other hand, a person may make a truthful confession, especially if he or she is dying or sentenced to death, in order to save an innocent person.

One confession to the Bridgewater crime and several confessions to the South Braintree murders surfaced during and after the Dedham trial. The Silva and Medeiros confessions and the Morelli gang involvement are the most compelling.

The Silva Story[1]

In 1922, Fred Moore was told by one of his investigators that according to an underworld source, there were rumors Vanzetti was innocent of the Bridgewater attempted holdup. Although Vanzetti's time for an appeal of that conviction had long passed, Moore believed pursuing this lead would be helpful in his public relations campaign promoting the innocence of the two Italians.

Moore learned that in 1917 Frank Silva planned to rob the L. Q. White Shoe Company in Bridgewater with Jimmy "Big Chief" Mede, a crook, who owned a cigar store in Boston used as a gangster hangout. Silva and Mede recruited a third confederate, Joe San Marco, to do the job. Mede,

Silva, and San Marco cased the company and the town of Bridgewater. The conspirators aborted the plan after the Commonwealth charged and convicted Mede of a different crime and sent him to Charlestown State Prison, and Silva joined the army.

The army released Silva from service in 1919, after the war had ended. He revived the plan to steal the L. Q. White payroll. Silva renewed his connection with San Marco, and they cased the company and the Bridgewater locale. The plan was to steal the Christmas payroll on December 24, 1919.

San Marco and Silva recruited "Guinea" Oates and "Doggy" Bruno, two local stickup men, to join them. Silva stole license plates and put them on Oates's touring car, which they used in the planned holdup. Oates was the driver, Bruno carried a shotgun, and San Marco and Silva carried pistols. The four tried to pull off the Bridgewater holdup, but they failed. After the attempted holdup, the Commonwealth convicted San Marco of murdering a police officer, and he was sentenced to life in prison. While in Charlestown State Prison, San Marco met up with Mede, who was still serving time. He told Mede of his involvement with Silva, Bruno, and Oates in the Bridgewater attempted robbery. San Marco would later deny that he took part in that crime.

According to Mede, after the Bridgewater crime, Silva and Bruno shaved off their moustaches, and Bruno and Oates went into hiding. Silva, under the alias of Paul Martini, met up with Jake Luban, a small-time thief. The two traveled to New York and joined another thief, Adolph Witner. The three formed a partnership for crime. They were caught looting post office boxes. Witner turned state's evidence against Silva and Luban in return for a thirty-day sentence. Silva and Luban were convicted and sent to prison for long terms.

Witner's legal problems did not end with his thirty-day sentence. The authorities later charged him with another crime and sent him to Boston for processing. While Witner was in Boston, Moore, with the help of his investigators, tracked him down. This is when Moore learned about Silva's participation in the Bridgewater crime from Witner, and Witner learned about Moore's involvement with Sacco and Vanzetti. Witner offered to help Sacco and Vanzetti if Moore would help him. Surprisingly, Moore was able to free Witner from his latest run-in with the law.

As a follow-up to his bargain to help Sacco and Vanzetti, Witner suggested that Moore and John Jocomo, a Moore investigator, join him for a trip to the federal prison in Atlanta, Georgia. The purpose of the trip was to introduce Moore to Luban and Silva and work out a plan to aid the two Italians.

Initially, Silva and Luban would have nothing to do with Moore because Witner had double-crossed them. However, following several more visits with Moore, Silva and Luban offered to confess to the Bridgewater and the South Braintree crimes as a way to obtain a new trial for Sacco and Vanzetti. Their willingness to do so was conditioned on Moore paying each of them ten thousand dollars. Once a new trial was obtained, the plan called for Silva and Luban to recant their confessions. Moore rejected their offer because it was absurd and corrupt.

Moore put the Silva story aside in order to concentrate on the Dedham posttrial motions. However, when Mede was released from prison in 1923, Moore urged him to tell all he knew about the Bridgewater crime to the authorities. Initially, Mede refused; however, William Thompson, upon learning Mede's story, used his powers of persuasion to have Mede tell what he knew to Governor Fuller. Mede agreed on the condition that the Commonwealth would not retaliate against him since he was then a licensed boxing promoter.

When Governor Fuller heard Mede's account, he told him to relate it to Captain Blye of the state police. Mede refused because he had not obtained the assurances he requested from the governor. Just days before the execution of Sacco and Vanzetti, Thompson persuaded Mede to relent. Mede went to Captain Blye, willing to tell everything, but Blye refused to hear him.

After the execution of Sacco and Vanzetti, Jack Callahan, a former bank robber turned journalist, encouraged Silva to disclose his involvement in the Bridgewater crime to the *Outlook and Independent* magazine, which he did for an undisclosed sum. Silva's confession, along with a full disclosure of the participation of San Marco, Bruno, and Oates in the Bridgewater attempted holdup, appeared in the October and November 1928 editions of the magazine. The article caused a minor sensation and was grist for Vanzetti's supporters bent on clearing his name. Some questioned the honesty of Silva's confession, suggesting he made it for the money.

The *New York Times* reported that Governor Fuller was not interested in the Silva confession, just as he was not interested in the Medeiros confession.

Silva's confession has remained a testament to Vanzetti's innocence of the Bridgewater attempted holdup.

The Medeiros Confession

One of the most dramatic events in the case occurred in the fall of 1925, when Celestino Medeiros, a self-confessed participant in the South

Braintree murders, attempted to exonerate Sacco and Vanzetti. Medeiros's confinement continued in the Dedham jail while his case for the murder of a bank employee was on appeal.[2] At that time, much of the activity in the jail centered on Sacco. Medeiros had observed Rosina Sacco, with her two children, visiting her jailed husband. He had privately confessed several times to friends that he knew Sacco and Vanzetti were innocent because he had been in on the South Braintree job and they were not involved.[3] Medeiros said that he hated to think Sacco's two children would grow up without their father should Sacco be sentenced to death.

On November 16, 1925, Medeiros tried to deliver a message to the *Boston American*, confessing to his participation in the South Braintree crime and indicating that Sacco and Vanzetti were not part of it.[4] The sheriff's office intercepted the message, and the newspaper never received it. Medeiros persisted, and on November 18, 1925, he had the following written message delivered to Sacco, who was in a nearby cell:

> I here by confess to being in the south Braintree shoe company crime and Sacco and Vanzetti was not in said crime.[5]
>
> Celestino Medeiros

A trusty at the jail reported that as Sacco read the note, he trembled uncontrollably and his eyes filled with tears.[6] Sacco immediately had the message delivered to his new lawyer, William Thompson, who rushed to meet with Sacco and Medeiros in order to investigate the matter.

Thompson shared what he learned from Medeiros with Assistant District Attorney Dudley Ranney. He advised Ranney that he intended to file a motion for a new trial based on the Medeiros confession. Because Medeiros's conviction for murder was on appeal, Thompson and Ranney agreed to keep the Medeiros confession confidential until that appeal was final.

The Medeiros appeal was successful. The court ordered a new trial;[7] however, it resulted in a second conviction for murder in May 1926. After that, Thompson obtained an affidavit and a deposition from Medeiros supporting Thompson's motion for a new trial for Sacco and Vanzetti.

Thompson wanted to avoid a battle of affidavits and counteraffidavits, which was certain to erupt between him and Ranney. Thompson offered to permit Ranney to cross-examine Medeiros during his deposition.[8] The attorney general, who was now involved, welcomed the suggestion, but Ranney opposed it and initially refused to cooperate. Eventually, Ranney accepted, and Thompson and Ranney deposed Medeiros. Thompson filed a motion for a new trial on May 26, 1926.

Of the many affidavits supporting the Medeiros motion, two of the most important were those of Fred Weyand and Lawrence Letherman, retired long-time agents of the Federal Bureau of Investigation.[9] These affidavits disclosed the involvement of the federal government in the Sacco and Vanzetti affair, which the Commonwealth had repeatedly denied. The affidavits confirmed that the federal government planted a spy in the prison cell adjoining Sacco's cell and a spy within the defense committee. There was also a plan, which Katzmann later aborted, to plant a spy in the home occupied by Sacco's wife and children. The affidavits revealed that the FBI had as many as twelve agents working on the case and that federal authorities had informed Katzmann of the radical activities of the two defendants.

Fred Weyand's affidavit, in part, also stated:

> Shortly after the trial of Sacco and Vanzetti was concluded I said to Weiss [another agent] that I did not believe they were the right men, meaning the men who shot the paymaster, and he replied that that might be so, but that they were bad actors and would get what they deserved anyway …It was the general opinion of the Boston agents of the Department of Justice having knowledge of the affair that the South Braintree crime was committed by a gang of professional highwaymen. [10]

Lawrence Letherman's deposition added:

> The Department of Justice in Boston was anxious to get sufficient evidence against Sacco and Vanzetti to deport them … that a conviction of Sacco and Vanzetti for murder would be one way of disposing of these two men … that Sacco and Vanzetti, although anarchists and agitators, were not highway robbers, and had nothing to do with the South Braintree crime.[11]

Medeiros testified in his deposition that at 4:00 AM on April 15, 1920, he was picked up in a Hudson auto by four Italians (later he corrected that to three Italians and a Pole) at his boarding house in Providence.[12] They then drove to South Boston to a saloon to get information for the holdup planned for that afternoon. After the saloon stop, they drove to Randolph, where they changed cars to a Buick, leaving the Hudson in the woods.

Medeiros's deposition correctly described some obscure facts regarding the South Braintree murders:

- The getaway car had to move up an incline when it picked up the bandits with the loot.[13]
- The bandits used two cars for their getaway; one was the Buick, later abandoned for a Hudson in the Manley Woods. [14]
- During their escape, they stopped at the home of a woman later determined to have been Mrs. Hewins, to ask directions to Providence (home base of the Morelli gang).[15]
- The driver of the Buick getaway car was "slim, light haired—not an Italian." He fit precisely the description of Steve "the Pole" Benkosky (a member of the Morelli gang). [16]

Medeiros provided Thompson with guarded information about the identity of his confederates in the South Braintree murders. Initially, he told Thompson only that they were Italians from Providence who stole shoes and textiles from freight cars. Following the code of silence, Medeiros would not give their names.[17] On a number of occasions, he said, "If I cannot save Sacco and Vanzetti by my own confession, why should I bring four or five others into it?"[18] Despite his refusal to provide the names of the other participants, it was obvious to Thompson that the Morelli gang members were the bandits Medeiros was protecting.

Thompson obtained an affidavit from James F. Weeks, who said he and Medeiros committed the Wrentham Bank robbery and murdered the clerk. Weeks revealed that Medeiros had admitted to him a number of times that he was part of the gang of bandits who committed the South Braintree holdup and killings and that Sacco and Vanzetti had nothing to do with it.[19]

The Morelli Gang

At the May 26, 1926, hearing on Thompson's motion for a new trial, additional facts surfaced implicating the Morelli gang in the South Braintree killings. The gang included five Morelli brothers: Joe, Mike,

Pasquale, Fred, Frank, and several non-Morelli family members, including Bibber Barone, Tony Mancini, and Steve "the Pole" Benkosky.

Joe Morelli and Sacco were look-alikes. Defense investigators showed pictures of the Morelli gang members to various persons who had been witnesses at the Dedham trial. Lewis Wade and Frank Burke identified Joe Morelli as looking like one of the bandits they had seen in South Braintree.[20] They acknowledged Joe Morelli looked like Sacco. An investigator said Mary Splaine also acknowledged the similar appearance of Joe Morelli and Sacco, although she later denied the investigator's claim.[21] Dominic DiBona, Emielio Falcone, Pedro Iscorla, Nicola Gatti, and Fortinato Antonello, all witnesses to the crime, thought Joe Morelli's picture looked like Sacco.[22] Donata DiBona said Mancini's picture looked like the man sitting next to the driver in the bandit car.[23]

A number of affidavits indicated several members of the Morelli gang were under indictment at the time of the crime.[24] All the indicted Morelli brothers, except Fred, were out on bond on April 15, 1920. Not only were members of the Morelli gang available to carry out the South Braintree robbery and murders, but they were in need of money for legal fees and bail.

The suspicious conduct of Mike Morelli driving a Buick touring car just before the South Braintree murders, as recorded by New Bedford police Inspector E. C. Jacobs in his notebook, was described in the affidavits.[25] (See chapter 6 for details of Inspector Jacobs's notes with respect to Mike Morelli and the Buick touring car.)

When Herbert Ehrmann joined Thompson's defense team, one of his first assignments was to verify the truthfulness of the Medeiros confession. This task took Ehrmann on a driving trip to Providence, Rhode Island, with an interim stop at the Blue Bird Inn at Seekonk, Massachusetts, where Medeiros had worked as a bouncer. It was there he learned from Barney Monterio, the owner, and his wife, May, that in January 1921 Medeiros had $2,800 and that he took a long driving trip with a circus girl to Mexico and back.[26] Interestingly, $2,800 for each of the five bandits at the scene of the crime, plus an additional partial share of $1,700 for the driver of the second car used by the bandits, would amount to $15,700, the exact amount of the stolen payroll. Monterio and his wife also provided affidavits that Medeiros told them he had been in on the South Braintree robbery and killings and that Sacco and Vanzetti were not involved.[27]

In Providence, Ehrmann confirmed from the police chief that a gang made up mostly of Morelli brothers operated in the New Bedford area during 1919 and 1920, stealing shoes and textiles from freight cars and fencing the loot in New York. The Morellis were American-born Italians who spoke English without an Italian accent.[28]

Ehrmann obtained a copy of the indictment against Joe Morelli that verified he was charged with the theft of hundreds of shoes from the Rice & Hutchins and Slater & and Morrill factories located in South Braintree. He determined that these thefts were carried out with the aid of a spotter in South Braintree, who identified the freight cars in which the shoes to be hijacked were loaded. Ehrmann concluded that the spotter would have had a perfect opportunity to learn when, where, and how the company delivered the payroll to the factories in South Braintree.[29]

One more bit of important information came to Ehrmann's attention. He was trying to piece together the identities of the Morelli gang members who might have pulled off the South Braintree job. Ehrmann learned that Anthony Mancini was a "big job" member of the gang. He was a cool, calculating killer in prison for murdering Alberto Alterio. Mancini committed that brazen act on Mulberry Street in New York, across the street from a police station.[30]

Ehrmann, accompanied by John Richards, a former United States marshal, visited Joe Morelli at the Leavenworth, Kansas, penitentiary where he was serving time. They questioned him about Mancini. At first, Joe denied he knew Mancini. When Ehrmann asked Joe Morelli about Sacco and Vanzetti, he answered, "Sacco? Sacco? See Mancini about that."[31] This unintentional slip by Morelli led Ehrmann to Mancini in the Auburn State Prison in New York.

During Ehrmann's interview of Mancini, it became apparent that he was very familiar with the Sacco and Vanzetti case. Mancini offered that Sacco and Vanzetti were not the kind of men who would engage in a South Braintree type of crime.[32] Ehrmann learned that Mancini murdered Alterio with a foreign-made 7.65-millimeter automatic. The gun used .32-caliber bullets, the same caliber bullets that killed Berardelli and Parmenter. That gun also produced right-twist markings on bullets, like the right-twist markings that appeared on five (all six according to Young and Kaiser) bullets fired into Berardelli and Parmenter.[33]

Ehrmann believed he was able to identify all six bandits who committed the South Braintree murders: Joe Morelli, the boss;[34] Anthony Mancini, the shooter; one other Morelli brother, a helper; Steve "the Pole" Benkosky, the driver; Celestino Medeiros, the backseat gunman; and Mike Morelli, the driver of the Hudson who waited in the Manley Woods.

Sacco and Vanzetti hoped that the Medeiros confession, with the surrounding facts and circumstances about the Morelli gang, would result in a new trial. Judge Thayer dashed their hopes on October 23, 1926, when he issued a fifty-five-page opinion that denied the motion. His principal reasons centered on various minor misstatements and errors by Medeiros. The judge concluded:

> Medeiros is, without doubt, a crook, a thief, a robber, a liar, a rum-runner, a "bouncer" in a house of ill fame, a smuggler, and a man who has been convicted and sentenced to death for the murder of one Carpenter, who was cashier of the Wrentham Bank.[35]

Six months later, the supreme judicial court affirmed Judge Thayer's denial as being within his discretion.

Corroboration of the Morelli gang's responsibility for the South Braintree murders occurred in 1973. Vincent Teresa, a self-confessed member of the Mafia, authored his autobiography, *My Life in the Mafia*. In it, he disclosed some startling admissions by Frank "Butsey" Morelli against his own interests. Teresa recalled:

> I remember ... that the Boston Globe printed an article that said Butsey was behind the robbery-murder in the Sacco-Vanzetti case. Butsey sued. I asked him, "What the hell are you suing them for? You can't beat a newspaper." He said: "They're implicating me in this Sacco-Vanzetti thing. What they said was true, but it's going to hurt my kid. I don't give a damn about myself. I'm ready to die anyway. But look what it's doing to my boy. He's a legitimate kid. He never knew what was going on before."
>
> I looked at Butsey. I didn't know much about the case except what I'd heard. But he was upset because of what was happening to his boy, not what happened to Sacco and Vanzetti. "We whacked them out, we killed those guys in the robbery," Butsey said. "These two greaseballs [Sacco and Vanzetti] took it on the chin. They got in our way so we just ran over them. Now after all these years some punch-drunk writer has got to start up the whole thing over again—ruin my reputation. I gotta sue even though

I don't expect to win. I gotta sue for my kid's protection."
I said: "Did you really do this?" He looked at me, right
into my eyes, and said: "Absolutely, Vinnie. These two
suckers took it on the chin for us. That shows you how
much justice there really is."[36] Reprinted with permission of
Random House, Inc.

Teresa was the federal government's principal witness whose testimony
sent more than fifty high-ranking Mafia bosses to prison. The accuracy and
honesty of his testimony in those cases have never been questioned.

Emil Moller, Joe Morelli's former cellmate, corroborated "Butsey"
Morelli's confession to Vincent Teresa. Moller recounted that on a number
of occasions, Joe admitted to him that the Morelli gang had committed the
South Braintree job. He said that they used a second car in the getaway and
were almost caught when changing cars in the woods because the second
car was stuck in the mud.

While in prison, Joe Morelli asked Moller to swear that he was with
him in New York on the day of the South Braintree crime and that he was
playing poker with Moller, Silva, and Luban at Luban's home that day. Moller
played along with Joe and said he would swear to the alibi. Unfortunately,
Vincent Teresa and Emil Moller did not corroborate "Butsey's" and Joe
Morelli's confessions in time to save Sacco and Vanzetti.

After Judge Thayer denied Sacco and Vanzetti's motion for a new trial
based on the Medeiros confession, their only hope was for clemency.

CHAPTER 12

A Plea for Clemency

With the Medeiros confession disposed of, the Commonwealth quickly moved to sentence the two Italians. At 10:00 AM on April 9, 1927, Winfield Wilbur, the district attorney of Norfolk County, moved the court for the imposition of the death sentence. He suggested that the sentence should be carried out some time during the week beginning Sunday, July 10, 1927.[1]

Sacco's Statement

Clerk R. B. Worthington spoke before a packed but stone silent courtroom: "Nicola Sacco, have you anything to say why sentence of death should not be passed upon you?"[2]

From within the steel cage that confined the two Italians, Sacco rose to his feet to address the court. Confinement in a small cell for seven years had robbed him of his youth. He looked pale, old, and tired. Hunger strikes had weakened his once sturdy peasant body. His spirit appeared broken. He spoke in halting and broken English:

> Yes, sir. I am not an orator. It is not very familiar with me the English language, and as I know, as my friend has told me, my comrade Vanzetti will speak more on, so I thought to give him the chance.

176

I never know, never heard, even read in history anything so cruel as this Court. After seven years prosecuting they still consider us guilty. And these gentle people here are arrayed with us in this court today.

I know the sentence will be between two class, the oppressed class the rich class, and there will be always collision between the one and the other. We fraternize the people with the books, with the literature. You persecute the people, tyrannize over them and kill them. We try to education of people always. You try to put a path between us and some other nationality that hates each other. That is why I am here today on this bench, for having been the oppressed class. Well, you are the oppressor.

You know it, Judge Thayer—you know all my life, you know why I have been here, and after seven years that you have been persecuting me and my poor wife, and you still today sentence us to death. I would like to tell all my life, but what is the use? You know all about what I say before, and my friend—that is, my comrade—will be talking because he is more familiar with the language, and I will give him a chance. My comrade, the man kind, the kind man to all the children, you sentence him two times in the Bridgewater case and the Dedham case, connected with me, and you know he is innocent. You forget all the population that has been with us for seven years, to sympathize and give us all their energy and all their kindness. You do not care for them. Among that peoples and the comrades and the working class there is a big legion of intellectual people which have been with us for seven years, but to not commit the iniquitous sentence, but still the Court goes ahead. And I think I thank you all, you peoples, my comrades who have been with me for seven years, and the Sacco-Vanzetti case, and I will give my friend a chance.

I forget one thing which my comrade remember me. As I said before, Judge Thayer know all my life, and he know that I am never been guilty, never—not yesterday nor today nor forever. [3]

Vanzetti's Statement

Clerk Worthington addressed Vanzetti: "Bartolomeo Vanzetti, have you anything to say why sentence of death should not be passed upon you?"[4]

Vanzetti stood erect. Prison life had been hard, and it showed on his aging face. He held a few notes in his hand as he addressed Judge Thayer. The judge did not look at him throughout Vanzetti's forty-five-minute oration. A truncated version follows:

> Yes. What I say is that I am innocent, not only of the Braintree crime, but also of the Bridgewater crime. That I am not only innocent of these two crimes, but in all my life I have never stole and I have never killed and I have never spilled blood. That is what I want to say. And it is not all. Not only am I innocent of these two crimes, not only in all my life I have never stole, never killed, never spilled blood, but I have struggled all my life, since I began to reason, to eliminate crime from the earth.
>
> ... Now, I should say that I am not only innocent of all these things, not only have I never committed a real crime in my life—though some sins but not crimes— not only have I struggled all my life to eliminate crimes, but crimes that the official law and the official moral condemns, but also the crime that the official moral and the official law sanctions and sanctifies—the exploitation and the oppression of the man by the man, and if there is a reason why I am here as a guilty man, if there is a reason why you in a few minutes can doom me, it is this reason and none else.
>
> ... Eugene Debs say that not even a dog—something like that—not even a dog that kill chickens would have been found guilty by American jury with the evidence that the Commonwealth have produced against us. I say that not even a leprous dog would have his appeal refused two times by the Supreme Court of Massachusetts—not even a leprous dog.
>
> ... We know, you know in your heart, that you have been against us from the very beginning, before you see us. Before you see us you already know that we were

radicals, that we were underdogs, that we were the enemy of the institution that you can believe in good faith in their goodness …

… We know that you have spoke yourself and have spoke your hostility against us, and your despisement against us with friends of yours on the train, at the University Club of Boston, on the Golf Club of Worcester, Massachusetts. I am sure that if the people who know all what you say against us would have the civil courage to take the stand, maybe your Honor—I am sorry to say this because you are an old man, and I have an old father—but maybe you would be beside us in good justice at this time.

… We were tried during a time that has now passed into history. I mean by that, a time when there was a hysteria of resentment and hate against the people of our principles, against the foreigner, against slackers, and it seems to me—rather, I am positive of it, that both you and Mr. Katzmann has done all what it were in your power in order to agitate still more passion of the juror, the prejudice of the juror against us.

… This is what I say: I would not wish to a dog or to a snake, to the most low and misfortunate creature of the earth—I would not wish to any of them what I have had to suffer for things I am not guilty of. But my conviction is that I have suffered for things I am guilty of. I am suffering because I am a radical and indeed I am a radical; I have suffered because I was an Italian, and indeed I am an Italian; I have suffered more for my family and for my beloved than for myself; but I am so convinced to be right that if you could execute me two times, and if I could be reborn two other times, I would live again to do what I have done already.

I have finished. Thank you. [5]

The Death Sentence

After Sacco and Vanzetti delivered their statements, Judge Webster Thayer, like Pontius Pilate, washed his hands of any responsibility for the death sentences he was about to impose:

Under the law of Massachusetts the jury says whether a defendant is guilty or innocent. The Court has absolutely nothing to do with that question. The law of Massachusetts provides that a Judge cannot deal in any way with the facts. As far as he can go under our law is to state the evidence.

During the trial many exceptions were taken. Those exceptions were taken to the Supreme Judicial Court. That Court, after examining the entire record, after examining all the exceptions—that Court in its final words said, 'the verdicts of the jury should stand; exceptions overruled.' That being true, there is only one thing this Court can do. It is not a matter of discretion. It is a matter of statutory requirement, and that being true there is only one duty that now devolves upon this Court, and that is to pronounce the sentences …

First the Court pronounces sentence upon Nicola Sacco.

It is considered and ordered by the Court that you, Nicola Sacco, suffer the punishment of death by the passage of a current of electricity through your body within the week beginning on Sunday, the tenth day of July, in the year of our Lord, one thousand, nine hundred and twenty-seven. This is the sentence of the law …

It is considered and ordered by the Court that you, Bartolomeo Vanzetti— [6]

Vanzetti interrupted, "Wait a minute, please your Honor. May I speak for a minute with my lawyer, Mr. Thompson?" [7]

Thompson, "I do not know what he wants to say."[8]

"I think I should pronounce the sentence—Bartolomeo Vanzetti, suffer the punishment of death—"[9]

Sacco broke in, "You know I am innocent. That is the same words I pronounced seven years ago. You condemn two innocent men." [10]

"—by the passage of a current of electricity through your body within the week beginning on Sunday, the tenth day of July, in the year of our Lord, one thousand nine hundred and twenty-seven. This is the sentence of the law. We will now take a recess."[11]

At 11:00 AM, the court adjourned. Vanzetti wanted to make a further statement about his friend, Sacco, but Judge Thayer would not allow it; it was clear he wanted the proceeding to end.

That evening, Vanzetti wrote a final statement about Sacco; a brief portion follows:

> ... [I]n considering his supreme sacrifice, remembering his heroism I felt small small at the presence of his greatness and found myself compelled to fight back from my eyes the tears, and quanch my heart trobling to my throat to not weep before him—this man called thief and assassin and doomed. But Sacco's name will live in the hearts of the people and in their gratitude when Katzmann's and yours bones will be dispersed by time, when your name ... your laws, institutions, and your false god are but a deem rememoring of a cursed past in which man was wolf to the man ... [12]

After the death sentences, there was nowhere to go, except to seek clemency from Governor Fuller.

The Clemency Petition

On May 4, 1927, Thompson and Ehrmann filed a petition for clemency on behalf of Sacco and Vanzetti.[13] Vanzetti authored the petition, and Thompson and Ehrmann assisted him by correcting his spelling and grammar. Sacco had fallen into a deep depression and had lost all hope that any procedure could save his life. He refused to sign the petition but did not object to his name being included.[14]

The hallmark of the petition was that the two Italians sought justice as men innocent of the crimes for which they were convicted. They did not ask for a pardon, as that would imply guilt on their part.

Although the petition did not argue their case in the detail of a legal brief, it summarized the principal points of contention. Attention was given to identification evidence, the guns and bullets disputes, Captain Proctor's misleading "consistent with" opinion, Sacco's cap, Katzmann's brutal cross-examination of Sacco, and the lies and conduct of the two Italians upon their arrest alleging consciousness of guilt.[15]

The petition embraced expressions of lofty humanitarian ideals. It drew upon philosophers and writers of western civilization, including Thomas Jefferson, Thomas Paine, Ralph Waldo Emerson, Abraham Lincoln, and Benjamin Franklin. The petition's closing captured its essence:

> [W]e would not have you believe that we are asking for mercy or for anything but justice; or that we would purchase our lives by the surrender of our principles or our self-respect. Men condemned to die may be forgiven for plain speaking. We would not urge upon you anything that might seem disrespectful or incredible; but in the long run the victims of public injustice suffer less than the government that inflicts the penalty. We can die but once, and the pang of death will be but momentary; but the facts which show injustice cannot be obliterated. They will not be forgotten; and through the long years to follow they will trouble the conscience of those whose intolerance has brought us to our death, and of generations of their descendants. A mistake of justice is a tragedy. Deliberate injustice is an infamy.
>
> Governor Alvan T. Fuller, we have been in prison seven years charged with a crime we did not commit, awaiting the fate that every day came nearer and nearer. Perhaps you can imagine what this has meant to us. And do you realize what this has meant to Sacco's wife and children, and to Vanzetti's father … and family at home in Italy? It is the thought not of our own approaching death, but of the suffering of those near and dear to us in the seven years that have passed, and of the greater suffering to come, that is the cause of our bitter grief. And yet we ask you not for mercy but for justice. We will not impose their sufferings or our own on you. You cannot justly consider their suffering or ours as a ground for your official action, except that that suffering may seem to you a reason for giving the most careful and unprejudiced consideration to the two grounds of our prayer—that we are innocent and that our trial was unfair. [16]

The following affidavits supplemented the petition:

Frank P. Sibley, a reporter for the *Boston Globe*, attended the Dedham trial.[17] He deposed that during the trial Judge Thayer spoke of Fred Moore, Sacco's attorney, in derogatory terms, such as, "I'll show them that no long-haired anarchist from California can run this Court." The judge frequently referred to counsel for the defense as "those damn fools." On several occasions, he said, "Just wait until you hear my charge."

Elizabeth R. Bernkopf, a reporter for the International News Service, often sat with Judge Thayer on the morning train into Dedham during the trial.[18] She deposed that Judge Thayer talked a great deal about the Sacco-Vanzetti trial; that he said he distrusted and had no sympathy for the kind of people supporting the defense financially and otherwise; and that he disliked and was suspicious of attorney Moore, whom he generally referred to as "that long-haired anarchist."

Robert Benchley, drama editor of *Life* magazine, testified in a deposition that he was acquainted with Mr. Loring Coes for many years.[19] Benchley said that in 1921, during the trial of Sacco and Vanzetti, Coes told him he had just been in the clubhouse of the Worcester Country Club with Judge Thayer, who said what he intended to do to Sacco and Vanzetti. In the presence of Coes and others, the judge referred to Sacco and Vanzetti as "those bastards down there … were Bolsheviki, trying to intimidate him and that … he would get them good and proper." Judge Thayer told him and the others that a "bunch of parlor radicals were trying to get these guys off and were trying to bring pressure to bear on the Bench," that he "would show them and would get those guys hanged," and that he "would also like to hang a few dozen of the radicals."

Nicholas Beffel, a correspondent for the *Federal Press* who attended the trial at Dedham, reported that the mention of Moore's name aroused hostility in Judge Thayer, and on one occasion, in the presence of other newspapermen, Judge Thayer shook his fist and said, "You wait till I give my charge to the jury. I'll show 'em!"[20]

Lois B. Rantoul, representing the Greater Boston Federation of Churches, attended the trial.[21] She stated that she had two private conversations with Judge Thayer at his request during the course of the trial.

In their first conversation at the end of the prosecution's case, the judge asked her how she thought the trial was going and what she thought of the government's case. She told him that she had not yet heard sufficient evidence to convince her that the defendants were guilty. Rantoul indicated the judge expressed dissatisfaction with this statement, by words, gestures, tone of voice, and manner. He said that after hearing the prosecution's arguments and his charge, she would certainly feel differently.

The second conversation occurred while defense counsel presented his case. Following the testimony of George Kelley, the Three-K shoe factory superintendent who had praised Sacco's character, Judge Thayer again asked Mrs. Rantoul what she thought of the case. She indicated that Kelley's statement in support of Sacco's character was important. Judge Thayer expressed contempt for her view and told her that Kelley did not mean what he said because he heard on the outside that Kelley had said Sacco was an anarchist and he could not do anything with him. She told Judge Thayer she had never before realized it was fair to judge a case by what a person said outside of court.

Mrs. Rantoul issued a report on the outcome of the case to the Greater Boston Federation of Churches and incorporated her interviews with Judge Thayer in the report. She concluded that Sacco and Vanzetti were innocent.[22]

In addition to the foregoing affidavits, Thompson attached a statement to the clemency petition by George U. Crocker, a distinguished lawyer and sometime resident at the University Club of Boston.[23] He stated it was his firm belief that the defendants did not receive a fair trial with an impartial judge.

Crocker told about an evening when Judge Thayer approached him and said all the talk about the government prosecuting Sacco and Vanzetti for being anarchists was utter nonsense. Crocker also told of a morning, during breakfast, when the judge came to his table uninvited, sat down, began reading from his proposed charge to the jury, and then said, "I think that will hold him, don't you?"

Crocker didn't know how many times Judge Thayer talked to him about the case during the trial, but he thought it was three or four times—and each time the judge showed what appeared to be a clear bias against the defendants. The judge spoke to Crocker about the failure of the defendants to establish an alibi and that because they were draft dodgers and anarchists, they were not entitled to any consideration. He also claimed that the matter of their being anarchists was "lugged in by the defendants and not by the government."

* * * *

Following the filing of the clemency petition, Governor Fuller began a review of the case.[24] His inquiry was not public, and he forbade counsel for Sacco and Vanzetti to be present during his examination of witnesses. However, the governor permitted defense counsel to suggest witnesses for him to call and to argue in favor of his clients.

On June 1, 1927, following extensive pressure from the press and civil rights organizations, Governor Fuller announced the appointment of an advisory committee to review the Sacco and Vanzetti case.[25] The committee's purpose was to provide the governor with advice as to the fairness of the trial and the guilt or innocence of the two Italians.

The committee consisted of Abbott Lawrence Lowell, president of Harvard University; Samuel W. Stratton, president of Massachusetts Institute of Technology; and Robert Grant, a retired probate judge.[26] Defendants' counsel objected to the makeup of the committee because President Lowell and President Stratton were not sufficiently knowledgeable in criminal law to be effective and because Judge Grant's background in probate was inadequate for the task. Moreover, defense counsel pointed out that Judge Grant had publicly expressed his prejudice against Italians in general and of Sacco and Vanzetti in particular.[27] The governor ignored these objections.

The committee held hearings beginning on July 11, 1927, and issued its eighteen-page report on August 7, 1927, along with the governor's decision denying clemency.[28] The report acknowledged and condoned the bias of New England Yankees:

> There has been presented by the Government a certain amount of evidence of identification, and other circumstances tending to connect the prisoners with the murder, of such a character that—together with their being armed to the teeth and the falsehoods they stated when arrested—would in the case of New England Yankees, almost certainly have resulted in a verdict of murder in the first degree—a result which the evidence for the alibis was not likely to overcome.[29]

The committee placed inappropriate weight on the identification evidence. Judge Thayer, no supporter of Sacco and Vanzetti, had made it clear that the prosecution's identification evidence was not determinative in this case. He had previously ruled that the defense produced more witnesses negating the identification of Sacco and Vanzetti as participants in the crime than the prosecution produced supporting the defendants' participation.[30]

Without clear identification of Sacco and Vanzetti as the murderers, what were the other circumstances that connected the two Italians to the crime? In Vanzetti's case, the gun found on him at the time of his arrest looked like the gun that Berardelli brought to Iver Johnson's repair shop three weeks before the crime. However, there was no evidence that Berardelli retrieved his gun before he was murdered, that Berardelli was carrying a gun that day, or that any witness saw a bandit pick up a gun from either victim. On what basis was it "almost certain" that a Yankee jury would convict Vanzetti—that he lied and was armed when arrested?

The evidence presented against Sacco was not much better. It consisted of inconclusive identification evidence that Sacco was the shooter. It relied on the Sacco cap testimony, which should have been discredited when it was learned that the cap was found the day after the crime and that Sacco wore a size 7-1/8 and the cap was 6-7/8. Moreover, in his attempt to tie the cap to Sacco, Katzmann claimed that a hole in the lining was made by a nail upon which Sacco hung his hat while at work. Officer Gallivan, however, testified he put the hole in the lining of the cap in an effort to find any evidence indicating who owned it. The ballistics testimony pitted two defense experts who opined that Sacco's gun was not the source of the fatal bullet against Proctor's misleading and discredited "consistent with" opinion and VanAmburgh's ambiguous "I'm inclined to believe" statement.

The Dedham testimony of Officer Connolly about Sacco's and Vanzetti's alleged attempts to draw their weapons after their arrest was negated by Connolly's earlier actions. He did not testify at the Plymouth trial that they tried to draw their guns, and his testimony before the grand jury flatly contradicted his Dedham testimony. The only evidence left to convict Sacco were his lies, the loaded weapon, and a cache of bullets he was carrying at the time of arrest.

The report reflected that the committee's members had essentially made up their minds the defendants were guilty at the outset of their investigation. It contained conclusions without analyses and dismissed serious matters of fact. For example, regarding sworn statements in affidavits about the judge's bias, the report simply stated, "[B]ut we do not believe that he used some of the expressions attributed to him, and we think that there is exaggeration in what the persons to whom he spoke remember."[31]

The committee gave no credence to the defendants' claim that the federal government was working with Katzmann to deport the defendants or find them guilty of murder as a way to get rid of them, despite the sworn affidavits of government agents Ruzzamenti, Weyand, Letherman, and Weiss.[32] The committee simply denied the claim.

The committee ignored Daly's testimony that Ripley, the jury foreman, said, "Damn them, they ought to hang them anyway," when Daly told Ripley he thought Sacco and Vanzetti were innocent. The committee dismissed the charge with an indifferent, "Daly must have misunderstood him."[33]

After the execution of the two Italians, many found the advisory committee's procedures problematic when it was learned that questionable evidence outside the trial record was considered by its members.

One instance involved Major Calvin Goddard's unauthorized ballistics examination with the comparison microscope, resulting in his conclusion that Bullet III and Shell W were fired from Sacco's gun.

Another instance involved Carlotta Tattilo, formerly known and referred to around town as Lottie Packard. Aside from the fact that her testimony was not presented at the trial by the prosecutor and was not tested by cross-examination, she was known for incoherent ramblings and contradictory charges. Police Chief Gallivan referred to Lottie Packard as a promiscuous "nut" who had sent many Braintree men to the doctor. She claimed that she had known Sacco since the two worked at the Rice & Hutchins factory in 1908. This was proved false when it was shown that Sacco was sixteen when he arrived at Milford in 1908 and that his employment record indicated he did not work at that factory until 1918. There were other inconsistencies in her testimony before the advisory committee. Nevertheless, its members believed that "her testimony is well worth considering."

* * * *

A charge of extreme bias fell on Lowell, chairman of the advisory committee, because of his treatment of Sacco's alibi. An indisputable alibi would be a perfect defense to the South Braintree murder charge. Sacco claimed just such an alibi. As disclosed at the Dedham trial, the defense produced a string of witnesses who swore under oath that Sacco was in Boston the day and time of the murders. Katzmann chose not to claim that Sacco had not been in Boston; rather, he attempted to raise doubts in the minds of the jurors whether April 15 was the day that Sacco met

Professor Felice Guadagni, Albert Bosco, Antonio Dentamore, and others in Boston. Katzmann was not successful in destroying Sacco's alibi, and it was obviously a matter for the advisory committee to examine. Sacco's alibi apparently disturbed Lowell to such an extent that he attempted to break it on his own.

At the trial, Katzmann asked the witnesses who testified to Sacco's presence at Boni's restaurant and Giordiani's coffee shop on April 15, 1920, how they fixed the date of their meetings.[34] The witnesses all fixed the date with reference to a banquet honoring James T. Williams, Jr., editor of the *Boston Transcript*, held that day at an Italian priory in the North End of Boston before hundreds of people.

President Lowell contacted James T. Williams, Jr., without informing Sacco's lawyer.[35] Williams indicated that he was honored at a dinner on May 13, 1920. Lowell was able to verify that dinner by obtaining a newspaper dated May 14, 1920, which reported on the event as having occurred the day before. Armed with this information, Lowell called Guadagni and Bosco to his office. They had previously testified at the Dedham trial and before the advisory committee in support of Sacco's alibi. Guadagni and Bosco had fixed April 15 as the date of the Williams banquet and claimed that it had been a topic of discussion with Sacco. Lowell confronted Guadagni and Bosco with his evidence that the Williams dinner was held on May 13, 1920. It now appeared that Lowell had broken Sacco's alibi.

Bosco and Guadagni were in disbelief.[36] Bosco was certain of the date, and he told Lowell he would return the next day with proof that the Williams banquet occurred on April 15, 1920. After Guadagni and Bosco left, Thompson expressed his thought to Lowell that there may have been two dinners honoring Williams. Lowell scoffed at Thompson, "I don't know whether you are trying to reach the truth or not ..."[37]

Bosco returned the next day with copies of the *La Notizia* newspaper of April 16, 1920, reporting on an April 15 banquet honoring James T. Williams, Jr., editor of the *Boston Transcript*, just as Bosco claimed.[38] Lowell had an aide phone Williams at his office in Washington, D.C., and Williams then recalled the April 15 banquet.[39] There were, indeed, two dinners. Bosco sought permission from Lowell to publish the facts covering the incident in *La Notizia*, with a disclosure of the two dinners honoring Williams. Lowell forbade Bosco from doing so.

Lowell, for all his professed integrity as the leading citizen of Boston—indeed, of all Massachusetts—suppressed evidence of his mistake. He directed that the minutes of the committee reflect only the following:

Executive Chamber, State House, Boston

Friday, July 15, 10:30 a.m.

Investigation resumed with all the Members of the
Committee present. [The witness Bosco] who was on the
stand yesterday afternoon again appeared with the editions
of the paper *LaNotizia*, requested by the Committee,
and the Committee, all counsel present, and the witness
looked in the books produced by the witness.[40]

More than a year after the execution of Sacco and Vanzetti, Bernard
Flexner and Charles Burlingham were in the process of preparing the
official record of the Sacco and Vanzetti case. They were at a loss as to how
to deal with the testimony of Guadagni and Bosco regarding the Williams
incident. On November 27, 1928, they wrote to Lowell, Thompson, and
Ehrmann for advice.[41]

On December 8, 1928, Lowell briefly responded to Flexner and
Burlingham that Bosco produced files of *La Notizia* indicating that Mr.
Williams had attended a luncheon on April 15 at an Italian priory in the
North End.

Lowell never corrected the official public record of the advisory
committee to reflect these facts. He would not admit his error in favor of
Sacco's alibi, a reflection of his arrogance and bias.

It came to Thompson's attention that Governor Fuller, during his
investigation, inquired of his personal lawyer about the lack of documentary
evidence supporting Vanzetti's claim that he delivered eels in Plymouth on
December 24, 1919, at the time of the Bridgewater crime.[42]

The inquiry moved Thompson and Ehrmann into action. They made
a desperate search for evidence showing that Vanzetti had purchased a
quantity of eels for sale and delivery on Christmas Eve, 1919. The two lawyers
visited Italian fish markets along Atlantic Avenue in Boston. They sought
bills, orders, or receipts reflecting large purchases of eels shortly before the
Christmas holiday of that year. Their persistence paid off. They discovered
an old box of American Express receipts. Under the date of December 20,
1919, they found a receipt for the shipment of eels to "B Vanzetti, Plymouth
Massachusetts." Delivery would have occurred on December 22 or 23, just
as the testimony at the Plymouth trial had indicated.[43] They delivered the
receipt to the governor's personal attorney, but nothing was ever heard about
it again, at least not from the governor's office.

Thompson learned later that with reference to that receipt, Governor Fuller commented, "It is only twenty miles from Plymouth to Bridgewater.[44] A pretty clever ruse—start with eels in Plymouth, then dash to Bridgewater for the holdup, then back to Plymouth to sell eels! Could there be a neater alibi?"

The final days approached.

CHAPTER 13

THE FINAL DAYS

After Governor Fuller denied the petition for clemency on August 3, 1927, Thompson was in a state of despair and disillusionment with the Massachusetts institutions to which he had devoted his life. On August 6, Thompson and Ehrmann withdrew from the case in what they believed was in the best interests of Sacco and Vanzetti:

> We feel that the defendants are now entitled to have the benefit of the judgment of counsel who can take up the case untrammeled by the commitments of the past and less disturbed than we are by a sense of injustice.[1]

Thompson arranged to have Arthur D. Hill, a highly respected Boston attorney who had previously assisted the defense, take over the case. Hill was adamant that Sacco and Vanzetti did not receive a fair trial. He moved into action quickly; the executions were set for midnight on August 10.[2]

A few days before Hill took over, Sacco and Vanzetti were returned to the death house.[3] They were both weak from their hunger strikes. Sacco stopped eating on July 17; Vanzetti joined the hunger strike at that time, but later, on July 26, broke his fast. Vanzetti again refused food beginning on August 2 to show his solidarity with Sacco.

Hill, with the assistance of attorneys Elias Field, Richard Evarts, and Michael Musmanno, engaged in one of the most extraordinary legal efforts in American history to save Sacco and Vanzetti.[4] During the final

191

days, Hill and his legal team filed a blizzard of papers with the federal and Commonwealth courts and with Governor Fuller.

On Saturday, August 6, Hill filed three motions in the superior court of Norfolk County. One motion called for a revocation of the sentences and the second for a new trial on the grounds of Judge Thayer's prejudice. Hill filed the third motion with Chief Judge Walter Perley Hall of the superior court for a speedy hearing on the first two motions and to assign the hearing for a new trial to a neutral judge. Judge Hall assigned both motions to Judge Thayer for hearings on August 8. In addition to the three motions, Hill filed a petition with the Massachusetts Supreme Judicial Court for a writ of error to reverse the convictions.

Monday, August 8, was another day of exceptional activity. Judge Thayer held a hearing on a motion for a new trial on grounds of his prejudice. Hill vigorously objected. He argued that Judge Thayer could not fairly rule on his own prejudice. Judge Thayer denied the motion. Judge George A. Sanderson of the supreme judicial court heard Hill's earlier petition for a writ of error that day. He denied the petition. Later that day, Hill appealed Judge Thayer's and Judge Sanderson's denials to the full supreme judicial court. Because the executions were to take place in two days, Hill sought a stay from Governor Fuller in order to argue his appeals.

On August 8, Hill also filed for a writ of habeas corpus before Justice Oliver Wendell Holmes of the United States Supreme Court to free the two Italians from prison. That same day, he sought a separate writ of habeas corpus from Judge George W. Anderson of the United States court of appeals. The courts denied each writ.

On Tuesday, August 9, Judge Thayer denied Hill's motion for a revocation of the sentences imposed on the defendants. Wednesday, August 10, was the day set for the executions. Governor Fuller conferred the entire day with his staff regarding Hill's motion for a stay. Sacco and Vanzetti suffered the anxiety of death by electrocution until the last half hour. Governor Fuller finally announced a stay thirty-six minutes before midnight. The governor spared their lives until midnight, August 22, in order to permit a hearing on Hill's pending appeals before the supreme judicial court. Defense counsel spent the following days preparing their arguments before that court on August 16.

On Friday, August 19, the Massachusetts Supreme Judicial Court denied Hill's appeals. Hill immediately filed a writ of certiorari, asking the United States Supreme Court to review the case. Certiorari may be granted by the United States Supreme Court if it finds that petitioner makes a substantial claim that he was denied a federal right by a lower court. Hill needed the entire record of the trial in order to perfect the filing of that writ. The record, however, would not be available until October 1927. Hill sought another stay of execution until October 1, this time from the United States Supreme Court, in order to obtain the record of the Dedham trial. In the meantime, Hill's team sought another writ of habeas corpus from Judge James M. Morton of the United States district court in Boston. Judge Morton denied the writ.

Time slipped away. In desperation, on Saturday, August 20, Hill filed for a writ of certiorari without the full record of the trial. Then he sought a stay of execution from Justice Oliver Wendell Holmes for time to produce the record. Justice Holmes denied the stay.

As the lawyers worked feverishly those last days to save them, Sacco and Vanzetti prepared for the end with their loved ones. The two Italians could do little more than write letters. Even that became difficult for Sacco, who was in his last hunger strike. He pressed on with letters to his children, Ines and Dante.

To six-year old Ines he wrote:[5]

> My Dear Ines:
> I would like that you should understand what I am going to say to you … for I love you so much … as you are the dearest little beloved one …
>
> I will bring with me your little and so dearest letter and carry it right under my heart to the last day of my life. When I die, it will be buried with your father who loves you so much, as I do also your brother Dante and holy dear mother …
>
> It was the greatest treasure and sweetness in my struggling life that I could have lived with you and your brother Dante and your mother in a neat little farm, and learn all your sincere words and tender affection. Then in the summer-time to be sitting with you in the home nest under the oak tree shade—beginning to teach you of life and how to read and write, to see you running, laughing, crying and singing through the verdent fields picking the wild flowers here and there from one tree to another, and from the clear, vivid stream to your mother's embrace …

> ... You are in my heart, in my vision, in every angle
> of this sad walled cell, in the sky and everywhere my gaze
> rests ...
> [Used with permission of Viking Penguin, a division of Penguin Group
> (USA) Inc.]

Dante was thirteen and approaching manhood. To his son, the little boy he had played catch with by throwing a ball back and forth over prison walls, he wrote:[6]

> My Dear Son and Companion:
> ... I knew ... what here I am going to tell you will touch
> your sensibilities, but don't cry Dante, because many tears
> have been wasted, as your mother's have been wasted for
> seven years, and never did any good. So, Son, instead
> of crying, be strong, so as to be able to comfort your
> mother ... But remember always, Dante, in the play of
> happiness, don't you use all for yourself only, but down
> yourself just one step, at your side and help the weak ones
> that cry for help, help the prosecuted and the victim,
> because that are your better friends; they are the comrades
> that fight and fall as your father and Bartolo fought and
> fell yesterday for the conquest of the joy of freedom for all
> and the poor workers. In this struggle of life you will find
> more love and you will be loved.
> ... And you will also not forget to love me a little
> for I do—O, Sonny! thinking so much and so often of
> you ...
> [Used with permission of Viking Penguin, a division of Penguin Group
> (USA) Inc.]

Although Vanzetti lost all hope to escape execution, he achieved a last wish—to see his sister Luigia before he died. Luigia arrived from Italy just days before the end.[7] Rosina and a group of the faithful met Luigia in Boston and escorted her to the prison.

Warden William Hendry relaxed prison rules and permitted Vanzetti out of his cell to sit alone with Luigia for an hour.[8] They embraced, held hands, sat close to each other, and talked of their happy years together in Villafelletto. They recalled how they swam in the waters of the Magra and played among the fields of the Piedmont.

194

Following her visit with Bartolomeo, Luigia sought the aid of William Cardinal O'Connell at his summer home in Marblehead.[9] That resulted in a cup of tea and the cardinal's platitudes about God's mysterious ways.

As the last few days slipped away, Vanzetti wrote a letter to Sacco's son:[10]

> Remember Dante, remember always these things; we are not criminals; they convicted us on a frame-up; they denied us a new trial; and if we will be executed after seven years, four months and seventeen days of unspeakable tortures and wrong, it is for what I have already told you; because we were for the poor and against the exploitation and oppression of the man by the man ...
>
> Now Dante, be brave and good always. I embrace you.
>
> P.S. I left the copy of *An American Bible* to your mother now, for she will like to read it, and she will give it to you when you will be bigger and able to understand it. Keep it for remembrance ...
>
> [Used with permission of Viking Penguin, a division of Penguin Group (USA) Inc.

Nicola Sacco and Bartolomeo Vanzetti met with their families and friends the morning of Monday, August 22, 1927, amidst alternating waves of despair, fear, anger, and resignation. Not so for Governor Alvan Fuller. He arrived at his office that morning, offering waiting reporters a cheerful, "Good morning gentlemen. It's a beautiful day, isn't it?"[11]

Gardner Jackson reported the same "callous cynicism" permeated the governor's staff. He recalled that he and other sympathizers waited with heavy hearts in the governor's antechamber that morning while Luigia made her last plea to the governor for her brother's life. The governor's secretary, Herman MacDonald, offered cigars to the men who were waiting and told them to take it easy, not to take it so hard, that "after all they were just a couple of wops."[12]

Later that last day, Hill sought a stay of execution from Justice Louis Brandeis of the United States Supreme Court. The justice recused himself from any participation in the case because his wife and daughter were caring for Sacco's wife and children. Hill then traveled to an island resort in Maine, where Justice Harlan Stone of the United States Supreme Court was vacationing. Hill sought, but Stone denied, a stay of the executions. Meanwhile, Musmanno pursued the two most powerful men in America. He sought a stay of execution from Chief Justice William Howard Taft, who was in Canada. He made a similar plea to President Coolidge. Both efforts were unsuccessful.

Hill was relentless. He persisted late into the day. He sought separate stays from Judge James Sisk of the Commonwealth court and Judge James Lowell of the federal district court in Boston. Both courts denied these motions. Hill made a plea that evening to Governor Fuller to spare Sacco and Vanzetti. The governor denied the plea.

That last evening, Rosina made a final visit to her husband, and Luigia to her brother.[13] Each was given five minutes for a final embrace, a kiss through prison bars, and a last good-bye. Vanzetti wept while Luigia prayed. Sacco clasped Rosina's hand and told her, "I love you and always will."[14] She responded tearfully, "Nick, I'm dying with you."[15]

There was yet one final visitor, William Thompson.[16] He came not as a lawyer but as a friend. When he received a message that Vanzetti wanted to see him once more before he died, Thompson quickly left for Charlestown State Prison. This Harvard-educated, Brahmin-bred Mayflower descendant shed the influence of generations of Puritan bigotry and found common ground with an uneducated Italian immigrant, a wretch in the eyes of the establishment.

When Thompson reached the prison, he went directly to the death house.[17] The authorities decided to execute Celestino Medeiros at the same time as the Sacco and Vanzetti executions. Medeiros's cell was nearest the electric chair, Sacco's cell was next, and Vanzetti was in the third cell. "[Vanzetti] seemed to be expecting me; and when I entered he rose … with his characteristic smile reached through the space between the bars and grasped me warmly by the hand." The guard told Thompson that he could sit in a chair in front of Vanzetti's cell but not closer than a mark painted on the floor.

Thompson sought reassurance from Vanzetti of his and Sacco's innocence, which Vanzetti provided.[18] Vanzetti asked Thompson to "clear my name." Thompson later wrote of his meeting with Vanzetti:[19]

> … [Vanzetti] spoke with eloquence of his sufferings, and asked me whether I thought it possible that he could forgive those who had persecuted and tortured him through seven years of inexpressible misery… I had asked

him to reflect upon the career of One infinitely superior to myself and to him … I said that in the long run the force to which the world would respond was the force of love and not of hate, and that I was suggesting to him to forgive his enemies …

There was another pause in the conversation. I arose and we stood gazing at each other for a minute or two in silence. Vanzetti finally said that he would think of what I had said.

* * * *

At midnight, Medeiros went to the electric chair without incident and with no words spoken.[20] He went quietly to death like a sleepwalker.

At 12:11 AM, the guards took Sacco to the chair.[21] As he was strapped in, he called out, "Long live anarchy," and then, "Farewell my wife and child," and to the witnesses, "Good evening, gentlemen. Farewell." Finally, in Italian, "Mother."

Following Sacco, Vanzetti entered the death chamber, where he stopped and declared to Warden Hendry, who stood nearby:

I wish to say to you that I am innocent. I have never done a crime, some sins, but never a crime. I thank you for everything you have done for me. I am innocent of all crime, not only this one, but of all, of all. I am an innocent man. [22]

Vanzetti shook hands with Warden Hendry and the guards standing by, and then he sat in the chair. Vanzetti's execution was difficult for Warden Hendry. He sympathized with the plight of the two Italians. Sacco and Vanzetti were his "good boys." He had treated them kindly and with respect.[23]

As the guards placed contact pads on his legs, Vanzetti spoke his final words, "I now wish to forgive some people for what they are doing to me."[24]

Warden Hendry, with tear-filled eyes, gave the signal.

So ended the life of Bartolomeo Vanzetti.

Vanzetti spoke and wrote many notable words during the seven years of his confinement. The following may be the most memorable:

If it had not been for these thing, I might have live out my life talking at street corners to scorning men. I might have die, unmarked, unknown, a failure. Now we are not a failure. This is our career and our triumph. Never in our full life could we hope to do such work for tolerance, for joostice, for men's onderstanding of man, as now we do by accident. Our words—our lives—our pains—nothing! The taking of our lives—lives of a good shoemaker and a poor fish peddler—all! That last moment belong to us— that agony is our triumph! [25]

* * * *

When the end came, reporters sent word by phone and wire to the world. Few among the waiting would soon forget that night. The cries and tears of millions joined those of Rosina Sacco and Luigia Vanzetti. Protests, strikes, and riots broke out in principal cities of the world.[26] Overseas, American embassies were stoned, American cars overturned, American flags burned.

The loyal supporters of the two Italians were determined to give them a proper funeral. The authorities released the bodies of the two Italians on Tuesday. The defense committee decided on cremation; no one was sure why. Perhaps it was an antireligious symbol, since cremation was against rules of the Catholic Church at that time.

Viewings of the bodies began Thursday evening and continued through Sunday morning, with the funeral set for Sunday afternoon.[27] City officials barred the defense committee from using its headquarters for viewing the bodies, as the building was old and not strong enough to accommodate the anticipated crowds. Langone's funeral home held viewings of Sacco and Vanzetti. Giant wreaths of flowers surrounded the two caskets and lined the walls of the parlor. Some of the wreaths contained messages—"Revenge" and "Massachusetts the Murderer"—some in English, some in Italian. [28]

At the opening of the first viewing on Thursday, August 25, Mary Donovan, a staunch and loyal supporter of the two, stood at the entrance holding a placard with a statement by Judge Thayer that became a rallying call:

DID YOU SEE WHAT I DID TO THOSE
ANARCHISTIC BASTARDS?
Judge Webster Thayer [29]

In fear of losing his license, Langone asked Mary to leave, which she did, but she continued to display the placard in front of Langone's.[30] The police promptly arrested Mary and destroyed the placard.

On Sunday, the final line of sympathizers formed outside of Langone's at 6:00 AM. It took four hours to reach the caskets. At 2:30 PM, a lead car and two hearses, each carrying a casket, left Langone's. Cars overflowing with flowers followed the hearses. Two limousines were next, one with Sacco and Vanzetti family members and the other with members of the defense committee. Behind the last limousine, thousands of mourners trailed on foot, eight abreast, with arms linked.

Over one hundred thousand people viewed the bodies, and an additional two hundred fifty thousand to a million lined the streets as the cortege moved through Boston for the eight-mile trip to the crematory at Forest Hills Cemetery.[31] The mourners strode defiantly amidst a falling rain that likened the streets to a valley of tears. They called it "the march of sorrows." It was a funeral of regal dimensions, but it had a dark side.

There were five hundred police on foot, seventy mounted officers, and many more in cars and motorcycles, all armed with guns and batons.[32] The city dug up streets and set up barricades and roadblocks so the procession could not pass the Massachusetts State House. The police forbade a musical band and the display of any placards or signs. Thousands of mourners began their procession with armbands hidden in their pockets. When they were near Scolly Square, on a signal they put them on, and a virtual sea of "Justice Crucified" in black letters against a red background burst onto the scene.

The police then became openly hostile.[33] The mounted officers repeatedly charged directly into the marchers and sympathetic bystanders, and some of whom were pushed through plateglass storefronts in the crush. Police battered defiant mourners with their batons, and officers with drawn guns kicked and beat the marchers who had fallen. While these police atrocities have been recounted by reporters, there are no known films of these events. Will Hays, chief censor of movies, had ordered the destruction of all newsreel footage covering the funeral.[34]

As the remnants of the marchers approached Forest Hills Cemetery, they passed through an Irish enclave.[35] They were jeered by hostile faces appearing in the windows and doorways of the flats and walk-ups lining the streets, with shouts of "Guineas, wops, dagoes go home."

When the caskets reached the crematory, thousands of rain-drenched followers surrounded the small chapel, which could hold only one hundred mourners. Mary Donovan read a eulogy over their caskets:

You, Sacco and Vanzetti are the victims of the crassest plutocracy the world has known since ancient Rome—and now Massachusetts and America have killed you—murdered you because you were Italian anarchists—In your martyrdom we will fight on and conquer.[36]

A thin line of smoke arose from the crematorium, sending a message that the spirit, the memory, and the ashes were all that remained of Nicola Sacco and Bartolomeo Vanzetti.

It was over!

CHAPTER 14

AFTERWARD

Earthly matters for Nicola and Bartolomeo came to an end. It was different for those who remained.[1] Rosina, widowed in her early thirties with two young children, faced an uncertain future. Traumatized from seven years of what she saw as unspeakable cruelty against the man she loved—the man she knew in her heart was innocent—left an indelible mark on her psyche. She turned inward and lost trust for outsiders. She built a wall of protection around herself and the children.

Rosina was determined to survive and to give Dante and Ines as normal a life as possible. Out of respect for her beloved Nicola, there would be no change of surname, no escape to a distant locale. She and the children would remain and live in the area under the Sacco name.

Rosina established a strict rule for herself and the children. There would be no discussions with outsiders, and very little among themselves, regarding the tragedy. They would put the last seven years behind them and live for the future. There were few exceptions to this rule of silence. Rosina kept to herself to such an extent that outsiders labeled her a recluse.

Although Rosina lost all faith in the God of her convent training, providence sent her a friend and protector in her time of need. Ermano Bianchini, a member of the defense committee, provided Rosina and the children with friendship and support during the time of Nicola's imprisonment. Two years after Nicola's death, Rosina and the children moved into Ermano's modest home in Watertown, a suburb of Boston. Ermano and Rosina started a small poultry business and married in 1943. When Ermano died in 1985, Rosina moved into grandson Spencer's home for a short while. Later, she moved to a nursing home. Rosina passed away in the early 1990s. She and Nicola left a progeny of honorable citizens.

Ines was remembered by one of her elementary school classmates as a quiet little girl who never mixed with her classmates. Dante and Ines each married and raised families in the Boston area. Ines and her family led very private lives, never publicly commenting about the tragedy. Dante's life was a bit more public because he was constantly pursued by reporters, writers, and historians for information—the kind that might solve the mystery of guilt or innocence of his father.

During the early years of the Great Depression, Dante held odd jobs in and around the Boston area. He and his girlfriend, Mildred, quietly eloped in 1939. They married in Friendship, Maine, 175 miles north of Boston, to avoid publicity. They raised three sons.

Dante, like his father, was skilled in mechanical matters. He became an airplane mechanic and an aviator as well. He worked for twenty-seven years as the airplane parts manager at the local airport. Dante was active in local clubs, a stellar member of his church and community, a devoted father and husband. Dante died in 1971, at the age of 58, of a blood clot in his lungs. Over 450 people attended his funeral.

Apologists for the Commonwealth persisted in their efforts to prove that at least Sacco was guilty. Francis Russell, a noted writer who had spent a significant part of his adult life researching and writing about the Sacco-Vanzetti affair, was at the forefront of this activity. Russell claimed a single theme in his writings and lectures. Over and over, he argued that the Sacco family's rule of silence was to hide a great secret—the guilt of Nicola Sacco. He bolstered his argument with the charge that Dante's failure to engage in public debate defending his father was further proof of his thesis. He carried his claim to an extreme when he wrote a letter to Dante while he was on his deathbed, hounding the man to disclose this so-called Sacco family secret.

After Dante's death, Spencer, Dante's son, responded to Russell's accusations at a public meeting on the Sacco-Vanzetti case, at which Russell was a participant. Spencer charged Russell, "You have confused and have abused my family and upset my family ..."[2] Spencer defended his father's silence as a way of protecting his family. He listed specific errors in Russell's writings. When Spencer finished, there was thunderous applause from the audience and silence from Russell. Later, Russell continued with his obsession that the Sacco family's conduct, and in particular Dante's silence, was proof of Sacco's guilt.

Luigia Vanzetti internalized the tragedy and brought it home with her when she returned to Italy. Vincenzina, Luigia's younger sister, recalled the affect Bartolomeo's suffering and death had on Luigia:

> My sister became prematurely old. She suffered and cried so much that something went out in her brain. She kept getting more and more depressed. She could not move her legs, her back. She had a total nervous breakdown, but she was conscious to the end. [3]

Judge Thayer retired a few years after the execution of the two Italians. His retirement was not peaceful. He and his wife were subjected to constant threats. Even though a police guard was stationed at his home, it was bombed in 1932, causing extensive damage and injury to his wife. Thayer died a year later.

Katzmann continued practicing law in the Boston area. He never realized his ambition to become attorney general. Ironically, he suffered a heart attack and died in 1953 during a civil trial in the Dedham courthouse in which Sacco and Vanzetti were convicted.

William Thompson's death in 1935, at the age of seventy, deeply affected Herbert Ehrmann, his co-counsel in the Sacco-Vanzetti case. At a memorial for Thompson before the Boston Bar Association, Ehrmann extolled Thompson's career, especially his efforts to save Sacco and Vanzetti in the face of disparagement from the establishment and personal economic loss. Ehrmann spoke passionately about the case. He noticed that Justice Edward Pierce had entered the room during his presentation. Justice Pierce had sat as one of the five justices on the supreme judicial court during some of the appeals of the Sacco-Vanzetti case. Ehrmann felt uncomfortable because his discussion of the case would be understood by Justice Pierce as critical of the court's decisions. Ehrmann recalled:

> After the proceedings were concluded, I saw the Justice approaching me, apparently under stress of a powerful emotion. The tears were pouring down his cheeks. To my amazement he grasped my hands warmly and said in a rather broken voice, "Thank you! Thank you! Thank you!" [4]

This account offers insight into what the world had believed was a unified Supreme Court regarding the Sacco-Vanzetti decisions. Justice Pierce's tears were eerily reminiscent of assistant prosecutor Williams's tears and words following the guilty verdicts at the end of the Dedham trial when he shunned McAnarney's congratulations and declared, "For God's sake, don't rub it in, this is the saddest thing that ever happened to me in my life."

CHAPTER 15

THE BALLISTICS CONTROVERSY

The Commonwealth's claim that Sacco was Berardelli's killer rested on two assumptions: 1) Bullet III in evidence was the authentic bullet that killed Berardelli; and 2) Bullet III was shot through Sacco's gun. I now completely leave my role as an observer and will elaborate on my theories about the case. I will use clues already developed by others, as well as my own, to respond to the Commonwealth's assumptions.

The Counterfeit Bullet

Proctor's contrived "consistent with" opinion regarding Bullet III and Bostock's suspicious claim of finding Shell W at the crime scene were only the beginning of the ballistics controversy. Rumors abounded after the conviction of the two Italians that the prosecution had engaged in misconduct during the trial.[1] These rumors took on an air of certainty after Proctor's admission of complicity with the prosecution in providing his misleading ballistics opinion. Arguments that Sacco and Vanzetti were framed erupted then and have continued to this day for that and the following reasons.

The testimony provided by Dr. Jones at the inquest, and by Dr. Magrath before the grand jury, was in accord with the theory that all six bullets shot into the victims were fired from the same gun and that it was not a Colt.[2] And because the trial evidence indicated that five of those bullets showed a right twist and one, a left twist, some observers of the case have concluded that the left-twist bullet was a counterfeit.[3]

The following four prosecution witnesses and one inquest witness, each with an excellent opportunity to observe the Berardelli shooting, provided testimony that only one shooter with one gun shot Berardelli multiple times. This too, supported the counterfeit bullet analysis.

James McGlone, a teamster, was across the street from where the shooting occurred.[4] He testified at the inquest, when events were fresh in his mind and before there was any pressure to convict the two Italians:

> A: [by McGlone] I saw one fellow have hold of the guard [Berardelli] and when I looked over two shots were fired at him ... He had hold of the guard and put two shots into him ... A couple of shots before that were fired ... four or five altogether. Five shots were fired.
>
> Q: [Mr. Adams] The man that shot the guard was the only one of the three [bandits] you saw with a weapon in his hand?
>
> A: The only one with a weapon in his hand ...

McGlone's testimony a year later at the trial as a prosecution witness was in accord with his inquest testimony. At the trial, McGlone testified, "[A]nd this fellow [the shooter] had him [Berardelli] by the shoulders.[5] He had a black pistol in his hand, flat on both sides. There was a couple of shots he fired when he held him this way. I saw him ... Berardelli going down like that." McGlone's testimony asserted that there was one shooter, one weapon, and two or more shots into Berardelli by the killer.

Lewis Wade, a shoemaker at Slater & and Morrill, was a bit down the road from the crime scene. He testified at the inquest, "I heard a shot ... as I looked I saw Berardelli and Parmenter.[6] I stood there and after the first shot Berardelli sank to the ground ... Two fellows went across the road after Parmenter, leaving this Italian alone with Berardelli. As he stood over him he took a gun and shot twice ... After the two shots were over Berardelli lay very still with his arm out."

Wade's testimony at trial as a witness for the prosecution provided more detail:[7] "I looked at Berardelli, and he was in a crouching position. That means his left arm was up here ... And this man was standing, well, not at the most over five feet, anyway from him and ... saw him shoot. Then I saw him shoot again ... Towards the man on the sidewalk, Berardelli."

Wade's testimony gave no indication that the killer used two guns or that any other bandit shot Berardelli. His testimony confirmed that the killer fired multiple shots into Berardelli while he was in a crouching position.

James Bostock, another prosecution eyewitness, confirmed the testimony of McGlone and Wade. He testified at the trial that he spoke to Parmenter and Berardelli as they walked on their way to deliver the payroll.[8] After a brief encounter, Bostock continued in the opposite direction on Pearl Street when he heard shots. Bostock stated that he turned and "As I looked down there, this Berardelli was on his knees in a crouched position as though he was guarding himself, and this man ... shot at Berardelli probably four or five times."[9]

The next witness to the shooting who testified for the prosecution was Lewis Pelser, a Rice & Hutchins shoe worker.[10] He testified at the trial that he heard shots while he was at work, and when he looked out of the window, he saw Berardelli's killer shoot him: "He put four bullets into him."[11]

Another eyewitness to the shooting was Annie Nichols, who testified at the inquest.[12] She said she was sitting at her kitchen window facing directly toward the crime scene. She testified that the same man who shot the detective [Berardelli] put two shots into Parmenter. Asked if more than four or five shots were fired, she answered, "Yes, but I can't say how many."[13] The following exchange with Mrs. Nichols indicates only one shooter was involved:

> Q: [by Deputy District Attorney Adams] Did the same man who shot the detective [Berardelli] shoot Parmenter?
> A: I think that he chased him when he ran across the street.
> Q: Who did shoot at him?
> A: That same man. I think it was him.
> Q: Did another man also shoot Parmenter?
> A: No, I don't think so.

However, in his opening statement to the Dedham jury on June 6, 1921, Williams charged:

> [B]ut the bullet, gentlemen, that caused Berardelli's
> death ... was fired from a .32 Colt automatic pistol. And
> when Sacco was arrested three weeks afterwards, he had
> on his person ... a fully loaded Colt automatic pistol of
> .32 calibre ... [14]

Williams later introduced Bullet III, with its left-twist markings, into evidence.[15] The prosecution's claim that the fatal bullet was shot from a Colt pistol was in direct conflict with the testimony of the foregoing five witnesses who established that only one shooter with one gun fired multiple shots into Berardelli, making it impossible for only Bullet III to show a left twist. That evidence was supported by doctors Jones and Magrath, who ruled out the possibility that Bullet III could have shown a Colt left twist when the other three Berardelli bullets showed right twists.[16] These factors were the principal grounds in 1985 for Young and Kaiser, in *Postmortem*, to conclude that Bullet III was a counterfeit and that it was substituted for the original fatal bullet in order to frame Sacco.[17]

Young and Kaiser also concluded that the substitution must have occurred sometime after September 10, 1920, when inquest and grand jury testimony conformed to the claim that all four Berardelli bullets originally showed right-twist markings.[18]

The testimony of the autopsy surgeons Magrath and Frazer, relating to the path of Bullet III shot into Berardelli, also was consistent with the testimony of McGlone, Wade, and Bostock.[19] The doctors testified at the trial that Bullet III hit Berardelli on the right side of his upper back, near his right shoulder, about six inches to the right of his spine, and three inches from the top of the shoulder. They said that the bullet had gone through his torso diagonally and downward, from right to left passing through his right lung, aorta, left kidney, and finally lodging against his left hip.

McGlone also testified at the trial that one of the bandits, while standing on the running board of the getaway car as it moved away, fired a shot in the direction of Berardelli.[20] Could this lone shot explain the one bullet in Berardelli with a left twist? At the time of that shot, Berardelli had fallen onto his back, with his head pointing in the direction the car was moving.[21] In this position, a shot from someone on the running board of the getaway car could not have hit Berardelli in his back and traveled downward through his body diagonally, from right to left, the way the fatal shot did.

One witness at the trial and one witness at the inquest testified that two bandits shot Berardelli. Edgar Langlois, a foreman at the Rice & Hutchins factory, was at his workbench on the second floor when he heard shots from the street below.[22] He opened a nearby window and said he saw two men shooting at Berardelli as he was standing—one man shot into the front of Berardelli's body and the other shot into his back. Langlois said he ran some seventy-five feet to a telephone and called the police. He returned to the window looking out and in as he held back his employees.

Langlois was unable to describe the bandits, their clothing, and whether they were clean shaven or if either one had a moustache. Langlois did not identify Sacco as one of the killers. Langlois's description of how the two bandits shot Berardelli does not conform to the path Bullet III and the other bullets took through Berardelli's body as described by the autopsy surgeons and the other eyewitnesses.

Langlois's testimony is also questionable when measured against his opportunity for an accurate view of the event and the details other witnesses provided regarding the shooting scene. McGlone, Wade, Bostock, and Pelser were a short distance from Berardelli when the shooting began, and Nichols was not much farther away. Each of those witnesses provided details of the shooter's and the victims' actions. Their testimony was consistent with one another and corroborated by the autopsy results; Langlois's testimony was not.

Sam Akeke, a shoe worker at Rice & Hutchins, testified at the inquest that, "Two fellows were shooting, it looked like ... two men, each had a revolver and shot the man carrying the money. I got excited and I would not keep looking at them."[23] This testimony, with Akeke's admitted lack of attention to the entire event and his use of the phrase "it looked like" was inconsistent with the autopsy findings as to the path of the fatal bullet as it traveled through Berardelli's body. This witness did not testify at the trial.

The pressure on prosecutor Katzmann to convict the two Italians was enormous. Leading citizens of the Commonwealth and the nation demanded a conviction of both defendants; they feared anything less would rally the radicals to commit further acts of violence. Katzmann needed conclusive physical evidence to eliminate any doubt in the minds of the jurors and the public that the defendants were guilty.

The evidence against Vanzetti was weak. Among other shortcomings, no one identified him as being at the scene of the shooting. Moreover, his .38-caliber revolver could not be connected to any of the six bullets fired into the victims because they were shot with .32-caliber bullets from an automatic. Sacco, however, was vulnerable; he was arrested carrying a Colt .32 automatic. The prosecutor could build a case against Sacco if he tied the fatal bullet to his gun. However, in order to accomplish that, a counterfeit bullet had to be substituted before the trial showing left-twist markings, but it also had to conform to the shape and condition of the fatal bullet.

There is offered here a refinement to the Young and Kaiser theory. Although Bullet III was probably produced and substituted after the grand jury hearing on September 10, 1920, it was *not* produced from Sacco's Colt .32. This author's theory holds that another Colt .32 produced counterfeit Bullet III and that it was substituted for Sacco's gun in order to cover up the plot that produced the counterfeit bullet.

The Sacco Switched Gun Theory

The obvious way to forge Bullet III would be to use Sacco's gun. However, a different approach was necessary. Shortly after the crime, Captain Proctor took possession of Sacco's gun and he maintained custody of it until the Dedham trial, when it was turned over to the sheriff and then to the court.[24] It would have been difficult, if not impossible, for the perpetrators of the plot to gain unrestricted access to Sacco's gun prior to the trial for the time necessary to create a credible counterfeit. Proctor had a falling out with the prosecutor's office. He insisted Katzmann had arrested the wrong men for the South Braintree murders.[25] Katzmann reacted by demoting Proctor as the lead investigator in the case, turning instead to Captain Michael Stewart for that role.[26] He also refused to honor Proctor's five-hundred-dollar expert witness fee for his "consistent with" ballistics opinion.[27] In view of these circumstances, Proctor would likely have been reluctant to cooperate with anyone seeking free rein to experiment with Sacco's gun outside of his presence.

Ballistics technology at the time of the Dedham trial could not establish whether a particular gun shot a particular bullet. Since a Colt .32 automatic always produced left-twist markings, any Winchester .32-caliber bullet shot from any Colt .32 automatic pistol could be linked to Sacco's Colt .32 if the counterfeit was made to look like the fatal bullet.

To that end, the conspirators shaped Bullet III through multiple experimental shots or with a tool and marked its base with a roman numeral III to look like the genuine fatal bullet, except that it had left-twist rather than right-twist markings. The perpetrators made the substitution, the plot held up through the trial, and the jury found Sacco and Vanzetti guilty. It is undisputed that the ballistics evidence was essential to those convictions.

However, an unforeseen event threatened disclosure of the plot. Ballistics technology had advanced by the late fall of 1923. The comparison microscope had entered the scene, and Major Calvin Goddard, a ballistics expert, was in the process of popularizing its use.[28] He claimed it was able to determine, with certainty, whether a particular gun fired a particular bullet.

The comparison microscope then operated as it does now, on the principle that striae (not to be confused with right- or left-twist markings) are produced in bullets from metal rubbing against metal when a cartridge is discharged and its bullet is spun through the barrel.[29] These striae are not visible to the naked eye but are detectable by the comparison microscope. For example, the microscope allows an expert to match one-half of a test bullet fired from a suspected gun with one-half of a fatal bullet. If the striae of the two halves, as seen under the comparison microscope, run together and match so that the two halves appear as a single bullet, then experts claim that the same gun shot both the test bullet and the fatal bullet.

The conspirators would have been concerned that the striae of the test bullets fired through Sacco's genuine gun during the June 18, 1921, Lowell tests would not match the striae in counterfeit Bullet III if the new microscope was used to examine those bullets. If the striae did not match, then a new trial would be inevitable, and the convictions might be set aside. If so, the judicial leaders of Norfolk County would be disgraced, and some of them might even face jail for evidence tampering and obstruction of justice.

Their fears would have increased upon the introduction of this new technology because that was also the time when Thompson requested Judge Thayer to allow one hundred new test shots to be fired through Sacco's gun.[30] Judge Thayer deferred responding to the request, but it was not certain how long he would delay his ruling. Immediate steps had to be taken by the conspirators to protect the plot and its perpetrators.

It is revealing that Judge Thayer first deferred, then later denied, defense counsel's request for one hundred new tests on Sacco's gun. If Bullet III had been shot through Sacco's gun as Katzmann claimed, one would think he and Judge Thayer would have wanted that fact confirmed by the new microscope.

Switching the barrels of the two guns—that is, replacing the barrel in Sacco's gun with the barrel of the Colt .32 that produced Bullet III—was not an answer for the conspirators because that would not give cover to Shell W, the spent Winchester shell supposedly found at the scene and claimed by the prosecution to be the shell to Bullet III. Since the theory holds that Shell W was a plant, it would be necessary for the perpetrators to connect it, too, to Sacco's gun if it was examined under the comparison microscope. Switching barrels would not assure this, since the firing mechanism of a gun, which is not part of the barrel, produces striae on a shell. The striae caused by the firing mechanism on a new test shell had to match the striae on Shell W if the plot was to remain undetected. This could be assured only if the entire gun that produced Bullet III was switched for Sacco's gun.

To avoid detection of the plot, the test bullets and the spent shells shot through Sacco's gun during the Lowell tests, including photographs of those items, if any, would need to be replaced with bullets and shells shot through the Colt .32 that produced counterfeit Bullet III, including photographs of those items.

Several factors would have aided the decision to switch guns. The hand-carved initials "MS" were identification marks made by officer Merle Spear on Sacco's gun at the time of his arrest.[31] Forging those marks on the Colt .32 that produced Bullet III would have been simple. Sacco had not maintained a record of the serial number of his gun, and the serial number was supposedly not taken down by the police the night Sacco was apprehended.[32] Sacco's gun was identified and introduced into evidence at the trial by the MS initials carved on its handle and not by its serial number.[33] It is not credible that the police failed to record the serial number to Sacco's gun that night. This appears to be a contrived afterthought by members of the cabal to remove any evidence of the serial number in the police files in order to facilitate without detection the substitution of a different Colt .32 for Sacco's pistol. With no record of the serial number, it would be difficult to prove that Sacco's gun was switched. This author filed a Freedom of Information request with the city of Brockton, Massachusetts, for a copy of the police report regarding the arrest of Sacco and Vanzetti the night of May 5, 1920. No trace of the police report was found.

The following events provided the perpetrators with the perfect opportunity to carry out their scheme. Following the conviction of Sacco and Vanzetti on July 14, 1921, defense attorney Moore filed a series of motions that prolonged the case at the trial level for several more years. On April 30, 1923, Moore reopened the debate regarding the controversial ballistics evidence offered by the prosecution during the trial, by filing a fifth supplementary motion for a new trial.

On November 8, 1923, the last day of arguments on that motion, Albert Hamilton, one of Sacco's ballistics experts, conducted a courtroom demonstration to illustrate and support Moore's arguments that Sacco's gun was not the source of the fatal bullet.[34] Hamilton used three guns: Sacco's Colt .32, which contained an old and foul, rusty barrel, and two new Colt .32s owned by him, which contained clean, shiny barrels. He would use these guns to explain and demonstrate those parts of a Colt .32 relevant to his affidavits supporting Moore's arguments, including, but not limited to, lands and grooves, marks made by ejectors and firing pins, and the character of flowback.

In the course of the demonstration, Hamilton disassembled the guns, including their barrels. When he completed his demonstration, he reassembled the guns in open court before the eyes of Judge Thayer, the prosecutors, defense attorneys, and others present. All three guns were returned to the evidence custodian for safekeeping, with instructions from Judge Thayer that the guns were not to leave his possession under any circumstances.

While the three guns were in an evidence locker, the conspirators had the opportunity to, and did, covertly engage in the following actions:

- They forged Sacco's Colt .32 by duplicating an "MS" mark on the handle of the Colt .32 that produced counterfeit Bullet III.
- They switched Sacco's gun for the forged Colt .32.
- They substituted the bullets and shells (including related photographs) produced by the forged Colt .32 for the Lowell test bullets, shells, and photographs.
- They artificially treated the barrel of the forged Colt .32 to look like the old and foul, rusty barrel of Sacco's gun. Then they placed that barrel into one of Hamilton's guns, and the shiny, new barrel of Hamilton's gun was placed into the forged Colt .32.

The pieces were now in place for someone to discover a substitution of a barrel that looked like the genuine barrel to Sacco's gun but in reality was the barrel of the Colt .32 that produced counterfeit Bullet III.

* * * *

Later events gave support to the counterfeit bullet claim. On July 25, 1927, attorney Herbert Ehrmann made a presentation on behalf of Sacco and Vanzetti before the advisory committee appointed by Governor Fuller.[35] Ehrmann charged that Bullet III was a forgery. He indicated that each of the four bullets extracted from Berardelli's body was marked by Dr. Magrath with parallel lines. He noted that the lines marking bullets 1, 11, and 1111 were clean and firm, but that the lines marking Bullet III were made by a "[C]lumsier hand and a blunter instrument …"

A firearms expert who examined the four Berardelli bullets in 1927 also noticed that the markings on the base of Bullet III were very different from the markings on the other three bullets.[36] Wilbur Turner, a defense expert, told the advisory committee that there was a "tremendous difference in the markings, as though they were made with a different tool or scratched with a different instrument."

In 1988, Charles Whipple, a former *Boston Globe* editor, revealed that police Sergeant Edward J. Siebolt admitted to him in 1937 that the Commonwealth's ballistics experts had switched Sacco's Colt .32 and that Sacco's gun had gone in and out of police custody a number of times.[37] Sergeant Siebolt's disclosure is an important clue supporting the Sacco switched gun theory. Why would there have been any reason to switch Sacco's gun? It was a Colt .32 that produced left-twist markings like those on counterfeit Bullet III. Sacco's gun had to be switched because it was not the right Colt .32—the one that produced counterfeit Bullet III. In view of the comparison microscope and Thompson's demand for one hundred new test firings of Sacco's gun, the switch of guns became necessary to protect the plot that created counterfeit Bullet III.

Notwithstanding the foregoing, the governor's advisory committee developed its own theory to tie Sacco to the murders through a "matching" analysis:

> The fatal bullet [a Winchester] found in Berardelli's body was of a type no longer manufactured and so obsolete that the defendants' expert witness, James Burns, testified that, with the help of two assistants, he was unable to find such bullets for purposes of experiment; yet the same obsolete type of cartridge [a Winchester] was found in Sacco's pockets on his arrest … Such a coincidence of the fatal bullet and those found on Sacco would, if accidental certainly be extraordinary.[38]

The advisory committee's conclusion was wrong because the so-called obsolete Winchester fatal bullet and the six Winchester cartridges found on Sacco were not obsolete.[39] Defense expert Albert Hamilton had no trouble test firing sixteen of the Winchester bullets claimed to be obsolete in tests he performed in 1923, three years after the South Braintree murders. Even more to the point, the Select Committee on Sacco and Vanzetti of the Massachusetts State Police was chaired by the renowned Dr. Henry C. Lee. In 1983, that committee and its panel of firearms experts performed tests on the Colt .32 that supposedly fired the fatal bullet, with six rounds of those supposedly obsolete Winchester cartridges. In addition, Marshall Robinson, a member of the select committee, had an ample supply of those Winchester bullets in 1983. It is clear that the failure of the defendants' expert Burns and his two assistants to find comparable Winchester cartridges was due to a lack of diligence.

What should have been a winning argument that Bullet III was a counterfeit and that someone switched Sacco's gun was never fully developed during Sacco and Vanzetti's lifetime.

* * * *

Despite the convictions of Sacco and Vanzetti, most of the world has never accepted their guilt.[40] Questions about every aspect of the evidence against them have persisted to this day. The credibility of the prosecution's evidence regarding the authenticity of Bullet III and whether it was fired through Sacco's gun has been the most doubtful. When these doubts are combined with the posttrial discovery of exculpatory evidence concealed by the prosecution, the coercion of prosecution witnesses, and the obvious bias of Judge Thayer, most independent scholars of the case have concluded that a new trial should have been granted.

The history of the ballistics analysis demonstrates that it has never met the test of proof beyond a reasonable doubt. Otherwise, there would not have been, for ninety years, repeated ballistics tests and challenging analyses of this evidence as well as questions about the competency of the prosecution's ballistics experts. A summary of the ballistics evidence presented during the trial, and new evidence uncovered thereafter, makes this point:

1921—The Dedham Trial:[41] The prosecution had the burden to prove beyond a reasonable doubt that Bullet III was the fatal bullet and that it was shot from Sacco's gun. Proctor testified that Bullet III was "consistent with" it having been fired through Sacco's gun, and VanAmburgh testified that he was "inclined to believe" it was fired through Sacco's gun. Defense experts Burns and Fitzgerald were unequivocal that Sacco's gun was not the source of Bullet III.

1923—Fifth Supplementary Motion:[42] During that motion for a new trial, defense experts Hamilton and Gill provided evidence that Bullet III was not shot through Sacco's gun. Prosecution experts VanAmburgh and Merton Robinson provided contrary testimony.

1923—Proctor's Affidavit:[43] In connection with the fifth supplementary motion for a new trial, the defense presented Proctor's affidavit of self-impeachment that his "consistent with" opinion on behalf of the prosecution was not intended to mean that he found any evidence Bullet III was shot through Sacco's gun but only that it was shot through a Colt .32. He deposed that prior to the trial he repeatedly told Katzmann he found no evidence the fatal bullet came from Sacco's gun and that the prosecution prearranged his "consistent with" opinion.

1924—VanAmburgh:[44] VanAmburgh's credentials and his competency as a ballistics expert were dubious, and he was discredited in the 1924 Reverend Dahm murder case. He opined in that case, after using the comparison microscope, that Harold Israel's gun shot the fatal bullets that killed the Reverend Hubert Dahm. District Attorney Homer Cummings (later attorney general of the United States) was suspicious of VanAmburgh's findings, and he commissioned six firearms experts for their opinions. All six unanimously agreed that Israel's gun was not the source of the fatal bullets. The district attorney rejected VanAmburgh's findings and exonerated Harold Israel.

1924—Judge Thayer's Investigation:[45] The judge's so-called investigation to determine whether a disputed gun barrel was the genuine barrel to Sacco's gun resulted in his 1924 decision, which is challenged in chapter 16, "The Rosetta Stone."

1927—The Governor's Advisory Committee:[46] Herbert Ehrmann and William Thompson argued that Bullet III was a counterfeit because the roman numeral III identification markings on the base of that bullet were very different from the identification markings on the base of the other bullets extracted from Berardelli's body. Defense ballistics expert Wilbur Turner agreed with this conclusion.

1927—Major Calvin Goddard:[47] Goddard performed unauthorized tests with the comparison microscope and concluded that Bullet III came from Sacco's gun. Assuming the accuracy of this author's switched gun theory, this is an expected result. It is virtually certain that the results of those tests were improperly shared with the advisory committee and Governor Fuller to the prejudice of Sacco.

Goddard's competency was discredited in another case. Shortly after the tests on Sacco's gun, Goddard was engaged to use the comparison microscope to test a pistol found on Frank Milazzo at the time of his arrest for the murder of Ernest Yorkell. Goddard concluded the bullets that killed Yorkell came from Milazzo's gun. Since Milazzo purchased his gun after Yorkell was murdered, that would have been impossible. A magazine article referred to Goddard's tests as a "complete fiasco." Goddard sued for one hundred thousand dollars claiming a libel. He later withdrew the claim without any recovery.

1944—Anonymous Ballistics Tests:[48] Apparently, the Commonwealth never released the details or results of these tests. Since the ballistics evidence was in its possession and control, it must have been aware of the results of the tests. Unless there is some other explanation for the lack of such information, it would appear that the results were adverse to the interests of the Commonwealth.

1961—The Francis Russell Tests:[49] In yet another attempt to support Sacco's guilt, Russell sponsored Frank Jury and Jac Weller, firearms experts, to perform tests on the supposed Sacco's gun. They opined that Bullet III came from Sacco's gun. Four years before these tests, Jury and Weller, together with Julian Hatcher, a ballistics expert, published a treatise on firearms. In that book they stated, "There can be no doubt that Sacco's pistol fired one cartridge case and one of the fatal bullets." Jury and Weller made the statement before they examined the ballistics trial evidence. As a result, Jury and Weller's independence and impartiality were compromised, and their findings should be discredited.

Moreover, Jury and Weller's competency was challenged. In 1954, a jury convicted Earl Saunders of murdering John Neeluns. Initially, the police found no murder weapon. In 1957, authorities arrested Franklin Wright for armed robbery. While working in the local crime laboratory at that time, Frank Jury tested Wright's gun under the comparison microscope. Jury concluded that Wright's gun was the source of the fatal bullets that killed Neeluns. Saunders was about to be released when an astute chief of police sought and obtained a second opinion that contradicted Jury's results. Jury then conducted a second test and concluded that Wright's pistol was not the source of the fatal bullets. Saunders was not released.

It became common knowledge in 1961 that although Jac Weller offered himself as a firearms expert, he spent most of his time since graduating from college in the real estate and insurance businesses.

1961—Dr. Boyd:[50] Francis Russell also engaged Dr. William Boyd of the Boston University Medical School to test Bullet III for traces of human blood and tissue in an attempt to verify that it was the genuine fatal bullet. The results were negative. They concluded that no traces were found on the bullet because too many years had passed.

1983—The Select Committee:[51] In a continuing effort to resolve sixty years of doubt and conflicting ballistics evidence, a Boston television station sponsored tests on Sacco's gun and Bullet III by a select committee chaired by the renowned forensic scientist, Dr. Henry Lee. The committee issued an ambiguous report on October 11, 1983, as to whether Bullet III and Shell W were genuine and whether they were shot through what was supposedly Sacco's gun.

1985—Professor Starrs:[52] James Starrs, professor of law and forensic science at George Washington University, conducted an exhaustive review and study of the select committee's report. He found that it was inconclusive as to whether Sacco's gun shot Bullet III and whether it was the genuine fatal bullet.

Professor Starrs, however, was not willing to concede Sacco's innocence. He noted that the committee, through the use of the comparison microscope, found that two cartridges discovered at the scene of the crime were manufactured by the same machine that produced six of sixteen cartridges Sacco possessed the night he was arrested. Professor Starrs concluded from this match that Sacco was involved in the crime. Starrs did not take into account that during the war years that same machine produced and probably sold thousands of cartridges throughout New England.

1985—Young and Kaiser:[53] In response to all this activity, support for Sacco's innocence increased. In 1985, researchers Young and Kaiser uncovered new evidence and made a penetrating analysis of the testimony of four witnesses to the shooting. They concluded that Bullet III was a counterfeit and that the prosecution framed Sacco and Vanzetti.

1988—Charles Whipple:[54] Whipple, a former *Boston Globe* editor, revealed a conversation he had as a reporter in 1937 with police Sergeant Edward J. Siebolt. According to Whipple, Siebolt admitted that the police ballistics experts had switched Sacco's gun, but Siebolt indicated that he would deny this if Whipple ever printed it. Siebolt also said that Sacco's gun had gone in and out of police custody a number of times and that the police dismantled it several times.

1996—Kadane and Schum:[55] Joseph Kadane, professor of statistics at Carnegie Mellon University, and David Schum, professor of engineering and law at George Mason University, authored *The Probabilistic Analysis of the Sacco and Vanzetti Evidence*. They developed inference networks and used complex mathematical and statistical formulas to analyze 395 pieces of evidence in the case, including the ballistics evidence. They concluded that Vanzetti was innocent and that the charges against Sacco "were not proven."[56]

The jurors relied heavily on the validity of the ballistics evidence in reaching their guilty verdicts against Sacco and Vanzetti. This stunning catalogue of conflicting and discrediting events regarding that evidence and the competency of the Commonwealth's ballistics experts puts those verdicts under a cloud of reasonable doubt.

CHAPTER 16

THE ROSETTA STONE

In 1799, French troops quartered near Rosetta, a town along the Nile in Lower Egypt, made an extraordinary discovery.[1] They found a stone tablet with inscriptions that appeared in parallel versions of several ancient languages that included Egyptian hieroglyphics and Greek. Scholars translated the Egyptian symbols by matching them to their known Greek counterparts. What had previously been incomprehensible characters was a decree praising King Ptolemy V, and the mysteries of Egypt were unlocked for the modern world. Since then, "Rosetta Stone" has been a metaphor for a clue that solves a mystery.

The Sacco-Vanzetti story is a ninety-year mystery. In response to Cambridge University Professor Lowes Dickinson's query, "Is immortality desirable?" poet Ferris Greenslet responded, "I almost think it is if only to get at the truth of the Sacco-Vanzetti case."[2]

There still remains the need for an answer to the unauthorized substitution of the barrel in Sacco's gun for the barrel of a different Colt .32. Clues to that mystery can be found in Judge Thayer's decision of March 25, 1924 (hereafter the "Decision") which addresses that issue. Critical scholars of the case have essentially ignored the Decision, which I believe is the Rosetta Stone to the entire case.

* * * *

The transcript of the trial and its subsequent proceedings were published by Henry Holt & Company in 1928. Its six thousand pages include stenographic minutes of both trials, as well as related pleadings, motions, affidavits, briefs, and court rulings regarding the Dedham trial.

My discovery of the following Docket Entries in the published record of the Dedham trial is the starting point of my analysis of the Decision.[3] My review of the vast literature covering this case has not found any mention by another author of the conflict between the following Docket Entries and Judge Thayer's Decision:

> 1924 Mar. 25 Decision—In re substitution of gun barrels.

> 1924 Mar. 27 Defts' Appeal to S.J.C. [Supreme Judicial Court] from Decision of date March 25, 1924.

> 1924 Mar. 27 Defts' Notice to Dist. Atty of Appeal from Decision.

> 1924 Mar. 27 Mo. of deft Sacco for ext. of time for filing exceptions in connection with Court's Decision: Dist Attys Assent-Time ext. to April 12, 1924.

> 1924 Mar. 27 Mo. of dft. Vanzetti for ext. of time for filing excep. in connection with Court's Decision: Dist. Atty's Assent—Time ext. to April 12, 1924.

> 1924 Apr. 5 Defts' claim of exceptions.

No further entries regarding the Decision, its appeal to the supreme judicial court, or the appeal papers appear in the Docket sheets. Moreover, the Henry Holt published record of the Dedham case does not contain a copy of the Decision, the appeal papers, or any order or response by the high court regarding an appeal of that Decision. These Docket Entries establish that court authorities initially treated the Decision and its related appeal papers as part of the Sacco-Vanzetti case.

The telltale Docket Entries are clear evidence that someone deliberately excluded the Decision and the appeal papers from the record without any explanation. Whoever was responsible for that obstruction neglected to eliminate the Docket Entries; the only mistake to an otherwise perfect alteration of the record of this case.

Some of these documents may be found among the Massachusetts archives. Several writers have acknowledged the existence of the Decision and Judge Thayer's characterization of it as his investigation into who had switched the barrel of Sacco's gun while it was in safekeeping in an evidence locker.[4] However, none of those writers indicated an awareness of the Docket Entries or the Decision's related appeal papers.

Since Judge Thayer, defense attorney Moore, and prosecutor Williams were present at the hearings that resulted in the Decision, it and the missing appeal papers must have passed through their hands, and they must have participated in, or condoned, the nullification of the appeal of the Decision to the supreme judicial court. Because Judge Thayer and the trial attorneys failed to provide an explanation, it appears likely they reached a sub-rosa agreement that resulted in this aberration.

In an effort to unravel this mystery, I filed a request with Massachusetts' authorities in 2006 to search for and provide me with a copy of the Decision. A copy was found and is set forth in Appendix A. Because my review of the Decision raised many questions, I followed with requests to state authorities for the missing appeal papers. The office of the supreme judicial court found none. However, the state archivist found four of the five appeal documents but did not find any action taken by the high court regarding the appeal or an explanation why the appeal was nullified.

The third appeal document, the district attorney's assent for an extension until April 12, 1924, for Sacco to file his bill of exceptions regarding the appeal, is the most telling.[5] A copy is set forth in Appendix B. The importance of this document rests on Judge Thayer's handwritten order and signature regarding Sacco's extension request to file his bill of exceptions in his appeal in these words: "Time extended until April 12, 1924—Webster Thayer—Justice of the Superior Court—March 27, 1924." A match of the date of this order with Judge Thayer's March 25, 1924, Decision (signed by him on March 21, 1924) reveals a serious conflict.

It is indisputable, by virtue of Judge Thayer's handwritten order of March 27, 1924, that he acknowledged that his Decision and its related appeal papers were a part of the Sacco-Vanzetti case and that an appeal of his Decision to the supreme judicial court was in process. Yet, Judge Thayer asserted otherwise on March 21, 1924, when without any mention of the appeal documents, he stated in his Decision that it related to an investigation initiated on his own motion and that his "investigation had nothing to do with the trial on the indictments before the jury, nor upon motions for new trials ... (Par. 6. Paragraph references relate to the Decision set forth in Appendix A) and that his investigation was not "a public trial or a hearing, within the meaning of the Constitution ..." (Par. 10). Those holdings completely disassociated his Decision from the Sacco-Vanzetti case and thereby eliminated jurisdiction or standing for anyone to appeal his Decision.

Judge Thayer's inconsistent positions, combined with the surreptitious removal or unexplained exclusion of those court documents, reflect an alteration of dates, documents or both in order to achieve the appearance of events different from what had actually occurred.

Like the discovery of the telltale Docket Entries that exposed the existence of the missing appeal papers, the discovery of the third appeal document points to the deliberate manipulation of material court records in a capital murder case. These mendacious actions compelled me to make an in-depth analysis of the Decision.

* * * *

Judge Thayer's Decision began:

> On or about February 13, 1924, District Attorney Williams informed the Court that Capt. VanAmburgh had told him [that] upon examination, the barrel in the Sacco ... pistol ... was not the ... barrel that belonged in the Sacco pistol. After this communication ... counsel for the defendants were notified of this [fact] ... (Par. 1)

The Decision does not disclose who authorized VanAmburgh, the prosecution's ballistics expert, apparently alone and certainly outside the presence of defense counsel, to examine Sacco's gun, which was in safekeeping in an evidence locker. The case was still pending, decisions on five supplementary motions for a new trial were forthcoming, and the case was subject to appeal. Judge Thayer did not provide an explanation for this anomaly, although paragraph 37 of his Decision indicates that VanAmburgh's ex parte examination of the barrel of Sacco's gun followed defense attorney Thompson's second request for one hundred new test firings of that gun. I argue that Thompson's persistent motions to test fire Sacco's gun at a time when the new comparison microscope had been introduced to the police, motivated VanAmburgh to announce his discovery of a substituted barrel in that gun in order to avoid the tests Thompson requested. Thompson's requests for new tests on Sacco's gun were denied by the judge.[6]

Judge Thayer continued:

> On February 15, 1924, two boxes, in the presence of counsel on both sides, and Capt. VanAmburgh and Mr. Hamilton, were opened by the Court ... and therein were found Hamilton's two new Colt automatic pistols, excepting there was an old rusty and foul barrel in one of his new pistols. In the Sacco pistol there was apparently a new barrel, which Mr. Hamilton said was his and that it belonged in his new pistol ... (Par. 4)
>
> But a dispute has arisen between the two experts Capt. VanAmburgh and Mr. Hamilton, as to whether or not the old rusty, and foul barrel found in the Hamilton pistol was the Sacco barrel. (Par. 5)
>
> Capt. VanAmburgh has testified that it was. As soon as the Court learned of this difference of opinion of experts on the substitution of barrels, an investigation was started at once, upon my own initiative and motion. This investigation had nothing to do with the trial on the indictments before the jury, nor upon motions for new trials ...(Par. 6)

Judge Thayer further characterized his investigation:

> [I]t then became my duty to ascertain ... whether or not there had been an innocent substitution of barrels ... or was it a wilful, intentional or planned substitution of barrels, with a view of interfering with and defeating the ends of justice ... If it was an intentional substitution, then it was a fraud upon me ... [and] clearly a contempt of court. (Par. 7)
>
> This investigation, however, was not a contempt proceeding, for no person should be held for contempt ...

without complaint and full hearing upon said complaint ...
(Par. 8)

In my judgement an investigation of whether or not a
fraud had been perpetrated upon the Court by tampering
with exhibits is not a public trial or hearing, within the
meaning of the Constitution ... (Par. 10)

By his own judicial bootstraps, Judge Thayer freed himself
from providing due process to anyone adversely affected by a judicial
determination he might make pursuant to his investigation. His judicial
holdings in paragraphs 6 and 10 posed a bar to any attempt to appeal his
Decision. The judge continued:

I have commenced no contempt proceedings, but have
simply ordered an investigation, with the purpose of
ascertaining whether or not a contempt of court has
been committed. If the Court has the inherent power to
order contempt proceedings on its own motion, certainly
there should be no complaint made because I ordered an
investigation of this most important question, especially,
when we consider the fact that counsel on both sides were
given the fullest opportunity to cross-examine every single
witness called. (Par. 12)

Judge Thayer justified his investigation by comparing it to a contempt
proceeding. He did not go too far with the analogy because that would
have required a complaint against the party committing the contempt,
followed by a public due process hearing, something he would probably
not have wanted. Judge Thayer defended his proceedings even though the
public, the press, and Sacco and Vanzetti were barred from the hearings.[7]
He tried to rationalize this procedure on the grounds that counsel on both
sides had the opportunity to cross-examine all the witnesses. By referring
to "counsel on both sides," Judge Thayer unwittingly acknowledged, by
implication, that the hearings were part of the Sacco-Vanzetti case.

Judge Thayer indicated that counsel for the defendants claimed someone
favorable to the Commonwealth made the gun barrel substitutions, while
the district attorney claimed the substitutions were the act of Hamilton.
The judge held, "But, no matter who made the substitutions ... [t]he

Commonwealth claimed that the barrel found in Hamilton's new pistol was the original Sacco barrel" (Par. 15).

The judge noted that after Hamilton compared the land and groove measurements he had previously made on the genuine Sacco barrel with the current land and groove measurements he made on the disputed barrel, "he [Hamilton] was unqualifiedly of the opinion that the disputed barrel was not the Sacco barrel" (Par. 19).

Judge Thayer responded to Hamilton's claim:

> I noticed particularly that Mr. Hamilton without measurements of the land and grooves and without hesitation [on February 15, 1924], testified that the new barrel taken out of the Sacco pistol was his. Did that act on his part indicate or did it not any knowledge? (Par. 20)

Judge Thayer made an unexpected disclosure:

> On the 12th day of November, 1923, District Attorney Williams filed an affidavit of Captain VanAmburgh, to which was attached a plug gauge. This was done at the request of the Court. A plug gauge is an instrument used to determine the diameter of the bore of pistols. At that time District Attorney Williams, in the presence of Mr. Everett [assistant Clerk of the Court] put said plug gauge in the barrel that was in the Sacco pistol and from his description I am satisfied that the barrel in the Sacco pistol was Hamilton's new barrel and not the Sacco barrel. (Par. 22)

Four days after the close of the oral arguments on the fifth supplementary motion for a new trial and three months before VanAmburgh claimed Sacco's barrel was switched, prosecutor Williams, outside the presence of defense counsel, experimented with and measured the barrel in Sacco's gun, which was supposed to be in safekeeping. Judge Thayer did not explain why defense counsel was not present during this experiment with an exhibit in evidence nor the reason for Williams's actions, particularly since they were "done at the request of the Court."

The next day, Judge Thayer, Clerk Worthington of the superior court, and prosecutor Williams took additional extraordinary actions:

> On November 13, 1923, when Mr. Worthington informed me that the plug gauge had been filed with an accompanying affidavit, I requested him to bring it to my room with the Sacco pistol. At that time the Sacco pistol was fully assembled. I could not disassemble it; so, accompanied by Mr. Worthington, I went to the District Attorney's office and while there in our presence at my request, Mr. Williams disassembled the Sacco pistol and after this was done both Mr. Worthington and I returned to my room, where I experimented with the plug gauge by pushing it into the barrel that had been dismantled from the Sacco pistol. After finishing my examination Mr. Worthington took the plug gauge and the component parts of the disassembled Sacco pistol back to his office. I am satisfied now that this barrel in the Sacco pistol was the new Hamilton barrel. I noticed at that time the barrel was a shade larger than the plug gauge. (Par. 23)

This was another experiment with Sacco's gun, again outside the presence of defense counsel, but this time by Judge Thayer. It is difficult to imagine greater disqualifying conduct than a sitting judge engaging in ex parte experiments with evidence relevant to a case pending before that judge. Moreover, permitting Worthington to return to his office alone, with the component parts of Sacco's pistol, leaves open the opportunity for tampering with evidence. Again, no explanation was given for these actions.

Judge Thayer then found:

> Mr. Hamilton in his affidavit affirmed that the diameter of the Sacco barrel measured .2924, while Captain VanAmburgh affirmed that it measured .3045. It now appears from the testimony of Mr. Hamilton that the diameter of his new barrel in the Sacco pistol measured .0009 greater than Captain VanAmburgh's plug gauge. This being true, the barrel in the Sacco pistol must have

been the Hamilton new barrel, because a plug gauge that measured .3045 could not have been pressed into a barrel that measured .2924. (Par. 24)

Judge Thayer's findings require some interpolation. He indicated that Hamilton measured the diameter of Sacco's barrel at .2924 inch while VanAmburgh measured the diameter of the supposed Sacco barrel at .3045. Then the judge determined that the diameter of Hamilton's new barrel found in what was supposed to be Sacco's pistol was .0009 greater than VanAmburgh's plug gauge that measured .3045. This means that the diameter of Hamilton's new barrel measured .3054 inch. This analysis is consistent with the judge's findings:

> Mr. Hamilton affirmed in his first affidavit on the fifth supplementary motion that the … diameter of the Sacco barrel last spring was .2924, while Captain VanAmburgh said it was .3045. The diameter of the new barrel in the Sacco pistol measured .3054, so that the diameter of the new barrel Mr. Hamilton examined on December 4 at Dedham was .0009 larger than even the VanAmburgh plug gauge. (Par. 47)

Judge Thayer devoted eight paragraphs of the Decision (Pars. 25–32) to suggesting that the security at the Dedham courthouse would have made it virtually impossible for a breach in the custody of the Sacco and Hamilton pistols. This set the stage for Judge Thayer's suggestion that the barrel switch occurred when Hamilton conducted his court demonstration with the three pistols on November 8, 1923.

Judge Thayer wrote:

> [T]he substitution would seem to have been made during the time Mr. Hamilton reassembled them [the three pistols] in Court. But notwithstanding this evidence obtained at Dedham, which seems to me to be convincing, Mr. Hamilton still maintained that the barrel in the new Hamilton pistol is not the Sacco barrel. (Par. 34)

The judge set forth competing arguments as to who had the better motive to substitute a new barrel for Sacco's original barrel. He indicated that counsel for the defendants claimed the Commonwealth's motive for switching the barrels was to defeat the one hundred new test firings requested by defense attorney Thompson (Par. 38).

Then Judge Thayer stated:

> On the other hand the Commonwealth claimed from a consideration of all the evidence that it was a "tricky" substitution by Mr. Hamilton with the ultimate motive of securing a new trial when the substitution was discovered ... and the plan was to have it discovered by him—then the claim would be made that the new barrel in the Sacco pistol was not the Sacco barrel, and then, on that account, a motion for a new trial would be filed. (Par. 39)[8]

The Commonwealth claimed that Captain VanAmburgh's discovery of the switched barrels defeated Hamilton's plan (Par. 40). The Commonwealth's argument was disingenuous. Hamilton would not have obtained a new trial even if he had discovered the substitutions of the barrels rather than VanAmburgh. The prosecution would have made essentially the same responses, and Judge Thayer would have issued essentially the same decision. There was no likelihood Judge Thayer would grant a new trial based on a transparent and obvious scheme to switch barrels.

Judge Thayer continued to assert Hamilton's motive:

> On this question of motive I have already been asked by counsel for the defendant to ... rule as follows:
> "(2) If the foul barrel found in one of Mr. Hamilton's pistols is not the original barrel of the Sacco pistol, then the defendants are entitled to a new trial as a matter of law." (Par. 41)
> Does this request or does it not tend to prove the claim of the Commonwealth that the motive behind the substitution was the securing of a new trial? (Par. 42)

Judge Thayer's claim that Hamilton switched the barrels during his court demonstration (Par. 34) raises significant questions. If Hamilton had switched the barrels on November 8, 1923, why didn't Williams discover the switch on November 12, 1923, when he experimented on and measured the barrel to Sacco's gun (Par. 22)? Indeed, why didn't Judge Thayer make that discovery when he experimented the next day with the Sacco gun barrel (Par. 23)? A shiny new barrel in Sacco's gun that was supposed to have an old, rusty and foul barrel would have been obvious.

During Judge Thayer's so-called investigation, defense counsel called Williams to the stand and cross-examined him on this issue (Par. 43). Williams had no justifiable excuse for not identifying a switch when he examined and measured the Sacco barrel on November 12, 1923. His claim of ignorance of how a plug gauge fits into a barrel is unconvincing (Par. 44). And Judge Thayer never provided an explanation for his own failure to discover Hamilton's supposed barrel switch when he experimented with the disputed barrel on November 13, 1923. Does this establish that the switch of barrels occurred after November 13, 1923, while the guns were in the care and custody of the Commonwealth, or that Williams, Judge Thayer or both were not truthful? Why were District Attorney Williams and Judge Thayer, separately, outside the presence of defense counsel, measuring and experimenting with the barrel to Sacco's gun a few days after final arguments on the fifth supplementary motion for a new trial? Certainly, this presented an opportunity for someone to switch barrels, guns or both.

In Hamilton's affidavit dated October 15, 1923, in support of the fifth supplementary motion for a new trial, he deposed that the diameter of the barrel to Sacco's gun measured .2924 inch.[9] VanAmburgh countered with his affidavit dated October 24, 1923, that the diameter of the barrel to Sacco's gun "is found to be .3045 inch."[10] This discrepancy presents a challenge to reconcile these different barrel measurements.

My theory holds that the conspirators planned to switch Sacco's gun for the forged Colt .32 with its .3045 barrel at a convenient time. After the switch was completed, any test using the comparison microscope would match Bullet III and Shell W with what was supposed to be Sacco's gun, but in reality, was the Colt .32 with a .3045 inch barrel that produced Bullet III.

The opportunity to switch guns probably occurred after November 8, 1923, when Hamilton completed his demonstration using Sacco's gun and his two Colt .32s. Either November 12 or 13, the days that Williams and Judge Thayer experimented with Sacco's gun, would have provided someone with the opportunity to switch Sacco's gun while it was outside the custody of the clerk of the court. The conspirators took an additional step to further the plot and discredit Hamilton. They artificially treated the .3045 inch barrel in the forged pistol to look like the old, rusty, and foul Sacco barrel, placed it in a Hamilton pistol, and transferred the shiny new barrel of that Hamilton pistol into the forged Sacco pistol. This was done as a predicate to the claims Judge Thayer, VanAmburgh, and Williams would make that Hamilton switched the barrels and would serve as a diversion from the real plot.

Hamilton's supposed involvement was advanced by Judge Thayer when he approvingly stated in his Decision that the Commonwealth claimed, "The substitution [of the barrels] would seem to have been made during the time Mr. Hamilton reassembled them [the three guns] in court ..." (Par. 34). Also, this was supported by VanAmburgh when he claimed to have discovered the switch three months later, and Williams charged the switch was:

> a tricky substitution by Mr. Hamilton with the ultimate
> motive of securing a new trial when the substitution ...
> was discovered ... (Par. 39)

Hamilton deposed in an affidavit dated December 6, 1923, that in an effort to reconcile the different barrel measurement in VanAmburgh's October 24, 1923, affidavit from his [Hamilton's] measurement, he visited the Colt Company on December 4, 1923, and sought a plug gauge like the one used by VanAmburgh in his measurement of the disputed barrel.[11] The company denied his request without explanation. Consequently, Hamilton went directly to the Dedham courthouse, and in the presence of Clerk Worthington (Par. 46), he examined VanAmburgh's plug gauge. Hamilton found it was impossible to measure the diameter of the barrel with the gauge rod because it had a reverse taper. Hamilton, apparently based on measurements he made with another instrument, found that, "The present diameter of the [barrel] of the Sacco pistol is .3054" ... .0130" larger than last April [.2924], and is .0009 larger than the large end of the VanAmburgh plug gauge [.3045]" (Par. 46).

Hamilton's affidavit also indicated that on April 6, 1923, the entire interior of the Sacco barrel was foul. However, when he examined that barrel on November 8, 1923, during his court demonstration, the lands for three-quarters of an inch were clean and bright while the grooves were foul. This was in contrast to what he found on December 4, 1923. At that time, when he examined the barrel of what he thought was Sacco's gun, the entire interior of the lands and grooves were free of fouling and were bright and shiny (Par. 46).

This suggests that someone had tampered with Sacco's barrel before Hamilton examined it on November 8, 1923, causing the lands (but not the grooves) for three-quarters of an inch to be clean, bright, and shiny. During Hamilton's cross-examination by Judge Thayer described below, Hamilton explained how this could have happened. He indicated that if someone attempted to wedge VanAmburgh's .3045 plug gauge into Sacco's .2924 barrel at just a fraction of an angle and pressed it against the metal in a wiggly motion, the plug gauge would make the lands shiny (Par. 49—first two questions by the court). This is consistent with the argument that on November 8, 1923, the barrel to Sacco's genuine gun measured .2924 inch, and the Colt .32 that produced Bullet III, with a .3045-inch barrel, was substituted later for Sacco's gun.

Judge Thayer's investigation became a game of "gotcha." Following the cross-examination of Williams (Pars. 43–44), Judge Thayer stated, "Now, it's only fair to the Commonwealth to put the same test to Mr. Hamilton"(Par. 45).

With this introduction, Williams cross-examined Hamilton for several pages of the transcript, followed by an intense cross-examination by Judge Thayer covering five more pages. The purpose of these interrogations was to show that Hamilton's claimed failure to recognize someone had switched the barrel to Sacco's pistol when he examined it on December 4, 1923, was not truthful. Judge Thayer attempted to establish that Hamilton knew the barrel in Sacco's gun had been switched, and his effort to hide the switch showed his consciousness of guilt (Pars. 45–55).

Hamilton answered why he did not recognize a switch of the barrel to Sacco's gun when he examined it on December 4, 1923. He explained that he went to the clerk's office on that day to examine the plug gauge used by VanAmburgh to measure the Sacco barrel and that he had only that purpose in mind. He said he was working on many other matters, so he focused only on that limited purpose and assumed the correct barrel was in Sacco's gun. Hamilton admitted he noticed that the entire barrel was bright and shiny on December 4, but he concluded that the judge, or some court personnel, had cleaned the barrel, even though he admitted that would have been unusual. He said he disclosed that matter to Mr. Thompson (Pars. 49–54).

Hamilton's failure to disclose that someone switched Sacco's barrel, if he actually knew otherwise, completely undercuts the prosecution's argument that it was Hamilton's plan to discover the switched barrels in order to obtain a new trial for Sacco (Par. 39). There was no reason for Hamilton not to have disclosed a switch of the barrels at that time if he had been responsible for it and if he intended to discover his own switch of the barrels and use that to gain a new trial as the prosecution claimed. This argues in favor of Hamilton's claim that he was not aware the barrels had been switched when he examined Sacco's gun on December 4, 1923.

At this point, we can draw some conclusions and reconcile the various barrel measurements. First, the different measurements of the Sacco barrel related to the following three different barrels:

- The shiny barrel of one of Hamilton's new guns: VanAmburgh found this barrel in what was supposed to be Sacco's pistol. Its diameter measured .3054 inch.
- The disputed barrel: This barrel was found in one of Hamilton's new pistols. It was artificially treated to look like the old, rusty, and foul barrel of Sacco's gun. It was the barrel of the Colt .32 that produced counterfeit Bullet III. Its diameter measured .3045 inch.
- The genuine barrel to Sacco's gun: This barrel was measured by Hamilton on April 6, 1923, and in October 1923 with a diameter of .2924 inch. This barrel was disposed of and replaced by the disputed barrel. The conspirators switched the disputed barrel and the shiny barrel as a distraction and to create a sham argument that blamed Hamilton for the barrel switches.

Second, there is further support that the prosecution's claim that Hamilton switched barrels during his court demonstration on November 8, 1923, does not ring true. In his Decision, Judge Thayer stated that from District Attorney Williams's description of the measurements he made on November 12, 1923, of the barrel in Sacco's gun:

I am satisfied that the barrel in the Sacco pistol was Hamilton's barrel and not the Sacco barrel. (Par. 22)

If that finding was so obvious to Judge Thayer, why didn't Williams recognize that fact on November 12, 1923, when he was measuring the barrel to Sacco's gun, and charge Sacco's barrel was switched?

Even more telling is Judge Thayer's conclusion set forth in his Decision following his examination of the barrel in Sacco's gun on November 13, 1923:

> I am satisfied now that this barrel in Sacco's pistol was the new Hamilton barrel. *I noticed at that time* [i.e., November 13, 1923] the barrel was a shade larger than the plug gauge. (Par. 23) (Emphasis added)

Why didn't Judge Thayer immediately open an inquiry on November 13, 1923, into why, and by whom the barrel to Sacco's gun had been switched, particularly since he noticed then that the barrel in Sacco's gun was a shade larger than the plug gauge (.3045)?

These two findings were intended to support the prosecution's claim that Hamilton made the barrel substitutions during his November 8, 1923, court demonstration. However, the findings suggest the opposite.

Judge Thayer rejected Hamilton's claim that the disputed barrel had been artificially treated to make it look like Sacco's old, rusty, and foul barrel (Pars. 56–57). This could have been an easy matter for the judge to resolve credibly. He could have called an independent ballistics expert to either verify or reject Hamilton's claim.

Instead, Judge Thayer made Hamilton's claim appear incredible:

> Mr. Hamilton further testified that this artificial treatment was a very bad job. And he was asked why, whoever did it, did not get an old rusty, foul Colt automatic barrel of .32 caliber, for substitution, rather than do a bad job by artificially treating a new barrel so as to make it look like the old Sacco barrel. Mr. Hamilton said he could not say why. (Par. 57)

Hamilton's inability to provide an answer on the spot gave the judge justification to quickly reject the claim. Judge Thayer's question is answered by the Sacco switched gun theory: That particular Colt .32 barrel had to be made to look like the old, rusty, and foul barrel to Sacco's gun because it belonged to the Colt .32 that produced counterfeit Bullet III. And that barrel had to be connected to, and eventually find its way into, what everyone was supposed to believe was Sacco's gun. This was accomplished when the judge found the disputed barrel to be the genuine barrel to Sacco's gun and ordered it to be placed into what he claimed was the genuine Sacco gun (Par. 73), but which in reality was the forged Colt .32 that produced Bullet III.

Finally, switching the barrels was made to look like a clumsy and "tricky" attempt by Hamilton to gain a new trial for Sacco and Vanzetti, making it less likely for anyone to discover the real plot.

Judge Thayer advanced a specious argument to justify his unwillingness to recognize the evidence supporting Hamilton's claim that the disputed barrel was not the genuine barrel to Sacco's gun:

> [A]ssuming that the disputed barrel is not the Sacco barrel, what effect would that have upon the motions for new trials? In my judgment none. This is so because all that remained for me to do was to file my decisions upon the motions for new trials. Suppose somebody had broken into the clerk's office and had stolen all of those exhibits. That would not mean the granting of a new trial. This is so because there had been a full trial before a jury on the indictments, and verdicts were rendered by the jury. And ... even the stealing of all the firearm exhibits would not as matter of law affect the verdicts already rendered by the jury ... (Par. 67)

Judge Thayer's willingness to assume that even if the disputed barrel was not the genuine Sacco barrel and would therefore not affect the verdicts, smacks of an unintended admission that the disputed barrel was not the genuine barrel of Sacco's gun.

Moreover, Judge Thayer's example comparing stolen exhibits in a theoretical case involving a noncontroversial verdict with a switch of the gun barrel of the murder weapon, the most crucial evidence in the Sacco-Vanzetti capital murder case, which was on appeal, is not a valid comparison.

Judge Thayer reviewed an additional relevant matter. It related to a dispute as to whether a photograph of the muzzle to Sacco's gun taken by Mr. Eckman in October 1923 and a photograph of the muzzle of Sacco's gun taken by Mr. Turner in March 1924 were of the same barrel.

Hamilton and Turner said they were not; VanAmburgh and Eckman said they were photographs of the same barrel. Hamilton claimed that the conspirators used the Eckman photograph as a model to treat the disputed barrel to look like the old, rusty, and foul barrel of Sacco's gun (Pars. 68–70).

Judge Thayer resolved this issue in a most unscientific way:

> [A]ll I can say is that I can only use to the best of my ability the eyes that I have been endowed with; and using them, with a strong magnifying glass … I am of the opinion that the Eckman photographs and the Turner photographs were taken of the same object, and that object was the Sacco barrel. (Par. 71)

Following that questionable finding by Judge Thayer, acting as an expert, he entered his finding regarding the disputed barrel:

> I find that the old rusty and foul barrel that was in Hamilton's new pistol is the original Sacco barrel and the new barrel in the Sacco pistol belongs in Mr. Hamilton's new pistol. It is therefore ordered that these two barrels be transferred to their respective pistols. (Par. 73)

* * * *

In 1946, VanAmburgh provided an interesting footnote to Hamilton's three-gun court demonstration of November 8, 1923, the antecedent to Judge Thayer's Decision of March 25, 1924.

VanAmburgh indicated that he had visited Judge Thayer in 1932 and asked the judge what had happened on November 8, 1923, when the barrels had been switched. VanAmburgh reported that Judge Thayer indicated that after Hamilton reassembled the three guns, he turned Sacco's pistol over to the court and proceeded to leave with his two pistols. The judge ordered Hamilton to stop and said, "Hand me your pistols." Hamilton did so, and the judge impounded them along with Sacco's pistol.

VanAmburgh claimed that Judge Thayer said:

I have thanked God many times since that I did so. And then the astounding discovery made later that the original barrel in the Sacco pistol was missing and an entirely different barrel substituted for it. [12]

The effect of VanAmburgh's story, twenty-three years after the event, provided belated support for the claim that Hamilton was responsible for switching the barrels—a theme repeated throughout the Decision and echoed by the Commonwealth's allies for years thereafter.

VanAmburgh's report about Judge Thayer's recollections appears contrived. Judge Thayer had never previously indicated the barrel to Sacco's gun was missing. He claimed it had been switched for the barrel of one of Hamilton's guns; he specifically found, "that the old rusty and foul barrel that was in Hamilton's new pistol is the original Sacco barrel ..." (Par. 73).

VanAmburgh was fully aware of what happened on November 8, 1923. He was intimately involved with the fifth supplementary motion for a new trial, which was argued that day, because he submitted three important affidavits in support of the Commonwealth's position, and he would have known of the testimony and evidence presented during Judge Thayer's so-called investigative hearings regarding the events of that day. The Decision specifically indicates that at all relevant times, "Mr. Hamilton was present at all hearings, and so was Capt. VanAmburgh ..." (Par. 13). VanAmburgh would not have needed to ask Judge Thayer what happened on November 8, 1923. He already knew what happened that day. However, more important is the fact that Judge Thayer did not mention the incident in his Decision—an indication of the insignificance of the event in his mind or that VanAmburgh's 1946 story about his 1932 conversation with Judge Thayer was a fabrication, and perhaps a cover, for his own involvement in the events related to switching Sacco's gun.

* * * *

Judge Thayer engaged in conflicting executive and judicial functions in this matter. He acted as a one-man grand jury when he opened an investigation into the substitution of the gun barrels; he acted as a prosecutor when he examined witnesses and sought evidence to determine who was responsible for the barrel substitutions; he acted as an expert when he opined on the Eckman and Turner photographs; and he acted as a judge when he determined that the disputed barrel was the genuine barrel to Sacco's gun. He ruled that his investigation was not a hearing under the Constitution and not part of the Sacco-Vanzetti trial, thus barring any appeal of his Decision. Can one man constitutionally carry out such a combination of conflicting functions?

My discovery of the overlooked Docket Entries and the third appeal document demonstrates that court authorities acted improperly. Those actions alone place a cloud of doubt over Judge Thayer's Decision. Doubt turns to certainty when it is determined that Judge Thayer's investigation went beyond the limits of his judicial authority.

A recent federal case involving a trial judge's investigation into what he claimed was improper conduct in the United States Attorney's office is instructive. The Seventh Circuit Court of Appeals *In The Matter of: United States of America*, 398 F. 3d 615 (2005), outlined the limits of judicial authority relevant to a situation substantially similar to the situation faced by Judge Thayer:

> We conclude the inquiry is inappropriate and must cease; ... Judges often are tempted to seek a larger role in the conduct of litigants that appear frequently before them ... But temptation must be resisted in order to maintain separation between executive and judicial roles ... the judge must turn the [investigation] over to a prosecutor rather than assume an inquisitorial role inappropriate to the Judicial Branch ... Our legal system does not contemplate an inquisitorial role for federal judges.

To show the serious nature of the matter, the appeals court entered a sharp rebuke to the district court judge:

> [T]he district court is directed to close its investigation ... The Office of Professional Responsibility [of the Justice Department] is free to proceed as it chooses, but it need not investigate at the behest of the Judicial Branch—nor are its findings ... to be reported to the Judicial Branch. This is a matter for the Executive Branch to handle initially using its own judgment ...

The case admittedly was not binding precedent on Judge Thayer, since the court decided this case many years after the events of March 25, 1924. However, it pronounces concepts of constitutional separation of powers—that the judicial branch is separate from the executive branch—that were applicable to the Massachusetts judicial and executive branches of government in 1924 under its constitution.[13]

Judge Thayer should have turned the inquiry regarding the substitution of the barrels over to the executive branch—to a prosecutor who, with a properly impaneled grand jury, could make an independent investigation of the matter and take appropriate action. Under the circumstances, Judge Thayer's finding that the disputed barrel was the original barrel to Sacco's gun should be rejected as beyond the scope of his judicial authority and because it was wrong.

* * * *

Nearly a century has passed since the South Braintree murders. The usual closure that follows a jury-produced guilty verdict is absent in this case because of the prosecutorial and judicial misconduct that took place during the trial. Posttrial disclosures and new evidence and analyses contrary to guilt have added to the impropriety of the jury's verdicts.

Absolute certainty of Sacco's and Vanzetti's innocence may have rested with only eight people: Sacco, Vanzetti, and the six culprits who committed the crime. Their voices from the past have spoken, leading to virtual certainty that the South Braintree murders were the work of the following six members of the Morelli gang, all of whom, although under indictment, were available at that time and in need of money for bail and legal fees:

- Frank "Butsey" Morelli admitted to Vincent Teresa that Morelli gang members were responsible for the South Braintree robbery and murders.[14]
- Joe Morelli, Sacco's look-alike, admitted to his cellmate Emil Moller on a number of occasions that the Morelli gang had committed the South Braintree murders and robbery.[15]
- Celestino Medeiros, a confessed participant in the crime and a member of the Morelli gang, identified his

confederates in ways that clearly pointed to the Morelli gang as the culprits.[16]

- Steve "the Pole" Benkosky, a member of the Morelli gang, precisely fit the description of the driver of the getaway car as provided by the sworn testimony of many witnesses, some for the prosecution, others for the defense.[17]

- A few days before the crime, Inspector Jacobs saw Mike Morelli in New Bedford, driving a Buick touring car that fit the description of the getaway car found two days after the murders.[18]

- Joe Morelli implicated Tony Mancini, a convicted murderer and member of the Morelli gang, of participating in the South Braintree crimes. Mancini possessed a foreign made automatic that used .32-caliber bullets like the bullets shot into the victims. Moreover, the five bullets not in controversy, that were shot into the victims, were fired from a 7.65 millimeter foreign made gun that put right-twist markings on bullets fired through its barrel.[19]

Identifying the Morelli gang as the killers was only one strand of many that wove a pattern of a deliberate frame-up of Sacco and Vanzetti.

The evidence that Bullet III was a counterfeit and that Sacco's gun was switched, as set forth in Chapter 15: The Ballistics Controversy, explains the otherwise inexplicable conduct of assistant prosecutor Williams and Judge Thayer, disclosed in the judge's own words in his March 25, 1924, Decision.

The weak identification of Sacco and Vanzetti as the killers, the prosecutorial misconduct, and the prejudice of Judge Thayer, together with the following specific actions, give further support to the claim that the Commonwealth contrived a case against the two Italians:

1. The police suppressed the report regarding fingerprints found on the getaway car.[20] If the report had revealed the prints of either Sacco or Vanzetti on that car, such information would certainly have been revealed. Since the prosecution did not release the report, it means that Sacco's and Vanzetti's prints were not on the getaway car. This was exculpatory evidence that should have been released to the defendants.

2. Prosecutor Katzmann never made the inquest minutes of April 17, 1920, or the grand jury testimony of September 10, 1920, available to the defense lawyers during the Dedham trial.[21] He argued that the inquest minutes were private and available only to the Commonwealth. The minutes contained testimony supporting the argument that one bandit shot all six bullets extracted from the bodies of Parmenter and Berardelli from the same gun. Information obtained during the inquest was also consistent with other evidence that the gun used by Berardelli's killer put right-twist markings on bullets. Sacco's Colt .32 put left-twist markings on bullets.

3. According to the grand jury minutes, Officer Michael Connolly's testimony at the Dedham trial that Sacco and Vanzetti tried to draw their weapons when arrested, was false.[22] This also showed subornation of perjury by the prosecution.

4. Captain Michael Stewart wrote a memorandum dated February 18, 1921, released by the state police in 1977.[23] The memo established that the revolver found on Vanzetti was not Berardelli's revolver, as the prosecution claimed in its attempt to connect Vanzetti to the crime. The Commonwealth suppressed the memo for over fifty years—an obstruction of justice.

5. Prosecutor Harold Williams's trial notebook, dated January/February 1921, identified nine matters that might suggest a frame-up of the defendants.[24] The notebook also established that Bostock found only three spent shells at the scene of the crime, not four as the prosecution claimed. The prosecution connected the fourth shell, surely a Winchester, to Sacco because of the Winchester cartridges found on him when he was arrested. The Commonwealth suppressed this information until 1977, when it was released to the public. To have permitted Bostock to testify as he did, while the prosecution possessed contrary evidence in its trial notebook, is a clear case of perjury and obstruction of justice.

6. Captain Proctor's repeated statements to prosecutor Katzmann that he found no evidence Bullet III was shot through Sacco's gun before Proctor issued his misleading "consistent with" ballistics opinion consisted of two offenses: suppression of those exculpatory statements and subornation of perjury.[25]

7. Finally, Fred Loring's testimony that he found Sacco's cap next to Berardelli's body right after the shooting was proven false six years after the trial.[26] It bears the mark of perjured testimony fostered by the prosecution.

* * * *

The Massachusetts institutions of justice failed Sacco and Vanzetti in their primary responsibility to provide them, as they were required to provide all defendants, with a fair trial. This case teaches that in times of national crisis, persons of alien origin who express unpopular political views are vulnerable to abuse from an all-powerful government.

Lord Acton, nineteenth-century British historian and philosopher, warned, "Power tends to corrupt and absolute power corrupts absolutely." His admonitions were echoes of the poet Shelley, "Power like a desolating pestilence, pollutes whatever it touches."

The Puritan-bred leaders of Massachusetts instituted a judicial system that placed all the power of the law in a criminal case into the hands of one trial judge, subject only to the supreme judicial court finding an abuse of his discretion, an abuse that court could not find even when Judge Thayer sat in judgment of his own bias and prejudice.

From the shame of the Sacco-Vanzetti trial, the Massachusetts legislature, some nine years after their execution, amended its criminal procedures in ways that would have provided the two Italians with a new trial if such legislation had been in effect in 1920.

The leaders of Massachusetts, who stood by for years and sanctioned a judicial system that allowed the death penalty to be imposed and carried out as it was in this case, were collectively guilty of a tragic miscarriage of justice. But that collective guilt cannot absolve the individual guilt of the police and the prosecutors who manipulated testimony, fabricated evidence, concealed exculpatory information, and suborned perjury, all of which led to the conviction and execution of the two Italians.

A special place in the dark recesses of injustice should be reserved for prosecutors Frederick Katzmann and Harold Williams and for Judge Webster Thayer as the persons primarily responsible for the tragedy of Nicola Sacco and Bartolomeo Vanzetti, two innocent men, whose ashes remain an indelible blot upon the Constitution's promise of due process for all persons in America.

"A mistake of justice is a tragedy. Deliberate injustice is an infamy."[27]

Bartolomeo Vanzetti

EPILOGUE

THE JUDGMENT OF HISTORY

The execution of Sacco and Vanzetti on August 23, 1927, brought finality to the Dedham case and to the lives of the two Italians but not to whether they were guilty or innocent and whether they received a fair trial. Historians, sociologists, lawyers, and literati continue to argue over these issues. New evidence disclosed in posttrial proceedings, as well as new information and analyses since the executions, have fostered much of the debate.

The judgment of history stands in opposition to the guilt of Sacco and Vanzetti despite the jury's guilty verdicts, Judge Thayer's confirmatory rulings of guilt, the affirmation of Judge Thayer's rulings by the Massachusetts Supreme Judicial Court, the advisory committee's concurrence of guilt, Governor Fuller's denial of clemency, the refusal of federal officials—including members of United States Supreme Court and President Coolidge—to intervene, and the initial acceptance and acclaim of the guilty verdicts by a majority of the press and the public.

This epilogue is a representative summary of the leading books, plays, articles, poetry, and art that have expressed the judgment of history on the Sacco-Vanzetti affair. It is by no means a complete collection of the vast amount of legal critiques, literature, and art on this subject. Professors Louis Joughin and Edmund Morgan, in *The Legacy of Sacco and Vanzetti*, have identified seven categories of this material in their extensive bibliography that references one hundred forty-four poems, six plays, eight novels, hundreds of books, journal articles, and newspaper stories published from 1920 to 1948. Professor Richard Newby, in *Kill Now, Talk*

Forever: Debating Sacco and Vanzetti, has assembled a catalogue of many such materials, and he has added more through 2006.

The conservative *Boston Herald*, in F. Lauriston Bullard's Pulitzer Prize editorial of October 26, 1926, reversed its long-held view of the guilt of the two Italians and foreshadowed the involvement of many civil rights activists:

> As months have merged into years and the great debate over this case has continued, our doubts have solidified slowly into convictions, and reluctantly we have found ourselves compelled to reverse our original judgment. We hope the Supreme Judicial Court will grant a new trial on the basis of new evidence not yet examined in open court ... We have read the full decision [of] Judge Webster Thayer ... and we submit that it carries the tone of the advocate rather than the arbitrator ... (Reprinted with permission of the Boston Herald.)

Professor Felix Frankfurter awakened the public's conscience to the Sacco-Vanzetti case in an article published in the *Atlantic* in the spring of 1927. He criticized Judge Webster Thayer's and prosecutor Frederick Katzmann's conduct during the Dedham trial. The article was followed by his book published a few months later.[1] In that year, two other authors stirred the public's interest: Eugene Lyons published *The Life and Death of Sacco and Vanzetti* and John Dos Passos released *Facing the Chair*.

Lyons and Dos Passos were strong advocates for the two Italians, but the Frankfurter exposé was more powerful and acted as a catalyst for intellectuals and civil rights advocates to take notice that the Commonwealth of Massachusetts was prepared to execute two immigrant workers whose political beliefs differed from those of the establishment.

Frankfurter's criticism of Judge Thayer and Katzmann, along with the changed views of the *Boston Herald*, created deep fissures in the wall of guilt the establishment had built around Sacco and Vanzetti. The supporters of the two Italians were no longer limited to a cadre of defense committee members and a ragtag group of Italian immigrants mixed with an assortment of ethnic workers and impecunious radicals. Frankfurter's charges and cogent arguments pointing to a tragic injustice jarred many from the educated and upper levels of society. His arguments spilled over into news accounts, journals, and law reviews. Many responses to Frankfurter's views were positive. Anatole France, author and Nobel laureate, made a plea to save Sacco and Vanzetti for the honor of America.[2]

The debate moved into high gear on April 25, 1927, when John Henry Wigmore, dean of the Northwestern University Law School, attacked Professor Frankfurter's arguments in a series of letters published in the *Boston Transcript*. Wigmore, an 1883 graduate of the Harvard Law School, was the country's foremost scholar on the law of evidence and a supporter of the Commonwealth's case.[3]

Frankfurter responded to Wigmore's charges, and their differences raged for several weeks amid headlines in the *Transcript* and leading newspapers. The debate became national in scope and brought the Sacco and Vanzetti story to millions beyond New England.

In several instances, Wigmore had not carefully reviewed the record of the case. Instead, he relied on misstatements made by Judge Thayer. When challenged by Frankfurter, Wigmore warned that if Massachusetts accepted Frankfurter's criticism, it would deserve the contamination of its judiciary by radicals.

Wigmore's arguments were a disappointment to A. Lawrence Lowell, president of Harvard, who had been the leading member of the governor's advisory committee that confirmed the guilt of the two Italians. After the executions, Lowell wrote to Chief Justice Taft of the United States Supreme Court that it seemed Wigmore had nothing favorable to say about the decision of the Massachusetts high court confirming the death sentences.

In retrospect, Wigmore's entry into the fray looks suspiciously like it was orchestrated by Judge Thayer, or perhaps by Lowell, to offset the momentum of Frankfurter's article and book. In any event, the debate brought unfavorable worldwide attention to how Massachusetts treated immigrant workers who espoused unpopular political views.

In the midst of the growing debate, noted American commentators spoke. On August 5, 1927, Heywood Broun, columnist with the *New York World*, said: "It is not every prisoner who has the President of Harvard University throw on the switch ... at least the fish peddler and his friend the factory hand ... will die at the hands of men in dinner coats ..."

Walter Lippman followed on August 19, 1927, and wrote in the *New York World* that "The Sacco-Vanzetti case is ... full of doubt ... so pervasive, so unsettling, that it cannot be denied and it cannot be ignored.[4] No man ... should be put to death where so much doubt exists." Shortly before the executions, poet Brent Dow Allison published verses titled

"For the Honor of Massachusetts."[5] On the day of the execution, Edna St. Vincent Millay saw to the first printing of her poem "Justice Denied in Massachusetts."[6] Both poems were sympathetic to Sacco and Vanzetti.

Following the executions, new information burst on the scene. A compelling disclosure of Vanzetti's innocence of the Bridgewater attempted holdup surfaced in the October and November 1928 issues of the *Outlook and Independent* magazine. Frank Silva (alias Paul Martini) confessed that he, together with three other gangsters, were responsible for the attempted holdup of the L. Q. White Shoe Company on Christmas Eve, 1919, and that Vanzetti had no part in that crime.

Efforts were made to debunk the Silva confession, principally because he was paid for making it, but according to F. R. Bellamy, in his article in the same issue of the *Outlook*, Silva's story had too many statements of fact to be so easily dismissed. He concluded that Vanzetti did not commit the Bridgewater crime.

Presidential politics provides an interesting footnote to the Sacco and Vanzetti affair.[7] Shortly before Governor Fuller denied clemency for the two Italians, rumors swirled in the community that the governor was going to grant a new trial. Then, President Calvin Coolidge announced in late summer 1927 that he would not seek a second term for the presidency. Governor Fuller followed that announcement with a tough law-and-order stand by denying Sacco and Vanzetti's petition for clemency, just as Coolidge took a tough law-and-order stand against the Boston police strike that propelled him to national prominence in 1920. Predictably, Governor Fuller's supporters placed his name into nomination for President at the 1928 Republican convention. The delegates rejected his ambition, stating, "The Republican party cannot afford to spend the summer debating the Sacco-Vanzetti case."[8]

In 1928, Upton Sinclair, the indefatigable aspirant of social justice, published *Boston*, a historical novel about the Sacco and Vanzetti case. Remarkably accurate as to the facts of the case, Sinclair expressed his thoughts:

> No more would Boston be the place of the tea-party and the battle of Bunker Hill; Boston would be the place where Sacco and Vanzetti were put to death!
> ... A hundred million toilers knew that two comrades had died for them. Black men, brown men, yellow men— men of a hundred nations and a thousand tribes—the

prisoners of starvation, the wretched of the earth—
experienced a thrill of awe. It was the mystic process of
blood-sacrifice, by which through the ages salvation has
been brought to mankind!

... To a hundred million groping, and ten times as
many still in slumber, the names of Sacco and Vanzetti
would be the eternal symbols of a dream, identical with
civilization itself, of a human society in which wealth
belongs to the producers of wealth, and the rewards of
labor are to the laborers ... [9] (Reprinted with permission of www.
BentleyPublishers.com.)

The Sacco-Vanzetti story soon found its way to theater. *Gods of the Lightning*, a dramatization of the suffering of the two Italians, made its appearance in New York in late 1928. Written by Maxwell Anderson and Harold Hickerson, the play fictionalized the Dedham trial with composite characters representing Sacco and Vanzetti and other participants in the case.

Professor Louis Joughin argued that the central idea of the play was to show that the Sacco-Vanzetti tragedy reflected "the inherent cruelty of man-made institutions."[10] Joughin provides an insight into the lingering animosity toward Sacco and Vanzetti among Boston officials. He noted that when the producers of the play made plans to perform *Gods of the Lightning* in Boston, the License Division sent the manuscript to the corporation counsel for an opinion. Boston's counsel replied that the play was "anarchistic and treasonable," an attempt to discredit Massachusetts because of the Sacco-Vanzetti trial.[11] He viewed the play's attacks as dishonorable.

The year after the execution of the two Italians followed with a publication of importance to their story—*The Letters of Sacco and Vanzetti*. During their seven-year ordeal, Sacco and Vanzetti wrote many letters in English, in addition to letters they wrote in Italian that were not included in the publication. Marion Denman Frankfurter, wife of the professor, and Gardner Jackson, a publicist and long-time supporter of the two Italians, compiled, organized, and edited *The Letters*. They were careful to limit their work to deciding which of the many missives should be included and which portions were redundant or immaterial. They also made minor grammatical corrections they deemed necessary for a reader's better understanding. Jackson, heir to a fortune, devoted his life trying to prove Sacco and Vanzetti innocent. Marion Frankfurter was equally dedicated to establishing their innocence. The original effort by Marion Frankfurter and Jackson was followed by the republication of *The Letters* in 1997.

Richard Polenberg's introduction to the republication of *The Letters* provides an insight into Governor Fuller's reaction to that book.[12] Polenberg reported that after Governor Fuller had completed his term of office, he followed the tradition of walking down the many steps of the capitol building to the sidewalk below to bid farewell to an awaiting crowd of loyalists. Jackson was among the assembled crowd, carrying a copy of *The Letters*. He offered it to the governor, who was not aware of its contents. When the governor recognized what it was, he threw it to the ground with contempt.

The year 1929 and the early 1930s brought forth the publication of additional books and plays sympathetic to Sacco and Vanzetti: Nathan Asch's *Pay Day*, Jeanette Mark's *Thirteen Days*, Samuel Behrman's *Rain from Heaven*, Lola Ridge's *Three Men Die* (in "Dance of Fire"), Bernard DeVoto's *We Accept with Pleasure*, Fredrick Allen's *Only Yesterday*, John Dos Passos's *U.S.A.*, Pierre Yrondy's *Seven Years of Agony*, and James Thurber's and Eugene Nugent's *The Male Animal*.

In 1931, Osmond K. Fraenkel, counsel for the newly created American Civil Liberties Union, edited the transcript in *The Sacco-Vanzetti Case*. The book presented the Commonwealth's charges and the defense's responses with relevant portions of testimony and Fraenkel's commentaries.

In 1932, artist Ben Shahn created twenty-three gouaches relating to the Dedham trial. Shahn declared the executions were "a crucifixion itself—right in front of my eyes."[13]

Sylvester Gates, a former Frankfurter pupil and author of the biography of Sacco and Vanzetti for the *Dictionary of American Biography*, reviewed the Sacco-Vanzetti case in the December 9, 1931, edition of the *New Republic*. He wrote, "The authorities, judicial and executive alike, remained obdurate to the end, inflicting on the two men that irrevocable sentence which has made Vanzetti in his prophetic words 'a vanquished man but a formidable shadow.'"

If Sacco and Vanzetti were innocent, who were the culprits responsible for the South Braintree murders? Herbert Ehrmann, appellate counsel for the two Italians, answered in 1933 with the publication of *The Untried Case: The Sacco-Vanzetti Case and the Morelli Gang*.

Ehrmann made a convincing argument that members of the Morelli gang of Providence, Rhode Island, were, as Celestino Medeiros implied, the perpetrators of the South Braintree murders and that Sacco and Vanzetti were not involved. So convincing was Ehrmann's effort, that Massachusetts Governor Joseph B. Ely, successor to Governor Alvan Fuller, wrote Ehrmann that he had some doubt as to the guilt of Sacco and Vanzetti, but after reading his book, he had no doubt of their innocence.[14] That response is particularly impressive since Governor Ely was formerly a leading prosecutor in Massachusetts.

Initially, Ehrmann's new book was not well received in all quarters. Professor E. M. Morgan, in the January 1934 *Harvard Law Review*, thought it failed to furnish proof of the Morelli gang's guilt, as the author promised. Given an opportunity to review the evidence and to study the record, Morgan's opinion changed. In 1948, he together with Professor Louis Joughin published *The Legacy of Sacco and Vanzetti* and concluded that history's judgment was that Sacco and Vanzetti were innocent men sent to death.

It is not clear what drove Maxwell Anderson to be so taken with the Sacco and Vanzetti story, but his interest in the case continued and resulted in the creation of one of his most elegant dramatic works, *Winterset*, a 1935 Broadway production for which Anderson was awarded the Drama Critics' Circle Award of 1936. Anderson wrote the play, mostly in verse, comparable to a Shakespearean tragedy.

The plot centers on Mio Romagna, whose mission in life is to prove the innocence of his father, Bartolomeo, who was executed for a murder and robbery he did not commit. The character of Bartolomeo is a fusion of both Sacco and Vanzetti. The dramatization is steeped in philosophical concepts of justice, duty, faith, and love.

A powerful rendition of distorted justice and a plausible explanation of Judge Thayer's conduct and attitude in the Dedham trial is made in the play by Judge Gault (Judge Thayer's character) when he declared it well to be rid of anarchists, and that the "dignity of the established order is more worthy of preservation than the life of a fish peddler."[15]

In the 1936 film production of *Winterset*, Burgess Meredith, in his screen debut, played the idealistic son with a mission to prove his father's innocence. The film was more successful than the theatrical version.

Robert M. Lovett, an editor of the *New Republic* and former chair of the Sacco-Vanzetti National League, made his thoughts known in "Sacco-Vanzetti—After Ten Years" in the August 26, 1937, edition of *Unity*. He concluded that based on the *Outlook* story, Vanzetti was innocent of the attempted robbery at Bridgewater, and he commented:

> [T]he sober second thought of mankind ... has all
> but unanimously convicted the Commonwealth of
> Massachusetts of the crime of shedding innocent blood ...
> Governor Fuller ... was a man of large ambition, of little
> education, and almost no common sense.

In 1937, William Allen White, a respected journalist, wrote in *Forty Years on Main Street* that Sacco and Vanzetti were innocent and that the case diminished America's stature in the world. Like many early observers of the case, White had initially concluded in 1927 that Sacco and Vanzetti were probably guilty.

The tenth anniversary of the executions reflected the continued vitality of the case.[16] A labor group led by Gardner Jackson, a long-time supporter of Sacco and Vanzetti, offered Massachusetts Governor Hurley and Boston Mayor Mansfield a bronze bas-relief memorial of the two Italians designed by Gutzon Borglum. The group asked that the plaque be permanently placed on the Boston Common. Borglum, world famous for his works, was in the process of sculpting the faces of the four presidents on Mount Rushmore. The plaque contained the following statement by Vanzetti:

> What I wish more than all in this last hour of agony is
> that our case and our fate may be understood in their
> real being and serve as a tremendous lesson to the forces
> of freedom so that our suffering and death will not have
> been in vain.

Massachusetts Governor Hurley claimed he had no authority to accept the plaque, and Boston Mayor Mansfield was opposed to accepting or displaying the plaque on the Common.[17] The bronze version of the plaque was lost. However, a plaster draft was saved and the Boston Public Library accepted it. The library now displays the plaster draft of the plaque on the upper floor of its main branch in the Back Bay.

In 1938, George Seldes, journalist and author, found Sacco and Vanzetti to be genuine libertarians who were unjustly convicted and executed.[18] He concluded Massachusetts failed to arrest the real murderers for fear that an admission of its mistake would bring contempt upon the courts.

In 1939, Michael Musmanno, then a Pennsylvania Court of Common Pleas judge (later a justice of the Pennsylvania Supreme Court), published *After Twelve Years,* a compelling account of the Sacco-Vanzetti story that supports their innocence. Musmanno was an active member of the defense team during the final days of the case.

While virtual unanimity of the innocence of Sacco and Vanzetti grew among journalists and legal observers during the thirty years following their execution, others within the intellectual community followed in like fashion. The perceived miscarriage of justice became fertile ground for expression in poetry, literature, theater, and art. The Sacco-Vanzetti story soaked into all levels of society. It was, as Ehrmann predicted, *The Case That Will Not Die*.

In 1942, Henry Fonda starred in the movie production of *The Male Animal*, which had as its theme the issue of academic freedom to present Vanzetti's famous "If it had not been for these thing ..." statement.

Bennett Cerf, editor of the *Saturday Review*, wrote in its December 11, 1943, edition that the Sacco-Vanzetti case was unjust and that Massachusetts "put two innocent men to death."

The twentieth anniversary of their executions saw the release of a manifesto inspired by the Sacco-Vanzetti case.[19] It was signed by 150 prominent persons urging resistance to all forms of tyranny in the world. Gardner Jackson and Professor Arthur M. Schlesinger, Jr., of Harvard drafted the manifesto. Signers included Franklin D. Roosevelt, Jr.; Representative Helen Gahagen Douglas of California and her actor-husband Melvyn Douglas; Robert M. Hutchins, chancellor of the University of Chicago; former Governor Herbert H. Lehman of New York; Senator Wayne Morse of Oregon; and labor leaders Philip Murray and Walter P. Reuther.

In the 1955 *Antioch Review*, Francis Russell, researcher and author, argued that Sacco and Vanzetti were innocent. He reversed his opinion in later publications for reasons noted hereafter.

Writers and artists spawned more paintings and dramatic presentations in 1960 that were sympathetic to Sacco and Vanzetti. In May, Armand Aulicino and Frank Field announced plans to write, and Lee Nemetz to direct and produce, *The Shoemaker and the Peddler*, a musical drama about the two Italians.[20] The musical opened off-Broadway on October 14, 1960.

The Sacco and Vanzetti Story, a two-hour NBC television series written by Reginald Rose, followed the announcement of Aulicino's musical.[21] The series aired on June 3 and 11, 1960, and featured Martin Balsam as Sacco and Steven Hill as Vanzetti. This production, in turn, stimulated interest by Robert Alan Aurthur to bring the NBC production to Broadway. The competition from other pending and proposed Sacco and Vanzetti productions put a hold on Mr. Aurthur's plans.

In 1960, the Metropolitan Opera in New York announced that pursuant to a Ford Foundation grant, it would produce a Sacco-Vanzetti opera composed by Marc Blitzstein.[22] The production, however, was voted down on September 1, 1960, by the National Federation of Music Clubs because of Blitzstein's membership in the Communist Party from 1938 to 1949. The death of Blitzstein in 1964 prevented the completion of his opera for thirty-seven years. Leonard Lehrman, Blitzstein's associate, finally completed the opera, *Sacco and Vanzetti,* and it premiered in 2001.

After more than thirty years of virtual unanimous support by writers and artists of the innocence of Sacco and Vanzetti, four writers responded in opposition.[23] The four, who Nunzio Pernicone, professor of history at Drexel University, labeled the "revisionists," were Robert H. Montgomery, Boston corporate lawyer and friend of Governor Fuller; James Grossman, attorney and frequent contributor to *Commentary*; and Francis Russell and David Felix, both researchers and writers on the Sacco-Vanzetti case. Each, in his own way, came to the defense of the Commonwealth.

Montgomery's *Sacco-Vanzetti: The Murder and the Myth*, published in 1960, was the first effort by the quartet. Rutgers University law professor Robert E. Knowlton, in the *Rutgers Law Review*, Winter 1961, found the book wholly inadequate, a catalogue of unfounded conclusions, and a display of personal vengeance.

Montgomery was obsessed with Vanzetti's failure to take the stand and defend his innocence in the Plymouth trial. He was so taken with the issue that in 1958 he instigated a war of letters with Felix Frankfurter, who was then an associate justice on the United States Supreme Court.[24] This was an obvious effort to discredit Frankfurter's 1927 article and book, the flashpoint that energized the intellectual community and others against the unfairness of the Dedham trial. He chewed on the following sentence contained in a footnote in Frankfurter's book:

> The circumstances of the [Plymouth] trial are sufficiently revealed by the fact that Vanzetti, protesting innocence, was not allowed by his counsel to take the witness stand for fear his radical opinions would be brought out and tell against him disastrously.[25]

Montgomery asked Frankfurter to identify the source of that statement. Frankfurter responded with his assurance of its accuracy, but Montgomery would have none of it. He demanded the source.

Dissatisfied with Frankfurter's response, Montgomery sought the aid of James Graham, co-counsel with John Vahey as Vanzetti's attorney in the Plymouth trial. Graham gave Montgomery his assurance, by letter, that he and Vahey properly advised Vanzetti of the risk he faced if he failed to take the stand. Ultimately, Graham said Vanzetti concluded, "I don't think I can improve upon the alibi which has been established. I had better not take the stand."

In Montgomery's letter of March 25, 1958, to Frankfurter, he arrogantly suggested that he should add a correction to Frankfurter's statement in his forthcoming book. Frankfurter sharply responded that his article and book were the products of meticulous preparation and accuracy, which President Lowell had verified. Frankfurter forbade Montgomery from making any corrections to the statement in question.

Montgomery persisted with further correspondence. Finally, Frankfurter put an end to it. He insisted that should Montgomery ever publish a book about the Bridgewater crime and reference attorney Graham's letter, then he (Montgomery) should publish Frankfurter's reply regarding the matter.

Montgomery's version of Vanzetti's failure to take the stand ignored Vanzetti's own words, which he set forth in *The Background of the Plymouth Trial*, written while he was in Charlestown State Prison. Vanzetti complained of Vahey's advice:

> He asked me how I would explain from the stand the meaning of Socialism, or Communism, or Bolshevism …
> I would begin by an explanation on those subjects and Mr. Vahey would cut it off at its very beginning. "Hush, if you will tell such things to the ignorant, conservative jurors, they will send you to state prison right away."[26]

Both versions of the controversy were probably correct. The final decision whether to take the stand was technically Vanzetti's, but an uneducated immigrant, ignorant of the law, the language, and the customs, would certainly have relied on the advice of his counsel.

Just two months before the Plymouth trial, Katzmann's office tried Sergie Zagroff, a professed anarchist, before Judge Thayer, for advocating the overthrow of the government.[27] The jury acquitted Zagroff even though he took the stand and admitted he was a Bolshevik advocating revolution.

The jury acquitted Zagroff because he did not act on his beliefs and was only expressing his opinion.

Vanzetti's failure to take the stand was repeatedly claimed an indication of his guilt by Governor Fuller and President Lowell, chairman of the governor's advisory committee.[28] Montgomery and other critics of Vanzetti failed to acknowledge that Vanzetti's lawyers did not provide complete information to him so that he could make an informed decision. Vanzetti's belief that Vahey sold him out was reinforced when Vahey and Katzmann became law partners after the Dedham trial.[29]

Judge Michael Musmanno's review of Montgomery's book in the *University of Pittsburgh Law Review*, March 1961, indicated the book was disorganized and lacked any sense.

Even attorney James Grossman, one of Professor Pernicone's four revisionists, took Montgomery to task in 1962.[30] He charged that Montgomery's arguments were unconvincing because he not only tried to prove Sacco and Vanzetti were guilty but that they received a fair trial.

James Grossman followed Montgomery's book with his article "The Sacco-Vanzetti Case Reconsidered" in the January 1962 issue of *Commentary*. Grossman conceded that Sacco and Vanzetti did not receive a fair trial, but he argued to separate the issue of guilt from the question of a fair trial. Grossman expressed a popular argument advanced by supporters of the Commonwealth's conduct: Sacco and Vanzetti were guilty in fact even if their trial was unfair. Grossman later retreated, admitting that without a fair trial, one cannot, in truth, be found guilty. His ambivalence found ultimate expression in his conclusion that Sacco was guilty and Vanzetti was innocent. He based Sacco's guilt on the prosecutor's version of the ballistics evidence and on Sacco's failure to sufficiently profess his innocence.

Sacco had claimed his innocence many times during his seven-year ordeal.[31] He professed his innocence to the jury immediately after the Dedham verdicts, in Italian, *"Sono innocente! Sono innocente!"* which he repeated in English, "They kill an innocent men. They kill two innocent men." Sacco responded at the time of sentencing, "As I said before, Judge Thayer know all my life, and he know that I am never guilty, never—not yesterday, not today, nor forever."

Grossman's reliance on the ballistics evidence to support Sacco's guilt is seemingly reasonable. However, he dismissed too easily all evidence to the contrary, including Proctor's misleading "consistent with" opinion, the inconsistent markings on the base of Bullet III compared to the markings on Bullets I, II, and IIII, the likelihood that Shell W was a plant, and that only Bullet III showed left-twist markings, notwithstanding that Berardelli's killer shot him multiple times with one gun.[32]

There were more reasons to question Sacco's guilt, which Grossman ignored: the Medeiros confession exonerating Sacco and Vanzetti; Joe Morelli's striking physical resemblance to Sacco; the Morelli gang's previous theft of shoes from factories located in South Braintree; the description of the driver of the getaway car precisely fit Steve "the Pole" Benkosky, a member of the Morelli gang; and Mike Morelli's possession of a Buick touring car shortly before the South Braintree murders that fit the description of the getaway car.

The third revisionist, Francis Russell, authored a number of articles on the Sacco-Vanzetti affair as well as two books: *Tragedy in Dedham* in 1962 and *Sacco &Vanzetti: The Case Resolved* in 1986. *Tragedy in Dedham* is a detailed chronicle of the case. Roger N. Baldwin, in his 1962 *Saturday Review* of the book, offered that it was an engrossing story; however, he charged that Russell provided nothing new about the Sacco-Vanzetti case. He believed that Russell failed to resolve even his own doubts about the case. Baldwin concluded that the executions were the product of "class prejudice and fear of alien radicals."

Justice Musmanno, in the 1963 *Kansas Law Review*, was more negative than Baldwin about *Tragedy in Dedham*. He charged that Russell's book was a confused maze of contradictions. Russell had changed his position on Sacco's innocence upon learning of the double hearsay statements attributed to a defense committee member and his son claiming Sacco was guilty.[33]

Professor A. J. Ayers, in the July 1963 *New Statesman,* wrote that he believed Vanzetti was innocent by virtue of the lack of evidence against him and the quality of his character. He seriously questioned the credibility of the 1961 ballistics tests on Bullet III, which was sponsored by Francis Russell.

In a telling comment in the January 1963 edition of the *American Historical Review,* Louis Joughin concluded that Russell's *Tragedy in Dedham* was useless because it failed to provide any sources; nothing could be verified.

The dramatists were not to be outdone. Robert Noah's previously announced play, *The Advocate*, opened on October 14, 1963. The play espoused the innocence of Sacco and Vanzetti, but its main theme centered on William Thompson, the patrician Boston lawyer who entered the case after the conviction of the two Italians.[34] Thompson devoted three years and sacrificed his law practice in an effort to save their lives.

In support of the four revisionists, Professor David Felix, in 1965, published *Protest: Sacco-Vanzetti and the Intellectuals*. Felix took a unique angle on the case. He argued that the Sacco-Vanzetti case belonged to the intellectuals. Felix, not a lawyer, concluded that the intellectuals got it wrong. He believed Sacco and Vanzetti were both guilty and that they received a fair trial. Even though he thought the intellectuals were wrong, he found that the case brought them together in America for the first time and prepared them for the important work they would be called upon to perform during the Great Depression to advance the liberal agenda of the New Deal.

Protest stimulated opposition to the so-called Sacco-Vanzetti myth that the two Italians were innocent and the subject of a political execution.[35] David Cort's "The Intellectual Mob for the Defense," a review of *Protest* in the March 1966 issue of *Commonweal*, argued that intellectuals supporting Sacco and Vanzetti favored mercy for them rather than the death penalty. In "Knights-Errant in Error?" in the *New York Times* book review, January 30, 1966, Robert J. Clements joined Cort and a growing chorus of critics of what they concluded was a mawkish group of bleeding heart intellectuals that included Edna St. Vincent Millay, Maxwell Anderson, John Dos Passos, Heywood Broun, and Ben Shahn. Along the same theme, Philip R. Toomins's review of *Protest* in the 1966 *DePaul Law Review* concluded that the Sacco-Vanzetti case changed what was essentially a criminal matter into a misleading argument that the two Italians were innocent and unjustly convicted because of their political beliefs.

These attacks on what Montgomery had labeled the "myth of innocence" brought forth a strong rebuke. Louis Joughin's review of *Protest* in the June 1966 *Journal of American History* criticized Professor Felix for selecting only evidence in support of the guilt of Sacco and Vanzetti and for ignoring evidence to the contrary. In particular, Joughin admonished Felix for not considering the views of Professor E. M. Morgan, foremost expert on the law of evidence and a critic of the conduct of prosecutor Katzmann and Judge Thayer during the Dedham trial.

A review of *Protest* in the *UCLA Law Review* of 1966 concluded that Felix presented only one side of many critical issues involved in the case and did not consider evidence against the verdict.

Michael Musmanno's review of *Protest* in the annals of the *American Academy of Political and Social Science*, July 1966, was critical of Felix's effort. He found that the book added nothing to the continuing arguments about the case and that it was beyond Felix's understanding. Musmanno concluded that next to Montgomery's book, it was the most worthless book in the Sacco and Vanzetti bibliography. *Protest* suffers the same infirmity of its predecessor, *Tragedy in Dedham*, by not containing any source notes.[36] A reader is at the mercy of the author's interpretations and accuracy of the facts.

The debate continued during the 1960s with more claims of guilty, not guilty; a fair trial, a travesty. Then, as if to respond to the four revisionists and their followers, Herbert B. Ehrmann, William Thompson's protégé and co-appellate counsel, published *The Case That Will Not Die* in 1969. The book is a trove of information, facts, and analyses supporting the innocence of the two Italians. It accused Judge Thayer and Katzmann, respectively, with judicial and prosecutorial misconduct.

Armand Aulicino's 1960 musical drama of the Sacco-Vanzetti story made a revised opening on February 8, 1969, to glowing reviews. This ended the 1960s roller coaster of commentaries on the case.[37]

Francis Russell's 1971 edition of *Tragedy in Dedham* acknowledged the continued existence of the "myth of innocence" of the two Italians in the forward to his book. Russell rejected the myth and clung to his then split theory—Sacco guilty, Vanzetti innocent.

In 1977, author Roberta S. Feuerlicht presented a strong defense of the innocence of the two Italians in *Justice Crucified: The Story of Sacco and Vanzetti*. Her exhaustive research confirmed many of Ehrmann's findings and added several new insights. Feuerlicht asserted that not only were Judge Thayer, prosecutor Katzmann, and Governor Fuller responsible for the injustice but that the Puritan philosophy that infected New England contributed to the tragedy. Most important, she labeled Justice Oliver Wendell Holmes, Jr., and A. Lawrence Lowell, president of Harvard, additional villains in the event.

Her reasons for these accusations were pointed. Justice Holmes refused to stay the executions even though he proclaimed, "I am convinced that these men did not get a square deal."[38] He rationalized his stance by saying, "but we cannot take the United States government into state affairs and undermine the basic principle of the separate sovereignties of the state and federal governments."[39] His was a form-over-substance argument of federalism in a capital murder case. The promise of the Fourteenth Amendment that "no person shall be deprived of life, liberty, or property without due process of law" should have been kept then, as it should be today.

President Lowell's sophistry in his advisory committee report was more than Feuerlicht could accept, and she challenged many findings in the report.[40] Feuerlicht questioned the advisory committee's conclusion, "On the whole, we are of the opinion that Vanzetti also was guilty beyond reasonable doubt."[41] She argued that Lowell's "on the whole" phrase were words of uncertainty and that Vanzetti could not "on the whole" be guilty beyond a reasonable doubt.

The next major event was Governor Michael Dukakis's proclamation and report that compelling grounds existed "for believing that the Sacco and Vanzetti legal proceedings were permeated with unfairness ..."[42] The report was the product of Alexander J. Cella, Esq., Professor Alan M. Dershowitz, Esq., and others. On the fiftieth anniversary of the execution of the two Italians, the governor proclaimed August 23, 1977, Nicola Sacco and Bartolomeo Vanzetti Memorial Day and declared:

> Any stigma and disgrace should be forever removed from the names of Nicola Sacco and Bartolomeo Vanzetti, from the names of their families and descendants ... and ... the people of Massachusetts [should] pause to reflect upon these tragic events, and draw from their historic lessons the resolve to prevent the forces of intolerance, fear, and hatred from ever again uniting to overcome the rationality, wisdom, and fairness to which our legal system aspires.[43]

In anticipation of Governor Dukakis's proclamation, the Massachusetts senate first voted to condemn it by a vote of twenty-one to fourteen on August 8, 1977, but then, a week later, the state senate reversed itself and tabled the condemnatory resolution by a vote of twenty-three to twelve.[44]

Just when it seemed the ongoing controversy might have found resolution by the Dukakis proclamation, the Sacco-Vanzetti story stimulated historians into new directions. On October 26, 1979, the Boston Public Library sponsored a conference upon the presentation of the Felicani collection of Sacco-Vanzetti papers to the library. Aldino Felicani had been treasurer of the Sacco-Vanzetti Defense Committee.

The two-day event brought leading historians and scholars together for a review titled *Sacco-Vanzetti: Developments and Reconsiderations—1979*. Professor William Salomone, University of Rochester; Philip J. McNiff, Director, Boston Public Library; author Norman Thomas diGiovianni; and Professor Nunzio Pernicone presented introductory remarks. Professor and historian Louis Joughin made a presentation, "Beyond Guilt or Innocence: The Responsibility of History." Barbara Miller Solomon, of Harvard University, explored underlying New England prejudices in "Brahmins and the Conscience of the Community." Daniel Aaron, also of Harvard, covered "The Idea of Boston: Some Literary Responses to the Sacco-Vanzetti Case." Professors Paul Avrich and David Wieck explored "The Anarchist Connection" of Sacco and Vanzetti. Researcher and long-time Sacco-Vanzetti scholar, Robert D'Attilio, probed the bombings and violent aspects of anarchism in "LaSalute e in Voi: The Anarchist Dimension." The conference included panel discussions with other notable followers of the Sacco-Vanzetti case.

The conference concluded with five presentations by noted scholars covering a variety of subjects growing out of the Sacco-Vanzetti affair. These included: the impact of the case on the labor movement, the role of the Roman Catholic Church, the prosecution of the two defendants because of their Italian ethnicity, the antifascism of Sacco and Vanzetti, and the continuing effort to reconvict the two Italians and expel them from the hall of fame of the radical left.

The late 1970s and early 1980s continued to stir doubts about the guilt or innocence of the two Italians. Various writers raised the Carlo Tresca declaration, reported by Max Eastman and others, that Sacco was guilty and Vanzetti was innocent.[45] That such second and third-hand hearsay statements had vitality in the 1980s was a sign that historians found the Dedham jury's guilty verdicts unconvincing.

William Young and David E. Kaiser made significant legal disclosures in 1985 with the publication of *Postmortem: New Evidence in the Case of Sacco and Vanzetti.*[46] The authors analyzed the Dedham trial transcript and other evidence and made a powerful argument that Bullet III was a forgery. They also uncovered documentary evidence that Vanzetti's gun was not Berardelli's gun, thereby destroying Katzmann's claim that Sacco took Berardelli's gun when Sacco shot him and gave it to Vanzetti.

In 1986, in an almost rapid-fire response to *Postmortem*, Professor James E. Starrs published "Once More unto the Breech: The Firearms Evidence in the Sacco and Vanzetti Case Revisited," a two-part series in the *Journal of Forensic Sciences*. Francis Russell followed Starrs's publication in the same year with *Sacco & Vanzetti: The Case Resolved.*

Russell took great pains to justify his changes of position concerning the guilt of the two Italians: originally, both Sacco and Vanzetti were innocent; then Sacco guilty, Vanzetti innocent; and finally, Sacco guilty and Vanzetti guilty as an accessory after the fact. Russell was swayed by the statement of Giovanni Gambera, an original member of the defense committee, who was reported by his son to have said, "Everyone knew that Sacco was guilty and that Vanzetti was innocent as far as the actual participation in the killings."[47]

Professor Starrs's 1986 article on the firearms evidence is faithful to the facts and acknowledges the ambiguities in the ballistics evidence presented at the Dedham trial. Starrs analyzed the efforts of the select committee of ballistics experts commissioned in 1983 by Westinghouse Broadcasting and Cable Inc. of Boston in yet another attempt to seek a definitive answer to the guilt or innocence of Sacco and Vanzetti.[48]

The renowned forensic scientist, Dr. Henry Lee, chaired the select committee. He appointed Anthony I. Paul, Marshall K. Robinson, and George R. Wilson, each a well-known ballistics expert, to the committee. The committee issued its report on October 11, 1983.

As a prelude to analyzing the report, Starrs pointed out the unreliability of ballistics technology at the time of the Sacco-Vanzetti trial. In particular, he declared useless the practice of pushing bullets through a gun's barrel, measuring lands and grooves, and comparing markings on bullets and shells to determine if a particular gun shot a particular bullet. Starrs asserted that only matching striations on bullets, using a comparison microscope, could determine if a particular gun shot a particular bullet.[49] He noted that the technology, however, was not available at the time of the Sacco-Vanzetti trial. Starrs concluded that the ballistics evidence at the Dedham trial was carelessly assembled, incomplete, confusingly presented, and beyond the comprehension and judgment of the ordinary intelligent layman.

Starrs analyzed the findings of the select committee and acknowledged it was unable to determine whether the .38-caliber Harrington & Richardson found on Vanzetti was in reality Berardelli's gun, as the prosecutor claimed.

Starrs also acknowledged that the committee was unable to determine if Bullet III was fired from Sacco's gun by comparing Bullet III to the committee's 1983 test-fired bullets through that gun because of the "poor condition" and "heavy oxidation" of Bullet III.[50] Starrs, however, stated the committee identified Bullet III as having been fired from Sacco's gun by matching a photograph of the striae on Bullet III with the striae on one of the Lowell Winchester test-fired bullets. The committee compared Bullet III with the Lowell test bullets in default of comparing Bullet III with the 1983 test bullets.

The committee did not definitively answer the question whether Bullet III was a counterfeit. The most the committee did was find that, after a comparison of Bullet III to the original Hamilton defense photographs, "it is the opinion of this Panel ... that Bullet III ... is the same as appears in the original defense photographs."[51]

Despite the select committee's limited findings, Professor Starrs pointed out that new and different evidence found by the committee, in his opinion, linked Sacco to the South Braintree crimes.

The new evidence consisted of two spent Peters shells found at the crime scene and Sacco's possession, upon his arrest, of sixteen Peters cartridges.[52] The select committee examined these items and found that six of the sixteen cartridges bore the same striations as the two spent Peters shells. Starrs concluded that because six Peters cartridges were manufactured by the same die-cutting tool that manufactured the two spent Peters shells, the match established Sacco's presence at the crime scene. Starrs made this conclusion without any knowledge of the quantity of cartridges manufactured by the same machine and their geographic distribution during the 1920s and earlier years. The probative value of this evidence and Starrs' expansive conclusion is questionable because those cartridges were manufactured during the time of the Great War. Perhaps hundreds of thousands were manufactured by the same tool and distributed throughout New England during this time period, making Starrs's conclusion unreliable and not provable beyond a reasonable doubt.

An equally important reason to question Starrs's matching argument is found by reviewing the writings of Dr. Henry Lee, the select committee's chairman. In 2001, Dr. Lee and Dr. Jerry Labriola authored *Famous Crimes Revisited*. The lead chapter analyzed and discussed in detail the ballistics evidence in the Sacco and Vanzetti case. Nowhere in the ninety-six pages devoted to the case does Dr. Lee mention Professor Starrs's matching theory. If the select committee had found evidence dispositive of Sacco's participation in the crime, based on Starr's matching theory, one would expect that Dr. Lee would have referenced that argument.

Many encyclopedias published during the 1980s carried these themes regarding the Sacco-Vanzetti case:[53] "the prejudice of the judge and the jury against immigrants and radicals appeared to have more weight than the evidence"; the case "revealed ethnic bias"; "Sacco and Vanzetti were convicted because they were radicals and because they were Italian"; "evidence ... pointed to the guilt of Morelli and his gang"; "Sacco's alibi was strong ... the opinion rests mainly on ballistics tests made many years after the trial, which were not conclusive"; "many historians believe that Sacco may have been guilty and that Vanzetti was probably innocent. But in either event ... the evidence was insufficient to support conviction."

On the other hand, *Time-Life Books*, in 1989, offered that "Sacco and Vanzetti made no secret of their interest in anarchist ideas" and that the "authorities opined that anyone capable of subscribing to such a dangerous philosophy was equally capable of murder in cold blood."

In 1991, Melvin I. Urofsky, professor of history at Virginia Commonwealth University, posited in his book, *Felix Frankfurter: Judicial Restraint and Individual Liberties,* that Sacco and Vanzetti were tried because they were aliens and anarchists and that Katzmann and Thayer's conduct in the Dedham trial subverted justice.

The 1990s brought forth two important books: *Sacco and Vanzetti: The Anarchist Background* by Professor Paul Avrich in 1991 and *A Probabilistic Analysis of the Sacco and Vanzetti Evidence* by Professors Joseph B. Kadane and David A. Schum in 1996.

Avrich's book provides an excellent study of the anarchist background of Sacco and Vanzetti. With exquisite details, Avrich paints a picture of the Italian anarchist movement in America and places Sacco and Vanzetti in the middle of it as active participants, suggesting that they were militant and dedicated anarchists capable of using violence to achieve the goals of the "Idea."[54] However, Avrich provides no hard evidence that either of the two Italians ever used violence to further the aims of that movement, although he provides detailed evidence of violence by many other anarchists.

In the end, Avrich concluded that even though the case against Sacco and Vanzetti remained unproven, "their innocence [had not been] established beyond any shadow of doubt."[55] Under American law, it is not a defendant's obligation to establish innocence beyond "any shadow of doubt." It is the government's obligation to prove guilt beyond a reasonable doubt.

Professors Kadane's and Schum's book used statistical methods to evaluate the relevance, credibility, and probative force of the evidence in the case. In the preparation of their book, the authors studied and reviewed the facts of the case and the trial evidence in detail. They relied on the expertise of renowned professionals in the fields of law, history, and psychology. In particular, they sought advice regarding forensic matters from Professor Starrs and factual details from Francis Russell, among others.

The authors identified 395 pieces of relevant evidence. They placed each piece of evidence under a microscope of logic pursuant to which a chain of reasoning was constructed within inference networks pioneered by Dean John Henry Wigmore. The probability of correct conclusions reached on the evidence was computer tested using complex statistical formulas. Professors Kadane and Schum concluded that the case against Vanzetti was "almost preposterously weak ... Vanzetti's guilt was not even an issue."[56] The authors found the issue of Sacco's guilt more complicated. In the end, they reaffirmed their conclusion that Vanzetti was innocent and found that Sacco's guilt was "not proven."[57]

Many Sacco and Vanzetti observers have been persistent in their vigor to continue publicizing the case into the twenty-first century. The Jersey City Museum put on a show titled "Ben Shahn and the Passion of Sacco and Vanzetti" in the fall of 2001.[58] The exhibition showed sixteen of twenty-three paintings of Shahn's works relating to the Sacco-Vanzetti story. The exhibition contained books, news articles, and a CD of music about the two Italians, including songs by Woody Guthrie.

In addition to the Jersey City showing of Ben Shahn's paintings and the 2001 publication of *Famous Crimes Revisited*, Professor Richard Newby, in 2006, published *Kill Now, Talk Forever: Debating Sacco and Vanzetti*. Bruce Watson's book *Sacco and Vanzetti: The Men, the Murders, and the Judgment of Mankind* followed in 2007.

Kill Now, Talk Forever is a comprehensive compilation covering key parts of the official Dedham trial transcript and a summary relating to many leading books and publications on the case from its beginning until 2003. The book contains topics for discussion and debate, along with fifty-two research topics with probing suggestions. It also provides an annotated bibliography, a trove of information for anyone interested in the details of the case. One cannot determine Newby's view of guilt or innocence, although the unfairness of the trial appears evident.

Bruce Watson's *Sacco and Vanzetti* reads like a detective story. Factually, it is meticulously accurate. While Watson seems clear that the two Italians should have been given a new trial, he guards against declaring either Sacco or Vanzetti innocent or guilty, leaving that for the reader to decide.

* * * *

We look to the law for justice and often find it. There are, however, times when justice eludes us. It is then we must turn to the high court of history for whatever is left of justice for us to find.

The law is great and glorious
It frees the innocent and condemns the guilty
But, when
One officer can lie,
One prosecutor can trick,
One juror can damn,
One judge can hang,
Then, the law is not great and glorious
It frees the guilty and condemns the innocent

In the end, it was history and not the law
That saved their names.
Even then, it was only words on paper
And not the lives of the two that history saved.

Theodore W. Grippo

APPENDIX A

COMMONWEALTH OF MASSACHUSETTS

Norfolk, ss

COMMONWEALTH VS. BARTHOLOMEO VANZETTI

and

COMMONWEALTH vs. NICOLO SACCO

In re Substitution of Barrels in Court Exhibit Pistols.

STATEMENT

(1) On or about February 13, 1924, District Attorney Williams informed the Court that Capt. VanAmburgh had told him that upon examination, the barrel in the Sacco Colt automatic pistol of 32 calibre, was not the Sacco barrel that belonged in the Sacco pistol. After this communication was made to the Court by Mr. Williams, counsel for the defendants were notified of this statement made by Capt. VanAmburgh concerning said barrel.

(2) On the last or next to the last day of the hearing on the 5th supplementary motion for a new trial, Mr. Hamilton, an expert on fire arms and ammunition, used as exhibits two new Colt automatic pistols of 32 calibre, which were filed with the clerk of the Superior Court at Dedham, with an affidavit, some time before said hearing. The Sacco pistol was also there at that time, and was used by Mr. Hamilton as an exhibit.

(3) It is admitted that Mr. Hamilton at this hearing on said motion disassembled all three pistols, and some time after he had finished his explanation and comparison between the two new Colt pistols belonging to him and the Sacco pistol, he reassembled said three pistols, in the presence of the Court and counsel on both sides, and by order of the Court, delivered them to Mr. Everett the assistant clerk of said Superior Court. The two new pistols were brought to the office of the clerk of said court in boxes, and Mr. Everett put them in the same boxes, after they had been reassembled by Mr. Hamilton. Mr. Hamilton also testified positively that at that time he put the Sacco barrel in the Sacco pistol and the two new barrels in his two new Colt pistols. So far, there seems to be no dispute.

(4) On February 15, 1924, said two boxes, in the presence of counsel on both sides, and Capt. VanAmburgh and Mr. Hamilton, were opened by the Court, after they had been brought to the Court by Sheriff Capen, and therein were found Hamilton's two new Colt automatic pistols, excepting there was an old rusty and foul barrel in one of his new pistols. In the Sacco pistol there was apparently a new barrel, which Mr. Hamilton said was his and that it belonged in his new pistol. The question then immediately arose, how did the new barrel of the Hamilton pistol, which he says he put into his new pistol when he reassembled its parts in court, get into the Sacco pistol, and how did the old rusty, foul barrel get into the new Hamilton pistol.

(5) It is an admitted fact by Mr. Hamilton that the new barrel in some way got into the Sacco pistol. But a dispute has arisen between the two experts, Capt. VanAmburgh and Mr. Hamilton, as to whether or not the old rusty, foul barrel found in the Hamilton pistol was the Sacco barrel.

(6) Capt. VanAmburgh has testified that it was. As soon as the Court learned of this difference of opinion of experts on the substitution of barrels, an investigation was started at once, upon my own initiative and motion. This investigation had nothing to do with the trial on the indictments before the jury, nor upon motions for new trials, for all the hearings upon the said motions had been closed, as I shall show later.

(7) Having ordered, as heretofore stated, these three pistols as exhibits to be placed in the custody of the clerk of courts, it then became my duty to ascertain whether or not there had been an interference with that order, and whether or not there had been an innocent substitution of barrels, (as it was admitted there had been some substitution), or was it a willful, intentional or planned substitution of barrels, with a view of interfering with and defeating the ends of justice and with the administration of the criminal law in this Commonwealth. If it was an intentional substitution,

then it was a fraud upon me, a presiding justice of the Superior Court, who heard all of the evidence at the trials upon the indictments, and all of the motions for new trials, and as a judicial agency of the government of this Commonwealth. If it was such a substitution and could be successfully accomplished, it would be a most serious assault upon the administration of the criminal law in this Commonwealth. This being true, willful substitution of these barrels, irrespective of successful accomplishment, by whomsoever made, would be clearly a contempt of court.

(8) This investigation, however, was not a contempt proceeding, for no person should be held for contempt (not committed in the presence or hearing of the Court), without complaint and full hearing upon said complaint. Whether this investigation may result in any future proceedings, I do not now know. Before taking up the merits of this investigation, I wish to refer to a certain matter.

(9) Soon after the Court had been informed of this substitution and after the newspapers published interviews with counsel on both sides, each counsel was not satisfied with what the other was alleged to have said. A reporter came to me one night to settle between attorneys a dispute as to the evidence that was introduced in court. I told him that this investigation was going to be conducted only in court. I also told the lawyers the same thing the next morning, and requested that there be no more interviews in newspapers.

(10) I was asked to have what was called a public trial. I did not grant this request, because by so doing, I might have defeated the very purpose for which this investigation was started, for at Dedham each witness was sworn and testified separately. The very publication of the testimony of the first witness, who was clerk of the Court, Mr. Worthington, might have conveyed information to every witness called thereafter. At the time this request was made, counsel and the Court had been at work for several weeks in the main judges' lobby. This room was used with the consent of Chief Justice Hall. The hearings on this investigation were all conducted there, excepting one whole week which was spent at Dedham. In my judgment an investigation of whether or not a fraud had been perpetrated upon the Court by tampering with exhibits is not a public trial or hearing, within the meaning of the Constitution. A public trial, generally speaking means a trial by jury or some trial upon the merits, between the parties.

(11) In the case of Commonwealth v. Wakelin, 230 M. 567, which was an indictment for murder, the defendant objected to the hearing on motions for leave to file a motion to dismiss and to quash the indictment, either in chambers or in the absence of the jury. The judge of the Superior Court

overruled the objection and the defendant excepted. In a very few words the Supreme Judicial Court overruled this exception, without giving any reasons therefor. It must have been on the ground that it was purely procedural, and not a public trial upon the merits, within the meaning of the Constitution.

(12) The public had a right to hold me responsible for a thorough, painstaking and efficient investigation of this important question, and this being true, I felt that I had a right to conduct it in my own manner in order that the most efficient results might be obtained. In Telegram Newspaper Co. v. Commonwealth, 172 M. 294, the Supreme Judicial Court said that when a contempt has been called to the attention of the Court, the Court, of its own motion can institute proceedings for contempt, and it does not depend upon the complaint of any of the parties litigant. This is so, because when a contempt had been committed, it was a contempt of the <u>judge trying the case</u>. Of course I have commenced no contempt proceedings, but have simply ordered an investigation, with the purpose of ascertaining whether or not a contempt of court has been committed. If the Court has the inherent power to order contempt proceedings on its own motion, certainly there should be no complaint made because I ordered an investigation of this most important question, especially, when we consider the fact that counsel on both sides were given the fullest opportunity to cross-examine every single witness called.

(13) Three weeks and two days have been devoted to this investigation. The daily hearings lasted until nearly 5 o'clock every afternoon. Mr. Williams, District Attorney representing the Commonwealth, and Mr. Moore (Mr. Thompson a very short time) representing the defendants, were present at all of the hearings and took part in the examination and cross-examination of witnesses. Mr. Hamilton was present at all hearings, and so was Capt. VanAmburgh, excepting the week at Dedham. They were allowed in the courtroom at all times, when all other witnesses appeared alone and were sworn separately, and no two of them were in the court room at the same time. I think I am perfectly safe in saying that during this entire hearing counsel for the defendants consumed more than two thirds of the time in cross-examination, for with only one exception, every witness was subjected to a long and exhaustive cross-examination. And let me say here that the counsel for the defendants went to the limit of his capacity in seeking to obtain some evidence that tended in some way to show that somebody connected with the Commonwealth might have or did substitute these barrels.

(14) Let me now consider the salient features of the evidence. At the outset it should be borne in mind that the Commonwealth has strenuously opposed every motion that has been filed by the defendants up to the

present time. This fact may or may not be of some importance on the question of motive. In other words, would anyone connected with the interest of the Commonwealth be likely to change the barrels of those pistols, which might under some circumstances result in assisting the defendants in filing more motions for new trials?

(15) Counsel for defendants has argued that it must have been somebody directing the interests of the Commonwealth in making these substitutions, while the District Attorney has argued that it was done by Mr. Hamilton. But, no matter who made the substitutions, whether innocently or intentionally, the Commonwealth claimed that the barrel found in Hamilton's new pistol was the original Sacco barrel.

(16) Therefore, the only question that I am going to determine now is, whether or not the barrel in Hamilton's new pistol is the original Sacco barrel.

(17) At this point it should be remembered that it was Mr. Hamilton who brought the two new pistols to the clerk's office. Of course it cannot be claimed that the Commonwealth had anything to do with that act. Whether or not this fact has any probative value depends upon its connection or association with other facts that may or may not be established.

(18) Now, Mr. Hamilton has testified that he knew that he put the Sacco barrel in the Sacco pistol and his two new barrels into his two new pistols. If this statement is true, then nobody could have meddled with the barrels of these two pistols before November 8, 1923, because he reassembled them on that day and also, because he put his two new barrels into his two new pistols at that time. On this account, Mr. Hamilton testified that the substitution must have taken place after that date and while the pistols were in the possession of the Clerk of the Court or his assistants.

(19) This statement then of Mr. Hamilton, put the issue squarely up to the Clerk's office. At first Mr. Hamilton was rather of the opinion that it was the Sacco barrel that was in his new pistol, but after a very suggestive question was put to him he became doubtful, so that he required a compound microscopic examination to ascertain the measurements of the lands and grooves of the Sacco barrel and those of the disputed barrel. After making these measurements and for other reasons given by him he was unqualifiedly of the opinion that the disputed barrel was not the Sacco barrel.

(20) In connection with the necessity of these measurements to determine whether or not the old barrel in his new pistol was the Sacco barrel, I noticed particularly that Mr. Hamilton, without measurements of the lands and grooves and without hesitation, testified that the new barrel

taken out of the Sacco pistol was his. Did that act on his part indicate or did it not any knowledge?

(21) Again it should be borne in mind that in all human probability the barrel in Hamilton's new pistol was removed first because the disputed barrel could not have found its way into the Hamilton new pistol until after the new barrel had been removed, and neither could the new barrel have found its way into the Sacco pistol until the barrel in the Sacco pistol had been removed. This being true it would seem to follow that the hand that removed the new barrel from the Hamilton pistol and put it into the Sacco pistol would be the same hand that put the old rusty and foul barrel into Hamilton's new pistol, whether it was Sacco's or some other. If one can determine accurately who removed the new barrel from Hamilton's pistol he can come pretty close to solving this entire controversy.

(22) After Mr. Hamilton had squarely put this substitution up to the Clerk's office the Court with counsel adjourned to Dedham. It took one full week there to take all the evidence. While there the Court was able to determine within what time, if made at the Clerk's office, this substitution must have been made. The hearing closed on November 8, 1923, on the supplementary motion for a new trial, when the three pistols were reassembled. On the 12th day of November 1923, District Attorney Williams filed an affidavit of Captain VanAmburgh, to which was attached a plug gauge. This was done at the request of the Court. A plug gauge is an instrument used to determine the diameter of the bore of pistols. At that time District Attorney Williams, in the presence of Mr. Everett, put said plug gauge in the barrel that was in the Sacco pistol, and from his description I am satisfied that the barrel in the Sacco pistol was Hamilton's new barrel and not the Sacco barrel.

(23) On November 13, 1923, when Mr. Worthington informed me that the plug gauge had been filed with an accompanying affidavit, I requested him to bring it to my room with the Sacco pistol. At that time the Sacco pistol was fully assembled. I could not disassemble it; so, accompanied by Mr. Worthington, I went to the District Attorney's office and while there in our presence and at my request, Mr. Williams disassembled the Sacco pistol and after this was done both Mr. Worthington and I returned to my room, where I experimented with the plug gauge by pushing it into the barrel that had been dismantled from the Sacco pistol. After finishing my examination Mr. Worthington took the plug gauge and the component parts of the disassembled Sacco pistol back to his office. I am satisfied now that this barrel in the Sacco pistol was the new Hamilton barrel. I noticed at that time the barrel was a shade larger than the plug gauge.

(24) Mr. Hamilton in his affidavit affirmed that the diameter of the Sacco barrel measured .2924, while Captain VanAmburgh affirmed that it measured .3045. It now appears from the testimony of Mr. Hamilton that the diameter of his new barrel in the Sacco pistol measured .0009 greater than Captain VanAmburgh's plug gauge. This being true, the barrel in the Sacco pistol must have been the Hamilton new barrel, because a plug gauge that measured .3045 could not have been pressed into a barrel that measured .2924.

(25) At Dedham more than twenty witnesses were called and examined. They included Mr. Worthington, Clerk of the Court, and his assistant, Mr. Everett, Sheriff Capen, Mr. Drummond, janitor of the court house, and his assistant, Mr. Ralph Law, Mr. McAuliff, night fireman, Mr. Delaney, day fireman, Samuel Law, painter, the Misses Foley and Delaney, matrons of the court house, Mr. Cobb, County Treasurer, Mr. Reynolds, night watchman from 12 p.m. until after 7 a.m., who went into the clerk's office every hour with a time clock that registered, Mr. Lovering, watchman from 4 p.m. until 12 p.m., who went every hour into the Clerk's office and registered the time, District Attorney Williams and his assistant, Mr. Keith, Mr. Henderson, clerk in Mr. Worthington's office, the Misses Clark and Hill, clerks in the office of Mr. Worthington, Frank J. Squires, Clerk of the District court, who had a key to his office in the court house, Miss Buckler, stenographer in Mr. Worthington's office, Mr. Pilling, civil engineer, who sometimes went into the fire-proof room to see records belonging to the county commissioners, Miss Brewerton, stenographer for the Superior Court, and Mr. Coulter, a deputy sheriff who went to Bridgeport, Connecticut, with Mr. Keith, Assistant District Attorney, to have pictures taken of certain bullets, and where one picture was taken of the muzzle of the Sacco pistol.

(26) Let us now consider the room where the firearms were kept. It was called the fireproof room. There were two steel shutters on the two outside windows, which were bolted overnight from the inside. There was also a steel shutter which was drawn down every night in front of the door that led from Mr. Worthington's main office into the fireproof room and was fastened with some kind of a pin on the side toward the main office. In the fireproof room there were tiers of lockers but only fourteen of them were equipped with a lock, for these fourteen lockers were kept locked with one lock. It appeared in evidence that at times one or more of the lockers if not pushed clear in would not lock, and when this was observed they would be pushed clear in and then they would lock. On the day of the view there appeared to be one locker that did not lock and that locker was labeled upon the outside "canceled checks."

(27) Now, Mr. Everett testified that when Mr. Hamilton handed to him the three pistols reassembled, he put the Sacco pistol into one of these lockers and locked it, and the two Hamilton new pistols were put by him into what was called a cupboard, where some of the exhibits in the case were kept. Mr. Everett also testified that on the 12th day of November when he took from the locker the Sacco pistol for Mr. Williams, the locker was then locked, and he locked it when he put the pistol back in its place. The evidence was that Mr. Williams had the pistol less than a minute or about a minute and during all of this time it was in the view of Mr. Everett.

(28) Now, Mr. Worthington testified that when he brought the Sacco pistol and the plug gauge to my room the pistol was then locked in the locker and when he returned it he locked the locker. If this testimony is believed it would seem to be incredible that there could be any substitution of barrels between November 8 and November 12 or 13, 1923. This is so, because one must unlock the locker before he can put Hamilton's new barrel into the Sacco pistol.

(29) But this is not all of the evidence on this point, for both Mr. Worthington and Mr. Everett testified that they had the sole charge of the Sacco pistol and they never found the locker where the Sacco pistol was kept, unlocked. They also testified that the two new Hamilton pistols were never called for nor touched by anybody from the time when they were reassembled and delivered to Mr. Everett, until February 13, 1923, when Mr. Everett brought them to the District Attorney's office, where they were disassembled by Mr. Brouilliard, a member of the State Police, in the presence of Mr. Worthington, Mr. Everett, Mr. Williams and Sheriff Capen, and when disassembled an old rusty and foul barrel was found in one of the new Hamilton pistols. Sheriff Capen brought to me at the judges' lobby these two pistols the next day.

(30) In addition to this testimony every person who had a key to the building and the different offices and all others having any relationship to the court house, testified that they never saw the slightest sign of a break anywhere, that they never by night or by day saw any suspicious person around the building, inside or outside, and they could not give me any help whatsoever in regard to any substitution of barrels.

(31) Inasmuch as Mr. Hamilton testified that the substitution must have taken place after the pistols and been delivered into the custody of Mr. Everett and after hearing all of the evidence and using his vast experience—as he had testified in 174 murder cases—I asked him if he could help me in any way in solving this problem. In substance he replied it could not have taken

place during the night time because the building was too well guarded then, but it might have been in the day time and must have been accomplished by two or more persons acting in concert together. He gave this opinion notwithstanding the testimony established that at no time during the day was the office of the Clerk of Court ever left alone and the further fact that no one could get into the locker file unless he knew where the key was kept. He also said that he did not think that anyone connected with the Clerk's office was connected in any way with any conspiracy to substitute barrels.

(32) If this is so it would seem almost incredible that a person or persons could get the key, go to the locker room, unlock the files, then disassemble two pistols, substitute one barrel for another and then get away with these acts without being seen by somebody in the office.

(33) Again, if the purpose of the person was to get rid of the Sacco barrel, it might be asked why did he not substitute an old one in its place and let Hamilton's new pistol alone. By substituting a new barrel in the Sacco pistol it was a complete give-away and was bound sooner or later to be discovered. It was only a question of time. This being true, the question would naturally arise which party—the Commonwealth or the defendants—would be likely to receive the greater benefit from this discovery of the substitution of barrels?

(34) Taking into consideration all of the evidence heard at Dedham I am unable to find a single fact that would warrant me in finding that there was any substitution of barrels after they were delivered into the custody of Mr. Everett by Mr. Hamilton. This being true, the substitution would seem to have been made during the time Mr. Hamilton reassembled them in court. But notwithstanding this evidence obtained at Dedham, which seemed to me to be convincing, Mr. Hamilton still maintained that the barrel in the new Hamilton pistol is not the Sacco barrel.

(35) Let us now consider further some of the other evidence that has a bearing upon this question. Motive is always a strong controlling factor in ascertaining the truth in all human investigations. Let me briefly state the claims of both parties.

(36) The Commonwealth claimed that having obtained verdicts of guilty at the hands of the jury and in asmuch [*sic*] as the hearings of all the motions for new trials had been fully heard and closed, it was satisfied with the evidence as it then stood without the substitution of any barrels, which might enable the defendants to file still another motion for a new trial.

(37) At the close of the hearing of the fifth supplementary motion for a new trial, counsel for the defendants said that he would reserve the

right to be heard on a request to fire one hundred cartridges through the Sacco pistol. This request was made with a view of showing that the location of the firing pin indentation on the primer surface established an individuality of the firing pin in the pistol. About six or seven weeks ago Mr. Thompson called on me at the court house and made a similar request. District Attorney Williams said at that time that he should oppose it until he had communicated with Captain VanAmburgh. Some time afterwards Captain VanAmburgh came to the Judges' lobby, examined the then supposed Sacco barrel, and told Mr. Williams, who informed the Court later, that it was not the Sacco barrel.

(38) Counsel for the defendants claimed that the motive on the part of the Commonwealth was to defeat and render ineffective the firing of cartridges through the Sacco pistol, as requested by Mr. Thompson, if the Court allowed the motion to do more firing through the Sacco pistol. At any rate, if the substitution was intentional, it was claimed by counsel for the defendants that it would eventually result in injury to the defendants.

(39) On the other hand the Commonwealth claimed from a consideration of all the evidence that it was a "tricky" substitution by Mr. Hamilton with the ultimate motive of securing a new trial when the substitution was discovered, as it was bound to be sooner or later; in other words, after the substitution was discovered—and the plan was to have it discovered by him—then the claim would be made that the new barrel in the Sacco pistol was not the Sacco barrel, and then, on that account, a motion for a new trial would be filed.

(40) The Commonwealth claims that this plan was defeated by the discovery by Captain VanAmburgh.

(41) On this question of motive I have already been asked by counsel for the defendant to allow a motion to be filed nunc pro tunc, that is to date its filing before this investigation was ordered, which motion should be based upon the same evidence. This motion I denied.

I have also been requested to rule as follows:

> (2) If the foul barrel found in one of Mr. Hamilton's pistols is not the original barrel of the Sacco pistol, then the defendants are entitled to a new trial as a matter of law.

(42) Does this request or does it not tend to prove the claim of the Commonwealth that the motive behind the substitution was the securing of a new trial?

(43) District Attorney Williams was called as a witness by the Court and was subjected to a vigorous and lengthy cross-examination by Mr. Moore. The District Attorney, in response to questions propounded by the Court, stated that he went to Bridgeport, Connecticut, to procure a plug gauge from Captain VanAmburgh at the requestof [sic] the Court. On November 12, 1923, in the presence of Mr. Everett, the District Attorney tried the plug gauge by pushing it into the barrel that was in the Sacco pistol. The diameter of the plug gauge was .3045, while the diameter of the barrel, according to Mr. Hamilton, was .2924.

(44) Mr. Moore in his cross-examination asked Mr. Williams why he did not know from the ease with which the plug gauge went into the barrel that it did not inform him that the barrel then in the Sacco pistol was not the Sacco barrel. Mr. Williams replied that in substance he did not know because he had never seen a plug gauge before, that he did not know how one should fit into a barrel, and that he came away believing that the barrel then in the Sacco pistol was the real Sacco barrel. Mr. Williams was there a very short time; not over a minute as I recollect it. The examination would have been very effective provided knowledge was established on the part of Mr. Williams. This was because knowledge of the substitution of these barrels not communicated to the Court would be evidence of guilty consciousness.

(45) Now, it is only fair to the Commonwealth to put the same test to Mr. Hamilton, who was a man of extraordinary experience in the field of firearms and ammunition. He has testified in almost every state in the Union in 174 murder cases, and his entire time is devoted and has been for years to murder cases and criminology.

(46) On the 4th day of December, Mr. Hamilton went to Dedham Court House and there, in the presence of Clerk Worthington, examined what he then thought was the Sacco barrel but now says it was undoubtedly his new barrel. He was there between fifteen and twenty minutes. He said that he went there to see Captain VanAmburgh's plug gauge. Mr. Hamilton and Captain VanAmburgh did not agree as to the diameter measurement of the Sacco barrel. As bearing upon the question of his knowledge of the substituted barrel let me read from his affidavit:

> On December 4, 1923, at Dedham, I examined and measured the plug gauge referred to by Mr. VanAmburgh in his last affidavit and attached thereto as an exhibit. I compared it with and attempted to determine by it the present muzzle diameter of the barrel of the Sacco pistol.

It was impossible to make this determination because of the following facts: The gauge rod or measuring end of it is a reverse taper, that is to say, the end diameter is .3048"; near the middle the diameter is .3046"; and at the handle end it is .3045". The present diameter of the muzzle of the Sacco pistol is .3054". The muzzle diameter of the Sacco pistol at the present time is .0130" larger than it was last April, and is .0009 larger than the large end of the VanAmburgh plug gauge.

Last April the entire interior of the Sacco pistol was foul from standing uncleaned after it had been used for the test shots. When I examined the barrel on November 8 last in court at Dedham, the top of the lands at each end for a distance of about three-quarters of an inch down into it were clean and bright, while the grooves were foul. Today the entire interior lands and grooves are free of fouling, and bright and shiny. Since November 8 the interior of the Sacco pistol has been quite thoroughly cleaned, both lands and grooves, so that the relation of diameter between this barrel and the VanAmburgh gauge rod is quite unlike the condition existing in April last, when I first saw the Sacco pistol.

(47) Mr. Hamilton affirmed in his first affidavit on the fifth supplementary motion that the diameter of the Sacco barrel last spring was .2924, while Captain VanAmburgh said it was .3045. The diameter of the new barrel in the Sacco pistol measured .3054, so that the diameter of the new barrel that Mr. Hamilton examined on December 4 at Dedham was .0009 larger than even the VanAmburgh plug gauge.

(48) Now then with this knowledge that he says he had on said date, the question is did he or did he not know from his large experience that the new barrel was not the Sacco barrel? For if he knew it, as I have said, and did not communicate the fact to the Court or to counsel, that would be important evidence upon guilty consciousness.

(49) It should also be borne in mind on this question that there were a great many pits, rust pits, in the original Sacco barrel. Now, let me read what he says on page 149 of the record of this investigation: Cross examination of Mr. Williams,

Q But, Mr. Hamilton, when you examined the barrel that was in the Sacco pistol on December 4, you then found that a barrel which you had measured in March [April 6] 1923, as .2924 appeared to be .3053 [.3054], did you not? A. Not then, I didn't, not then. It did, when I examined it down here December 4, it did appear then to be, but I know now I was measuring my own barrel.

Q And the barrel you were measuring was—had a bore diameter of .3053 [.3054], didn't it? A. Yes.

Q And you knew the Sacco pistol barrel in March [April 6], 1923, was .2924? A. Yes, sir.

Q And how did you account in your own mind for that sudden increase in bore diameter of the barrel which you then assumed to be the Sacco barrel? A. I was unable to satisfactorily account for it in my own mind, because while I saw that what appeared to be the barrel had been thoroughly cleaned, it did not satisfy my mind that that was the cause of its enlargement, and I could not possibly conceive, or, in fact, I was satisfied that the Court had never applied any cleaning process to the extent that the barrel had. I had never yet found a Court presuming to clean a barrel that was a Court exhibit, and I assumed this Court was no exception.

Q Well, you made affidavit on December 6 stating that that Sacco pistol barrel had been cleaned by someone, did you not? A. That I did state, and I have also corrected me now. That was based on the assumption that I had examined the actual original Sacco barrel.

Q And at that time you were willing to accept as a fact that the barrel which you were then examining on December 4 and which measured .3053 [.3054] bore diameter was the Sacco pistol, were you not? A. I did take it and supposed it was the Sacco pistol, although I could not satisfactorily explain to myself why the diameter had been changed nor why it had been cleaned.

Q But you recognized as a possibility at that time that it might have expanded to that size, did you not? A.

No, I did not accept it as a possibility. I immediately reported and called to the attention of Mr. Thompson the inconsistency of what I had found and put the question to him who I supposed had cleaned that barrel. I informed him that certainly the court did not do it, and certainly I did not believe any clerk of the court would dare do such a thing.

Q Did you state anywhere in your affidavit of December 6 that that was not the Sacco barrel or in your opinionwas [*sic*] not the Sacco barrel? A. No, sir.

Q Why didn't you, if you did not do so? A. Because I had no thought in my mind that it was not.

Q How could you help having a thought in your mind if you say it was impossible to increase the bore diameter from .2924 to .3053 [.3054]? A. The easiest thing in the world. My mind is carrying a good many subjects, a good many different exhibits, and I have on my mind most of the time details of five to seven murder cases.

Q Well, wasn't that particular examination of sufficient importance to you that you would use every care at that time to ascertain the truth? A. No, sir, because I was on a specific errand, on a specific purpose to obtain just the information to complete my affidavit, and that was the relationship between the VanAmburgh plug and the interior of the barrel, and my mind wasn't on anything else. I am familiar with the working of my own mind. I am capable of concentrating it upon a given subject or not concentrating it upon a given subject, and at that time it was concentrated upon that one problem and nothing else.

The COURT. May I ask this question: In what way would the VanAmburgh plug gauge have "to be used so that it would be possible that it is responsible for the bright and shiny appearance of the surface of the lands of the Sacco pistol which has changed its diameter from .2924 last April to .3045 now?

Mr. HAMILTON. That is easy. By simply inserting it into a given barrel and instead of making a true insertion straight ahead, inserting it at just a fraction of an angle and it would naturally wedge and bind as it went in and out due to the holding of the plug not in perfect alignment with the interior of the barrel.

The COURT. You don't mean that would cut the barrel itself?

Mr. HAMILTON. No.

The COURT. It would not make the barrel any larger?

Mr. HAMILTON. It would wedge it.

The COURT. And simply eliminate the fouling, wouldn't it?

Mr. HAMILTON. It would press it down against the metal sometimes a wiggling motion.

The COURT. Then that would not make the difference, would it?

Mr. HAMILTON. It would not make the difference.

The COURT. Would make it look more shiny?

Mr. HAMILTON. Would make it look more shiny, yes, sir. That is what I understand your question—

The COURT. But it would not account for the difference?

Mr. HAMILTON. It would not—it would account for the shininess, but it would not account for the difference in diameter.

Also let me read: Page 198

The COURT. Have you taken, Mr. Hamilton, the size of the barrel that was found in the Sacco pistol?

Mr. HAMILTON. I have, your Honor.

The COURT. Is that larger than the plug gauge of Captain VanAmburgh. .3045?

Mr. HAMILTON. It is.

The COURT. Larger?

Mr. HAMILTON. It is larger, and I think my records, as I have measured them it is three ten-thousandths or four ten-thousandths of an inch larger.

The COURT. Now, let me ask you this question. When you ascertained that fact that this barrel was considerably larger than Captain VanAmburgh's plug gauge, what thought came to your mind with reference to that difference?

Mr. HAMILTON. I can tell you exactly what I thought at that time.

The COURT. That is what I want. Anything different than what you said in your affidavit?

Mr. HAMILTON. Yes, sir, because I did not care to state it here, what went through my mind. I remember distinctly, and from what occurred here I now know I was unwarranted in entertaining that thought, and I will tell you what it was. I entered that plug and I looked through this barrel and the first thought came in my mind that the Court had been possibly, possibly the Court had been cleaning this barrel. I could not conceive to my mind why you would do it and did not think you would do it, but I said to myself no one else could have done it, cleaned that barrel. I looked at that barrel and admitted to myself it was a good job of cleaning.

The COURT. Even for a justice of this court to do?

Mr. HAMILTON. It impressed me. I remember at that time. I says that the Court must be familiar with fire arms and has cleaned it well. I immediately dispelled it because I said, 'No Court would alter an exhibit.'

The COURT. But you already said that the removal of the fouling would not account at all for that difference, haven't you?

Mr. HAMILTON. It wouldn't, it wouldn't account for it.

The COURT. Then if the Court had even done a good job in cleaning it, thatcouldn't [*sic*] have accounted for the difference?

Mr. HAMILTON. That couldn't account for that difference, and the thing I thought of at the time, I remembered the testimony about pittings and I looked in here and there were no pittings in this barrel, and that I took into account, and I am frank to admit to you.

The COURT. Do you think the Court by good cleaning could remove those pittings?

Mr. HAMILTON. I was satisfied you couldn't or anyone else couldn't do it.

The COURT. And you are satisfied that by the removal of the rust or dirt even under those circumstances you couldn't bring the old Sacco barrel up to—

Mr. HAMILTON. To that condition. There was one other thing went through my mind at that time; when I saw this barrel in this condition I immediately coupled it, the condition of this barrel and the possibility of somebody having cleaned it, with what I saw in a barrel in Montreal recently when I went in to buy—

The COURT. When was that?

Mr. HAMILTON. That was—I can give you the data that day I was there.

The COURT. It was since December, anyway?

Mr. HAMILTON. No, I was in Montreal before December, and I went into a store and purchased a Bayard 32 pistol, and as I looked into it it was very foul. I wanted it for a court exhibit. The man in charge took a brush, dipped it into a flour, and he simply cleaned the interior of it presto! It came out bright and clean. And I says, "Is it possible that that court or somebody for him has removed those rust spots?"

The COURT. And that is the only difference, that is the reason that entered into your mind?

Mr. HAMILTON. Yes, that went through my mind.

The COURT. That the Court did all those things, that the Court cleaned it?

Mr. HAMILTON. I did not think you did do it. I entertained it as a possibility.

The COURT. Oh, I see, and the same time you knew that by cleaning that barrel—

Mr. HAMILTON. Ordinarily it would not do it.

The COURT. Well, anyway, it wouldn't account for that difference, would it?

Mr. HAMILTON. No.

The COURT. Even though the Court did an excellent job in cleaning?

Mr. HAMILTON. Even though he done a job better than I had ever seen done or was able to do myself.

The COURT. Even then that would not have accounted for it?

Mr. HAMILTON. Would not have accounted for it, no, sir.

(50) Now, let me read on page 8 of the record of this investigation:

Mr. THOMPSON. Of course, Mr. Hamilton, you had in mind the desire, I think suggested by you but certainly in our minds all through these hearings and since then frequently reiterated, that a further experiment should be made for the purpose of seeing whether the firing pins made dents in the middle or not? You knew we were in hopes of having that experiment made?
Mr. HAMILTON. Yes. I might say that any substitution would be almost immediately detected by even a lay examiner. There is no possible chance of mixing up those two new barrels with the Sacco barrel.

(51) Now, then, the Commonwealth claims if he knows now that there could have been no mixup of these barrels which would not have been discovered, he must have known it on December 4 at Dedham, because he has no more information on the measurements of these diameters and the rusty pits now than he had then. Therefore, if he had this knowledge on December 4, 1923, the question would naturally be asked why he allowed Mr. Thompson, who was acting in the most perfect good faith, to ask the court to fire more cartridges through the barrel of a pistol the diameter of which measured .3053 [.3054] while the Sacco barrel measured only .2924, knowing that "any substitution would be immediately detected by even a lay examiner"? And why did he not tell Mr. Thompson that any further experiments with firing pin indentations on the primer of a cartridge fired in a barrel the diameter of which measured .3053 [.3054] would be prejudicial to the defendants, if the claim of prejudice now set up is true? Again is it or is it not possible for a man of the experience of Mr. Hamilton, knowing that the Sacco barrel was an old one filled with many rust pits, dirty and foul in its chamber, with cuts, scratches and marks on the outside of its muzzle and with a barrel diameter of .2924, to examine a new barrel for 15 or 20 minutes with no rust pits in its chamber, with no marks, cuts or scratches on its outside muzzle and with a diameter of .3054 and "not have a thought in his mind that it was not the Sacco barrel" as appears from his testimony on page 151 of this record of this investigation? If he

had this knowledge at that time he must have known that the experiment could have been of no assistance to the Court.

(52) Now, the Commonwealth claims that the discovery of a new barrel by Mr. Hamilton before or at the time the firing took place, would under these conditions lay the foundation for another motion for a new trial, and this foundation so laid it is claimed reveals the true motive, [sic]

(53) Again, it was argued before me with much force that Mr. Hamilton would not have set forth in his affidavit these facts about the condition of this new barrel or have written to Mr. Moore to have measurements made of this barrel before any firing was done, if he was not acting in good faith. In answer to this argument the Commonwealth claims it was a planned or "tricky" substitution, and Mr. Hamilton set forth these facts in his affidavit as a matter of self-protection.

(54) To both of these arguments I have asked myself many times this question—"Where would it have left Mr. Hamilton if he had not set forth these facts as he did? Would it or would it not have been evidence of guilty consciousness? Was it preparing the way to the final discovery of a new barrel in the Sacco pistol, which discovery he believed would have been a cause for a new trial, as claimed by the Commonwealth, or was it simply the calling in good faith, of the attention of the Court to the actual condition of the substituted barrel without any knowledge on his part?"

(55) It should be remembered that I am now merely stating the claims of counsel on both sides. It is not my purpose now to decide any of these disputed questions that bear upon the issue of intentional substitution. Before so doing I must examine all of the evidence with the treatest [sic] care, caution, and intelligence at my command. It is my purpose now to decide simply the question of whether or not the disputed barrel is the Sacco barrel, and in the determination of this question I am reviewing the salient features of the evidence.

(56) There is another piece of testimony of Mr. Hamilton to which I should refer, as bearing directly upon the identity of the old rusty and foul barrel in Hamilton's new pistol. He testified that this old rusty and foul barrel was a new barrel but that the extreme end of its muzzle had been artificially treated so as to make it look like an old muzzle. Because of this artificial treatment Mr. Hamilton distinguishes the disputed barrel from the Sacco barrel. In other words, whoever did this job of artificial treatment of the muzzle end, did so for the purpose of making the muzzle of the disputed barrel look like the old Sacco muzzle. If anyone connected

with the Commonwealth substituted this barrel, then, according to the testimony of Mr. Hamilton, he must have treated it artificially to make it look like an old muzzle after Mr. Hamilton had delivered his new pistol to Mr. Everett.

(57) Mr. Hamilton further testified that this artificial treatment was a very bad job. And he was asked why, whoever did it, did not get an old rusty, foul Colt automatic barrel of .32 caliber, for substitution, rather than do a bad job by artificially treating a new barrel so as to make it look like the old Sacco barrel. Mr. Hamilton said he could not say why.

(58) On Tuesday last, for the first time, on this disputed barrel Mr. Hamilton discovered what he said was a human hair imbedded [sic] in some substance which covered it. Pictures of this barrel were taken at the Turner studio. On Thursday that particular hair was gone but Mr. Hamilton made a new discovery of two more. The Court asked Mr. Hamilton to fix some definite time within which the first hair must have become attached to the muzzle of that pistol. He finally replied, "After November 8, 1923," the time when he reassembled the pistol. Although he admitted that he knew nothing about the prior history of the disputed barrel, yet he testified that the first hair became attached to the muzzle after November 8, 1923. Of course the purpose of this testimony was to show that the disputed barrel in the new pistol was not the Sacco barrel, because that barrel had never received any artificial treatment.

(59) Some time in October 1923, a photograph was taken of the muzzle of the Sacco barrel by Mr. Eckman of Bridgeport, Ct. Photographs, as I have already said, were taken of the disputed barrel by Mr. Turner. There appeared to be certain similarities between the Eckman photograph and the Turner photographs. Mr. Hamilton accounts for those similarities by claiming that whoever treated the muzzle of the disputed barrel for the purpose of making it look like the Sacco barrel, used the Eckman photograph for that purpose as a model.

(60) Let me consider now the request of counsel for the defendants to fire 100 or any substantial number of cartridges through the Sacco pistol for the purpose of proving that the location of the firing pin indentations off center on the primer established the individuality of the firing pin that made the indentation. In the first place it should be known that a certain shell (Winchester) was picked up near the dead body of Berardelli. At the trial it was known as the Fraher shell Ex. 4. The firing pin indentation on this shell was less off center than any of the test shells fired at Lowell. The question was raised whether or not the difference in the off center

indentations indicated any individuality in the firing pin of the Sacco pistol. In my judgment the motion should not have been allowed and would have been refused. My reasons are as follows: During the trial Messrs. Burns and Fitzgerald, two firearm experts called by the defendants, and Captain VanAmburgh and Captain Proctor fired at Lowell 14 test cartridges. The shells and bullets were used at the trial on the indictment before the jury as exhibits, excepting two of the bullets that were lost. If the Supreme Judicial Court should grant a new trial, then the Commonwealth and the defendants might be both prejudiced thereby, because the result on the bullets and the shells fired through the Sacco pistol in its present condition, would be entirely different on account of the present condition of the barrel, than when the test cartridges were fired at Lowell.

(61) Again, there is an additional important reason. This question of the individuality of the firing pin indentation was thoroughly tried out before the jury. Messrs. Burns and Fitzgerald testified that the firing pin indentation was no evidence of the individuality of the pistol that fired the shell. They both testified that the off center indentations and the flow back were common to all pistols. This off center indentation was due, in their judgment, to the varying pressure developed at the time of the explosion, which varied between 12,000 and 15,000 pounds to the square inch. In other words, because the tolerance or play between the cartridge and the chamber and the difference in firing pressure from 12,000 to 15,000 pounds per square inch at the time of the explosion, caused the indentations to vary in their off center locations upon the primer surface in proportion to the varying pressure then exerted.

(62) Mr. Fitzgerald, who had charge of the testing room in the Colt factory, testified that on all of the test shells fired at Lowell the indentations were in different locations on all the shells, which tended to prove that the firing pin indentations were not evidence of the individuality of the particular firing pin.

(63) It would seem as though Mr. Fitzgerald, who has been in the employ of the Colt Manufacturing Company for years and who had charge of its testing department, ought to be well qualified to express an opinion in regard to the individuality of the firing pin indentation of the pistol manufactured by the company for which he had worked for years. Mr. Hamilton testified that five cartridges fired would be just as good as more. This being true, why should I allow more cartridges to be fired when I had in my possession as exhibits at the time the request was made, more than that number of test shells that were fired at Lowell, which Mr.

Hamilton had previously examined, and based upon that examination made an affidavit in which he affirmed that by comparison between the indentation on the picked-up shell and the test shells fired at Lowell, he was of the unqualified opinion that the picked-up shell was not fired by the Sacco pistol.

(64) If there was any individuality about the location of the indentation on the shell picked up near the dead body of Berardelli, because it was nearer the center of the primer than on the test shells, why would not two men of the experience of Messrs. Burns and Fitzgerald, who were employed by the defendants, have discovered it, and why should they have testified against the interests of the defendants that the location of these firing pin indentations carried with them no individuality of the firing pin that made said indentations?

(65) After Mr. Hamilton had formed this unqualified opinion that the picked up shell or Fraher shell Exh. 4 was not fired through the Sacco pistol, the question might be asked whether or not the request for more firing through the Sacco pistol, after his discovery of the condition of the barrel in the Sacco pistol, was not made for the purpose of allowing him to discover the new barrel in the Sacco pistol?

(66) In my judgment, this issue having been fully, fairly and thoroughly tried out before the jury, it ought to be considered closed.

(67) There is another matter to which I wish to refer, and it is this: assuming that the disputed barrel is not the Sacco barrel, what effect would that have upon the motions for new trials? In my judgment none. This is so because all that remained for me to do was to file my decisions upon the motions for new trials. Suppose somebody had broken into the clerk's office and had stolen all of those exhibits. That would not mean the granting of a new trial. This is so because there had been a full trial before a jury on the indictments, and verdicts were rendered by the jury. And this being true, even the stealing of all the fire-arm exhibits would not as matter of law affect the verdicts already rendered by the jury. Therefore, if it cannot affect the verdicts, it ought not as a matter of law to require a new trial, because the only question involved is whether or not those verdicts of the jury should be set aside. If a new trial should be granted, then the loss of the Sacco barrel (if it has been lost) might be of importance to both sides. But that question is not now under consideration. If the only question involved was the right of the court to go ahead with the decisions on the motions for new trials now pending, I should in all probability have so proceeded without much delay. But I have been dealing with a question

of the greatest importance, that affects the very life of our courts, a very important branch of the government of this Commonwealth. The willful substitution of barrels in exhibits used in the trial of murder cases is of such great importance to defendants, as well as to the Commonwealth, that it demands on the part of the court a most searching investigation.

(68) There is one more matter to which I desire to refer briefly. It is the photographs. As I have already stated, Mr. Eckman, sometime in October 1923, took a picture of the Sacco barrel, at Bridgeport, Connecticut, where Captain VanAmburgh lived. Deputy Sheriff Coulter took the barrel there, accompanied by Mr. Keith, Assistant District Attorney. At that time many pictures were taken of some of the bullets that were exhibits used at the trial and which were to be filed and were filed by Captain VanAmburgh attached to his affidavit. Only one picture was taken of the muzzle of this barrel and this one was taken for the purpose of photographing the lands of the barrel. On this account the camera was very much out of focus. This one photograph was introduced for the purpose of proving it was a photograph of the Sacco barrel. Captain VanAmburgh testified to this effect and pointed out to the court marks and cuts on the disputed barrel that appeared to him to be on the photograph. Photographs were also taken in the last week of this hearing by Mr. Turner. Comparisons were then made by all the experts between the Eckman photograph and the Turner photographs. Messrs. Hamilton and Turner testified that Mr. Turner's photograph did not correspond with the Eckman photograph and therefore could not have been the photograph of the Sacco barrel. Captain VanAmburgh and Mr. Eckman testified that the Eckman photograph and the Turner photographs were those of the same object, and therefore the Turner photographs were those of the Sacco barrel. On this disputed question it might be well to inquire why District Attorney Williams, who has been charged inferentially with knowledge of this substitution of barrels, should offer in evidence a photograph of the muzzle of a barrel that he knew had been artificially treated to make it look like the Sacco pistol. The defendants knew nothing of this photograph. Captain VanAmburgh wrote for it, and Mr. Eckman sent it to him by mail. Captain VanAmburgh testified that the barrel that Mr. Eckman took a picture of was the original Sacco barrel. If Mr. Williams knew that this photograph represented an artificially treated muzzle and was not the Sacco barrel, would he have introduced that photograph in evidence, when its very introduction would have been a contemptuous fraud upon the court?

(69) The experts called by the defendants testified that they could not see any similarities between the Eckman and the Turner photographs that appeared to them. But one or both of them were asked if I could not see similarities between them. The reply was in substance that while they would look similar to me, to the trained and skillful eye of the expert they would look dissimilar. Let me quote from page 26 of the record of this investigation an answer by Mr. Hamilton in reply to a question.

> Q You will have to make me an expert almost as good as Mr. Turner and some of these others. A. I want to clear it for this reason. To the untrained eye—I am analyzing these 2 spots for the reason that to the untrained eye those 2 spots would appear to be, of course, the same thing. The moment those spots are analyzed, as I will later show when I analyze some other spots, there is no question in my mind at the present moment but what the barrel that photograph 6-H (Turner) was made from, that photograph 1-H (Eckman) was the model from which that barrel was put in its present condition. There is no question in my mind about that whatever. Instead of 1-H (Eckman) being a photograph of the disputed barrel, the disputed barrel was modeled on its muzzle after photograph 1-H (Eckman) and it [*sic*] easy to be led astray. If you look at those 2 squares ...

(70) In other words, the claim is made that some one in order to defeat the desire of Mr. Hamilton to fire more cartridges through the Sacco barrel took the Eckman photograph as a model and artificially treated the muzzle end of the disputed barrel for the purpose of making it look like the Eckman photograph and then claim that it was the photograph of the Sacco barrel. When one throws the searchlight of human probabilities upon this opinion it almost forces one to the conclusion that when expert testimony gets started on its way with its momentum of enthusiasm, interest and bias behind it, there would seem to be no mountain of perplexing difficulties too steep for it to ascend.

(71) To this answer of the experts that marks may look similar to me but dissimilar to them, all I can say is that I can only use to the best of my ability the eyes that I have been endowed with; and, using them, with

a strong magnifying glass and with the naked eye I could see marks and things upon the Turner pictures that to me appeared upon the Eckman photograph. I could do this without even suggestions from either Captain VanAmburgh or Mr. Eckman, both of whom called my attention to many similarities. It would seem to be unprofitable for me to state in detail all of the similarities that I observed. Suffice it to say that after a thorough study of all the evidence and a careful examination of all the photographs I am of the opinion that the Eckman photographs and the Turner photographs were taken of the same object, and that object was the Sacco barrel.

(72) There are other matters to which I might refer, but it would seem to be to no purpose so far as this investigation is concerned. Connected with this investigation the evidence in some respects has been very disturbing. Conditions have arisen that have been very distressing to me, but they were not of my creation, and neither were they created by the defendants themselves. Therefore there should not be in any quarter whatsoever the slightest prejudice against them nor should their legal rights in the remotest degree to be affected thereby. But although these conditions were not created by me, yet I have tried to meet and decide them according to the best of my ability and judgment and in conducting this investigation as I have tried to serve the best interests of all the people of the Commonwealth.

Decision

(73) I find that the old rusty and foul barrel that was in Hamilton's new pistol is the original Sacco barrel and the new barrel in the Sacco pistol belongs in Mr. Hamilton's new pistol. It is therefore ordered that these two barrels be transferred to their respective pistols. It is further ordered that the order made by this court on November 8, 1923, to the effect that these three pistols be delivered into the custody of the Clerk of the Superior Court for the County of Norfolk be continued in force and said pistols shall remain impounded with him until the further order of this Court.

March 21st 1924   WEBSTER THAYER
                                 JUSTICE OF THE SUPERIOR COURT

(Filed March 25, 1924)

A true copy, Attest:
ss: Willard E. Everett Assistant Clerk

196 The paragraph numbers have been added by the author.

204 The references to March 1923 in the first and third questions in paragraph 49 should be April 6.

204 The references to .3053 in the first, second, and fifth questions should be .3054.

205 The references to .3053 in the fourth and fifth questions should be .3054.

208 The references to .3053 in paragraph 51 should be .3054.

APPENDIX B

Sacco's motion for time to file exception to Judge Thayer's March 25, 1924, Decision re switching of gun barrels. Notice his handwritten order of March 27, 1924, extending time until April 12, 1924.

#132

COMMONWEALTH OF MASSACHUSETTS

Norfolk, ss.   Superior Court
                                               Criminal Session

Commonwealth of Massachusetts   )   No. 5545

            vs.   ) MOTION FOR EXTENSION OF TIME
                                       TO FILE BILL OF EXCEPTIONS IN
Nicola Sacco and Bartolomeo Vanzetti) CONNECTION WITH COURT'S ORDER

            "In re substitution of Barrels in Court Exhibit Pistols".

          Comes now Fred H. Moore appearing for and on behalf of

Nicola Sacco one of the defendants in the above entitled cause, and

moves that the statutory time to file his Bill of Exceptions to the

Court's order or finding in connection with "In re Substitution of

Barrels in Court Exhibit Pistols" of date March 25th, 1924, be

extended for 30 days on and after March 3 1924.

                              Fred Moore
                              Wm. J. Callahan
                              Attorney for Nicola Sacco. per J W

          I, Harold P. Williams, District Attorney of Norfolk County,

Commonwealth of Massachusetts hereby assent to the defendant's

motion for an extension of time for filing Bill of Exceptions

to the Court's order "in re substitution of Barrels in Court Exhibit

Pistols" for 30 days on and after March 3 1924.

          Dated this 27th day of March 1924.

                              _H. J. W_
                              District Attorney Norfolk County

Time extended until
April 12th 1924.
          Nichols Frazer, justice of the superior court
Mch. 27th 1924

COMMONWEALTH OF MASSACHUSETTS.

APPENDIX C

Chronology of Major Events

1880

- Huge Italian immigration began and lasted until 1920.

1886

- The Chicago Haymarket Affair was a defining event for the anarchist movement in America. Seven policemen were killed. Seven German immigrants and one American, all anarchists, were arrested. Seven were given the death penalty.

1888

- Bartolomeo Vanzetti was born in Villafalletto, in the Piedmont district of northern Italy.

1891

- Nicola Sacco was born in Torremaggiore in southern Italy.

1892

- New Orleans citizens lynched eleven Italians following the unsolved murder of Chief of Police D. C. Hennessey. A prelude to over fifty lynchings and many serious assaults against Italian workers and their families over the next thirty years.

1901

- President McKinley was assassinated by Leon Czolgosz, an avowed anarchist.

1902

- Luigi Galleani, a leader of the Italian anarchist movement, arrived in America. He began publication of *Cronaca Sovversiva* (*Subversive Chronical*) the following year.

1908

- Sacco and Vanzetti separately immigrated to America.

1912

- Sacco participated in the strike at the giant American Woolen Mills in Lawrence, Massachusetts.
- Eugene V. Debs, the socialist candidate, received an unexpected large vote in the presidential election.

1913

- Sacco participated in the strike at Draper Company, in Hopedale, Massachusetts.

1914

- The Ludlow massacre resulted in the deaths of twelve adults and thirteen children during a strike at the Ludlow, Colorado, company mines owned by John D. Rockefeller. Anarchists vowed revenge.
- The Great War begins in Europe.

1915

- Anarchists were blamed for New York bombings at St. Alphonsos Church, St. Patrick's Cathedral, the Bronx courthouse, and the Tombs police court.

1916

- Mooney-Billings bombing in San Francisco and the reprisal bombing at the Boston Salutation Street Station occurred.
- Vanzetti participated in the Plymouth Cordage Company strike in Plymouth, Massachusetts.

1917

- United States entered World War I.
- The Espionage Act was adopted.
- Sacco and Vanzetti fled to Mexico with other anarchists to avoid conscription. They returned to America shortly thereafter.
- The Russian Revolution started.
- The Milwaukee bomb tragedy killed ten policemen and one woman. Anarchists were blamed.

1918

- The Sedition Act was adopted.
- Galleani was arrested and *Cronaca Sovversiva* was outlawed.
- Judge Kenesaw Mountain Landis, in Chicago, sentenced 101 radical members of the Wobblies to long prison terms.
- Eugene V. Debs was convicted under the Sedition Act and sentenced to ten years for an earlier antiwar speech.
- World War I ended.

1919

- A plot to assassinate President Wilson was uncovered.
- The May Day celebration followed a series of bombings intended to force America to recognize Soviet Russia.

- Galleani was deported and *Cronaca Sovversiva* was put out of business.
- Following Galleani's deportation, bombs were set off in seven cities in retaliation.
- Bombs were mailed to thirty leading citizens and officials. They were intercepted and defused, with one casualty.
- Attorney General Palmer ordered the first Red Raid of radical groups.
- Radicals were rounded up and deported to Russia on *The Buford*, nicknamed the "Soviet Ark."
- Governor Calvin Coolidge broke the Boston police strike.
- A failed holdup of the L. Q. White Shoe Company payroll in Bridgewater, Massachusetts, was attempted by four bandits on Christmas Eve.

1920

- Attorney General Palmer ordered a second raid on radicals in thirty-three cities.
- Justice Department arrested and detained Andrew Salsedo and Roberto Elia, New York printers of radical literature.
- Payroll robbery and murder of a paymaster and his guard occurred in South Braintree, Massachusetts.
- Inquest and grand jury investigations conducted for South Braintree crimes.
- Vanzetti was sent to New York to determine the fate of Salsedo and Elia.
- Salsedo's dead body was found on the pavement below the fourteenth-floor detention center where he had been confined. Government claimed suicide; anarchists claimed murder.
- Sacco and Vanzetti were arrested for the South Braintree murders; both were held without bond.
- Katzmann prosecuted Vanzetti alone, in Plymouth, before Judge Webster Thayer, for the Bridgewater attempted holdup. Vanzetti was convicted and sentenced for that crime.
- Fred Moore took over the defense of Sacco and Vanzetti at the murder trial in Dedham. He represented Sacco and appointed the McAnarney brothers to represent Vanzetti.
- Wall Street bombing occurred.

1921–1923

- Angelina DeFalco attempted to shake down Sacco and Vanzetti in 1921.
- Sacco and Vanzetti were tried and convicted of first-degree murder at Dedham, in 1921.
- Five supplementary motions for a new trial were filed in 1921, 1922, and 1923.
- Sacco had a mental breakdown in 1923. He recovered in 1924.

1924

- Judge Thayer denied all five pending motions for a new trial.
- Moore and the McAnarney brothers withdrew their representation of Sacco and Vanzetti.
- William Thompson, as appellate counsel, joined by Herbert Ehrmann as his co-counsel, took over the appeal and further defense of Sacco and Vanzetti.

1925

- Celestino Medeiros confessed to having participated in the South Braintree murders. He absolved Sacco and Vanzetti from any involvement in the crime.
- Vanzetti had a mental breakdown and recovered shortly thereafter.

1926

- Supreme judicial court affirmed convictions of Sacco and Vanzetti and denied Thompson's appeal of Judge Thayer's rejection of all five supplementary motions for a new trial.
- Thompson filed a motion for a new trial based on the Medeiros confession.
- Judge Thayer denied the Medeiros motion for a new trial.

1927

- Thompson appealed the denial of the Medeiros motion for a new trial to the supreme judicial court.
- Supreme judicial court affirmed Judge Thayer's denial of the Medeiros motion for a new trial.
- Vanzetti filed a petition for clemency with Governor Fuller.
- Governor Fuller appointed an advisory committee for recommendations regarding the clemency petition.
- Advisory committee found the trial fair and confirmed the guilt of Sacco and Vanzetti.
- Governor Fuller denied the petition for clemency.
- Thirteen days of defense efforts to stay the execution of Sacco and Vanzetti failed.
- Sacco and Vanzetti were executed at midnight on August 23.

APPENDIX D

Principal Characters

Berardelli, Alessandro: Payroll guard murdered at South Braintree.

Boda, Mike: Anarchist friend of Sacco and Vanzetti and South Braintree murder suspect, but never charged.

Callahan, William: Assistant defense attorney for Vanzetti during Plymouth trial.

Coacci, Ferruccio: Anarchist friend of Sacco and Vanzetti and South Braintree murder suspect, but never charged.

Connolly, Michael: Officer who arrested Sacco and Vanzetti.

DeFalco, Angelina: Court interpreter who tried to shake down Sacco-Vanzetti Defense Committee.

Ehrmann, Herbert: Assistant appellate defense counsel for Sacco and Vanzetti in Dedham trial.

Frankfurter, Felix: Harvard law professor, advisor to defense committee, critic and author, condemned practices of Judge Thayer and prosecutor Katzmann. Professor Frankfurter was appointed to the United States Supreme Court by President Roosevelt in 1939 and was awarded the Presidential Medal of Freedom in 1963.

Fuller, Alvan T.: Governor of Massachusetts, denied clemency for Sacco and Vanzetti.

Galleani, Luigi: Leading proponent of anarchism in America, publisher of *Cronaca Sovversiva,* and advocate of violence if necessary to achieve goals.

Katzmann, Frederick: District attorney and prosecutor of Vanzetti in the Plymouth trial and Sacco and Vanzetti in the Dedham trial.

Lowell, A. Lawrence: President of Harvard University, chairman of the governor's advisory committee.

McAnarney, Jeremiah: Dedham trial counsel for Vanzetti.

Medeiros, Celestino: Confessed to participating in the South Braintree murders. Declared Sacco and Vanzetti were not involved.

Moore, Fred: Dedham trial counsel for Sacco and chief counsel for both defendants.

Morelli, Frank ("Butsey"): Confessed to Vincent Teresa that Morelli gang members were responsible for the South Braintree crimes.

Morelli, Joseph: Sacco look-alike, confessed to his cellmate that Morelli gang members were responsible for the South Braintree crimes.

Orciani, Ricardo: Anarchist friend of Sacco and Vanzetti and South Braintree murder suspect, but never charged.

Palmer, Mitchell: United States Attorney General during Red Scare.

Parmenter, Frederick: Paymaster murdered at South Braintree.

Proctor, William: Veteran Massachusetts State Police captain, initial lead investigator, ballistics expert for the Commonwealth, and provider of misleading "consistent with" opinion that Bullet III was shot through Sacco's pistol.

Sacco, Nicola: Convicted at the Dedham trial for the Berardelli murder at South Braintree.

Stewart, Michael: Captain of Bridgewater's two-man police department and successor to Captain Proctor as lead investigator.

Thayer, Webster: Judge during the Vanzetti Plymouth trial and the Sacco-Vanzetti Dedham trial.

Thompson, William: Chief appellate defense counsel for Sacco and Vanzetti for Dedham murder verdicts.

Vahey, John: Vanzetti's Plymouth trial lawyer.

VanAmburgh, Charles: Retired army captain and ballistics expert for the Commonwealth in the Dedham murder trial.

Vanzetti, Bartolomeo: Convicted at the Dedham trial for the Berardelli murder at South Braintree.

Williams, Harold: Prosecutor and successor to Katzmann as district attorney in Dedham murder trial.

SOURCES

I have relied principally on the following sources in the preparation of this book:

The five volumes of the transcript of the record regarding the Dedham trial of the South Braintree murders and subsequent proceedings, published by Henry Holt and Company, 1928, and identified by reference to page numbers Tr. 1-5621.

The supplemental volume of the incomplete transcript of the record regarding the Plymouth trial of the Bridgewater attempted holdup, the preliminary hearing regarding the Bridgewater crime, certain Pinkerton reports and the inquest regarding the South Braintree murders, published by Henry Holt and Company, 1928, and identified by reference to page numbers Supp. Tr. 1-143.

Federal Bureau of Investigation files regarding the Sacco-Vanzetti matter, released under the Freedom of Information Act (14 parts), approximately 2000 pages.

Responses from Massachusetts authorities and the FBI regarding missing fingerprints on the Buick getaway car.

Response from Brockton authorities regarding the Brockton Police report of May 5, 1920, relating to the arrest of Sacco and Vanzetti.

Files maintained by the Harvard Law School regarding hearings relating to Judge Webster Thayer's investigation into the substitution of the barrel of Sacco's gun.

Judge Webster Thayer's March 25, 1924, Decision In re: The Substitution of Barrels in Court Exhibit Pistols.

Four appeal papers relating to the aborted appeal to the Massachusetts Supreme Judicial Court of Judge Thayer's March 25, 1924, Decision: In re The Substitution of Barrels in Court Exhibit Pistols.

Several hundred news stories in the *New York Times* circa 1920–1928.

Books and Periodicals:

Allen, Frederick Lewis. *Only Yesterday.* New York: John Wiley & Sons, Inc., 1931.

Aron, Paul. *Unsolved Mysteries of American History.* Chapter 18: "Were Sacco and Vanzetti Guilty?" New York: John Wiley & Sons, Inc., 1997.

Asch, Nathan. *Pay Day.* Detroit, Michigan: Omnigraphics, Inc., 1990. Originally published, *New York Times*, 1930.

Avrich, Paul. *Anarchist Portraits.* Princeton, New Jersey: Princeton University Press, 1985.

Avrich, Paul. *Sacco and Vanzetti: The Anarchist Background.* Princeton, New Jersey: Princeton University Press, 1991.

Barone, Michael. *The New Americans.* Washington, D.C.: Regnary Publishing, Inc., 2001.

Beffel, John. "Eels and the Electric Chair," *New Republic*, December 1920.

Behrman, S. N. *Rain From Heaven.* New York: Random House, 1934.

Borsella, Cristogianni. *On Persecution, Identity & Activism: Aspects of the Italian-American Experience from the Late 19th Century to Today.* Wellesley, Massachusetts: Dante University Press, 2005.

Bortman, Eli. *Sacco & Vanzetti.* Beverly, Massachusetts: Commonwealth Editions, 2005.

Boston Public Library. *Sacco-Vanzetti: Developments and Reconsiderations–1979.* Conference Proceedings. Boston: Trustees of the Public Library of the City of Boston, 1979.

Caputo, Jr., Silvio J. *The Death of Spring.* Port Washington, New York: Ashley Books, Inc., 1984.

Colp, Ralph, Jr. "Bitter Christmas," *Nation,* December 1958.

Colp, Ralph, Jr. "Sacco's Struggle for Sanity," *Nation,* August 1958.

Cook, Fred J. "Sacco and Vanzetti," *Nation,* August 1929.

D'Alessandro, Frank M. *The Verdict of History on Sacco and Vanzetti.* New York: Jay Street Publishers, 1997.

Dos Passos, John. *Facing the Chair: Story of the Americanization of Two Foreign Born Workmen.* Boston: Sacco-Vanzetti Defense Committee, 1927.

Ehrmann, Herbert B. *The Untried Case: The Sacco-Vanzetti Case and the Morelli Gang.* New York: The Vanguard Press, 1933.

Ehrmann, Herbert B. *The Case That Will Not Die: Commonwealth vs. Sacco and Vanzetti.* Boston: Little, Brown, 1969.

Evans, Colin. *Murder Two: The Second Casebook of Forensic Detection.* Wiley, 2004.

Fast, Howard. *The Passion of Sacco and Vanzetti.* New York: The Blue Heron Press, Inc., 1953.

Felix, David. *Protest: Sacco-Vanzetti and the Intellectuals.* Bloomington, Indiana: Indiana University Press, 1965.

Feuerlicht, Roberta Strauss. *Justice Crucified: The Story of Sacco and Vanzetti.* New York: McGraw-Hill, 1977.

Fraenkel, Osmond K. *The Sacco-Vanzetti Case.* New York: Alfred A. Knopf, 1931.

Frankfurter, Felix. "The Case of Sacco and Vanzetti," *Atlantic*, March 1927.

Frankfurter, Felix. *The Case of Sacco and Vanzetti: A Critical Analysis for Lawyers and Laymen.* Boston: Little, Brown, 1927.

Funk & Wagnall's New Encyclopedia, 1971.

Gambino, Richard. *Blood of My Blood: The Dilemma of the Italian-Americans.* Garden City, New York: Doubleday & Company, Inc., 1974.

Gambino, Richard. *Vendetta: The True Story of the Largest Lynching in U. S. History.* Toronto: Guernica, 1998.

Gerber, Samuel and Richard Saferstein, Editors. *More Chemistry and Crime: From Marsh Arsenic Test to DNA Profile.* American Chemical Society, Washington, D.C., 1997.

Hason, Erica. *The 1920s.* San Diego: Lucent Books, 1999.

Higham, John. *Strangers in the Land: Patterns of American Nativism 1860–1925.* New York: Atheneum, 1969.

Jackson, Brian. *The Black Flag.* London: Routhedge & Kegan Paul, 1981.

Joughin, G. Louis and Edmund M. Morgan. *The Legacy of Sacco and Vanzetti.* New York: Harcourt, Brace, 1948.

Kadane, Joseph B. and David A. Schum. *A Probabilistic Analysis of the Sacco and Vanzetti Evidence.* New York: John Wiley & Sons, Inc., 1996.

Kornbluh, Joyce L., Editor. *Rebel Voices: An IWW Anthology.* Ann Arbor, Michigan: The University of Michigan Press, 1964.

LaGumina, Salvatore J. *WOP!: A Documentary History of Anti-Italian Discrimination.* Toronto: Guernica, 1999.

Landau, Elaine. *Sacco and Vanzetti: Cornerstones of Freedom.* New York: Scholastic, Inc., 2004.

Lee, Dr. Henry, Chairman. Report of Firearm Examination Panel—Select Committee on Sacco and Vanzetti, 1983.

Lee, Dr. Henry and Dr. Jerry Labriola. *Famous Crimes Revisited: From Sacco-Vanzetti to O.J. Simpson.* Southington, Connecticut: Strong Books, 2001.

Lyons, Eugene. *The Life and Death of Sacco and Vanzetti.* New York: International Publishers, 1927.

Marks, Jeannette. *Thirteen Days.* New York: Albert & Charles Boni, 1929.

Monroe, Judy. *The Sacco and Vanzetti Controversial Murder Trial.* Berkeley Heights, New Jersey: Enshaw Publishers, Inc., 2000.

Montgomery, Robert H. *Sacco-Vanzetti: The Murder and the Myth.* New York: Devin-Adair, 1960.

Moquin, Wayne, Charles Van Doren and Francis A. J. Ianni. *A Documentary History of the Italian Americans.* New York: Praeger Publishers, 1974.

Musmanno, Michael J. *After Twelve Years.* New York: Alfred A. Knopf, 1939.

Newby, Richard. *Kill Now, Talk Forever: Debating Sacco and Vanzetti.* Bloomington, Indiana: Author House, 2006.

Nickell, Joe and John F. Fischer. *Crime Science: Methods of Forensic Detection.* University Press of Kentucky, 1999.

Owen, David. *Hidden Evidence.* Firefly Books Ltd., 2000.

Porter, Katherine Anne. *The Never-Ending Wrong.* Boston: Little, Brown, 1977.

Rappaport, Doreen. *The Sacco-Vanzetti Trial.* New York: Harper Collins Publishers, 1992.

Richards, David A. J. *Italian American: The Racializing of an Ethnic Identity.* New York: New York University Press, 1999.

Ridge, Lola. *Dance of Fire,* "Three Men Die." New York: Smith and Haas, 1935.

Roediger, David R. *Working Toward Whiteness.* Cambridge, Massachusetts: Basic Books, 2005.

Rolle, Andrew. *The Italian Americans: Troubled Roots.* Norman, Oklahoma: University of Oklahoma Press, 1980.

Russell, Francis. *Tragedy in Dedham: The Story of the Sacco-Vanzetti Case.* New York: McGraw-Hill, 1962.

Russell, Francis. *Sacco & Vanzetti: The Case Resolved.* New York: Harper & Row, 1986.

Sacco, Nicola and Bartolomeo Vanzetti. *The Letters of Sacco and Vanzetti.* Ed. Marion Denman Frankfurter and Gardner Jackson. New York: Viking, 1928.

Silva, Frank. "The Frank Silva Story," *Outlook and Independent,* 1928.

Sinclair, Upton. *Boston: A Documentary Novel of the Sacco-Vanzetti Case.* New York: Albert and Charles Boni, 1928.

Solomon, Barbara Miller. *Ancestors and Immigrants: A Changing New England Tradition.* New York: John Wiley & Sons, Inc., Science Editions, 1956.

Starrs, James E. "Once More Unto the Breech: The Firearms Evidence in the Sacco and Vanzetti Case Revisited," *Journal of Forensic Sciences.* April/July 1986.

Teresa, Vincent with Thomas C. Renner. *My Life in the Mafia.* New York: Doubleday & Company, Inc., 1973.

Thompson, William. "Vanzetti's Last Statement". Boston: *Atlantic,* 1928.

Topp, Michael M. *The Sacco and Vanzetti Case: A Brief History with Documents (The Bedford Series in History and Culture).* Boston: Bedford Books, 2004.

Tuchman, Barbara W. *The Proud Tower.* New York: Random House, 1962.

Urofsky, Melvin I. *Felix Frankfurter: Judicial Restraint and Individual Liberties.* Boston: Twayne Publishers, 1991.

Vanzetti, Bartolomeo. *The Story of a Proletarian Life,* translated by Eugene Lyons. Boston: Sacco-Vanzetti Defense Committee, circa 1921.

Vanzetti, Bartolomeo. *Background of the Plymouth Trial,* written while in Charlestown State Prison.

Watson, Bruce. *Bread & Roses: Mills, Migrants and the Struggle for the American Dream.* New York: Viking, 2005.

Watson, Bruce. *Sacco and Vanzetti: The Men, the Murders, and the Judgment of Mankind.* New York: Viking, 2007.

Weeks, Robert P., Ed. *Commonwealth vs. Sacco and Vanzetti.* Englewood Cliffs, New Jersey: Prentice-Hall, 1958.

Wilson, Edmund. *Letters on Literature and Politics.* New York: Farrar, Straus & Giroux, 1977.

Young, William and David E. Kaiser. *Postmortem: New Evidence in the Case of Sacco and Vanzetti.* Amherst, Massachusetts: The University of Massachusetts Press, 1985.

NOTES

See sources for full titles and information regarding publications abbreviated in the notes below.

CHAPTER 1

An Overview

1   Lyons, *The Life and Death*, 68.

2   Wilson, *Letters on Literature and Politics*, 154; Avrich, *Sacco and Vanzetti*, 5.

3   Watson, *Sacco and Vanzetti*, 365.

4   Vanzetti's words, Russell, *Tragedy*, 387-388 (and note).

5   Vanzetti's words, see Ehrmann, *The Case*, 459.

6   Vanzetti's metaphor, see Russell, *Sacco & Vanzetti*, 221.

CHAPTER 2

Boston in the 1920s

1   Higham, *Strangers*, generally; Feuerlicht, *Justice*, generally.

2   Feuerlicht, *Justice*, 31 et seq.

3   Ibid. 47.

4   Ibid. 59.

5   Ibid. 59.

6   Higham, *Strangers*, Chapters One, Two and 285 et seq.

7   Lyons, *The Life and Death*, 30–31; Watson, *Bread and Roses*, 9.

8   Watson, *Bread and Roses*, generally.

9   Lyons, *The Life and Death*, 29.

10   Moquin, et al., *A Documentary*, generally, and 99–110, 163–252, 253–270; Rolle, *The Italian Americans*, generally, and 71–72, 83–85, and 156; Higham, *Strangers*, 90–91; La Gumina, *WOP!*, generally, and 198–203.

11   Gambino, *Vendetta*, generally, and 77–88.

12   Ibid. 77.

13   Ibid. 79.

14   Ibid.

15   Ibid. 97.

16   Ibid.

17   Ibid.

18   Moquin, et al., *A Documentary*, 167–170; Gambino, *Blood of My Blood*, 119.

19   Moquin, et al., *A Documentary*, 259–262.

20   Barone, *The New Americans*, 143.

21   Feuerlicht, *Justice*, 79–80; Avrich, *Sacco and Vanzetti*, 46. For a detailed history of anarchism, see: Avrich, *Anarchist Portraits*, generally.

22   Avrich, *Sacco and Vanzetti*, 130.

23 Lyons, *The Life and Death*, 64.

24 *Funk and Wagnalls* (re: anarchism), Vol. 2, 81 (re: communism), Vol. 6, 358–366 (re: socialism); Vol. 21, 443–447.

25 Avrich, *Sacco and Vanzetti*, 48–51.

26 Avrich, *Sacco and Vanzetti*, 93–162; Topp, *The Sacco and Vanzetti Case*, 14; Lyons, *The Life and Death*, 36–42.

27 Rolle, *The Italian Americans*, 20, 71–72; Avrich, *Sacco and Vanzetti*, 99–100. See Avrich, *Sacco and Vanzetti*, 97–102, for more bombings in New York City, the poisoning at the University Club in Chicago, the Mooney-Billings incident in California and other acts of terrorism.

28 Avrich, *Sacco and Vanzetti*, 98–102.

29 Edward Cunha, who led the prosecution against Tom Mooney, interviewed by John A. Fitch of *Survey* magazine in July 1917.

30 Avrich, *Sacco and Vanzetti*, 93. For the bombings and other tumultuous events that followed America's entry into World War I, see Ibid. 93–162. See also Feuerlicht, *Justice*, 89–138, generally, and 93; Topp, *The Sacco and Vanzetti Case*, 14–17.

31 Avrich, *Sacco and Vanzetti*, 104–105.

32 Ibid. 94.

33 Ibid. 139.

34 Ibid. 140-143.

35 Ibid. 174 et seq.

36 Ibid. 175.

37 Feuerlicht, *Justice*, 132–135.

38 Ibid. 134.

39 Joughin and Morgan, *The Legacy*, 212.

40 Avrich, *Sacco and Vanzetti*, 177.

CHAPTER 3

Nicola and Bartolomeo

1 Lyons, *The Life and Death*, 11–16; Avrich, *Anarchist Portraits*, 162–175 re their anarchist background.

2 Avrich, *Sacco and Vanzetti*, 17.

3 Avrich, *Sacco and Vanzetti*, 21–22.

4 Joughin and Morgan, *The Legacy*, 456.

5 Avrich, *Sacco and Vanzetti*, 26.

6 Watson, *Bread and Roses*, 222.

7 Watson, *Sacco and Vanzetti*, 28–29.

8 Joughin and Morgan, *The Legacy*, 456.

9 Ibid.; Avrich, *Sacco and Vanzetti*, 70.

10 Avrich, *Sacco and Vanzetti*, 69.

11 Ibid.

12 Ibid. 228, Note 45.

13 Russell, *Tragedy*, 238–242 (re: Sacco); 266–267 (re: Vanzetti); see also, Ralph Colp, Jr., M.D., *The Nation*, "Sacco's Struggle for Sanity," August 15, 1958, 65–70; Colp, Jr., *The Nation*, "Bitter Christmas," December 27, 1958, 493–495.

14 Avrich, *Sacco and Vanzetti*, 37.

15 Vanzetti, *The Story*, 2.

16 Avrich, *Sacco and Vanzetti*, 18.

17 Vanzetti, *The Story*, 2.

18 Ibid. 3.

19 Vanzetti, *The Story*, 13.

20 Ibid. 3.

21 Ibid.

22 Ibid.

23 Ibid.

24 Ibid. 5.

25   Ibid.

26   Ibid. 9.

27   Ibid.

28   Ibid. 10.

29   Avrich, *Sacco and Vanzetti*, 34.

30   Vanzetti, *The Story*, 14.

31   Ibid.

32   Ibid.

33   Ibid. 14–16.

34   Avrich, *Sacco and Vanzetti*, 43.

35   Ibid.

36   Musmanno, *After Twelve Years*, 178; Tr. 4921–4922; Frankfurter and Jackson, *The Letters*, 81, 121, 204.

37   Sacco and Vanzetti, *The Letters*, 204.

38   Watson, *Sacco and Vanzetti*, 15.

39   Avrich, *Sacco and Vanzetti*, 42.

40   Ibid. 32.

41   Feuerlicht, *Justice*, 26.

42   Watson, *Sacco and Vanzetti*, 162.

43   Ibid. 346.

44   Russell, *Tragedy*, 266.

45   Ralph Colp, Jr., M.D., *The Nation*, "Bitter Christmas," December 27, 1958, 493.

46   Ibid.

47   Russell, *Tragedy*, 266–267; Joughin and Morgan, *The Legacy*, 471–472; Lyons, *The Life and Death*, 119–120.

CHAPTER 4

Bridgewater and the Plymouth Trial

1 Lyons: *The Life and Death*, 47–48; Topp, *The Sacco and Vanzetti Case,* 1–2.

2 Ehrmann: *The Case*, 3–19; Avrich, *Sacco and Vanzetti*, 199 et seq.

3 Ehrmann, *The Case*, 42, 89.

4 Ibid. 13.

5 Watson, *Sacco and Vanzetti,* 49-50; Young and Kaiser, *Postmortem,* 23-24.

6 Ibid.

7 Russell, *Tragedy*, 18.

8 Watson, *Sacco and Vanzetti*, 54; Russell, *Tragedy,* 63–64.

9 Supp. Tr. 155–156.

10 Tr. 1725; Watson, *Sacco and Vanzetti*, 59; Russell, *Tragedy*, 65.

11 Ehrmann, *The Case*, 59; Watson, *Sacco and Vanzetti*, 230; Feuerlicht, *Justice*, 180.

12 Avrich, *Sacco and Vanzetti*, 153; Russell, *Tragedy*, 84–85.

13 For details regarding the Elia-Salsedo affair, see Avrich, *Sacco and Vanzetti*, 181–195; Feuerlicht, *Justice*, 149–151; Russell, *Tragedy*, 88–91.

14 Supp. Tr. 38–43.

15 Supp. Tr. 43 et seq. (Bowles); Supp. Tr. 71 et seq. (Cox); Supp. Tr. 89 et seq. (Harding).

16 Supp. Tr. 48–49.

17 Supp. Tr. 366; Ehrmann, *The Case*, 6.

18 Supp. Tr. 17.

19 Supp. Tr. 65.

20 Supp. Tr. 75, 81.

21 Supp. Tr. 77.

22 Supp. Tr. 365; Ehrmann, *The Case*, 5.

23 Supp. Tr. 7.

24 Ibid. 9.

25 Ibid.

26 Supp. Tr. 15.

27 Supp. Tr. 81.

28 Supp. Tr. 367; Ehrmann, *The Case*, 7.

29 Supp. Tr. 388; Ehrmann, *The Case*, 8.

30 Supp. Tr. 23.

31 Supp. Tr. 101.

32 Supp. Tr. 129 and 136.

33 Supp. Tr. 313, 321, 327–328.

34 Supp. Tr. 349.

35 Supp. Tr. 42–43.

36 Supp. Tr. 140.

37 Ibid. 141.

38 Supp. Tr. 141.

39 Supp. Tr. 141–142.

40 Ehrmann, *The Case*, 14, 99.

41 Ehrmann, *The Case*, 14, 100.

42 Supp. Tr. 142.

43 Ehrmann, *The Case*, 14, 100; Feuerlicht, *Justice*, 179.

44 Supp. Tr. 209.

45 Ibid.

46 Supp. Tr. 42–43.

47 Tr. 1714–1715 (Vanzetti); Supp. Tr. 145; Tr. 756 (Connolly).

48 Supp. Tr. 145 et seq.

49 Supp. Tr. 145–148.

50 Supp. Tr. 107–108, 164 (Stewart takes cap from Vanzetti's room).

51 Supp. Tr. 364 (Graves); Supp. Tr. 365 (Cox); Supp. Tr. 366 (Bowles).

52 Supp. Tr. 7.

53 Supp. Tr. 75.

54 Supp. Tr. 46.

55 Ehrmann, *The Case*, 7.

56 Supp. Tr. 90.

57 Supp. Tr. 128.

58 Supp. Tr. 116 et seq.

59 Supp. Tr. 106–108.

60 Supp. Tr. 164, 167, 212.

61 Supp. Tr. 106–107.

62 Supp. Tr. 143.

63 These words have been attributed to Abraham Lincoln in the Lincoln-Douglas Debate of October 13, 1858. Lincoln's actual words were "Has it not got down as thin as the homeopathic soup that was made by boiling the shadow of a pigeon that had starved to death?"

64 Supp. Tr. 212–213; Ehrmann, *The Case*, 56–58.

65 Russell, *Tragedy*, 95–96.

66 Ibid. 124.

67 Ibid. 123–124.

68 Ibid. 103.

69 Ehrmann, *The Case*, 115 et seq.

70 Joughin and Morgan, *The Legacy*, 48.

71 Supp. Tr. 284–285.

72 Supp. Tr. 286–287.

73 Supp. Tr. 223 et seq.

74 Supp. Tr. 236 et seq.

75 Supp. Tr. 239 et seq.

76 Supp. Tr. 250 et seq.

77 Tr. 253 et seq.

78 Supp. Tr. 257 et seq.

79   Supp. Tr. 316 et seq.

80   Supp. Tr. 281 et seq.

81   Supp. Tr. 288 et seq.

82   Supp. Tr. 294 et seq.

83   Supp. Tr. 301 et seq.

84   Supp. Tr. 229.

85   Supp. Tr. 265.

86   Supp. Tr. 263–276, 281.

87   Supp. Tr. 269.

88   Supp. Tr. 277.

89   Supp. Tr. 243–244.

90   Supp. Tr. 274.

91   Supp. Tr. 298–299.

92   Supp. Tr. see unnumbered page 36, titled "Stenographic Minutes of Plymouth Trial."

93   Lyons, *The Life and Death*, 64; Joughin and Morgan, *The Legacy*, 220.

94   Ehrmann, *The Case*, 108, et seq.; Russell, *Tragedy*, 105.

95   Russell, *Tragedy*, 105–106.

96   D'Allessandro, *The Verdict*, 112.

97   Russell, *Tragedy*, 107–108.

CHAPTER 5

The Shakedown

1   The DeFalco affair has been reported upon by several sources: Ehrmann, *The Case*, 161–170; Russell, *Tragedy*, 118–121; Watson, *Sacco and Vanzetti*, 95–97.

CHAPTER 6

South Braintree and the Dedham Trial

1   Russell, *Tragedy*, 158; Ehrmann, *The Case*, 146–147.

2   Joughin and Morgan, *The Legacy*, 378.

3   Ehrmann, *The Case*, 19–39; Kadane and Schum, *A Probabilistic*, 4–7.

4   Ehrmann, *The Case*, 38–39, 89-90.

5   Tr. 626.

6   Tr. 634.

7   Tr. 635 (re: Ryan), 651–652 (re: bullet hole).

8   Starrs, "Once More," 1056.

9   Ehrmann, *The Case*, 19, Supp. Tr. 395 et seq.

10 Ehrmann, *The Case*, 20.

11 Supp. Tr. 426.

12 Ehrmann, *The Case*, 26.

13 Ibid. 30.

14 Supp. Tr. 412–413.

15 Tr. 798.

16 Young and Kaiser, *Postmortem*, 92.

17 Supp. Tr. 441.

18 Ibid.

19 Fraenkel, *The Sacco-Vanzetti Case*, 512–513, 520, 533.

20 Supp. Tr. 395.

21 Supp. Tr. 395; Tr. 757.

22 Supp. Tr. 414.

23 Ibid.

24 Young and Kaiser, *Postmortem*, 106, 108.

25 Joughin and Morgan, *The Legacy*, 83–84.

26 Tr. 109 et seq.

27   Young and Kaiser, *Postmortem*, 107.

28   Supp. Tr. 414.

29   Ehrmann, *The Case*, 42–43.

30   Ibid. 42.

31   Cook, *The Nation*, December 22, 1962, "The Missing Fingerprints," 450.

32   Tr. 223.

33   Letters of Theodore W. Grippo to Massachusetts authorities and the FBI in his files.

34   Ehrmann, *The Case*, 43.

35   Ibid.

36   Ibid. 43–44; Russell, *Tragedy*, 292–293.

37   Ehrmann, *The Case*, 44.

38   Ibid.

39   Ibid.

40   Ibid.

41   Ibid.

42   Ibid. 44–45.

43   Ibid. 44–46.

44   Tr. 74–76.

45   Lyons, *The Life and Death*, 39.

46   Ehrmann, *The Case*, 43–45, 409–419; Russell, *Tragedy*, 286 et seq.

47   Ibid. 414; see generally, Ehrmann, *The Untried Case*; Joughin and Morgan, *The Legacy*, 19.

48   Joughin and Morgan, *The Legacy*, 18-19, 115.

49   Ehrmann, *The Case*, 58–66.

50   *State of Kansas v. Cedric E. Hunt*, 275 Kan. 811, 69 P. 3d 571 (2003); *United States of America v. Melvin Telfaire*, 469 F. 2d 552, 152 U.S. App. D.C. 146 (1972); Ehrmann, *The Case*, 66–85.

51   Ibid.

52 Ehrmann, *The Case*, 68, 189; Russell, *Tragedy*, 68–69.

53 Russell, *Tragedy*, 68–69.

54 Ibid.; Ehrmann, *The Case*, 66-85; Young and Kaiser, *Postmortem*, Chapter 5; Fraenkel, *Sacco-Vanzetti*, 205 et seq.

55 Ibid.

56 Ibid.

57 Ehrmann, *The Case*, 49, 58-66.

58 Ibid.

59 Ibid.

60 Ibid.

61 Ibid.

62 Ibid.

63 Ibid.

64 Ibid.

65 Ibid.

66 Ibid.

67 Ibid.

68 Russell, *Tragedy*, 138; Lyons, *The Life and Death*, 71–72; Watson, *Sacco and Vanzetti*, 103.

69 Lyons, *The Life and Death*, 71–72.

70 Russell, *Tragedy*, 138.

71 Russell, *Tragedy*, 97–98; Watson, *Sacco and Vanzetti*, 116–118.

72 Ibid.

73 Russell, *Tragedy*, 25–26, 66–67; Watson, *Sacco and Vanzetti*, 59–60.

74 Feuerlicht, *Justice*, 188 et seq.; Ehrmann, *The Case*, 153–159; Watson, *Sacco and Vanzetti*, 85–88, 115.

75 Watson, *Sacco and Vanzetti*, 115.

76 Ibid.

77 Joughin and Morgan, *The Legacy*, 237–238.

78 Russell, *Tragedy*, 126.

79 *Commonwealth v. Wilkins*, 243 Mass. 356, 138 N.E. 11 (1923).

80 *Weeks v. United States*, 232 U.S. 383, 34 S. Ct. 341, 58L Ed. 652 (1914).

81 *State v. Slamon*, 73 Vt. 212, 50 A. 1097 (Vt. 1901); and in Iowa: *State v. Sheridan*, 121 Ia. 164, 96 N.W. 730 (1903). Both states later rejected their earlier pro-exclusionary positions.

82 *Henry v. United States*, 361 U.S. 98 (1959).

83 Ibid.

84 Ibid.

85 Tr. 752.

86 Ibid.

87 Joughin and Morgan, *The Legacy*, 116.

88 Ibid.

89 Feuerlicht, *Justice*, 348.

90 Tr. 76.

91 Tr. 64.

92 Tr. 76.

93 Russell, *Tragedy*, 45; Ehrmann, *The Case*, 191 (Note 1); Feuerlicht, *Justice*, 378.

94 Ehrmann, *The Case*, 506; Feuerlicht, *Justice*, 378.

CHAPTER 7

Dedham: The Case against Vanzetti

1 Tr. 417–418.

2 Tr. 1728; Feuerlicht, *Justice*, 208 (second note), 209.

3 Feuerlicht, *Justice*, 207–208; Fraenkel, *The Sacco-Vanzetti Case*, 39.

4 Tr. 2215.

5 Tr. 417.

6 Ibid.

7 Tr. 421–423.

8 Tr. 424.

9 Tr. 965.

10 Tr. 1371–1372.

11 Tr. 1076.

12 Tr. 425–427.

13 Tr. 433–441.

14 Tr. 1298-1308; Fraenkel, *The Sacco-Vanzetti Case*, 208.

15 Tr. 1275–1298; Fraenkel, *The Sacco-Vanzetti Case*, 208.

16 Tr. 490, 495; Ehrmann, *The Case*, 189–190; Joughin and Morgan, *The Legacy*, 73.

17 Tr. 594–597.

18 Tr. 595.

19 Tr. 615–616.

20 Ehrmann, *The Case*, 188.

21 Tr. 732–733.

22 Young and Kaiser, *Postmortem*, 86–89.

23 Tr. 806–811.

24 Tr. 1687.

25 Tr. 1687.

26 Tr. 1689.

27 Tr. 196.

28 Tr. 200, 2237–2238.

29 Tr. 813–814.

30 Tr. 816–819.

31 Tr. 823–825.

32 Ibid.

33 Ehrmann, *The Case*, 249.

34 Young and Kaiser, *Postmortem*: 88–89.

35 Ibid. 89.

36   Ibid.

37   Supp. Tr. 149.

38   Ehrmann, *The Case*, 103, 106.

39   Tr. 1714–1715.

40   Tr. 1747–1748.

41   Supp. Tr. 141.

42   Tr. 328.

43   Tr. 1701–1702.

44   Ibid.

45   Tr. 1702.

46   Tr. 1703.

47   Tr. 1702–1703, 1585–1586.

48   Tr. 1549.

49   Ibid.

50   Tr. 1587–1589.

51   Tr. 1522–1530.

52   Tr. 1538–1539.

53   Tr. 1634.

54   Tr. 1581–1585.

55   Tr. 1583–1585.

56   Tr. 1498, 1518–1519.

57   Tr. 1555.

58   Tr. 2192.

59   Tr. 1546–1547.

CHAPTER 8

Dedham: The Case Against Sacco

1   Lola Andrews, Tr. 337; Lewis Pelser, Tr. 294; Carlos Goodridge, Tr. 545; William Tracy, Tr. 501; William Heron, Tr. 520; Mary Splaine, Tr. 224; Francis Devlin, Tr. 464.

2 Hans Behrsin, Tr. 324–332; James Bostock, Tr. 195; Lewis Wade, Tr. 206; James McGlone, Tr. 274; Edgar Langlois, Tr. 284; Mark Carrigon, Tr. 176–177; Louis DeBeradinis, Tr. 482–483. (In the transcript and other sources, the name "Carrigon" is also spelled "Carrigan" and "Carrington.")

3 Tr. 334–336.

4 Tr. 336.

5 Tr. 337.

6 Tr. 2219.

7 Tr. 349–357.

8 Tr. 1309–1312.

9 Tr. 1327.

10 Tr. 1374–1375.

11 Russell, *Tragedy*, 147.

12 Tr. 1378.

13 Tr. 1383.

14 Tr. 1377.

15 Tr. 3892–3899.

16 Tr. 3950 et seq.

17 Tr. 4509, 4512–4513.

18 Fraenkel, *The Sacco-Vanzetti Case*, 317.

19 Ibid.

20 Ibid.

21 Tr. 292.

22 Tr. 294.

23 Tr. 300.

24 Ibid.

25 Tr. 301.

26 Tr. 322.

27 Tr. 303.

28 Tr. 320–321.

29   Tr. 1122 et seq. (Brenner); Tr. 1149 et seq. (McCullum); Tr. 1166 et seq. (Constantino).

30   Tr. 1172.

31   Tr. 5565–5577.

32   Ibid.

33   Ibid.

34   Tr. 5584–5585.

35   Fraenkel, *The Sacco-Vanzetti Case*, 255.

36   Tr. 543–545.

37   Ibid. 545.

38   Tr. 546-547; Tr. 3740.

39   Ibid; Fraenkel, *The Sacco-Vanzetti Case*, 52, 267–268.

40   Tr. 1353 (Arrogni).

41   Tr. 1357 (Magazu).

42   Tr. 1399.

43   Tr. 1490.

44   Joughin and Morgan, *The Legacy*, 14.

45   Ibid. 134–135.

46   Tr. 3807; Feuerlicht, *Justice*, 285.

47   Tr. 510–511.

48   Tr. 520.

49   Tr. 220–224 (Splaine); Tr. 460–463 (Devlin).

50   Tr. 223.

51   Russell, *Tragedy*, 345–346.

52   Ibid.

53   Ibid.

54   Ibid.

55   Ibid. 346.

56   Tr. 325–327.

57   Tr. 195.

58   Tr. 205.

59   Tr. 4469–4470.

60   Tr. 274.

61   Tr. 288.

62   Tr. 178.

63   Tr. 480–482.

64   Tr. 482.

65   Tr. 482–483.

66   Tr. 483–488.

67   Julia Campbell, Tr. 1331; Albert Frantello, Tr. 1011; William Foley, Tr. 1592; Emielo Falcone, Tr. 1080–1081; Pedro Iscorla, Tr. 1098; Henry Cerro, Tr. 1110; Sibriano Gudierres, Tr. 1114; Barbara Liscomb., Tr. 1191; Frank Burke, Tr. 977; Nicola Damato, Tr. 1488; Cesidio Magnerelli, Tr. 1254; Donato DiBona, Tr. 1260; Fortinato Antonello, Tr. 1271; Antonio Frabizio, Tr. 1273; Nicolo Gatti, Tr. 1212; Dominick DiBona, Tr. 1245; Joseph Cellucci, Tr. 1571; Elmer Chase, Tr. 1342; Wilson Dorr, Tr. 1368; Tobia DiBona, Tr. 1274; Winfred Pierce, 1044; Jennie Novelli, Tr. 1238–1239; Daniel O'Neil, 1393, 2101.

68   Lawrence Ferguson, Tr. 1070, 1074; Olaf Olsen, Tr. 1487.

69   Tr. 1006 et seq.

70   Tr. 1014 et seq., 1020, 1024, 1028.

71   Tr. 1033.

72   Tr. 1024.

73   Tr. 1020, 1024–1028.

74   Tr. 1191.

75   Ibid.

76   Ibid.

77   Tr. 71, 76.

78   Tr. 798.

79   Ibid.

80   Tr. 798–799.

81   Tr. 808 (Sarah Berardelli); Tr. 811 (Hattie Parmenter).

82   Tr. 853–854.

83   Ibid.

84   Tr. 854.

85   Tr. 857.

86   Ibid.

87   Tr. 1850–1851.

88   Ibid.

89   Ehrmann, *The Case*, 208, 210, 217, 514–516.

90   Ibid. 3, 403-404.

91   Tr. 1928–1929.

92   Ibid.

93   Tr. 1929.

94   Ibid.

95   Ibid.

96   Tr. 2064–2065.

97   Tr. 2092–2093.

98   Tr. 2094.

99   Tr. 5169–5170.

100 Young and Kaiser, *Postmortem*, 92.

101 Ibid.

102 Tr. 5170-5171, 5182.

103 Ibid.

104 Ehrmann, *The Case*, 208.

105 Ibid. 206; Tr. 2210.

106 Ehrmann, *The Case*, 206; Tr. 3517, 4765, 5555.

107 Ehrmann, *The Case*, 206; Tr. 4293, Tr. 4765.

108 Ehrmann, *The Case*, 250, 253–254, Tr. 5319.

109 Tr. 3641–3643.

110 Tr. 896.

111 Tr. 5185–5186; Ehrmann, *The Case*, 254–256.

112 Tr. 5186.

113 Tr. 911 et seq.

114 Young and Kaiser, *Postmortem*, 114–117.

115 Ibid. 117.

116 Ehrmann, *The Case*, 264.

117 Ibid. 264–265.

118 Ibid. 265.

119 Ibid.

120 Ibid. 273–274.

121 Tr. 884–896.

122 Tr. 911–921.

123 Russell, *Tragedy*, 212, 233; Ehrmann, *The Case*, 512.

124 Tr. 3641–3643.

125 Tr. 3681 (Katzmann); Tr. 3681–3682 (Williams).

126 Ehrmann, *The Case*, 267–269.

127 Tr. 5378u.

128 Ibid.

129 Joughin and Morgan, *The Legacy*, 127.

130 Ibid.; Tr. 2254.

131 Ehrmann, *The Case*, 268 (*Atlantic Monthly*); 173 Note 2c (Frankfurter, *The Case of Sacco and Vanzetti*).

132 Joughin and Morgan, *The Legacy*, 130–131.

133 Tr. 195.

134 Tr. 882.

135 Tr. 885.

136 Young and Kaiser, *Postmortem*, 109.

137 Ibid.

138 Tr. 195.

139 Tr. 882.

140 Ehrmann, *The Case*, 56–58.

141 Ibid.

142 Ibid. 478–480.

143 Tr. 2256 et seq.

144 Ehrmann, *The Case*, 531; Tr. 761-762.

145 Ibid.; Tr. 757-758.

146 Ehrmann, *The Case*, 53–54; Lyons, *The Life and Death*, 47–50.

147 Lyons, *The Life and Death*, 47–48.

148 Tr. 1715.

149 Tr. 1608; Tr. 1903.

150 Ibid.

151 Tr. 1858.

152 Ibid.

153 Tr. 1863.

154 Tr. 751 et seq.

155 Ibid.

156 Ibid.

157 Ibid.

158 Ibid. 752–753.

159 Tr. 761–762.

160 Minutes of September 1920, box 18 HLS: Young and Kaiser, *Postmortem*, 69.

161 Young and Kaiser, *Postmortem*, 70.

162 Tr. 2205.

163 Tr. 2259.

164 Fraenkel, *The Sacco-Vanzetti Case*, 469–470.

165 There is no record in the transcript of the serial number of Sacco's gun at the time of his arrest. At the trial, Sacco's gun was introduced into evidence as Exhibit 28 through the testimony of Officer Merle Spear as "a Colt revolver, automatic revolver." Spear testified that he later marked "the initials 'MS', I think," Tr. 781; Starrs, "Once

More," 636. Although a serial number is associated with what was supposed to be Sacco's gun much later in the transcript, by then a switch of Sacco's gun is believed by the author to have been made for the Colt .32 that produced counterfeit Bullet III.

166 Ehrmann, *The Case*, 54–58, 287–289.

167 Ibid.

168 Ibid. 57.

CHAPTER 9

Dedham: Katzmann's Victory

1 Ehrmann, *The Case*, 60–62.

2 Although Katzmann alluded that Coacci, Boda, and Orciani were members of the gang who committed the South Braintree crime, they were never indicted and no findings of their participation were made by Judge Thayer.

3 Feuerlicht, *Justice*, 150–151.

4 Ehrmann, *The Case*, 350, 373.

5 Tr. 1940.

6 Tr. 1679; Tr. 1823.

7 Tr. 1824; Tr. 1941.

8 Tr. 1824.

9 Ibid.

10 Ibid.

11 Ibid. Tr. 1991.

12 Tr. 1824.

13 Ibid.; Tr. 1825.

14 Ibid.; Tr. 2024.

15 Ibid.; Tr. 1826.

16 Ibid.; Tr. 2033–2034.

17 Ibid.

18 Tr. 2025–2027.

19 Tr. 2026–2028.

20 Tr. 2235.

21 Tr. 2033–2034.

22 Tr. 1645–1649.

23 Tr. 1661.

24 Tr. 1662–1664.

25 Tr. 1991–1994.

26 Tr. 1667–1669.

27 Tr. 1669–1670.

28 Tr. 1679–1683.

29 See calendar for months of April-December 1920.

30 Tr. 1817 et seq. (re: Sacco), Tr. 1689 et seq. (re: Vanzetti).

31 Tr. 1715.

32 Tr. 1845 (re: Sacco); Tr. 1726, 1731, 1808 (re: Vanzetti).

33 Tr. 1817 et seq. (re: Sacco); Tr. 1689 et seq. (re: Vanzetti).

34 Tr. 1737 et seq.

35 Tr. 1777 et seq.

36 Tr. 1747.

37 Tr. 1748.

38 Supp. Tr. 149.

39 Tr. 1721.

40 Tr. 1716.

41 Tr. 1745 et seq.

42 Ibid.

43 Tr. 2203–2204.

44 Ehrmann, *The Case*, 304.

45 Tr. 1818.

46 Tr. 1867.

47 Ibid. et seq.

48 Tr. 1867.

49 Ibid. et seq.

50 Tr. 1869.

51 Frankfurter, *The Case*, 46.

52 Tr. 1867–1961; Tr. 1969–1972.

53 Tr. 1950.

54 Tr. 1873 et seq.

55 Tr. 1873.

56 Tr. 4073.

57 Tr. 1875.

58 Tr. 1876 et seq.

59 Tr. 1879 et seq.

60 Tr. 1885 et seq.

61 Ehrmann, *The Case*, 322.

62 Tr. 1845 et seq. (re: Sacco); Tr. 1810 et seq. (re: Vanzetti).

63 Ehrmann, *The Case*, 56–58.

64 Tr. 4224 (Brief for the Commonwealth).

65 Tr. 3522–3523.

66 Joughin and Morgan, *The Legacy*, 220; Lyons, *The Life and Death*, 64.

67 Ehrmann, *The Case*, 469.

68 Ibid. 321 (the Weyand Affidavit).

69 Frankfurter, *The Case*, 46, 57.

70 Ibid. 46.

71 Ibid. 104.

72 Tr. 2145.

73 Tr. 2125.

74 Tr. 2140.

75 Tr. 2139.

76 Tr. 2142 et seq.

77   Tr. 2147.

78   Ibid.

79   Tr. 2148.

80   Tr. 2154 (re: Judge Thayer); Tr. 2154, Tr. 2175 (re: Katzmann).

81   Tr. 2178.

82   Tr. 2179.

83   Tr. 2239.

84   Tr. 2245.

85   Tr. 2254.

86   Tr. 2255, Tr. 2264, Tr. 2238.

87   Tr. 2255–2256. The only paragraph in Judge Thayer's charge to the jury relating to Sacco's cap makes no mention of Sacco's difficulty trying on the cap during the trial.

88   Tr. 2262–2263.

89   Tr. 2256–2257, 2259, 2261–2262.

90   Russell, *Tragedy*, 211–215.

91   Ibid.

92   Tr. 2266; Russell, *Tragedy*, 211–215; Watson, *Sacco and Vanzetti*, 166–170.

93   Ibid.

94   Ibid.

95   Ibid.

96   Ibid.

CHAPTER 10

Motions and Appeals

1   Ehrmann, *The Case*, 115.

2   Joughin and Morgan, *The Legacy*, 114; Tr. 5540, 5547 et seq.

3   Fraenkel, *The Sacco-Vanzetti Case*, 119.

4   Joughin and Morgan, *The Legacy*, 114.

5   Joughin and Morgan, *The Legacy*, 12–13, 115–117; Fraenkel, *The Sacco-Vanzetti Case*, 107.

6   Fraenkel, *The Sacco-Vanzetti Case*, 108.

7   Ibid.

8   Ibid. 109 et seq.

9   Ibid. 110–113.

10   Ibid. 113 et seq.

11   Ibid.

12   Ibid. 114 et seq.

13   Ibid. 115.

14   Ibid. 116.

15   Ibid. 116–117.

16   Ibid.

17   Ibid. 117; Joughin and Morgan, *The Legacy*, 14.

18   Ibid. 117–118; Joughin and Morgan, *The Legacy*, 14–16.

19   Tr. 3604 et seq.

20   Fraenkel, *The Sacco-Vanzetti Case*, 118.

21   Ibid. 118.

22   Ibid. 345 et seq.; Tr. 3698–3704.

23   Tr. 3698–3704.

24   Ibid.

25   Frankfurter, *The Case*, 76.

26   Watson, *Sacco and Vanzetti*, 252–253.

27   Feuerlicht, *Justice*, 106 et seq.

28   Watson, *Sacco and Vanzetti*, 335.

29   Ehrmann, *The Case,* 152 et seq., 402.

30   Ibid. 152–153.

31   Ehrmann, *The Case*, 402; Russell, *Tragedy*, 132-133.

32   Ibid.

33   Ibid.

34 Ibid.

35 Ibid.

36 Ibid. (for entry of Thompson and Ehrmann); see Ibid. 481–482 (for their withdrawal as counsel).

37 Joughin and Morgan, *The Legacy*, 16.

38 Ibid.

39 Ibid.

40 Ibid. 18.

CHAPTER 11

True Confessions?

1 A full account of the Silva story has been recounted by a number of authors. See Russell, *Tragedy*, 271–278; Watson, *Sacco and Vanzetti*, 201 et seq.; Ehrmann, *The Case*, 51–52; Fraenkel, *The Sacco-Vanzetti Case*, 199–200. The *Outlook and Independent* magazine carried Silva's confession in its October and November 1928 editions.

2 Ehrmann, *The Case*, 405.

3 Russell, *Tragedy*, 290, 299.

4 Feuerlicht, *Justice*, 313.

5 Ibid.

6 Russell, *Tragedy*, 279.

7 Ehrmann, *The Case*, 408.

8 Ibid. 409.

9 Tr. 4500 (re: Weyand); Tr. 4505 (re: Letherman).

10 Tr. 4503.

11 Tr. 4506.

12 Tr. 4615 et seq.; for a summary, see Ehrmann, *The Case*, 406–407.

13 Tr. 4688, 4711.

14 Tr. 4624, 4631, 4632, 4637, 4644.

15 Tr. 4643; Ehrmann, *The Case*, 506, 521; Russell, *Tragedy*, 44–45.

16 Tr. 4632; Ehrmann, *The Case*, 424-425.

17 Ehrmann, *The Case*, 411.

18 Ibid. 412.

19 Tr. 4401, 4403.

20 Tr. 4484–4485 with photo of Joseph Morelli attached (re: Burke); Tr. 4469–4470 with photo of Joseph Morelli attached (re: Wade).

21 Tr. 4470–4471; Tr. 4606–4607 (re: repudiation).

22 Tr. 4465.

23 Tr. 4565.

24 Tr. 4407 et seq.

25 Tr. 4419 et seq.

26 Ehrmann, *The Case*, 410.

27 Tr. 4474 (re: Barney Monterio); Tr. 4477 (re: May Monterio).

28 Ehrmann, *The Case*, 410–412.

29 Ibid. 413–414.

30 Ibid. 421–424.

31 Ibid.

32 Ibid.

33 Ibid. 421.

34 Ibid.

35 Tr. 4726.

36 Teresa and Renner, *My Life*, 45–46.

CHAPTER 12

A Plea for Clemency

1 Tr. 4895.

2 Ibid.

3 Tr. 4896.

4   Ibid.

5   Tr. 4896 et seq.

6   Tr. 4904–4905.

7   Tr. 4904.

8   Ibid.

9   Tr. 4905.

10 Ibid.

11 Ibid.

12 Russell, *Tragedy*, 363.

13 Tr. 4907 et seq.

14 Ibid.; Russell, *Tragedy*, 367–368; Feuerlicht, *Justice*, 341 et seq.

15 Tr. 4910 et seq.

16 Tr. 4923.

17 Tr. 4924.

18 Tr. 4926.

19 Tr. 4928.

20 Tr. 4929–4931.

21 Tr. 4932.

22 Tr. 4933–4945.

23 Tr. 4946–4947.

24 Ehrmann, *The Case*, 533 et seq.

25 Joughin and Morgan, *The Legacy*, 301 et seq.

26 Ibid. 302.

27 Ehrmann, *The Case*, 484; Watson, *Sacco and Vanzetti*, 311.

28 The blue cover sheet to Decision of Gov. Alvan T. Fuller at Tr. 5378a.

29 Tr. 5378j.

30 Tr. 3514.

31 Tr. 5378l.

32 Tr. 5378l–5378m.

33   Tr. 5378p–5378q.

34   Ehrmann, *The Case*, 358 et seq.

35   Ibid. 374, et seq.

36   Ibid.

37   Ibid. 378–379.

38   Ibid. 383.

39   Ibid. 384.

40   Ibid. 385.

41   Ibid. 386–387.

42   Ehrmann, *The Case*, 536.

43   Ibid.

44   Ibid. 537; see also Joughin and Morgan, *The Legacy*, 53.

CHAPTER 13

The Final Days

1   Russell, *Tragedy*, 411; Ehrmann, *The Case*, 481–482.

2   Ehrmann, *The Case*, 482–483; Russell, *Tragedy*, 388 (re: stay of execution by Gov. Fuller from July 10, 1927 to August 10, 1927).

3   Russell, *Tragedy*, 422.

4   Ehrmann, *The Case*, xviii, 482–483; see also Fraenkel, *The Sacco-Vanzetti Case*, 178–182.

5   Frankfurter and Jackson, *The Letters*, 67 et seq.

6   Ibid. 70 et seq.

7   Feuerlicht, *Justice*, 397.

8   Ibid.

9   Feuerlicht, *Justice*, 397–398.

10   Frankfurter and Jackson, *The Letters*, 321 et seq.

11   Feuerlicht, *Justice*, 401.

12   Ibid. 403–404.

13 Feuerlicht, *Justice*, 401.

14 Ibid.

15 Ibid.

16 Ibid. 404 et seq.; Russell, *Tragedy*, 443 et seq.; Frankfurter and Jackson, *The Letters*, 398 et seq.

17 Ibid.

18 Russell, *Tragedy*, 444 et seq.

19 Ibid.

20 Ibid. 449.

21 Ibid. 450.

22 Ibid.

23 Joughin and Morgan, *The Legacy*, 480.

24 Russell, *Tragedy*, 450.

25 Ibid. 387–388 (and note).

26 Feuerlicht, *Justice*, 410.

27 Ibid. 411.

28 Ibid.

29 Russell, *Tragedy*, 456.

30 Feuerlicht, *Justice*, 411.

31 Russell, *Tragedy*, 456 et seq.; Feuerlicht, *Justice*, 410 et seq.

32 Ibid.

33 Ibid.

34 Young and Kaiser, *Postmortem*, 6.

35 Ibid.

36 Russell, *Tragedy*, 460.

CHAPTER 14

Afterward

1   Russell, *The Case Resolved*, 183 et seq.; Feuerlicht, *Justice*, 426–428; Watson, *Sacco and Vanzetti*, 360; D'Alessandro, *The Verdict*, 440 et seq.; Avrich, *Sacco and Vanzetti*, 216–217.

2   Feuerlicht, *Justice*, 428.

3   Tr. 891-893; Young and Kaiser, *Postmortem*, Chapter 9.

4   Ehrmann, *The Untried Case*, 245.

CHAPTER 15

The Ballistics Controversy

1   Feuerlicht, *Justice*, 419; Joughin and Morgan, *The Legacy*, 157; Fraenkel, *The Sacco-Vanzetti Case*, 535–550.

2   Supp. Tr. 414 (re: Dr. Jones); Young and Kaiser, *Postmortem*, 107 (re: Dr. Magrath).

3   Tr. 891-893.

4   Supp. Tr. 420–424.

5   Tr. 268.

6   Supp. Tr. 441.

7   Tr. 203.

8   Tr. 187–189.

9   Tr. 188.

10   Tr. 292.

11   Ibid.

12   Supp. Tr. 396.

13   Supp. Tr. 398.

14   Tr. 76–77.

15   Tr. 119.

16   See second note above of this Chapter 15.

17   Young and Kaiser, *Postmortem*, Chapters 9 and 10.

18   Ibid. 112.

19   Tr. 117–118 (Magrath); Tr. 105–107 (Frazer).

20   Tr. 269.

21   Ehrmann, *The Case*, 22; Young and Kaiser, *Postmortem*, 104; Supp. Tr. 421.

22   Tr. 278–285; Supp. Tr. 444–446.

23   Supp. Tr. 446–447.

24   Tr. 887.

25   Ehrmann, *The Case*, 41–42, 49, 59, 146–149.

26   Ibid. 147.

27   Tr. 5085.

28   Evans, *Murder Two*, 303, Nickell and Fischer, *Crime Science*, 105; Owen, *Hidden Evidence*, 113; A. James Fisher, 1922–1923 "Time Line", Department of Political Science and Criminal Justice, Edinboro University of Pennsylvania. The early 1920s was the era of the comparison microscope. Evans sets 1923 as the time when Calvin H. Goddard refined Phillip O. Gravelle's comparison microscope for use in ballistics examinations. Nickell and Fischer assert that Charles Waite and Phillip Gravell developed the comparison microscope, and together with John Fischer in 1923, founded the Bureau of Forensic Ballistics in New York City. A. James Fisher states the comparison microscope was invented by Goddard and Waite in 1923. Although the comparison microscope technology was not available for use during the 1921 trial of Sacco and Vanzetti, there is no doubt that by 1923, the community of ballistics experts and big city police departments were well aware of the newly developed comparison microscope and the claim that its use could determine with certainty whether a particular gun fired a particular bullet.

29   Starrs, "Once More", 647–649.

30   Appendix A, par. 37.

31   Tr. 781-782.

32   Starrs, "Once More", 636.

33   Tr. 781–782.

34   Ehrmann, *The Case*, 277, Note 1; See also Appendix A.

35   Ehrmann, *The Case*, 504-505.

36   Ibid. 284.

37   New World Encyclopedia, "Sacco and Vanzetti", 8.

38   Tr. 5378w–5378x.

39   Hamilton obtained sixteen of those bullets in 1923: Ehrmann, *The Case*, 511–512. In 1962, Braverman obtained boxes: Ehrmann, *The Case*, 512, Note 23. See also: Starrs, "Once More," 1068.

40   See Epilogue, The Judgment of History; Watson, *Sacco and Vanzetti*, 351-372.

41   Tr. 896, Tr. 920.

42   Tr. 3604 et seq.

43   Tr. 3641–3643.

44   Russell, *Tragedy*, 249–251.

45   Appendix A.

46   Ehrmann, *The Case*, 504–505; Tr. 5317.

47   Ehrmann, *The Case*, 279–281 (re: tests), 281–282 (re: Milazzo incident).

48   While the results have been difficult to obtain, there is evidence that the Commonwealth engaged in ballistics tests on Sacco's gun in 1944. See Starrs, "Once More," 1052, where he discusses evidence of the 1944 tests and the select committee's findings regarding the same.

49   Young and Kaiser, *Postmortem*, 95; Russell, *Tragedy*, 464–465 (re: Jury and Weller); Ehrmann, *The Case*, 285–286 (re: Jury and Weller's competency).

50   Russell, *Tragedy*, 318.

51   Starrs, "Once More," 630 et seq.

52   Ibid. 1071 et seq.

53   Young and Kaiser, *Postmortem*, generally.

54   *New World Encyclopedia*, "Sacco and Vanzetti," 8.

55   Kadane and Schum, *The Probabilistic*, generally.

56   Ibid. 283.

CHAPTER 16

The Rosetta Stone

1   *Funk & Wagnalls New Encyclopedia*, Vol. 20, 396.

2   Russell, *Tragedy*, Fly Cover.

3   Tr. 5542.

4   Ehrmann, *The Case*, 277, Note 1; Morgan, *The Legacy*, 160 et seq.;
     Russell, *Tragedy*, 248–249; Watson, *Sacco and Vanzetti*, 237–239,
     241, 244, 246–247.

5   Appendix B.

6   Ehrmann, *The Case*, 277, Note 1.

7   Watson, *Sacco and Vanzetti*, 239–240; Russell, *Tragedy*, 249.

8   Appendix A, Par. 39. Hamilton's involvement as Sacco's ballistics
     expert raised challenges to Hamilton's background and character the
     more effective he became. Most of the attacks came from those who
     defended the Commonwealth's findings of guilt. Francis Russell
     claimed "his doctorate was self awarded" and that by trade, he was
     nothing more than a druggist hawking patent medicines. Russell,
     Tragedy, 233–234. Nevertheless, Thompson defended Hamilton as
     a man of honor; Ibid. 377. Hamilton's affidavits of April 14, 1923
     (Tr. 3563); October 3, 1923 (Tr. 3575); October 15, 1923 (Tr.
     3608); October 20, 1923 (Tr. 3643); October 24, 1923 (Tr. 3651);
     December 6, 1923 (Tr. 3685), should be examined, as they reflect
     the depth of Hamilton's expertise in ballistics.

9   Tr. 3632, Appendix A, Par. 47.

10   Tr. 3665, Appendix A., Par. 47.

11   Tr. 3692.

12   Russell, *Tragedy*, 248.

13   See Massachusetts Constitution in effect in 1920, dividing the
     Commonwealth into legislative, executive, and judicial branches.

14   Teresa, *My Life*, 44-46.

15   Russell, *Tragedy*, 278–279; Ehrmann, *The Case*, 192; Ehrmann, *The Untried Case*, 100.

16   Ehrmann, *The Case*, 404 et seq.

17   Ehrmann, *The Case*, 424–425; Ehrmann, *The Untried Case*, 80–83; Fraenkel, *The Sacco-Vanzetti Case*, 533.

18   Ehrmann, *The Case*, 43 et seq.

19   Tr. 4454; Russell, *Tragedy*, 294–298; Feuerlicht, *Justice*, 319; Fred J. Cook, *The Nation*, "The All American Frame-up," May, 1969, 607.

20   Ehrmann, *The Case*, 58–59, 399.

21   Ibid. 19–20.

22   Young and Kaiser, *Postmortem*, 69.

23   Ibid. 89.

24   Ibid. 160–161.

25   Tr. 3642–3643.

26   Ehrmann, *The Case*, 204–222, 515–516; Young and Kaiser, *Postmortem*, 92.

27   Tr. 4923.

EPILOGUE

The Judgment of History

1   Frankfurter, *The Case*, generally.

2   Russell, *Sacco & Vanzetti*, 118.

3   Russell, *Tragedy*, 371–372; Joughin and Morgan, *The Legacy*, 260-262.

4   Newby, *Kill Now*, 563, 564, 566. While Lippman's doubt regarding the guilt of Sacco and Vanzetti is accurately quoted, he later expressed reservations as to their innocence.

5   Joughin and Morgan, *The Legacy*, 282.

6   Ibid.

7   Feuerlicht, *Justice*, 383.

8   Joughin and Morgan, *The Legacy*, 314.

9   Sinclair, *Boston*, 754.

10   Joughin and Morgan, *The Legacy*, 409.

11   Ibid. 410–411.

12   Frankfurter and Jackson, *The Letters*, xxxvii.

13   Russell, *Sacco & Vanzetti*, 144.

14   Ehrmann, *The Untried Case*, photostat copy of the governor's letter opposite the title page.

15   Joughin and Morgan, *The Legacy*, 416, 419.

16   *New York Times*, "Offer Sacco Memorial," August 23, 1937; Watson, *Sacco and Vanzetti*, 353–354, 356–358; Bortman, *Sacco & Vanzetti*, 78.

17   Ibid.

18   Newby, *Kill Now*, 494.

19   *New York Times*, "Sacco Manifesto Attacks Tyranny," August 24, 1947; Joughin and Morgan, *The Legacy*, 350.

20   *New York Times*, "Nemetz to Stage 'Sacco-Vanzetti,'" May 31, 1960; "Theater: Sacco and Vanzetti Drama," October 15, 1960; and "Stage: A Sacco-Vanzetti Music Drama," February 9, 1969.

21   *New York Times*, "TV: Sacco-Vanzetti" reviews, June 4 and 11, 1960.

22   *New York Times*, "Ford Foundation Sponsors Opera," February 26, 1960. However, see *New York Times*, "Music Unit Attacks Opera by Blitzstein," September 2, 1960.

23   Russell, *Sacco & Vanzetti*, 5–6.

24   Newby, *Kill Now*, 508–512.

25   Frankfurter, *The Case*, 7, footnote 1; Montgomery, *Sacco-Vanzetti*, 30.

26   Watson, *Sacco and Vanzetti*, 74.

27   Russell, *Tragedy*, 123–124.

28   Ibid. 394 (as to Fuller).

29   Russell, *Tragedy*, 96.

30   Grossman, "The Sacco-Vanzetti Case Revisited," *Commentary*, January 1962.

31   Tr. 2266 (at conviction); Tr. 4896 (at sentencing).

32   Grossman, "The Sacco-Vanzetti Case Revisited," *Commentary*; January 1962.

33   Russell, *Sacco & Vanzetti*, 11–13.

34   *New York Times*, "Theater: The Advocate", October 15, 1963.

35   Montgomery, *The Murder*, generally.

36   Felix, *Protest*, 265 (no endnotes).

37   *New York Times*, "Theater: Sacco and Vanzetti Drama," October 15, 1960.

38   Feuerlicht, *Justice*, 388.

39   Ibid.

40   Ibid. 377 et seq.

41   Ibid. 380.

42   Report to Governor Dukakis, July 13, 1977, Taylor's cover letter (see Sinclair, *Boston*, 757).

43   Proclamation issued by Governor Dukakis, July 19, 1977.

44   *Lewiston Evening Journal*, "Bay State Swipes at Sacco-Vanzetti Proclamation," August 9, 1977; *New York Times*, "Sacco and Vanzetti Day Opposed," August 9, 1977; "Sacco-Vanzetti Vote Reversed," August 16, 1977.

45   Russell, *Sacco & Vanzetti*, 26–27.

46   Young and Kaiser, *Postmortem*, generally, Chapters 9 and 10.

47   Russell, *Sacco & Vanzetti*, 12.

48   Starrs, "Once More," 631 et seq.

49   Ibid. 634, 648.

50   Ibid. 644.

51   Ibid. 1069; Report of Firearm, 27–28.

52   Report of Firearm, 28; Starrs, "Once More," 1073–1074.

53 Newby, *Kill Now*, see the six opinions found on 583–584.

54 Avrich, *Sacco and Vanzetti*, 9, 45, 57.

55 Ibid. 5–6.

56 Kadane and Schum, *A Probabilistic*, 283.

57 Ibid.

58 *New York Times*, "Art Review", September 30, 2001.

Index

Page numbers in **bold** indicate photos.

six years of unsuccessful motions regarding Dedham convictions, 3, 22

Thayer's barring of, on his Decision, 238

Thompson to supreme judicial court regarding Dedham convictions, 104, 164–165, 297, 298

Arrogni, Harry, 105

Asch, Nathan, 248, 303

atheism, 14

The Atlantic/The Atlantic Monthly, 119, 244, 307

Aulicino, Armand, 251

Aurthur, Robert Alan, 251

Austro-Hungary, 4

automobiles
    Buick, 37, 38, 45, 48, 51, 52, 67, 68, 69, 71, 72, 73–74, 84, 85, 87, 88, 171, 172, 240, 255, 302
    Cole 8, 73
    Hudson, 38, 69, 85, 170, 171, 173
    Overland, 38, 39, 42, 43, 52, 82, 123, 144, 146, 147

Avrich, Paul, 32, 259, 262, 303

Ayers, A. J., 255

B

The Background of the Plymouth Trial (Vanzetti), 253

Backus, A. C., 17

Bagnetto, Antonio, 11

Balboni, Carlo, 55

Balboni, Joseph, 55

Balboni, Rosa, 55

Baldwin, Roger N., 255

ballistics. *See also* bullets; guns; shotgun shells.
    ambiguities in evidence, 259-262
    controversy around, 205–219
    evidence presented and thereafter uncovered, 215–219
    experts, 162, 260
    Goddard's unauthorized examination, 187

Moore's response to, 154

playing crucial role in jury decision, 118

Proctor's "consistent with" ballistics opinion, 162, 181, 186, 205, 216, 241, 254

Proctor's contrived and misleading ballistics testimony, 119

technology of, 115, 210, 211, 260

tests, 116, 217, 261. *See also* Lowell tests.

Thayer's misrepresentation of testimony on, 156

two defense experts against Proctor, 186

Balsam, Martin, 251

Barone, Bibber, 172

Barone, Michael, 12, 303

Barr, C. A., 36, 37

Barre VT, 14

Bastoni, Enrico, 55

Beffel, Nicholas, 183

Behrman, Samuel N., 248, 303

Behrsin, Hans, 93, 107

Bellamy, F. R., 246

"Ben Shahn and the Passion of Sacco and Vanzetti," 263

Benchley, Robert, 183

Benkosky, Steve "the Pole," 70, 103, 171, 172, 173, 240, 255

Berardelli, Allessandro, 67, 69, 70, 90, 104, 122, 156, 161, 186, 206, 207, 208, 209, 214, 299

Berardelli, Sarah, 90, 92

Berardelli bullets, **138**

Berardelli gun theory, 90–92

Berkman, Alexander, 18

Bernkopf, Elizabeth R., 183

Bianchini, Ermano, 201

bias
    against immigrants, 9
    against Italians, 54
    ethnic bias in case, 261
    of expert testimony, 288
    of A. L. Lowell, 187, 189

guilty verdicts, public questioning of, 159

guineas, 199

gun evidence, failure of defense to suppress, 45, 81

guns. *See also specific guns.*
  Berardelli gun theory, 90–92
  carrying of, 122, 123, 144
  claim of Sacco's and Vanzetti's attempt to draw when arrested, 122, 125, 126, 154, 186, 241
  disputes about, 181
  found on Sacco and Vanzetti when arrested, 39, 76, 126, 186
  found on Vanzetti, 93
  Magrath's testimony on, 71, 205
  Parmenter's Harrington and Richardson .32 caliber revolver, 92
  permit for Sacco's gun, 24
  Sacco's, 71, 187, 210-215
  Sacco's Colt .32, 70, 115–120, 210
  switched gun theory. *See* switched gun theory.
  Vanzetti's .38-caliber revolver, 70, 92, 124

Guthrie, Woody, 263

H

Hall, Walter Perley, 192

Hamilton, Albert, 119, 161, 162, 213, 215, 216, 224–237, 261, 265–266, 268–270, 272–285, 286, 287, 288, 289

Hamilton-Proctor motion, 161–162

Harding, Frank, 36, 38, 46, 48

Harding, Warren, 18

Hardwick, Thomas W., 18

Harrington & Richardson
  .38 revolver, 91, 92, 122, 260
  .32-caliber revolver, 91, 92

Hartford CN, 29

Harvard Law Review, 249

Hassam, George, 36

Hatcher, Julian, 217

Haymarket Square, 12

Hays, Will, 199

Hendry, William (warden), 194, 197

Hennessey, D. C., 10, 293

Henry Holt and Company, 221, 302

Henry v. United States, 82

Henry VIII, 5

Heron, William, 106

Hewins, Mabel, 85, 171

Hickerson, Harold, 247

Hill, Arthur D., 191–193, 195–196

Hill, Steven, 251

Hill, William, 68

historical perspective on guilt of Sacco and Vanzetti, 243, 263–264

Holmes, Mr., 94

Holmes, Oliver Wendell, Jr. (Justice), 18, 192, 193, 257

Homestead Strike, 1892, 18

Hopedale MA, 23, 24, 294

Hudson (car). *See* automobiles, Hudson

Hugo, Victor, 31

hunger strikes, 25, 26, 33, 176, 191, 193

Hurley, Charles F. (governor), 250

Hutchins, Robert M., 251

Hutchinson, Anne, 5

I

identification evidence, 46-48 (Vanzetti/Plymouth trial); 88-90 (Vanzetti/Dedham trial); 100-110 (Sacco/Dedham trial)

Il Proletario, 23

immigrant labor, 2, 3, 4, 7, 14, 15

injustice
  and Duke University lacrosse team, xiv
  FBI frame-up of Salvati, Lamone, Tameleo, and Greco, xiv
  Frankfurter on, 244
  and Katzmann, Williams, and Thayer, 242, 257
  and Puritans, 5-7, 257
  Sacco's rant against injustices of America toward working man, 151

Kurlansky, Harry, 102–103

L

L. Q. White Shoe Company, 35, 37, 166, 167, 246, 296
La Notizia, 140, 188, 189
labor movement, 2
labor syndicalists, 15
LaBrecque, Alfred, 103
Labriola, Jerry Dr. (and Dr. Henry Lee), 261, 306
Labriola, writings of, 31
Lamone, Peter, xiv
Landis, Kenesaw Mountain (judge), 17, 295
Langlois, Edgar, 108, 209
Langone's funeral home, 198, 199
language
    Sacco's difficulty with English, 144, 150, 176
    Vanzetti's difficulty with English, 40
Laplace, Pierre-Simon, 31
Lawrence MA, 7–8, 24
Lawrences, 6
Lee, Henry C., 215, 218, 260, 261, 306
left-twist markings on bullets, 70, 206, 208, 210, 211, 214, 241, 255
The Legacy of Sacco and Vanzetti (Joughin and Morgan), 34, 120, 243, 249, 305
Lehman, Herbert H. (New York governor), 251
Lehrman, Leonard, 252
Leopardi, Giacomo, 31
Letherman, Lawrence, 170, 187
The Letters of Sacco and Vanzetti (Sacco and Vanzetti), 247, 248, 307
Levangie, Michael, 88, 93
lies
    of Connolly, 126
    of Katzmann, 143
    of Sacco, 154, 186
    of Sacco and Vanzetti, 75, 76, 122, 126–127, 144, 152, 181
    of Vanzetti, 41, 45, 52, 87, 90, 94, 186
Life (magazine), 183
The Life and Death of Sacco and Vanzetti (Lyons), 34, 244, 306
The Life of Jesus, 31
Lincoln, Abraham, 182, 316
Lindbergh, Charles, 4
Lippman, Walter, 245
Liscomb, Barbara, 110
Lo Pizzo, Anna, 8
Lodge, Henry Cabot, 12
Lodges, 6
Longhi, Vincent, 55
Loring, Fred, 69, 110, 113, 114, 241
Lovett, Robert M., 249–250
Lowell, Abbott Lawrence, 113, 185, 187–188, 245, 253, 254, 257, 258, 300
Lowell, James (judge), 196
Lowell MA, 7
Lowell tests of Sacco's gun, 116, 211, 212, 213, 260
Lowells, 6
Luban, Jake, 167, 175
Ludlow Massacre, 16, 294
lynchings, 10–12, 293–294
Lynn MA, 15
Lyons, Eugene, 34, 244, 306, 308

M

MacDonald, Herman, 195
Madame X, 143
Mafia, 9, 174, 175
Magazu, Peter, 105
Magrath, George Burgess, 70, 71, 208, 214
Malaquci, Terese, 56
Malatesta, Errico, 31
The Male Animal (Thurber and Nugent), 248, 251
Mancini, Anthony "Tony," 172, 173, 240
manifesto, on twentieth anniversary of executions, 251

Ted Grippo is a retired Chicago lawyer with over fifty years experience in law enforcement and private practice. He has been active in promoting Italian American cultural and civic activities for many years. Ted and his wife, Marlene, spend weekends with family and friends at their summer home in Fontana, Wisconsin.

CPSIA information can be obtained at www.ICGtesting.com
Printed in the USA
235939LV00002B/4/P